RELIGION AND RURAL SOCIETY:
SOUTH LINDSEY 1825–1875

RELIGION AND RURAL SOCIETY: SOUTH LINDSEY 1825-1875

James Obelkevich

CLARENDON PRESS · OXFORD
1976

Oxford University Press, Ely House, London W.1

GLASGOW NEW YORK TORONTO MELBOURNE WELLINGTON
CAPE TOWN IBADAN NAIROBI DAR ES SALAAM LUSAKA ADDIS ABABA
DELHI BOMBAY CALCUTTA MADRAS KARACHI DACCA
KUALA LUMPUR SINGAPORE HONG KONG TOKYO

ISBN 0 19 822426 5

© *Oxford University Press 1976*

*Printed in Great Britain
by Cox & Wyman Ltd
London, Fakenham and Reading*

To
my Mother
and
the Memory of my Father

PREFACE

THIS work is intended as a case study in the social history of religion, focusing on a rural district in Lincolnshire in the middle decades of the nineteenth century. It has three related aims: to analyse the changing structure of agrarian society in this area; to explore the broad spectrum of local religious phenomena—popular superstition as well as the activities of the churches; and finally to place this multifarious religious life in its changing social context.[1]

That is not to suggest that I regard religion merely as an epiphenomenon of an underlying social reality or have sought to 'reduce' it to its social bases. Not only does religion shape society as well as reflect it, but religious organizations enjoy a certain institutional autonomy, and I have said much about their official ideals and aspirations and about their internal life and structure. In my account of the Church of England I necessarily discuss the clergy at some length, and my interpretation of Primitive Methodism allows relatively little weight to external factors. Nevertheless I have assumed that even the most 'autonomous' aspects of religion had a social context and a social resonance. Even the ancient superstitions of popular religion, 'timeless' responses to the human condition rather than to immediate social conditions, had their social distribution, their 'ethnography'. And the churches, whatever their internalities of doctrine or of ecclesiastical machinery, left very different imprints on the villages of south Lindsey. It is in any case not the religion of the professionals, religion in its doctrinal purity, that I have sought to recover, but rather concrete religious phenomena with all the impurities of a specific social context.

To bring this approach to the religious life of the English

[1] I have, however, excluded the few isolated Baptist and Congregational chapels, two localized centres of Roman Catholic strength, and the rather larger body of Wesleyan Reformers who seceded from the parent body after 1850 and affiliated with the United Methodist Free Churches.

countryside in the nineteenth century is to confront what has since come to be looked back upon as one of the high points in English religious history—the 'Victorian religious revival', the 'golden age of the country parish'. In this perspective the choice of south Lindsey for detailed study may have a certain strategic value; as one of the most agricultural districts in England, it provided what are generally regarded as favourable social conditions for organized religion and for the Established Church in particular. To isolate these conditions still further I have concentrated on the villages of the area and largely excluded the towns—which were no more than small market towns and did not powerfully affect the religious life of the countryside. Furthermore, the area was sheltered by geography from the urban and industrial centres of the 'new civilization'. In this setting the two most vigorous and important religious organizations of the century, the Church of England and Methodism, both were active, and they are studied here in their period of greatest impact, between the French wars and the onset of the agricultural depression. If south Lindsey was untypical of rural England as a whole, its strongly agricultural character also made it an optimum environment for organized religion; and an estimate becomes possible in this setting of something like the maximum range and depth of 'christianization', against which any subsequent—or antecedent—'dechristianization' or 'secularization' must be measured.

Yet the very features in this environment that made it hospitable to the churches—its agricultural economy and village social pattern—were themselves undergoing changes that made their relations with the churches increasingly problematic. For south Lindsey, no less profoundly than the industrial towns, was being transformed by capitalism. Under its impact, traditional village society, a society of ranks that preserved some of the communal qualities of a *Gemeinschaft*, dissolved into a society of classes. The farmers in particular withdrew from the village community, isolated themselves from the labourers, and formed themselves into a separate class, while the labourers, reluctant to accept the cash nexus and the breakdown of traditional reciprocities, clung to the older habits and values. The extension of capitalism from economic enterprise to social relations, the uneven emergence of classes, their contrasting circumstances and antagonistic outlooks—these constituted a dangerous challenge to organized religion. Indeed south Lindsey provides a relatively pure example, free of the complications presented by English towns of the period, of the interplay between Christianity and capitalism. The rural setting thus was congenial both to the churches, which were spared the effort of keeping pace with the more rapid population growth of the towns, and to a capitalist class structure, which was established more firmly and clearly in the villages than in the towns. One noteworthy aspect of this interplay was the process by which new classes developed a characteristic religiosity as part of their larger style of life; 'elective affinities' become apparent between particular social formations and religious doctrines or practices which in themselves had no explicit social content. These class styles expressed in subtle form the larger challenge confronting the churches: to maintain themselves as religious communities when the secular village community around them was dissolving into separate classes.

At the same time, however, the churches were forced into competition with each other. Though south Lindsey was a rural area, it was not dominated by the Established Church: indeed, if anyone dominated the religious scene, it was the Methodists, whose 'aggression' had taken them into virtually every parish and thrown the clergy on the defensive. The Anglican reforms and revivals were therefore directed as much at the Wesleyans and 'Ranters' as at the ungodly. There was, however, not only rivalry but also co-operation, and indeed convergence, as church and sects gradually evolved into denominations. South Lindsey thus affords an opportunity to examine the strategies and tactics of the churches in conditions of religious pluralism.

In the search for the social meaning of religion I have assumed, with Feuerbach, that the secret of theology is anthropology, and, by extension, that the secret of religious history is social history. Yet religion at the same time casts its own unique light on society. In the nineteenth century, at any rate, when secular modes of expression were scarce (or left few records), the concerns and aspirations both of individuals and of groups could express themselves—indirectly or symbolically if necessary—in religion as nowhere else. Religion thus offers privileged access to values and assumptions that might otherwise have remained unarticulated or invisible. To attempt a social history of religion is not therefore to ascend to a realm beyond experience—but to return to men's 'common thoughts on common things'.

To the many who helped me with this study I would like to express my gratitude. My greatest debt is to Mrs. Joan Varley, formerly County Archivist at Lincoln, whose kindness in guiding me to Lincolnshire sources went well beyond the call of duty. She and her staff, Mr. Michael Lloyd, Dr. Mary Finch, Dr. Richard Olney, and Miss Judith Cripps, provided a most congenial and helpful setting for local research. I am also indebted to the librarians and staffs of the British Museum, the British Museum Newspaper Library, the Public Record Office, the Methodist Archives and Research Centre, the Church Commissioners, the Folklore Library at University College, London, the Library of the English Folk Dance and Song Society, the Lincoln Cathedral Library, and the Lincoln City Library. A number of Methodist circuit superintendents and Anglican parish clergymen graciously allowed me access to records in their custody. Two Lincolnshire historians, Mr. Terence Leach and Mr. William Leary, were generous with advice and with materials from their private collections. This work had its origins as a Ph.D. thesis at Columbia University; I am indebted to my adviser, Dr. R. K. Webb, for his criticism and encouragement. Among the many others with whom I have discussed this work are R. W. Ambler, Graham Howes, Hugh McLeod, Carolyn Needleman, Martin Needleman, Richard Olney, Professor Trygve Tholfsen, Daniel Tuman, Professor W. R. Ward, Eileen Yeo, and Stephen Yeo. Of course I alone am responsible for the errors and shortcomings that remain. My final debt is acknowledged in the dedication.

ACKNOWLEDGEMENT

The author gratefully acknowledges permission from Routledge Kegan Paul, Ltd., to reproduce material from *English Peasant Farming* by Joan Thirsk.

CONTENTS

LIST OF MAPS

ABBREVIATIONS

Agri. Hist. Rev.	*Agricultural History Review*
ANC	Ancaster estate papers, L.A.O.
And.	Anderson papers, L.A.O.
Bodl.	Bodleian Library, Oxford
Cor.	Correspondence of the Bishops of Lincoln, L.A.O.
C.R.	Methodist circuit records, L.A.O.
Hornc. News	*Horncastle, Spilsby, and Alford News*
I.R.	Board of Inland Revenue records, P.R.O.
L.A.O.	Lincolnshire Archives Office
Linc. Gaz.	*Lincoln Gazette*
Lincs. N. and Q.	*Lincolnshire Notes and Queries*
Lincs. Times	*Lincolnshire Times*
Louth Adv.	*Louth and North Lincolnshire Advertiser*
M.A.R.C.	Methodist Archives and Research Centre
Mass.	Massingberd papers, L.A.O.
Mkt Rasen W.M.	*Market Rasen Weekly Mail*
MON	Monson MSS., L.A.O.
News. Cutt.	Newspaper Cuttings, Local History Collection, Lincoln Public Library
P.M.M.	*Primitive Methodist Magazine*
P.P.	*Parliamentary Papers*
P.R.O.	Public Record Office
Q.A.B.	Queen Anne's Bounty
Retf. News	*Retford, Worksop, Isle of Axholme and Gainsburgh News*
Stamf. Merc.	*Lincoln, Rutland, and Stamford Mercury*
V.R.	Visitation returns, Lincoln diocesan records, L.A.O.
White, *Directory*	William White, *History, Gazetteer, and Directory of Lincolnshire*, edns. of 1842, 1856, 1873.
Winn	Henry Winn papers, L.A.O.

I

SOUTH LINDSEY: THE BACKGROUND

IF religion cannot be understood apart from its social context, the ways in which society leaves its mark on religion are complex and multifarious, and it is convenient to explore the larger environment—the economic and social geography of south Lindsey—before examining the more immediate setting formed by the social classes. This secondary context exerted a strong but chiefly indirect influence on local religious life.

Nineteenth-century south Lindsey was overwhelmingly rural and agricultural, a district not only without large towns but entirely lacking in rural industry. It was therefore untypical of rural England of the time, and it represented something like an extreme case of an agricultural district undisturbed by urban influence. But that is not to say that it was unique or monolithic. Like most of rural England it was affected by the triumph of capitalist agriculture. And within it was a diversity of regional and local environments, most of which had parallels in other counties, and each of which exerted a different influence on religious life. Thus the local context was itself complex and multifarious, and its elements need to be examined separately: the county; south Lindsey as a whole; the regions within south Lindsey; the parishes; the agricultural economy; and the structure of the population.

GEOGRAPHY

South Lindsey naturally shared some of the characteristics of the county of which it was a part.[1] Lincolnshire, the second largest county in England, ranking only behind Yorkshire, had long been relatively isolated and little known. Indeed it was mis-known: it was popularly conceived to consist entirely of Fens, low, flat, wet, and unhealthy. In fact, with its great size it has great internal diversity, as does south Lindsey, encompassing a variety of upland and lowland terrain. For this reason it has

[1] See Map 1.

been grouped variously with the eastern counties and, more plausibly, with the east Midlands, while its northernmost parts have been claimed for the North of England; but it does not fit comfortably into any of the standard regions of England.

In the nineteenth century it was still an isolated county, largely surrounded by water and cut off from the rest of England: an island within an island. Its long coastline on the 'German Ocean', as the North Sea was known down to World War I, lacked natural harbours, and in the south it was separated from adjoining counties by the Fens. The river Trent in the north-west was spanned only twice in thirty miles, and even then by toll bridges, one of which was built as late as 1832, while the Humber to the north remains bridgeless to the present day. Until the coming of the railways in the 1840s, communications were better only in the south-west, where the Great North Road passed just inside the county borders. Yet geographical facts do not necessarily become cultural facts, and it would be wrong to assume that the county's geographical isolation meant cultural isolation. Its folklore diverged little from that of its neighbours, and in religion it was not slow to respond to the appeal of Methodism. The rest of the country knew little of Lincolnshire, but Lincolnshire was not cut off from the main currents of national life.

Internally Lincolnshire had been divided since before the Conquest into three great administrative and judicial divisions, the three parts of Lindsey, Kesteven, and Holland, each with its own Commission of the Peace and Quarter Sessions, but all under one lord lieutenant and one sheriff. Lindsey, occupying the north and much of the east of the county, was by far the largest of the three: with over a million acres it would rank as the twelfth-largest county. South Lindsey, the area under study, has been defined as the area south of a line joining Gainsborough, Market Rasen, Louth, and Mablethorpe, but excluding the former fenland in the south-east. With over 400,000 acres it would have ranked in size between Bedfordshire and Hertfordshire.

South Lindsey, thus defined, did not coincide with any administrative or ecclesiastical unit, though after the second Reform Act it roughly corresponded with the mid-Lincolnshire parliamentary constituency. Its geographical and social boundaries, however, were clear. To the south, the river Witham separating Lindsey from Kesteven was a recognized frontier:

MAP I. Lincolnshire and South Lindsey.

A	Till Basin	E	South Wolds
B	Cliff	F	North Wolds
C	Central Vale	G	Middle Marsh
D	Fen Margin	H	Outer Marsh

the 'highlanders' on the north bank looked across to the 'fensmen' on the south bank.[1] It also marked the linguistic boundary between the Lindsey and the south Lincolnshire dialects; in the Lindsey dialect, a person from south Lincolnshire was a 'yallow-belly'—'He's a real yallowbelly, you may tell it by his tongue.'[2] Farther east the Wolds and Marshes of south Lindsey were set off from the separate world of the Fens. To the north the boundary again was defined socially as well as geographically. North Lindsey was dominated by one great family, that of the Earls of Yarborough, with their great estate of some 55,000 acres; in south Lindsey no family possessed land, income, or influence remotely comparable.[3] South Lindsey thus occupied the social and geographical space between the Yarborough domain and the Fens.

As this is a study of rural religion, the towns have been excluded, but they cannot be ignored entirely, since they and the villages around them were interdependent, not only in their economic and social but also in their religious life. Nevertheless, most were essentially market towns, service centres for their agricultural hinterlands. Far from harbouring an alien or abrasive urban spirit, they complemented rural society and did not 'contradict' it. And apart from Horncastle, there was no important town in the 'interior' of south Lindsey: the largest ones, Lincoln, Louth, and Gainsborough, were located on the borders of the area and faced away from south Lindsey as well as towards it.

Lincoln, the county and cathedral town, was the largest in population in 1851 with 17,456; the others in order of size were Louth (10,467), Gainsborough (7,506), Horncastle (4,921), Alford (2,262), Market Rasen (2,110), Spilsby (1,461), and several 'small but ancient' market towns like Wainfleet (1,365) and Burgh-le-Marsh (1,215). Some of the smaller towns were

[1] Though the Lindsey side was no more than thirty feet above sea level and the south bank about seven or eight.

[2] Edward Peacock, *A Glossary of Words used in the Wapentakes of Manley and Corringham, Lincolnshire*, English Dialect Society, 1877, p. 278. See also G. S. Streatfeild, *Lincolnshire and the Danes*, 1884, pp. 266–7; James E. Oxley, *The Lindsey Dialect*, 1940, p. 5.

[3] See R. J. Olney, *Lincolnshire Politics 1832–1885*, 1973, pp. 13–15 and *passim*. The Brocklesby estate included only three small Wold parishes in south Lindsey—Cawkwell, Ruckland, and Worlaby—whose total area was less than 2,000 acres, and all of which were sold before 1856. (White, *Directory*, 1856, pp. 233, 733, 736.)

hardly to be distinguished from a 'considerable village' like Bardney, a 'large, well-built, and improving village' like Saxilby, or a village like Hogsthorpe, the 'metropolis of the Marsh'.[1] But the towns had the markets, professional men, bank branches, petty-sessional courts, and shops that conferred on them a precarious urbanity. Among the larger towns, only Lincoln and Gainsborough had any industry worth mentioning, the manufacture of agricultural machinery, which itself depended on the agricultural market. A wider range of heavy engineering industry developed in Lincoln from the 1850s and, with the growing population, tended to withdraw the town from the local agricultural world and to give it a life of its own. Something similar occurred, though in a lesser degree, at Gainsborough, aided by its position as a port town on the Trent. But even in Lincoln the dependence on agricultural markets, including the local ones, was still apparent in the last quarter of the century.[2] With these two partial exceptions the towns of south Lindsey were 'agricultural towns', embedded in the countryside.[3] Their corn merchants, attorneys, and bankers, their fairs and markets all catered primarily to the needs of local farmers and landlords. So closely were their fortunes tied to those of the countryside that when agriculture entered its 'Golden Age' after 1850, they attained their peak population, and when agriculture declined in the Great Depression they declined too.

In the realm of religion town and country stood more on even terms, with the influence of one on the other varying from denomination to denomination. In the Church of England, though the ideal and model of the village parish church continued to inspire town churchmen, towns and villages largely remained in separate compartments. Only through Methodism did the towns have much effect on village religious life. All of the larger towns and many of the smaller ones were 'capitals' of Methodist

---

[1] Most of these characterizations appear in White, *Directory*, 1856.

[2] See Sir Francis Hill, *Victorian Lincoln*, 1974, pp. 88, 118–22, 203. Earlier in the century Thomas Cooper (the Chartist, who was raised in Gainsborough and lived for a time in Lincoln) recounted a conversation between two local tradesmen: when one said there was '"nothing doing, and no money stirring", the other invariably rejoined, "No, nor won't be, till after harvest"' (*Wise Saws and Modern Instances*, 1845, ii. 111).

[3] K. C. Edwards, 'A Lincoln Industrial Centenary', *East Midland Geographer*, i (1954), p. 44; Ian Beckwith, 'The River Trade of Gainsborough, 1500–1850, *Lincolnshire History and Archaeology*, no. 2 (1967); Olney, *Lincolnshire Politics*, pp. 5–6.

circuits, which usually comprised one town and a dozen or more surrounding villages; the circuit, the key unit of Methodist organization, brought preachers and people from towns and villages into regular contact with each other and made it possible for the financial and human resources of the town chapels to contribute to the life of the outlying village chapels. But there was also influence in the reverse direction, and when the migration of villagers to the towns is considered, it is likely that the villages had a greater effect on the religious life of the towns than vice versa.

The social environment in south Lindsey was shaped less by the towns than by its internal geographic structure.[1] Its varied terrain was the basis for a well-defined set of eight regions which had their own economic, social, and sometimes religious character. The main distinction was between lowland and upland regions, which formed an alternating sequence from the Trent in the west to the North Sea in the east. In the west was the Till basin, a low, flat tract subject to flooding from the small river Till. To its east was the Lincoln Cliff or Edge, a limestone upland belonging to a much larger geological system that includes the North York Moors, the Northamptonshire Uplands, and the Cotswolds. Next was the third principal region, the central clay vale; like certain districts in the Midlands, its boulder clay was stiff, heavy, 'cold', and poorly drained. To its east rose the Wolds, part of a wider series of chalk uplands which included the Yorkshire Wolds, the Chilterns, and the downlands of southern England. Two regions can be distinguished here: the North Wolds, higher and bleaker, and the South Wolds, with smaller parishes and more valleys and trees. Lying between the Wolds and the sea was the Marsh, another low, flat district. The Middle Marsh at the foot of the Wolds was a strip of predominantly clay soils, rich but poorly drained. The Outer Marsh, along the coast, contained land of extreme fertility, highly prized as fattening grounds for cattle. One further region can be identified: the Fen margin, a tier of parishes along the southern edge of the Wolds that included both Wold and Fen soils but belonged

---

[1] See David L. Linton, 'The Landforms of Lincolnshire', *Geography*, xxxix (1954); Joan Thirsk, *English Peasant Farming*, 1957; D. R. Mills, 'Settlement Patterns in the Till Basin (Lindsey) Past and Present', Nottingham University unpublished undergraduate thesis, 1952.

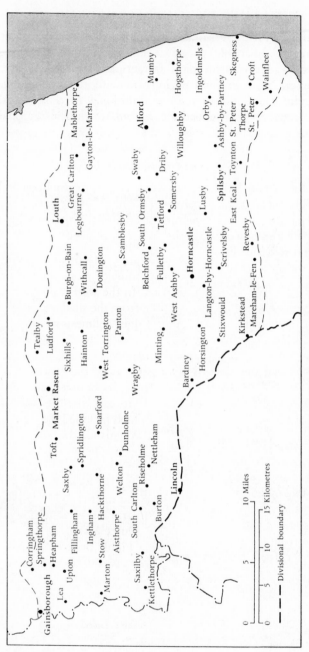

MAP 2. South Lindsey: places mentioned in the text

predominantly with the uplands. In general, the upland regions had soils more amenable to advanced agricultural methods, and boasted large, successful 'high' farmers and a more 'modern' social structure. The lowland regions were more backward in their agriculture and perhaps more traditional in their social relations. Together they constitute a framework for regional comparisons within south Lindsey.

PARISHES

Great as the regional differences were, still more fundamental were the differences at the parish level. The size of the parish, the settlement pattern, and the structure of landownership combined to exert the most powerful of the indirect influences on social relations and religious life.

South Lindsey's total area of 410,000 acres was divided into 237 parishes, with an average area of 1,736 acres.

Distribution of Parishes by Size

Acreage	Number of parishes
1–999	55
1,000–1,499	60
1,500–1,999	47
2,000–2,999	55
3,000–	20

Nearly half the parishes had less than 1,500 acres and were small by English standards. This pattern of small parishes was on the whole favourable to the Established Church; for though a small parish might also contain a small benefice inadequate to support a resident incumbent, there was a church in nearly every parish, and the smaller the parish, the more accessible the church was to the inhabitants and the more accessible they were to influence or pressure from the parson or squire. The size varied considerably, however, from region to region:

Average Size of Parish, by Region

Region	Acres	Region	Acres
Till basin	2,340	North Wolds	1,758
Cliff	2,165	South Wolds	1,197
Central vale	1,859	Middle Marsh	1,451
Fen margin	2,158	Outer Marsh	2,256

The average parish in the South Wolds was only half the size of parishes in the Till basin, Cliff, Fen margin, and Outer Marsh. But even in these regions the average parish size was, by national standards, favourable to the Establishment.

Many of these parishes were also small in population. In 1851 a fifth of the population lived in parishes of fewer than 200 souls, somewhat under a half were in parishes of 200 to 499, and a third were in large parishes of 500 and above. Again there were regional variations. In the South Wolds, with its small parishes, well over half the population was in parishes of 250 and below, while in the Fen margin and Outer Marsh the population was concentrated in large parishes of 500 and over. But the general distribution was probably favourable to the Church of England.

The pattern of settlement, whether concentrated or dispersed, also affected the fortunes of the churches. Dispersed settlement tended to favour the Methodists, who could organize a class and hold cottage or farmhouse services in an outlying hamlet more easily than the parson could. An estimate of the extent of dispersed settlement may be formed from a variety of evidence: the presence in a parish of a named hamlet or a second township; contemporary maps; census enumerators' books; and county directories, which refer to 'scattered' populations in particular parishes. This evidence suggests that there was a significant amount of dispersed settlement in about a third of the parishes; not surprisingly it was most frequent in large parishes. The regions most favourable to Methodism in this respect were the Till basin, the Outer Marsh, and the Central vale; but this advantage was probably outweighed by the many small parishes with nucleated settlement in south Lindsey as a whole.

The most powerful influence at the parish level was the structure of landownership and specifically the relative weight of large and small property. The 'New Domesday' survey of landowners in the early 1870s showed that in Lincolnshire, compared with England as a whole, relatively more land was held in very large and in very small estates, but the deviation from the national average was slight.[1]

[1] F. M. L. Thompson, *English Landed Society in the Nineteenth Century*, 1963, pp. 32, 113–15, 117, citing J. Bateman, *The Great Landowners of Great Britain and Ireland*, 1883.

Percentage of Total Area Occupied by Land in
Large and Small Estates

	10,000 acres and over	3,000–10,000	1,000–3,000	300–1,000	100–300	1–100
Lincolnshire	28	13	10	15	12	14
England	24	17	12·4	14	12·5	12

The county average, however, conceals much regional variation. An attempt has been made to compile the relevant figure for the eight regions of south Lindsey, using the same Return of Land-owners and local directories.[1]

Percentage of Area in Large and Small Estates

Region	Size of Estate			
	1,000 acres and over	100–999 acres	1–99 acres	Total
Till basin	34	25	9	68
Cliff	71	18	3	92
Central vale	53	17	6	76
Fen margin	33	19	10	62
North Wolds	63	21	3	87
South Wolds	52	26	7	85
Middle Marsh	25	30	13	68
Outer Marsh	2	20	24	46
South Lindsey	46	22	8	76

Though the figures are very incomplete for several regions, the general pattern is suggestive. The upland regions showed a high degree of concentrated ownership—at least two-thirds of the Cliff was in estates of 1,000 acres or more—as did the Central vale; there appears to have been a somewhat wider distribution of property in the other lowland regions, particularly in the Outer Marsh, with its host of small owner-occupiers.

This contrast between large and small property may be reformulated at the parish level as the distinction between concentrated and divided ownership, which in turn forms the basis for the familiar distinction between 'close' and 'open' parishes. By linking patterns in landownership with many aspects of economic, social, political, and religious life, it is an indispensable tool in the analysis of nineteenth century rural society.[2]

---

[1] P.P. 1874, lxxii; White, *Directory*, 1856 and 1872.

[2] See E. J. Hobsbawm and George Rudé, *Captain Swing*, 1969, pp. 182–3; D. R. Mills, 'English Villages in the Eighteenth and Nineteenth Centuries: A Sociological Approach', *Amateur Historian*, vi (1965); B. A. Holderness, '"Open" and "Close"

In a close parish all or most of the land was owned by a single landlord, who, particularly when resident in the parish, exercised a control over it that could approach total domination. Particularly important was his control over the supply of housing; in order to hold the poor rate down as low as possible, he would limit the amount of cottage housing available to labourers, who, unable to live in the parish, would be unable to gain a settlement in it and become a burden on the poor rate. Indeed landlords not only declined to build new cottages but also sometimes pulled down existing ones. Though it was the occupiers and not the owners of land who were assessed to the poor rate, a landlord who kept it low in this manner might pocket the difference in rent. In close parishes the shortage of cottage housing meant that there were not enough labourers residing in the parish to supply the needs of the farmers. Many labourers were thus forced to live some distance from their work, in open parishes. There the land was owned by many small owners who could not limit the amount of housing and who indeed were likely to build cottages as speculative investments. Most of the labourers living in an open parish would work there, but others would have to walk long distances to work in a close parish. They arrived at work already tired, a fact that led farmers eventually to criticize the system and demand that landlords provide more cottages in the close parishes. Contemporaries were of course well aware of the evils of the system; here they are described by the incumbent of an open parish:

The moral condition of such villages as Tealby, Binbrook, Middle Rasen very much need[s] the attention of great landed proprietors. Tealby is bounded by North Willingham, Walesby, and Kirmond, each the property of single proprietors who will not allow sufficient labourers to dwell on their estates. They are therefore driven to Tealby at a distance from their work, having to pay high rents for ruinous cottages, and by late Acts of Parliament chargeable to this parish when needing relief. All this is supposed by the farmers here to be a manoeuvre of the great landlords to relieve their estates of burdens ... There is a bad moral effect in having part of the population in a floating condition— over-worked, and unable to contract any genial attachment to the locality—without a *home*. . . . Young men with small families are placed

---

in comfortable spots in these favoured parishes—but when their families increase they are removed to Tealby—and they know the reason. ... Day after day a man leaves his children asleep in the morning, and returns to find them asleep in the evening.[1]

For closer analysis it is useful to refine the basic distinction, either by taking account of the residence and non-residence of squires or by registering intermediate degrees of concentration in landownership. The following classification, which takes the latter course, specifies four types of parish. Type A parishes are 'Squire's' parishes—close parishes in the strict sense—in which one landlord owned more than half the land.[2] In 'oligarchic' parishes, Type B, a few landlords owned most of the land, but none had more than half. In 'freeholders'' parishes, Type C, the land was owned by smallholders averaging less than 40 acres each—open parishes in the strict sense. Type D comprises 'divided' parishes—all the rest, in which there were often several large landlords with small or medium holdings and a larger number of smallholders. It is not always easy to decide between Types C and D, though true 'freeholders'' parishes were more likely to take on the characteristics of small towns.[3] Fortunately the basic distinction between close (Types A and B) and open (Types C and D) usually suffices.

With this classification it is possible to identify patterns in social geography at the parish level. Open parishes tended to be larger in area than close parishes: about 2,000 acres on the average, as against 1,600.

Parish Types: Total and Average Areas

Type	Number	Total area (acres)	Average area (acres)
A	130	200,443	1,542
B	27	45,754	1,695
C	34	71,209	2,094
D	46	92,357	2,008

Close parishes had smaller and less dense populations than open parishes; in 1851, 59 per cent of the area was in close parishes but only 44 per cent of the population.

[1] Flowers to Kaye, 30 Nov. 1848, Cor. B. 5/4/56/3.
[2] Parishes were classified on the basis of data from local directories and from the Land Tax returns of 1831 in the Lincolnshire Archives Office.
[3] Mills, 'English Villages', p. 276.

Parish Types: Population and Density of Population in 1851

Type	Total population	Average population	Population per square mile
A	22,149	170	71
B	7,276	169	102
C	16,708	491	149
D	19,220	418	133

And in the first half of the century, population grew much more rapidly in open than in close parishes.

Parish Types: Percentage Increase in Population, 1801–51

Type	
A	53·2
B	76·5
C	90·6
D	94·5

A larger proportion of the population was engaged in non-agricultural occupations in open than in close parishes. In 1831 there was a large minority in such occupations (more than a fifth of the families) in nearly two-thirds of the open parishes, compared with only a third of the close parishes. It is noteworthy that in most of these contrasts the greatest disparity is between Types A and C, with Types B and D falling in between; this pattern strongly suggests that the structure of landownership was indeed the key variable. There were also implications for the realm of faith and morals. If a landlord could prevent a cottage from being built he certainly could refuse land for a Methodist chapel. And he could scrutinize the religious behaviour of his tenants and their families, whether they were farmers or labourers, and evict anyone who displeased him. Close parishes, particularly those with resident squires, were thus the favoured terrain of the Established Church. Open parishes by contrast were more accessible to Methodism: larger in area and in population, with more hamlets and dispersed settlement, they were more independent of the influence of squires and parsons. Yet if they were friendlier to Methodism, they also tended to be 'rough' parishes, with more drunkenness and disorder. To this day clergymen deprecate the 'sullen' spirit in what formerly were open parishes. Yet the contrast should not be oversimplified. If close parishes tended to be Anglican, an unco-operative squire could obstruct the designs of the parson, and if open parishes tended to be

Methodist, their rough ways could also make them hostile to all forms of organized religion. Yet even in these variant cases the influence of landownership on religious life, as on social relations more generally, is unmistakable.

AGRICULTURE

Agriculture is the main prop. Neither the throne, the constitution, nor anything else is so strong a prop to this country, Old England, as her agriculture.

The Revd. Frederick Peel, at the tenth annual meeting of the Marton Agricultural Society, October 1850. (*Lincs. Times*, 22 Oct. 1850.)

Agriculture was indeed the main prop. In the villages of south Lindsey, where rural industry was minimal, it completely dominated the economy; and along with the ownership of land it was the chief determinant of social structure. Yet if agriculture was the basis of the economic and social order it also embodied the contemporary spirit of improvement and of capitalist rationality. Lincolnshire as a whole was one of the premier agricultural counties of the kingdom, important not for its mere size but for the quality of its arable farming; in the upland districts in particular farmers were renowned for their advanced methods. It was this view of agriculture in Lindsey that was expressed in another statement from the middle of the century, by a committee of the North Lincolnshire Agricultural Society:

Other counties, both in England and Scotland, may have entered earlier into the field of agricultural improvement, but in none has it been cultivated with greater energy and with more marked results than in this county, during the half century just concluded.[1]

Here then was an apparent paradox: a modern agriculture was credited with being the main prop of the social order of Old England. If the paradox was softened by the persistence of backward agricultural methods, particularly in the lowlands, the fact remained that nearly all farming, whether pursued by improvers or by traditionalists, was capitalist in outlook, oriented towards markets and profits.[2]

It was the upland regions, the Cliff and Wolds, that boasted the

[1] Report of the Committee of the North Lincolnshire Agricultural Society, 3 June 1851, Stubbs I/16/1/2, L.A.O.

[2] For general accounts of Lincolnshire agriculture, see Thirsk, *English Peasant Farming*, and John Algernon Clarke, *On the Farming of Lincolnshire*, 1852.

'spirited' methods of national reputation. Formerly their thin soils had been suited only for rabbit warrens, but by 1850 they had been transformed into regions of productive and profitable high farming. This involved a classic four-course rotation: turnips, barley, seeds and wheat. The turnips, nourished by expensive and sometimes exotic fertilizers, fed the sheep that fertilized the arable crops; and after 1850 the sheep became an increasingly important source of profit for their meat and wool.[1] Farms in the upland regions were large: in 1867 they averaged 139·3 acres in the North Wolds and 109·6 acres in the South Wolds, compared with the south Lindsey average of 86·5 acres.[2] Most of the land indeed was held in much larger farms—300 acres made a middling farm and farms of 1,000 acres were not uncommon. The North Wolds in particular had developed very rapidly in the first half of the century; making the land fit for crops had required much labour, as did the more intensive methods of cultivation, and the population of the region had grown rapidly. This 'frontier' character was less in evidence in the South Wolds and the Cliff, but the pattern of farming was similar in all three upland regions, as was the social pattern, with large estates, close parishes, low population densities, and resident gentry. Improving farmers had transformed social relations in these regions as well as the agriculture.

Conditions in the clay lowlands, the Central vale, the Till basin, and the Middle Marsh were not conducive to high farming, and the agriculture of these regions at mid-century was still backward if not benighted. As in similar districts in other counties, the soil was impractical for turnips, making a fallow necessary, and poor drainage allowed sheep rot to decimate the flocks in bad years.[3] From the Tithe Files there emerges a portrait of clay-land farming in the late 1830s that flatters neither the soil nor its cultivators. Snelland, in the Central vale, was 'almost throughout a tract of inferior clay and generally speaking not well cultivated'. Springthorpe, in the Till basin, was said to be capable of good

---

[1] A local newspaper noted in 1861 that 'sheep-breeding is the sheet anchor of the Lincolnshire farmer, and enables him to bear up against the vicissitudes of the seasons by relying more on sheep and wool than on his corn crops' (*Louth Adv.* 24 Aug. 1861).

[2] Calculated from the Agricultural Returns of 1867, M.A.F. 68/135, P.R.O.

[3] See R. W. Sturgess, 'The Agricultural Revolution on the English Clays', *Agri. Hist. Rev.* xiv (1966).

crops but was 'completely lost for want of underdraining and inclosing'. (It was one of several parishes in the neighbourhood in which some land lay in open fields until the 1840s.) Its arable was '*ruined* by water and the wretched system of cultivation universally adopted in open fields', and it had an 'insulated and lost appearance'.[1] As drainage became effective in the 1830s and after, the need for a bare fallow every third year relaxed but did not disappear completely. Lowland farms were smaller than those in the uplands; in 1867 they averaged 83 acres in the Till basin and 100·2 acres in the Central vale, and anything above 300 acres was exceptional. Rents were lower, the husbandry had little glamour or prestige. The intractable soil in a parish like Newton-by-Toft— 'it is hard to work, either a mire or baked'—naturally repelled the more ambitious farmers—'nobody with money will come and farm it'.[2] Yet by the end of the period progress was considerable.

In the Middle Marsh the soil was predominantly a boulder clay with properties similar to those of the other clay districts. And similar scenes of backwardness were the rule until the advent of deep drainage, though grazing was more successful there than in the central and western districts. Its arable, early in the century, was 'detestably managed. . . . a two-field rotation with a fallow every other year'.[3] Open fields retarded improvement in many parishes until the 1830s and 1840s. At Muckton in 1838 most of the parish was 'a *flat, cold*, unproductive soil. . . . With very little exception the land is extremely poor'; the arable was 'all heavy working, unfit for turnips'; the roads were 'almost impassable'; 'the principal Farms were untenanted during the great depression, indeed the land is of that character, that no man of capital and intelligence would hold them, at that time. The two largest farms are now let on lease to very spirited tenants, who are draining and improving the lands at a great outlay.'[4] After enclosure and drainage, much depended on ploughing up the poorer pastures; eventually, respectable yields were achieved. Still, pastoral husbandry remained important; the numbers of cattle and sheep in the district in 1867 were above the south Lindsey

---

[1] Pickering to Tithe Commissioners, 31 May 1839, I.R. 18/5267; Woolley to Tithe Commissioners, 30 Dec. 1837, I.R. 18/5284.

[2] William Bartholomew of Goltho, quoted in the minutes of the tithe commutation meeting, 8 Apr. 1840, I.R. 18/5153.

[3] Thirsk, *English Peasant Farming*, p. 244.

[4] Woolley to Tithe Commissioners, 27 June 1838, I.R. 18/5146.

average. As in the other lowland regions farms were small, averaging 61 acres in 1867, and there were few resident gentry.

The Outer Marsh, though linked with the farming systems of the Middle Marsh and Wolds, was a region apart. Its 'luxuriant grazing lands' were the 'glory of Lincolnshire'[1] and in a number of parishes over half the agricultural acreage was devoted to pasture, which brought rents exceeding forty shillings per acre. Sheep and cattle, reared elsewhere, notably on the Wolds, were fed and fattened in the Outer Marsh. Not surprisingly, it had the highest average numbers of cattle (22 per 100 acres) and sheep (145 per 100 acres) of any region in south Lindsey. Much of the land was rented by large Wold farmers, like Richard Dudding of Panton, who had a Marsh farm at Mablethorpe, twenty-two miles away; it was estimated that four-fifths of Winthorpe was occupied by non-residents.[2] The average holding, 42 acres, was the smallest in south Lindsey, and the majority of resident farmers were small freeholders. In 1831 nearly three-fifths of the resident farmers employed no labourers—compared with the south Lindsey average of 46 per cent—and over 90 per cent of the population lived in open parishes. The special social characteristics of the region persisted despite the invasion of 'out'ners' from the Wolds.

A survey of the agricultural regions leaves a strong impression of diversity, particularly in the earlier years, and of a basic contrast between upland and lowlands. By 1870, on the eve of the agricultural depression, the contrast had been reduced but not eliminated. The upland farmer was still a man of large capital, with a large farm, working a perfected technique of cultivation; the lowland farmer, a man of small capital, with a smaller farm, coping with unfavourable conditions.

POPULATION

Demographic events like birth, marriage, and death become occasions for religious events, but the influence of demography on religion does not end there. The size of a population; its growth and decline; its age, sex, and marital structure; its rates of fertility and mortality—all the basic demographic features of a society have their bearing on its religious life.

The rural population of south Lindsey grew rapidly in the

---

[1] Clarke, *Farming of Lincolnshire*, p. 76.
[2] White, Directory, 1872, pp. 263, 508; *P.P.* 1867–8, xvii, p. 303.

first half of the century, if less rapidly than the nation as a whole; from 37,234 in 1801 it reached 54,009 in 1831 and 65,553 in 1851, an increase of three-quarters since the beginning of the century, compared with a doubling of the national population. The rate of increase varied considerably from region to region: more than 100 per cent in the Outer Marsh, with its open parishes and proliferating small farms, and well above average also in the North Wolds, where the agricultural transformation required an expanding labour force. Growth was below average in the South Wolds and Fen margin—57 and 59 per cent respectively —owing perhaps to migration to the adjoining regions of growth. Population also grew faster in open than in close parishes. It would appear that the 'target' population for the Established Church was growing less rapidly than that of the Methodists.

The growth was due to natural increase: migration was causing a net outflow from rural districts in this period. At the middle of the century, fertility in south Lindsey was a little higher than the national average, mortality a little lower. Locally, infant mortality was at the high national level down to the middle of the century —it was 152·5 per 1,000 live births in 1850–2, virtually identical with the national average—but twenty years later had fallen to 131·8, while the national average had risen slightly to 155·7. The death rates for women aged 15 to 44, the years of child-bearing, exceeded those for men, which in every other age-group were higher than those of women.[1] What is most significant about the pattern of mortality is that death struck at the young and at people in the prime of life, and therefore had a greater impact on the survivors than it does in contemporary society.

Death rates were the chief determinant of the age structure, which itself has an important bearing on religious practice. Church attendance has often found to be highest among children and old people, and lowest among young married couples. In the south Lindsey population in 1851 more than a quarter of the population was under 10 years of age. This was favourable to religious practice, but it was counterbalanced by the sparsity of old people: only 7 per cent of the population was 60 or older.[2]

[1] Calculated from the *Annual Reports* of the Registrar-General and from the Censuses.

[2] Calculated from a sample of every twentieth household drawn from the enumerators' books of the 1851 Census (henceforth the '1851 Census sample').

Like the age structure, the proportions of males and females in a population are of interest in a study of its religious life, given the traditional propensity of women for religious practice. In 1851 the sex ratio (defined as the number of males per 100 females in a population) was 104·2 in south Lindsey, compared with 88·1 in England and Wales. Since the demand for labour in local agriculture was primarily for males, the figure is not surprising. There were some significant regional variations:

Sex Ratios by Region, 1851

Till basin	105·6	North Wolds	109·8
Cliff	107·7	South Wolds	100·7
Central vale	104·7	Middle Marsh	104·3
Fen margin	100·5	Outer Marsh	98·7

The heavy demand for farm labour in the Cliff and North Wolds is reflected in high sex ratios. It is noteworthy that in 1831 the proportion of farm labourers to the total male population aged 20 and over was highest in these two regions, despite the low population density and scarcity of labourers. The low sex ratio in the Outer Marsh may have been due to the predominance of pastoral agriculture. There is also evidence to suggest that the sex ratio was higher in close than in open parishes; since more of the workforce in open parishes was engaged in non-agricultural occupations, the link between agriculture and the predominance of males in the population is again confirmed.

The most important implication of the sex ratio is that substantial numbers of females were emigrating from the villages. Since there were many more women than men in the country as a whole, substantial numbers of them must have emigrated from south Lindsey to have left it with its male majority. If before emigration the local sex ratio may be assumed to have been the same as the national and if after emigration it was 104·1, then at least 15·5 per cent of the female population must have emigrated from the area. And since males too emigrated, and some females migrated into south Lindsey, the gross female emigration must have been even higher. This emigration was a steady, long-term phenomenon. More dramatic and conspicuous was the increase in emigration, male as well as female, that took place after 1851, which caused the beginning of absolute population decline in many parishes. Of 220 parishes reaching a definite peak in the course of the century (excluding, that is, some small squire's parishes whose population varied little), 92 had reached their Census maximum in 1851 or before, 53 in 1861, 48 in 1871, and 27 in 1881. A more precise index of the increase in emigration is provided by calculating the rate of emigration for rural registration sub-districts.[1] In ten sub-districts the rate of emigration was 7·2 per cent between 1841 and 1850, 14·1 per cent between 1851 and 1860, and 17 per cent between 1861 and 1870. This sharply increased outflow after 1850 does much to explain the complaints about the scarcity of labour and the rise in labourers' wages.[2] Regional variations were remarkable. Emigration rates were very high in the Wolds—24·4 per cent in the Binbrook sub-district between 1861 and 1870—and low in the Marshes, where there was less reliance on arable agriculture. An impression of the age of the emigrants may be obtained by expressing the 1871 age-groups as percentages of the corresponding figures for 1851.

1871 Population as a Percentage of 1851 Population, by Age-group, Wragby Sub-district

	Males	Females
0–4	96·8	96·7
5–9	101·1	114·4
10–14	111·1	114·2
15–19	114·4	91·1
20–24	76·8	87·5
25–29	82·0	88·0
30–34	89·4	85·7
35–39	95·7	100·0
40–44	88·0	103·3
45–49	134·5	108·0
50–54	130·6	118·0
55–59	98·4	131·9
60–64	132·1	100·0
65–	115·3	1·205
Total	101·2	100·8

[1] The actual intercensal increase in population less the natural increase yields net emigration; the rate of emigration is then net emigration as a percentage of the total population in the earlier census.

[2] In the 1870s the labourers' unions did much to promote overseas emigration overseas, particularly to Canada, the United States, and New Zealand. They urged labourers to emigrate, arranged public meetings for emigration agents, and collected money to assist emigrating families. See the *Labour League Examiner*, 1874, and the *Labourer*, 1875, *passim*; and Pamela Horn, 'Agricultural Trade Unionism and Emigration, 1872–1881', *Historical Journal*, xv (1972).

From this sub-district and others in which emigration increased sharply after 1850 a common pattern emerges: young women began to emigrate while still in their teens while young men tended to wait until their early twenties, but emigration continued among men at ages when it had ceased among women. This phase of acute emigration tended to reinforce both the younger and the older age-groups; the middle of the age structure was being hollowed out. The population remaining, both male and female, ought to have had a greater propensity for religious practice than the original population; otherwise the departure of the emigrants, chiefly unmarried young people, probably had little direct effect on the village religious scene, since they were rarely active in it at that stage in their lives. By the same token, their already low level of church attendance could only have fallen still lower in their new urban environment. Their migration reinforced the pattern of organized religion in both their old and their new homes, making the countryside more accessible to the churches, and the town still less.

CONCLUSION

The social and geographic background surveyed in this chapter exerted a complex influence upon institutional religion: some factors aided the Establishment, some Methodism, some, perhaps, indifference. What then was their relative importance?

At every level of analysis there were counteracting forces. Formal religious practice regardless of denomination was probably aided by emigration. But this was offset by the predominance of males in the population. 'Anglican' advantages were numerous: above all the small size of the parishes and the distribution of population mainly in parishes of less than 500 persons. Nationally the Established Church was strongest in areas of small parishes, weakest in areas of large parishes.[1] Small parishes tended to have nucleated settlement, small populations, concentrated ownership of land, and perhaps a resident squire: a series of reinforcing features that suited the machinery of the

[1] See Alan Gilbert, 'The Growth and Decline of Non-conformity in England and Wales, with Special Reference to the Period before 1850', unpublished D.Phil. thesis, University of Oxford, 1973.

Church of England. Other factors, however, favoured Methodism. The majority of the population was in open parishes, relatively immune from the pressure of parsons and squires. These were parishes that were large in area, with dispersed settlement and a large non-agricultural workforce, who tended to be more receptive to Methodism, or at least to be independent of Anglican control mechanisms. There were contrary forces at the regional level as well. The complexities of the parish were reproduced in the region, partly because each region took its character from the parish type that predominated within it. But in general upland areas were more congenial to the Establishment, lowland areas to Methodism. The South Wolds, for example, were a region of small parishes, concentrated settlement, large estates, and resident owners; the Outer Marsh was its Methodist antithesis, with large parishes, dispersed settlement, small estates, and non-resident owners. Other regions, however, were less clear-cut. The Till basin had the lowland pattern of large parishes and small estates, but also a fairly high sex ratio; the Cliff had the upland large estates, but also large parishes; the Central vale was 'Anglican' in its large estates and sparse population, but also 'Methodist' in its dispersed settlement and absentee landlords. If one of these features is to be singled out as the most important, it is the structure of landownership within the parish. But in a capitalist economy and class society it was above all the social classes that shaped religious life.

II

AGRARIAN SOCIETY: FROM COMMUNITY
CLASS SOCIETY

THE social structure of south Lindsey in the middle of the nineteenth century cannot be understood apart from the larger transformation of English rural economy and society during the previous two centuries.[1] In this transformation, peasant agriculture and the traditional village society were supplanted by capitalist agriculture—with its large estates, large farms, and production for profit in the market—and by a capitalist class society, in which class lines were drawn more sharply in the countryside than in most towns. The three classes in the new society were strictly defined by their relationship to the means of production, the landlords receiving rent from land, the farmers profits from capital, and labourers wages from physical work. Economic 'base' and social 'superstructure' did not, however, develop evenly or emerge simultaneously. Capitalist agriculture was established by the eighteenth century, but the social transformation was not complete until the second half of the nineteenth, elements of the old society coexisting with those of the new over a long transitional period. And not only did social change lag behind economic change, but the three classes within agrarian society developed at different rates of speed. Yet before the development of each individual class can be understood, it is necessary to trace in greater detail the development of the system as a whole, from community to class society.

It should be pointed out that 'community' and 'class society' are abstractions; they summarize key features but do not exhaust realities. Rural England in 1700 was not a pure specimen of a *Gemeinschaft*, nor was it a pure specimen of a class society in 1850, or 1875. What is involved is not a stark dichotomy but

[1] See Hobsbawm and Rudé, *Captain Swing*, chs. 1–3; J. D. Chambers and G. E. Mingay, *The Agricultural Revolution 1750–1880*, 1966; H. J. Habakkuk, 'La Disparition du paysan anglais', *Annales*, xx (1965); John Saville, 'Primitive Accumulation and Early Industrialization in Britain', in R. Miliband and J. Saville (eds.), *Socialist Register 1969*, 1969.

rather movement along a continuum. There is, however, no question about the direction or depth of change; not only was the economy of the village transformed, but also the character of its social relations.

It is therefore not necessary to romanticize the 'traditional village' to see how fundamentally it differed from the 'capitalist village' of the middle of the nineteenth century. Land in the older society was widely if unevenly distributed. There were of course aristocratic and gentry landlords on the one side and landless labourers on the other, but probably the majority of the families occupied land even if they did not own it. Subsistence was a more frequent aim of farming than profit. And common involvement in the land and co-operation in agriculture gave rise to common values and sentiments, which were expressed in the festivities at harvest and at other high points in the agricultural year. The village was therefore not an assemblage of individuals but a community. Inequalities of wealth, status, and power were great—though not as great as they were to become later—but the community or collectivity was in important ways prior to the individuals who composed it. The individual ownership of property was qualified by the existence of the commons and by common rights over the open fields; agriculture was subject to collective regulation. And to a considerable extent the village governed and policed itself and enforced moral sanctions upon its members.

The traditional village was also a face-to-face society, in which persons knew each other in more than one role—or rather knew each other as persons as well as actors in particular roles; social relations were therefore characteristically 'manystranded'.[1] In such a society, in which the collectivity prevailed over the individual and in which persons had significant relations with others outside the family, the family was inevitably less salient as an institution, less inward-looking, less 'psychological' than it was to become later. The same factors also shaped relations between superiors and inferiors in village society. Society was conceived as a hierarchy of ranks, which primarily expressed differences in status, rather than of class; the 'horizontal' solidarities, whether of rank or class were rarely more than 'latent', being overshadowed by the 'vertical' ties of the reciprocity of

[1] To adapt a term introduced by Eric Wolf, *Peasants*, 1966, pp. 81–6.

paternalism from above and deference from below. The rich lived among the poor and in principle at least were expected to take responsibility for their welfare. There was thus a systematic character to social relations and to the links between property, economy, and society.[1]

The subsequent history of the village community in the eighteenth and nineteenth centuries was the history of its dissolution, both of its material base and of its social and moral superstructure. Economic forces, above all the concentration of landownership and the triumph of capitalist agriculture, destroyed the viability of peasant agriculture. By the middle of the eighteenth century the three classes—landlords, tenant farmers, and labourers—were objectively present, but the subjective correlatives of class consciousness and class culture evolved over a longer period. Classes were made, or made themselves, not only by acting on common economic interests but also by withdrawing from the village community, from social contacts with those not of their own class, and by retreating into the private life of the family and of individual experience.

The first to emerge were the landowners, who indeed had formed something like a class long before 1700: their consciousness of common interests and the national range of their social interactions in the seventeenth century give plausibility to the notion of a 'one-class society'.[2] The stages of their withdrawal from community to class and to family are more visible and better recorded than for any other class. As early as the sixteenth century it has been noted that 'aristocratic funerals began to move from being a manifestation of the whole feudal community to more modest family affairs'. More generally, in the following century 'the gentry drew away from the lower classes' and drew their children away from those of the poor to give them a separate, segregated education.[3] And if seventeenth-century country gentlemen still 'examined samples of grain, handled pigs, and on market days, made bargains over a tankard with drovers and

[1] See Philippe Ariès, *Centuries of Childhood* (trans. Robert Baldick), 1962; Harold Perkin, *Origins of Modern English Society*, 1969, esp. p. 37.

[2] Peter Laslett, *The World We Have Lost*, 1965.

[3] Keith Thomas, *Religion and the Decline of Magic*, 1971, p. 604, citing M. E. James, 'Two Tudor Funerals', *Transactions of the Cumberland and Westmorland Antiquarian and Archaeological Society*, N.S. lxvi (1966); Lawrence Stone, 'Literacy and Education in England 1640–1900', *Past and Present*, no. 42 (1969), pp. 71–2.

hop merchants', by the eighteenth century they had largely turned over these active roles to the farmers. They also withdrew from the traditional recreations of the village.[1] To further distance themselves from the lower orders, they built their houses outside the villages and surrounded them with parks. Yet if they had withdrawn from village society, preferring class and family as the bases of their social life, they still controlled the villages; they were still landowners and magistrates, and they continued to perform the charitable duties of traditional paternalism. But in the long run their sense of responsibility to the poor was compromised by their economic dependence upon agricultural capitalism, and when the landowners in Parliament supported the New Poor Law, it was only a public and national version of an 'abdication' that was an accomplished fact within the village.[2] The imperatives of class ultimately prevailed over the traditions of community.

As gentry culture was entering its higher stages, in the late seventeenth and early eighteenth centuries, the economic basis of the traditional society was disintegrating. Squeezed by falling prices and rising taxes, smallholders sold their land, and the resulting concentration of ownership in the great landlords was decisive. The smallholders declined, and landless labourers multiplied; the graded ranks of the older society were compressed into the three classes of landlords, farmers, and labourers. Parliamentary enclosure only furthered these tendencies, ending common rights and placing further emphasis on individualist agricultural enterprise.

The farmers were next to withdraw from the village community and to emerge as a class. In the eighteenth century and first half of the nineteenth, they too became conscious of themselves as a class with common interests and a common culture. Enriched by agricultural 'improvement', 'new style' farming families adopted a more luxurious, and recognizably middle-class way of life. They began to develop their own political stance, independent of the direction of the gentry. They now shunned social

---

[1] T. B. Macaulay, *History of England*, 1858, i. 320; G. E. Mingay, *English Landed Society in the Eighteenth Century*, 1963, p. 168; Barbara Kerr, 'The Dorset Agricultural Labourer 1750–1850', *Proceedings of the Dorset Natural History and Archaeological Society*, lxxxiv (1963), p. 163; Robert Malcolmson, *Popular Recreations in English Society, 1700–1850*, 1973, p. 68.

[2] See Hobsbawm and Rudé, *Captain Swing*, pp. 47–8; Perkin, *Origins*, pp. 187–91.

intercourse with their labourers, expelling farm servants from the farmhouses, removing their children from village schools, discontinuing harvest suppers and other communal festivities, treating labourers as mere machines for labour. And as they withdrew emotionally from the community they cultivated the private life of the family.

The labourers were a proletariat in their objective economic conditions, but subjectively they were reluctant to accept the cash nexus and capitalist class relations, and they preserved, in a stunted form, much of the older outlook, including a less intense family life and a deferential goodwill to their superiors. There was thus a disjuncture between the class-conscious gentry and farmers on the one hand and the labourers on the other, with their lingering if unreciprocated 'communal' expectations. Finally, in the course of the nineteenth century, the labourers too developed something of a class consciousness, and in the process abandoned some of the 'rough' ways of the past for a more private and disciplined existence. Thus the village community, once its material base was undermined, dissolved, slowly and unevenly, into three classes, each in its own way coming to social terms with the new economic order.

THE GENTRY

If the landed gentry were scarce in south Lindsey, they were still men of considerable wealth and social influence. As landlords they were in a position to exert powerful pressure on their tenants, farmers as well as labourers, and they ruled their parishes without challenge. Their influence could well be exerted in the religious sphere, and indeed the Anglican ideal envisioned squires and parsons working in partnership to promote the interests of the Establishment. In south Lindsey, however, this ideal was seldom realized. In the first place gentry influence was confined to close parishes: the rather larger population in open parishes lay beyond their reach. And many landlords were absentees, with but little direct control over their parishes. Even if they resided, they found that while their power over the labourers had grown, they had lost some of their sway over the farmers, now more wealthy and independent. And if their power to serve Church interests was limited, there was also an ambiguity about their desire to do so. For the ideal of the gentleman and the ideal of the Christian ultimately diverged, despite efforts by Thomas Arnold and others to reconcile them, and the tension between them gave the religious identity of the gentry a divided, problematic character.

Who then were the gentry? The definition of a gentleman notoriously involved nuances and impalpable essences: a town gentleman was not the same as a country gentleman, and even in the countryside contemporaries disagreed.[1] In the present study the definition used varies with the question asked. For the question of the extent to which landlords were able to exert their economic and social influence to aid the Church, the relevant group is that of landlords owning at least one parish. For the question of the religious significance of gentry values and style of life, the relevant group is those generally acknowledged by contemporaries as bearing the 'port, charge, and countenance' of a gentleman.

The two groups overlapped but did not completely coincide, for there were some who had the life style without the land, and were therefore unable to exert influence over tenants, while others had the land without the life style: notably those farmers who owned and occupied an entire parish and who certainly wielded the influence of a squire but who did not move in 'county' society.

The gentry proper—gentry by virtue of their mode of life— were of diverse origins. There were old county families like the Andersons of Lea, descended from a Lord Chief Justice in the reign of Elizabeth I, and the Dymokes, Hereditary Champions of England since Edward II. Secondly there were newer families of local origin like the Tennyson d'Eyncourts of Tealby. In a third group were new families from outside the county, like the Liveseys of Baumber, whose origins were in Blackburn, and the Becketts of Corringham, influential bankers in Leeds. These families were converting urban wealth into rural status, but most of the outsiders who acquired their Lincolnshire estates in the nineteenth century did not reside on them, and presumably were also buying land as an investment. Diverse as their origins were, there is no evidence that the older families were con-

---

[1] In the early 1870s three lists of south Lindsey gentry were compiled, in Burke's *Landed Gentry*, Walford's *County Families*, and White's *Directory*; of the total of 115 names mentioned only twenty-two appeared on all three lists.

temptuous of the recent, commercial, or urban origins of the newer families; for wealth, and the adoption of an acceptable style of living, rather than antiquity, was the ticket of admission into county society.[1] Still, the gentry were far from homogeneous, and age and pedigree were not the only respects in which they varied. They ranged from magnates with many thousands of acres to petty squires who barely owned one entire parish. Some were deep in debt and distress, others had ample supplies of ready cash. The larger owners could play a part not only on the county scene but in London as well; in the 1840s most Lincolnshire squires owning estates of more than 7,000 acres had town houses.[2] But the smaller owners might have no weight beyond their own neighbourhood, or even outside their own parish. In politics they inclined to Toryism, but a large minority were Whigs. And in religion, if most were Church of England, there were also a few adherents of the Church of Rome—and of what Disraeli called the 'religion of all sensible men'.

Whatever his views, a landlord who was master in his parish could do much to shape its religious life—but only if he resided. And many had compelling reasons to live elsewhere. A number of large properties in south Lindsey simply lacked a house fit for the residence of a gentleman; they were outlying parts of estates whose seats were in a different part of Lincolnshire or in another county altogether. Kesteven, with its superior social attractions, was favoured by several owners of estates of this kind, including the Ancaster, the Brownlow, the Chaplin, and the Turnor. Several owners, like Lancelot Rolleston of Low Toynton, evidently came into residence solely for shooting in the autumn.[3] Others may have been deterred by the unfavourable reputation of the climate in Lindsey, however unjustified that may have been. Financial difficulties led several families to cut expenses by living abroad: Pau, in the lower French Pyrénées, was a favourite refuge for local distressed gentlefolk. And institutional owners like the Charterhouse or Bethlehem Hospital were non-resident by necessity.

[1] As in Essex around 1800. See Colin Shrimpton, 'Landed Society and the Farming Community of Essex in the Late Eighteenth and Early Nineteenth Centuries', unpublished Ph.D. thesis, University of Cambridge, 1965, pp. 152-3.

[2] Olney, *Lincolnshire Politics*, p. 21.

[3] *Hornc. News*, 24 Sept. 1870. Another sportsman and occasional resident was J. W. Fox of Burgh-on-Bain (White, *Directory*, 1856, p. 647).

An absentee owner could exert little influence over the religious life of his parish. At most he could screen out persons of the 'wrong' religious views—or refuse to do so—when he or his agent selected new tenants: the policy of Willoughby de Eresby, non-resident owner of the extensive Ancaster estate in the Marsh and southern Wolds.[1] And among the absentees the institutional owners appear to have been no more likely than the others to manage their parishes at all effectively by remote control. Magdalen College, Oxford, owned a considerable estate in Horsington, and was patron of the living, but was unable or unwilling to exert any pressure on the tenants for the sake of the church. The curate complained that

the Church, instead of deriving either support or credit from the tenants of the College estate at Horsington, suffers the greatest evils. The lands are leased to Mr. Burkinshaw, who sublets the larger part to Mr. Stones, a *Wesleyan Class Leader*, and a principal prop of the Meeting here. Of course all his influence is antagonistic to the Church. There are, unfortunately, still worse cases. A cottager, named Bowering, resides on the College estate; he has three adult sons, and three unmarried daughters under his roof: the daughters are *known to be Prostitutes*, and two of the sons are strongly *suspected of the murder of Mr. Dymoke's keeper.'*[2]

The effective influence of the non-residents was small; the critical question then is, how many resident squires were there?

Unfortunately, though chronic absenteeism is easy enough to detect, distinguishing between continuous and occasional residence often is difficult. In 1851 it appears that only seventeen parishes were blessed with resident gentry landowners while four more were occupied by farmer-gentlemen who were their sole owners. In these twenty-one 'primary' parishes with resident squires there were only 4,935 persons, 7·6 per cent of the total population of south Lindsey. On a broader definition of residence (including parishes in which the owners were occasional residents, parishes with resident gentlemen who did not own much if any land, and parishes owned by squires resident in adjoining parishes), forty-two 'secondary' parishes are added, making a grand total of sixty-three parishes with resident squires. They amounted to more than a quarter of the total parishes, but their population

[1] See below, p. 35.
[2] Watkin to Cholmeley, 29 Dec. 1852; Magdalen College, Oxford, estate records, Schools 1853.

was less than a quarter of the total, and the great majority of villagers lived in squireless parishes. South Lindsey was emphatically an area of sparse gentry settlement and of correspondingly limited gentry influence.

Distribution of Resident Squires in 1851, by Region

	Primary parishes	Secondary parishes	Parishes in region
Till basin	2	3	17
Cliff	3	10	21
Central vale	1	4	49
Fen margin	2	2	10
South Wolds	5	23	53
North Wolds	6	15	38
Middle Marsh	2	6	33
Outer Marsh	0	1	15

Percentage of Population Under Resident Squires in 1851, by Region

	Primary parishes	Secondary parishes
Till basin	11·3	13·0
Cliff	7·0	47·4
Central vale	0·7	5·4
Fen margin	16·1	16·1
South Wolds	10·1	42·6
North Wolds	19·5	41·6
Middle Marsh	6·9	19·2
Outer Marsh	0·0	4·5
Total	7·6	22·4

Within south Lindsey the geographical distribution of gentry families was most uneven, as is shown by the tables above and by the regional pattern of magistrates.[1]

Distribution of Magistrates by Region, 1824, 1856, 1872
(including clerical justices)

	1824	1856	1872	Total parishes
Till basin	4	4	7	17
Cliff	1	5	5	21
Central vale	7	7	6	49
Fen margin	2	2	2	10
South Wolds	14	11	16	53
North Wolds	5	7	6	38
Middle Marsh	0	6	4	33
Outer Marsh	0	2	2	15
Total	33	44	48	236

[1] Cragg 1/1, pp. 447–8, L.A.O.; White, *Directory*, 1856, pp. 11, 50; White, *Directory*, 1872, pp. 52–3.

The gentry had deserted the lowland regions, apart from the Till basin. And the area-wide shortage of gentry meant that clergymen had to be pressed into service as magistrates.[1] In 1824 clergymen and squarsons outnumbered plain squires on the bench 18 to 15; in 1856 laymen had the advantage, 24 to 20, while in 1872 numbers were equal at 24 each. These, it should be noted, were men empowered to act as justices: of those who actually did judicial work, the active magistrates, the majority were probably clergymen. Few of the larger resident owners troubled themselves with the weekly grind of petty-sessional cases. On the whole, then, landlord influence was weak in south Lindsey.

The 1851 Religious Census showed that church attendance was highest in close parishes with resident landlords.[2] Yet it is not clear that a squire could simply command his people to appear in church for the Sunday service. There is doubt particularly with respect to the tenant farmers, who were becoming richer, more independent, and more class-conscious. Unfortunately the influence of landlords over the religious activities of their tenant farmers is not well documented, and it is necessary to approach the subject indirectly, by considering the general state of the relations between landlords and farmers.

Their economic dealings with each other involved opportunities for conflict of interest, but both sides regarded agriculture as a co-operative enterprise. A model improving landlord like G. F. Heneage could spend over £100,000 on his estate over a period of twenty years.[3] When low prices destroyed the farmers' profits, landlords often either returned part of the rent or undertook to spend it on improvements on the estate.[4] Of course, abatements of rent and investment of capital were less frequent with landlords who were themselves in financial difficulty or less

---

[1] Urging the Lord Lieutenant to nominate a clergyman to the Commission of the Peace in the Marshland hundred of Calceworth, the Revd. W. Dodson pointed out that 'within this hundred there is not a single layman, ranking as a Gentleman, resident on his property' (Dodson to Brownlow, 7 Apr. [1842], 4 BNL, Box 3, L.A.O.).

[2] See below, p. 155.

[3] *Mkt Rasen W.M.*, 12 Jan. 1867.

[4] Many instances of abatements of rent were mentioned in local newspapers in 1830-1, 1834-5, and 1850-1; landlords like William Hutton of Gate Burton promised to spend 20 per cent of their rental on improvements (*Lincs. Tims*, 11 June 1850) and J. B. Stanhope claimed that many spent 30 per cent (*Hansard*, xii, col. 509, 25 Apr. 1853).

committed to the gospel of agricultural progress. But confidence and co-operation appear to have been the rule. Leases were rare, as most farms were let by the year, yet there were virtually hereditary tenancies on many estates. The custom of tenant right, by which the incoming tenant compensated the outgoing tenant for unexhausted improvements, also sustained confidence between owner and tenant. And landlords and farmers joined forces to counter threats from below, presenting a solid front to the labourers' unions in the 1870s. The confidence and co-operation were real, but the confidence was that of the tenant in the landlord the co-operation that of the landlord with the tenant: the balance in their partnership was shifting in favour of the farmers.

Landlords also sought to cultivate friendly personal relations with their tenants, at least with the larger ones. C. J. H. Massingberd-Mundy called upon his tenants at South Ormsby and Driby nearly every Sunday afternoon.[1] Many landlords treated their tenants to dinner at rent day, and old-style paternalism and deference revived in an atmosphere of beer and tobacco.[2] Some landlords appear to have inspired genuine affection; while testimonials no doubt could easily be rigged, it is notable that both G. F. Heneage and Sir Charles Anderson were presented with portraits by their tenants,[3] while Sir Thomas Beckett was honoured after his death by a memorial tablet in the parish church subscribed to by the local tenantry. Yet more than affection was involved, for all three had made large investments on their estates and had championed the cause of agriculture. Affection had to be earned—or purchased—by concrete favours and benefits.

If the economic balance was gradually tilting in favour of the tenants, how then did a landlord influence his tenants' politics?[4] When he selected a tenant for a farm, he could take care that his political views were congenial. For most landlords the first concern was that their tenants should have sufficient capital and farming ability, but a prospective tenant's political views would be elicited—if indeed a farmer was not deterred even from applying for a farm to a landlord of a different party.

[1] Diaries, M.M. 10/55, 58, 100–2, L.A.O.
[2] Examples include William Hutton of Gate Burton and Willoughby Wood of South Thoresby (*Stamf. Merc.*, 7 Dec. 1838, *Louth Adv.*, 22 Dec. 1866).
[3] *Mkt Rasen W.M.*, 5 Jan. 1861; *Retf. News*, 21 Feb. 1874.
[4] See the excellent discussion in Olney, *Lincolnshire Politics*, ch. 4.

The critical test, however, was at the elections, and the poll-books show that the landlords' political influence was still strong. On the Monson estate, for example, the tenants voted Tory in 1835 and 1841 under the Tory fifth lord, but when he was succeeded by a Whig, they swung over automatically to the other party.[1] And many farmers took little interest in politics—the agent on the Ancaster estate complained in 1840 that the farmers 'are such a sleepy set scarcely anything will stir them'.[2] But the question is more complicated than it seems. A closer look at the motives and at the voting patterns of both landlords and farmers suggests that the landlords were conceding more and the farmers deferring less than they had in the past. There is no doubt that most farmers tended to be Tory, so Tory landlords would seem to have had no need either for coercion or modesty about their political influence, yet they increasingly felt it desirable to make a show of tolerance or indifference when an election approached. Christopher Turnor, a Tory landlord, declared before the 1852 election that his Lindsey tenants could vote any way they pleased: he had stated the previous summer his intention to vote for Stanhope, the second Tory candidate, but did not wish to prejudice their vote and gave the Whig candidate permission to canvass his tenants. His profession of indifference—'"if they all vote for him I shall not be in the least displeased"'—was probably insincere, and he could convey his wishes to his tenants privately or through his agent.[3] Yet it was desirable to avoid any suggestion of coercion. Furthermore, voting was not mechanically regular: in election after election there were numerous dissenting votes, more on some estates than others, but enough to disprove any assumption of mechanical compliance.[4] While there may have been genuine apolitical deference, as well as instinctive Toryism, the suspicion arises that the farmers voted with their landlords because their 'deference' was being purchased, and rewarded, by material benefits.

What then of the landlord's influence over his tenants' religious practice? He could exclude Dissenters from his estate as easily as Liberals, and he could ultimately evict a religious as easily as a

---

[1] Lindsey poll books, 1835, 1841, and 1852.
[2] Booth to Kennedy, 2 Apr. 1840, 3 ANC 7/23/39/15.
[3] *Lincs. Times*, 3 Feb. 1852.
[4] See especially Olney, *Lincolnshire Politics*, p. 135.

political recalcitrant. The agent of the Ancaster estate noted of
one applicant for a farm that he 'would be a very good tenant
but there is one objection to him being a Dissenter', and when
the Ecclesiastical Commissioners acquired the parish of Lusby,
they ejected the four chief tenants because they were Methodists.[1]
But if the means of influence were the same, the objectives were
of quite different orders. Political influence was employed to
obtain votes at contested elections, of which there were only five
in the fifty years under study; religious influence on the other
hand was intended to promote regular attendance at the parish
church, or at least absence from the chapel, Sunday after Sunday.
Political influence mattered on only five days in fifty years,
religious influence on all 2,600 Sundays. Close personal supervision was therefore necessary if religious influence was to be
effective, and in south Lindsey the scarcity of resident squires
made that a rarity. Furthermore, Whig landlords like Lord
Yarborough in north Lindsey had many Methodist farmers on
their estates. Probably the most a squire expected of his tenant
farmers was to attend the Sunday morning service in the parish
church—which might be considered a 'civic' duty, an affirmation
of the unity of the village with the squire at its head, as much as a
religious one.

If the farmers had become more independent of landlord
influence, the labourers had become more vulnerable. Economic
and social change over the previous century had elevated the
landlord and debased the labourer, who was left powerless as
well as poor. A landlord who wished his labourers to attend
church could easily coerce them, but whether he wished to do so
in the first place is unclear, and it is necessary to consider other
aspects of landlord–labourer relations.

Traditional paternalistic charity had not disappeared, but it
was limited in extent and eroded by contrary motives.[2] The
ambiguities of landlords' dealings with labourers are especially
apparent in the system of open and close parishes. It was the landlords who were responsible for the evils of the system, since it

[1] Booth to Kennedy, 23 Jan. 1844, 3 ANC 7/23/44/10A; *Linc. Gaz.*, 28 June
1862.

[2] An American agricultural writer visiting England (including south Lindsey)
in the 1840s claimed more generally that 'the large establishments have lost that
patriarchal character ... Those strong personal ties ... have almost ceased to
exist' (Henry Colman, *European Agriculture and Rural Economy*, 1846, i. 140).

was they who curtailed the provision of cottages for labourers in their parishes. On the other hand, the cottages they allowed to stand were generally superior to those in open parishes, being well built and accompanied by gardens and allotments. Moreover, it was generally assumed that the labourer had greater security renting his cottage directly from a landlord than as a sub-tenant from a farmer.[1] And besides the traditional paternalist doctrine still urged by squires like James Whiting Yorke and James Banks Stanhope there was also a revised version for the age of affluent farmers: according to William Hutton, squire of Gate Burton, 'it was alike the duty of landlord and tenant to see that the wants of the labourer were cared for.' The practical application was carried furthest by G. F. Heneage, whose estate was considered a model of its kind, a miniature welfare state. He paid pensions to old people; and far from pulling down cottages to save on the poor rates, he had large numbers of good new ones built which were situated conveniently near the fields and provided with a rood of land for a garden.[2] Many squires and their wives gave blankets, calicoes, and coal to their labourers at Christmas and during the winter.

Paternalism took on still another form, for it was a matter of sentiment as well as charity. The squire and his relations were the parochial version of a royal family, and while they lived private lives, sheltered from the vulgar gaze, they translated events in their family history into public, communal celebrations. A wedding, the birth of an heir, his coming of age—all called for parish festivities.[3] When a death occurred in a gentry family, virtually the entire village would attend the funeral, and house-

---

[1] A Lindsey Yeoman, *A Farming Tour*, 1854; Clarke, *Farming of Lincolnshire*, p. 154; see also T. Hardy, 'The Dorsetshire Labourer', in H. Orel (ed.), *Thomas Hardy's Personal Writings*, 1967, pp. 181–2. Nevertheless, the landlord's power was arbitrary. Colman tells of one of the Lincolnshire landlords he visited, 'an excellent landlord and friend, distinguished for his integrity and philanthropy', who gave notice to some of his cottagers because 'they had taken lodgers into their families, who were not agreeable to him'. (*European Agriculture and Rural Economy*, i. 65.)

[2] *Lincs. Times*, 30 July 1850; *Linc. Gaz.*, 9 Nov. 1872; *Boston, Stamford, and Lincolnshire Herald*, 1 Aug. 1848; *Mkt Rasen W.M.*, 12 Jan. 1867.

[3] When Edward, son and heir of G. F. Heneage, was born in 1840, there was a christening dinner for the gentry and chief farmers and only gifts of food for the poor (*Linc. Gaz.*, 12 May 1840); when his own heir was born in 1866 the festivities were mainly for the poor (*Louth Adv.*, 6 Oct. 1866). Significantly, the more elaborate and more popular of these celebrations was held after 1850, when social tensions had eased.

holders drew their blinds to show their respect. On these occasions landlords cultivated the loyalty of the labourers with a 'dignified version' of parish society.

They gave a more economic turn to this strategy, encouraging the labourers' skills as well as their loyalty, in local ploughing and agricultural societies. Most of these societies were founded around 1840; each attracted men from all classes in a particular neighbourhood and beyond. Competitions for labourers were held in various agricultural tasks and prizes were awarded to the winners. And there was a prize too for the labourer with the longest period of service with the same farmer. To complete the appearance of an integrated society, farmers and clergymen attended, as well as landlords and labourers. The landlord received the deference proper to the leader of the neighbourhood; farmers and clergymen made speeches and proposed toasts; the labourers were seen but not heard. The societies were founded at a time when the tension between farmers and labourers was at its greatest, and when only the landlords could appeal to the labourers' loyalty. In other respects as well they were a phenomenon of the transition from traditional to class society.[1] Landlords sought to reward labourers' skills and their loyalty alike; not by traditional paternalism nor by appropriate wages but by a peculiar combination of a cash prize and a certificate. Thus both economic progress and social stability were to be assured.

In the long term the landlords' paternalism faded as their economic interests aligned them with the farmers and against the labourers. Nevertheless, they continued to cast themselves in a dignified role, projecting an image and ideal of paternalism, beneficence, and community across the social gulf.[2]

In the squire's dealings with the parson, however, it was the absence of a social gulf that created difficulties. Farmers and labourers were inferiors, but a parson could claim to be a gentleman,

[1] The labourers' unions, concerned for their members' dignity as well as their wages and hours, deprecated the societies and their prizes for length of service. In 1875 the Amalgamated Labour League was 'glad to notice that all the best class of labourers are beginning to stay away from the degrading exhibitions of these societies' (*Labourer*, 25 Dec. 1875).

[2] The duality of landlords' attitudes towards the labourers has been noted by Hobsbawm and Rudé, *Captain Swing*, and by Esther Moir, *The Justice of the Peace*, 1969, p. 99.

and therefore an equal. And their roles were not sharply distinct either, for if the parson was also a gentleman, the squire could claim to be a kind of pastor to his people, capable of doing everything the parson did except administer the sacraments.[1] Finally, ever since the Restoration it had been axiomatic with squires of every shade of churchmanship that they were masters in their own parishes and that the clergy must be kept in subordination, but the parson's freehold in his benefice made him independent of the squire and immune to his pressures. The relationship between squire and parson therefore teemed with opportunities for conflict, and the Anglican ideal of harmonious partnership was only one possibility among many, and not perhaps the most likely.

From the point of view of the squire, a judicious exercise of patronage would avert difficulties—but a wrong choice could plague him for life, since the parson's freehold made him immovable. Sir Charles Anderson could 'never ... sufficiently regret having appointed [R. T.] Lowe rector' of his parish of Lea; Anderson, a moderate High Churchman of traditional outlook, was angered and disgusted by Lowe's ritual innovations and felt that he 'had done more harm in the parish than the most Ultra puritan'.[2] It is noteworthy, however, that in a large minority of close parishes, the patronage was not in the hands of the squire; around 1851 this was the case in as many as 51 out of 130 such parishes, 40 per cent of the total. Thus a squire might have to deal with a parson not of his own choosing, a standing affront to his sovereignty in the parish.

When parson or church challenged that sovereignty too directly, squires did not hesitate on occasion to exercise it with *force majeure*. An incident from Revesby, the home parish of James Banks Stanhope, illustrates the point. The living was a donative, and on that authority Stanhope gave his clergyman, the Revd. Andrew Veitch, notice to quit. When Veitch refused to go, and continued to take services in the church, Stanhope directed his gamekeepers to occupy the church on Saturday and remain inside until it was time for services the following morning. Veitch entered the church, but when he began to

---

[1] See Owen Chadwick, *Victorian Miniature*, 1960.

[2] Diary, 13 Apr. 1869, Helmsley MSS. Richard Thomas Lowe was rector of Lea 1852–74.

read the prayers, the gamekeepers carried him out bodily.[1] This was an extreme case, but it may be suspected that most squires probably wished they could treat all church livings as donatives. At any rate a masterful squire could treat the church buildings on his estate as his private property. Edward Heneage had his workmen pull down the tower of the parish church at Sixhills and use the stone to repair walks in his garden and roads in the parish. This was perpetrated, needless to say, without a faculty, yet the archdeacon declined to prosecute. Heneage's power was not challenged in the entire affair.[2]

More serious was the streak of anti-clericalism running through gentry culture. Its most articulate exponent was the sixth baron Monson, whose views, expressed in letters to his eldest son, are not so much typical as archetypal. He disliked the 'Saints' who would 'make a row' about Princess Mary of Cambridge marrying a Roman Catholic.[3] An Evangelical preacher at Pau aroused his scorn: 'We have a clergyman here named Hedges but he always calls himself Edges. An extempore preacher!! you can fancy how charming of course I do not hear him but still as he preaches without any restraint of a written discourse it seriously incommodes me as to time.'[4] High churchmen were no better. When his sister-in-law gave her son the middle name Paul because he was baptized on 25 January, the Conversion of St. Paul (though he was born on 1 January), Monson remarked that 'whereas by all right and propriety as it was born on the first it ought to be called Edmund Circumcision Larken'. He belaboured the clerical zealots who were destroying moderate churchmanship:

The fact is as the principle of High Church is to throw an undisputed power into the hands of the parsons and make the laity nothing, weak minds are led astray by the intoxication of power. The good old days of the moderate Country Clergyman are passing away and we shall have only fanatics of both extremes.[5]

In more expansive moments he lashed out against all the clergy, but particularly those he suspected of pursuing money, his own or other people's. When Lady Henry Watson announced her

---

[1] *Stamf. Merc.*, 7 Dec. 1851.

[2] Anon. [C. A. Wilkinson], *The Last Act in the Drama of Sixhills*, n.d. Louth and Market Rasen newspapers, 1871–3, *passim*.

[3] Monson to Monson, 5 Dec. 1855, MON 25/10/4/1/11.

[4] 22 Dec. 1856, MON 25/10/4/2/4. He was hard of hearing.

[5] 3 Feb. 1853, MON 25/10/3/3/108; 10 June 1851, MON 25/10/3/1/89.

remarriage to a clergyman, he had 'no doubt the man marries her for *her money* as she cannot be very far off sixty. It is exactly what these fellows in black coats are doing everywhere . . . the Church at this time are more eager after money than any other profession'. His indignation rose when they imprudently asked him for donations. 'I declined being a Vice President of the Church Building Society. It was one of the clerical modes of extorting money.' Again: 'The impudent and extortionate begging letters from Clergy of whom I know nothing and which come in shoals perfectly disgust me.' 'You will find . . . what a fearful job it is one of these days to refuse begging letters of all kinds and descriptions but decidedly the worst are the mendicant clergy.'[1] Such views were more idiosyncratic in expression than in content. They represented more than a vein of Whig anti-clericalism; they sprang from a fundamental assumption of gentry culture. Just as the State controlled the Church of England on the national level, so the squire should dominate the parson and church at the parish level. Accustomed to having his own way in his parish, he resented opposition from the one man whom he was powerless to remove. High church, low church, or no church, in his own parish he was an erastian.

Still masters in their own parishes, the gentry eschewed strong-arm tactics in their dealings with their dependants: indeed they professed to act in accordance with principle, with the duties and responsibilities of their position. Of all the classes in rural society it was they who had gone furthest in elaborating a set of values and a conscious way of life. Two of its elements particularly relevant to gentry religious life deserve to be explored: their passion for blood sports and their ideal of the Christian gentleman.

What set off the gentry from all other classes and groups in Victorian society was their rejection of the gospel of work. If theirs was a privileged state, it was a state of being, not doing. There were, it is true, exceptions. In 1851—a bad year for agriculture—a number of squires are found managing farms on their own estates: Frederick Chaplin, 1,300 acres at Tathwell; James Banks Stanhope, 800 acres at Revesby; William Hutton, 600 acres at Gate Burton; Sir Henry Dymoke, 600 acres at Scrivelsby.[2]

---

[1] 30 Apr. 1853, MON 25/10/3/3/71; 30 Dec. 1856, MON 25/10/4/2/1; 1 Nov. 1855, MON 25/10/4/1/25; 24 Dec. 1851, MON 25/10/3/1/4.

[2] Noted in the Enumerators' books of the 1851 Census.

But in general the life of the gentry was a life of idleness which called for diversions and recreations.

Among their favourite forms of relief were field sports, which alone of the 'traditional' recreations involving cruelty to animals survived in the upper class. They also had religious overtones. It is true that shooting differed in important ways from hunting, the one a private affair for friends, the other a public chase open to all comers; yet both were pre-eminently gentry pastimes, and their chroniclers and interpreters wrote for a gentry audience.[1] Throughout the literature of both sports, local and national alike, were two themes of religious significance: the kinship between men and animals, and the desecration of Christianity. The kinship between men and animals—affirmed in different ways at every level of agrarian society—was felt perhaps most strongly by the élite. Upper-class sportsmen regularly attributed to animals, to dogs and horses, human characteristics, and bestowed upon them human feelings. It was an article of belief among sportsmen that animals were endowed with reason, and they cited examples in creatures ranging from the foxhound to the elephant. The feelings of gentlemen towards their dogs were particularly intense. Dogs had human traits like intelligence and loyalty; they dreamed —but happily were free of the fear of death. Hounds did not bark but were allowed to 'speak', and their 'music' delighted their human friends. Every hound had its name and responded to it when called; recognition and response were mutual between hounds and huntsmen.

> Their proudest joy, all thorough Sportsmen own,
> To know their dogs, and by their dogs be known.

The tie alas was inevitably broken at death, but a squire might vow to commemorate his departed hounds by building a shrine in the chapel and by carving their outlines in his gravestone.[2] Surprisingly, kinship with horses was less often expressed, though at Blankney in Kesteven the Chaplins erected gravestones to mark the graves of some of their hunters,[3] and a sportsman

---

[1] Thompson (*English Landed Society*, pp. 144, 149) notes that hunting attracted farmers and others in rural society above the ranks of the labourers.

[2] Delabere P. Blaine, *An Encyclopedia of Rural Sports*, 1840, pp. 220. 222–9, 474–6; Richard Ellison, *Kirkstead! or the Pleasures of Shooting*, 1837, p. 35.

[3] I am indebted to Mrs. Wendy Lloyd for directing me to these monuments— to Fidget, Sunbeam, and Dumps.

made sad when death had ended his 'brotherhood' with his horse might express a larger hope:

> There are men both good and wise who hold that
> in a future state
> Dumb creatures we have cherished here below
> Shall give us joyous greeting when we pass the
> golden gate;
> Is it folly that I hope it may be so?
> For never man had friend
> More enduring to the end,
> Truer mate in every turn of time and tide.[1]

Human traits were ascribed to animals, while at the same time men were made bestial in the heat of the chase. The emotional, overtones have a supra-rational, religious dimension.

Yet the religious essence of field sports was more specific than this: its desecration of Christianity. Some of the symptoms were minor. Perhaps it was no more than an innocent juxtaposition when Charles Anderson, son of the squarson of Lea, wrote in his diary on 21 January 1837, 'Shot. Read *Lyra Apostolica*.'[2] Anderson, then at the height of 'Newmania', passed for the leading High Church layman in the county. More serious was the piece-meal profanation of Christianity. 'The spires [of churches] form *objects* to the Yarborough family in *hunting*,' complained an archdeacon to his bishop about the great north Lindsey family.[3] Likewise, the Christian calendar and Christian holidays were adapted to mark the seasons of blood sports:

The 'time of grace' begins at Midsummer, and lasteth to Holyrood-day. The fox may be hunted from the Nativity to the Annunciation of our Lady; the roe from Michaelmas to Candlemas; the hare from Michaelmas to Midsummer; the wolf as the fox; and the boar from the Nativity to the Purification of our Lady.[4]

More flagrant still was the custom of 'blooding' a novice hunter with the 'brush' of the dead fox: a none-too-subtle parody of

---

[1] G. J. Whyte-Melville, *Songs and Verses*, 1924, p. 149.

[2] Diary, Helmsley MSS. *Lyra Apostolica* was a collection of religious verse by members of the Oxford Movement, chiefly by Newman.

[3] Goddard to Kaye, 9 Dec. 1834, Cor. B. 5/4/79/1.

[4] Joseph Strutt, *The Sports and Pastimes of the People of England*, ed. W. Hone, 1845, p. 23.

the sacrament of baptism, a substitution of the blood of the fox for the blood of the Lamb. The animals pursued by the devotees of field sports acquired a virtually religious character and were treated appropriately. A modern historian notes that the gentry of Dorset had a 'reverence' for the preservation of game, which 'assumed an almost ritual significance'.[1] The fox was transformed into a sacred animal; when Charles Anderson discovered a dead fox, the victim of foul play, his response was only half ironic: *"'horror horror!! most sacrilegious" "murder hath broken open the foxes anointed Temples!'"*[2] It is hard to avoid the conclusion that the blasphemy and desecration were consciously intended. On another occasion, when a fox was pursued into the city of Lincoln through the Minster Yard before being killed, Anderson noted that 'had the Cathedral gates been open he would probably have attended Divine Service'. And in an episode in Charles Kingsley's novel *Yeast* the hounds leaped over the walls of a churchyard, then 'swept round under the grey wall, leaping and yelling, like Berserk fiends among the crowded tombstones, over the cradles of the quiet dead'; there was 'a ghastly discord in it. Peace and strife, time and eternity—the mad noisy flesh, and the silent immortal spirit.'[3] Nor was the Established Church the sole victim of blood sport sacrilege. The hounds of the Handley Cross hunt, in Surtees's novel, were 'very steady and most musical. Their airing yard adjoins the Ebenezer chapel, and when the saints begin to sing, the dogs join chorus.' And in south Lindsey, when the Burton hunt was about to cross a small wheat field at Reepham, the occupier, 'a small farmer and staunch Wesleyan . . . held up a shovel in a threatening attitude to deter them from crossing,' but the Master, Lord Henry Bentinck, burst through regardless.[4] The theme reached fuller development in the poem *Kirkstead! or the Pleasure of Shooting*, by Richard Ellison, squire of Sudbrooke. The choice of Kirkstead was not

[1] E. W. Martin, *The Case against Hunting*, 1959, p. 45; Kerr, 'The Dorset Agricultural Labourer', p. 163.

[2] Anderson to Pepys, 4 Dec. 1826, Bodl. MSS. Wilberforce. Similarly a miscreant in a Trollope novel killed 'the demon' (a fox) 'whom the aristocracy and plutocracy worshipped' (*The American Senator*, 1940, p. 106).

[3] Anderson to Samuel Wilberforce, 8 Apr. 1828, Bodl. MSS. Wilberforce; *Yeast*, 4th ed., London, 1881, p. 16. Kingsley's first chapter, 'Philosophy of Fox-Hunting', abounds in incidents of desecration.

[4] R. S. Surtees, *Handley Cross*, 1843, i. 133; *Linc. Gaz.*, 22 Feb. 1862.

arbitrary. Its well-known ruins of a twelfth-century Cistercian abbey and the small surviving chapel *ante portas* formed an ensemble sanctified both to piety and to beauty[1]—and an irresistible attraction to hares, dogs, and shooters.

> First to the Abbey-yard and ruins near,
> (Hares love the Abbey-yard) our course we steer . . .
>
> The Abbot's Kitchen—(Monks knew what is good,
> Or fame belies the holy fathers!)—there,
> Where oft a Hare has smok'd, we find a Hare . . .
>
> Hard by the Chapel three more Hares we slay,
> While some are miss'd, and many steal away.[2]

The venerable setting added an extra thrill to the destruction of game. From north Lindsey came a still more daring and explicit account of massacre amidst monastic ruins: during a run of the Brocklesby hounds, 'the fox took refuge in the remains of the old Abbey Chapel, where he was sacrificed within five yards of the altar'.[3] The climactic experience for a sportsman was evidently to offer animal sacrifice at a Christian altar.

The two themes—kinship with animals and the desecration of Christianity—appeared frequently in conjunction; T. S. Eliot noted that 'bishops are a part of English culture, and horses and dogs are a part of English religion'. This indeed might have served as the text for the Master of the Southwold Hunt, who gave the two themes their ultimate expression. He kept two photographs on his desk, one of his favourite hound and one of Bishop King, the saintly Anglo-Catholic, explaining, '"they are the two on whom I place most reliance."'[4]

The passion for field sports was not the only element in gentry culture that created tension with their Christian professions. The ideal of the gentleman which lay at the heart of their class culture was even more problematic. Could a gentleman be a Christian? The Arnoldians and the gentlemen thought so, and argued

---

[1] See Nikolaus Pevsner and John Harris, *The Buildings of England: Lincolnshire*, 1964, p. 287.

[2] Ellison, *Kirkstead!*, pp. 15–16.

[3] Nelthorpe to Anderson, 31 Dec. 1845, And. 5/2/3/52. The 'old Abbey Chapel' was that of the former Augustinian abbey at Thornton Curtis.

[4] T. S. Eliot, *Notes Towards the Definition of Culture*, 1949, p. 31; Gilbert Walker, *Tales of a Lincolnshire Antiquary*, ed. W. A. Cragg, 1949, p. 9.

that the two ideals were identical; but it needs to be pointed out how divergent, indeed ultimately contradictory, they were.[1] The origins of the idea of the gentleman were pagan, not Christian; a gentleman was worldly in orientation, of the world as well as in it, had an ample supply of material wealth, respected traditional social status, cultivated pride in himself and his pedigree, prized temperament, moderation, balance, self-possession, and self-control. The Christian, on the other hand, is otherworldly, despises material wealth, is ascetic, denies all purely human distinctions and social categories, attacks human pride and self-sufficiency, and demands an immoderate devotion to ethical standards. When Francis of Assisi decided to take Christianity seriously, he gave his money away and ceased to be a gentleman. Now it can be argued that no one in any section of south Lindsey society came close to this definition of Christian, and that the landed gentleman was no further from it than anyone else. But there were two critical differences distinguishing the gentleman from men in other classes and occupations. The first was that no more was expected of the others than to perform certain actions—to be a farmer was simply to farm and to be a labourer was simply to labour, but to be a gentleman was to be in a certain state of mind, or soul. The second was that to be a gentleman was to commit oneself to a definite creed of belief and code of behaviour, a certain conception of human nature; but this was not true of a farmer or a labourer. That state of mind, that creed and code were inconsistent with Christianity. The incompatibility of the two value systems is suggested in the very phrase 'Christian gentleman', for to say baldly that someone is a gentleman does not necessary imply that he is a Christian. The same is true of *miles christianus* and 'Christian Scientist', but not of 'Christian farmer' or 'Christian labourer'. The tension between the Christian and the gentleman must have been felt by the more self-aware squires. It was one of the most devout of them, Sir Charles Anderson, the lay leader of moderate high churchmanship in the area, who expressed it most clearly; writing to his friend Bishop Samuel Wilberforce, he said that if he were a clergyman and 'had a Bishop forced upon me whose principles I didn't approve of' he would fight until he got his way, for he

[1] Karl Löwith, 'Can There be a Christian Gentleman?', *Theology Today*, v (1948).

had little belief in 'conscience. . . . Temper has often much more to do with it'.[1]

THE FARMERS

The farmers were the active capitalists in English agriculure: they rented farms, conducted farming operations, employed labour, and received the profits. Having transformed the agricultural economy, and taken on the economic role of a middle class, they also acquired its distinctive social role, and transformed agrarian social relations as well. And since there were so few resident squires, farmers acted as *de facto* rulers in most parishes, controlling village 'government' (in the parish vestries) as tightly as they controlled the village economy. Altogether the emergence of the farmers in rural society paralleled that of the urban middle class, and in both town and countryside there was a similar chronology across the middle decades of the century, with the social tension of the 1830s and 1840s followed after 1850 by an era of good feeling. In a district like south Lindsey, where resident gentry were scarce, the farmers enjoyed considerable freedom in their social as well as their economic activity, and it is their initiatives that dominate the social history of the period.

At first sight farmers constituted a large minority of the rural population. The Census figures suggest that about one family in three in south Lindsey was headed by a farmer.[2] But before the numbers of farmers are calculated it is necessary to examine the size of their holdings, in a district in which the range extended from mere cottage plots to the great Withcall farm of more than 2,000 acres.

The contrast between large and small holdings, and between regions of *grande* and *petite culture*, is a familiar one in agrarian societies and has often been found to underlie political, religious, and other differences. By continental standards, farms in south Lindsey, as in England as a whole, were very large. In 1867 the average for the area was 86·5 acres, though regional variation was considerable.[3]

---

[1] 16 Oct. 1869, Bodl. MSS. Wilberforce.

[2] In both the 1831 and the 1871 Census the number of farmers was almost exactly one-third the number of houses.

[3] Calculated from the Agricultural Returns of 1867.

	acres		acres
Till basin	83·0	South Wolds	109·6
Cliff	139·9	North Wolds	139·3
Central vale	100·2	Middle Marsh	60·8
Fen margin	54·5	Outer Marsh	41·5

Large farms dominated the upland regions, where estates too were large, while smaller farms (and estates) dominated the lowlands, with the Outer Marsh approximating most closely to a region of peasant holdings.

Whatever the size of the average holding, there was in every region a wide range between the smallest farms and the largest. The regional patterns of distribution compiled by Dr. Joan Thirsk for the whole of Lindsey in 1870 suggest that the majority of farmers cultivated holdings of less than 20 acres in every

Distribution of Farms by Size: Lindsey, 1870

	under 5 acres	5–19	20–49	50–99	100 and above
	%	%	%	%	%
Clays, etc.	26·5	29·4	13·7	11·0	19·3
Cliff	9·7	28·0	11·0	9·7	41·5
Wolds	31·7	22·9	8·2	9·3	27·9
Middle Marsh	23·4	35·9	18·0	10·5	12·2
Outer Marsh	24·6	39·9	19·5	8·1	7·8

Source: Thirsk, *English Peasant Farming*, pp. 242, 264, 298. Dr. Thirsk's 'Clays, etc.' includes the Till basin and the Central vale of South Lindsey.

region except the Cliff, but most of the cultivated area was occupied by the large farms. This impression is confirmed for south Lindsey by the 1851 Census sample, in which the average size of 118 farms was 128 acres: though the majority of holdings were of less than 60 acres and amounted to less than 8 per cent of the total sample area.

The contrast between large and small farmers is reinforced when the question of farm labour is considered. Among the majority of farmers with smallholdings, many relied entirely or predominantly upon family labour. In 1831 only a little over half the 3,213 farmers in south Lindsey employed any outside labour; in the 1851 sample the majority of farmers with 40 acres or more did so. Most labourers were employed on the large farms: in the 1851 sample, only 13 per cent of the farmers occupied more than 300 acres, but they employed 56 per cent of the labourers;

less than a quarter of the farmers had holdings of 200 acres or more but they employed nearly three-quarters of the labourers.[1] There was thus a sharp contrast between the larger farmers, who did no physical work themselves and employed considerable numbers of outside labourers, and the small farmers, whose whole families worked on the farm. Smallholders even described themselves in the Census enumerators' books as 'farmer-labourer' or 'cottager-labourer'. So great was the contrast that contemporaries routinely classified cottagers and small farmers with the 'poor' and not with the larger farmers. These small occupiers abounded in the Marsh, where a parish like Mumby was described by its incumbent in 1855 as being 'made up of small tenant farmers, or freeholders poorer than labourers'; a generation later the situation had not changed: 'most of the farmers are of the laboring class.'[2] In the lowland regions, where small farmers were especially numerous, many succumbed to the temptation of buying land, but in adding to their burdens they seem rarely to have escaped an essentially labouring life. At Sturton-by-Stow

many of the small farmers have become small freeholders, doing their own work with only occasional help. They are generally poor, having given too much for their land . . . the mortgagees of the land received more for it than did the landlords formerly, and were equally absentees. The work was done by men who had a little capital, and who, struggling for dependence, worked double tides, rather than by the special dependent class of laborers.

At Sturton and similar parishes in the Till basin there was consequently much unemployment, and much resentment at 'the class of poor farmers, against whom was levelled the mot that "they did their own work, and borrowed money to pay themselves wages"'.[3] In spite of this resentment these labourers with land—and mortgages—were much closer to ordinary labourers without land than they were to high farmers. Excluding the smallholders—those with less than 30 acres[4]—reduces the

[1] For the Census sample, see above, p. 18, n. 2.
[2] Entries for Mumby in A.T. Schools Questionnaire 1855, and 1886 V.R., L.A.O. See also *P.P.* 1867–8, xvii, p. 74.
[3] *P.P.* 1865, xxvi, pp. 228–30.
[4] As suggested by Barbara Kerr in 'The Dorset Agricultural Labourer', p. 160, and in *Bound to the Soil*, 1968, p. 11.

farming class to about 15 per cent of the total rural population. It was the larger farmers, who occupied most of the land and employed most of the labourers, who constituted the true farming class that will be the chief subject of this discussion.[1]

If the new class of large farmers that emerged in the first half of the nineteenth century had their origins in the older race of farmers, they also broke decisively with traditional ways; the differences were expressed conveniently by Tennyson—who was born and raised in south Lindsey—in the contrast between the 'Old Style' and the 'New Style' farmers.[2] Farmers of these contrasting types differed in their economic attitudes, their agricultural practice, their style of life, and their relations with landlords and labourers.

As farmers developed into a class, their attitudes to farming itself changed, becoming less 'social' and more 'economic'—what had been a way of life increasingly became a capitalist business. This can be traced in the changing conceptions of rent and farm revenue. For most of the eighteenth-century farmers considered that a normal return from farming amounted to 'three rents': one for the landlord, one to cover expenses, and one as profit. If evidence from Essex is representative, a more sharply defined capitalist attitude appeared towards the end of the century. The farmer now began to treat his capital, not his rent, as the primary economic datum; and rather than seeking a multiple of the rent, he now sought a certain rate of return, usually 10 per cent, on his capital investment.[3] The new approach, it should be noted, was adopted more quickly by landlords than by farmers, many of whom probably did not even keep accounts.[4] In Suffolk it was reported that until the agricultural depression in the last quarter of the nineteenth century, many farmers kept no accounts besides their pass-books at the bank: 'not one in ten had the foggiest notion of whether the corn or the cattle or

[1] It was also specifically the large farmers who were the target of criticism from the labourers' unions, e.g. at a meeting of the Amalgamated Labour League at Ludford in August 1875 (*Labourer*, 21 Aug. 1875).

[2] See his dialect poems, 'Northern Farmer: Old Style' and 'Northern Farmer: New Style' in ed. C. Ricks, *Poems*, 1969, pp. 1124–6, 1189–91.

[3] Mingay, *English Landed Society*, pp. 253–4; Shrimpton, 'Landed Society and the Farming Community of Essex', pp. 330–1.

[4] Perhaps because landlords were rentiers, they habitually analysed the economics of farming in terms of a return on capital; e.g. James Banks Stanhope, in a parliamentary debate (*Hansard*, cxxvii, p. 257, 12 May 1853).

the poultry were *each* paying their way.'[1] The very limited evidence for south Lindsey suggests that by the second half of the century farmers had abandoned the three rents doctrine and had arrived at or come very close to a fully capitalist perspective. John West of Dunholme drew up an annual balance sheet and calculated the profitability of individual crops; he also entered into the books his capital—£4,600 on a farm of 496 acres—but apparently did not calculate the rate of return, though he clearly was aware that his own substantial capital was at stake. William Scorer, farming at Burwell, entered in his accounts for 1860–1 a 'Loss on year's farming' of £200, 'interest of Capital not calculated'.[2] At the very least this was a recognition of capitalist accounting and may well have been shared by the larger farmers of the area.

The new-style farmer also took a different view of agricultural work itself. The old-style farmer was a villager among other villagers, most of whom did agricultural work, and like them he worked too; the new-style farmer however shunned physical work, which was associated with the labouring class. Mounted on his horse he rode over his farm issuing commands to the labourers as they tilled the soil. So great was the revulsion from physical labour that by 1859 a competition in practical skills for farmers' sons in one of the local ploughing and agricultural societies attracted only three entrants.[3]

Indeed the new-style farmer renounced not only physical work but also traditional farming methods, and embraced the cause of 'scientific' agriculture. That is not to suggest that advanced methods swept all before them. Even in the Wolds and Cliff regions, the centres of agricultural progress, 'improvers' in the boom years of the French wars had made their fortunes by the unsubtle practice of taking grain crop after grain crop, exploiting the virgin soil like American prairie farmers.[4] And in the lowland regions many cultivators struggled with obsolete rotations and

[1] J. G. Cornish, *Reminiscences of Country Life*, 1939, pp. 62–3, quoted by W. H. B. Court, *British Economic History, 1870–1914*, 1965, pp. 45–6.

[2] West papers, L.A.O. Scorer 1/6 and 1/21, L.A.O. In 1874 it was estimated that landlords received 2½ per cent on their capital, farmers 5 or 6 per cent on theirs (*Mkt Rasen W.M.*, 28 Mar. 1874).

[3] *Linc. Gaz.*, 19 Nov. 1859. This was the Horncastle Labourers' and Ploughing Society.

[4] B. A. Holderness, 'Rural Society in South-east Lindsey, 1660–1840', unpublished Ph.D. thesis, University of Nottingham, 1968, pp. 568–71.

methods down to the middle of the century and beyond. A farmer at Willoughby aroused the disgust of an estate agent by declining to single his turnips;[1] not everyone who dabbled in turnip husbandry knew, or followed, the rules laid down by the experts. And when technical advance did take place it was sometimes inspired by irrational motives. There were fashions in agricultural methods, and when new-style farmers indulged in the latest artificial fertilizers their expenditures were sometimes more conspicuous than considered. Perhaps the most rational instrument of agricultural advance was the North Lincolnshire Agricultural Society.[2] It was for the large farmers, whose leading role again is apparent; of 110 members from south Lindsey in

Membership in the North Lincolnshire Agricultural Society

	1838–44	1860
Till basin	6	5
Cliff	11	11
Central vale	29	29
Fen margin	1	5
Southern Wolds	3	19
Northern Wolds	9	33
Middle Marsh	0	4
Outer Marsh	2	4
	61	110

1860, 94 have been identified: none farmed less than 100 acres, only 15 farmed less than 300, and nearly half farmed 500 or more. The changing agricultural prospects in south Lindsey were reflected in the regional patterns in the Society's membership. Around 1840 nearly half the south Lindsey members were from the backward Central vale, which was just beginning to undergo improvement. By 1860 there had been an upsurge in membership among Wold farmers; with their growing preoccupation with pastoral agriculture they would have been interested in the farm animals featured in the Society's competitions and displays.[3] Yet

[2] He also sowed them broadcast and committed other howlers (Findlay to Kennedy, 30 June 1853, 3 ANC 7/23/65/21).

[1] List of Subscribers 1838–46, T.L.E. 2, L.A.O. *Rules of the Society . . . Annual Report*, 1861.

[3] A veritable cult of the fatted animal appears in these competitions. It doubtless had good economic and culinary reasons, but it may also have appealed to the capitalist farmer's taste for conspicuous investment. It was in any case their counterpart to the labourer's more traditional fascination with natural freaks. Arable husbandry by contrast was the realm of sober calculation and quiet virtue, where superior yields won no prizes and profit had to be its own reward.

whatever the problems they may have faced in this period, their accomplishments were not in doubt—the transformed upland regions, which a contemporary hailed as 'imperishable monuments' to their 'energy and ability'.[1] In that achievement the new-style farmers ranked with the entrepreneurs of the heroic age of industrialization.

With their capitalist attitudes and advanced methods the new-style farmers entered into their reward: they became men of substantial wealth. Unfortunately little is known about the year-to-year profits of farming, but an indication of farmers' wealth survives in their wills. A sample of about a hundred wills of south Lindsey farmers proved in the early 1850s[2] suggests that south Lindsey farmers were accumulating considerable fortunes, elevating their possessors far above the ranks of the labouring poor. And it was the largest farmers, operating with the

Value of Property in Wills of South Lindsey Farmers, 1851–5

	Number
£10,000 and over	3
5–9,999	15
1–4,999	26
500–999	20
100–499	34
1–99	9
	107

Farmers' Wealth per Acre, by Size of Farm, 1851–5
Total number of farmers: 92

	Acreage			
	1–49	50–99	100–299	300–
£7 and more per acre	15	5	9	17
less than £7 per acre	7	13	22	4

most capital, who appeared to have won the greatest rewards.[3] It was on this solid material base that the farmers developed the cultural superstructure of a new class.

With their wealth, new-style farmers and their families allowed themselves what was not merely a rising standard of living but

---

[1] Clarke, *Farming of Lincolnshire*, p. 76.

[2] In Lincoln Consistory Court, L.A.O.

[3] The smallest farms also yielded high ratios of wealth to acreage; the data paradoxically support the claims both of the advocates of high farming and of the advocates of spade husbandry and peasant farming. Similar results were obtained in J. R. Vincent's analysis of wills in Cambridgeshire, 1848–57 (*Pollbooks*, 1967, pp. 37–8).

one which at the same time expressed their rising social aspirations. The farmhouse itself took on a new role; with fewer farm servants and more domestic servants present it was transformed from a centre of production to a centre of consumption. Farmers' wives abandoned the dairy for the parlour, now adorned by a piano.[1] They and their daughters shed their sober black and, at a safe distance, followed the fashions of the metropolis, the vogue for crinolines arriving in south Lindsey in the early 1860s, four years after it had begun in London.[2] The style of the farmer too changed from plain to fancy. The older farmer was still close to farm work and as a matter of course wore 'top-boots'; his successor wore the more genteel shoes. When the old-style farmer and his wife rode to market, she sat on the pillion behind him; their horse was 'a good nag, for market service'.[3] The new-style farmer and his wife rode to market in a gig; he had more refined horses, including expensive hunters—no longer was it acceptable to ride to hounds on a nag. New-style farmers took up shooting as well as hunting; many had shooting rights over their farms when their landlords were non-resident.[4] Altogether new-style farmers were less concerned with work, more with consumption, less with village society, more with family and with others in their class.

Education was another aspect of the new style. Probably not all the older farmers were even literate; of 160 farmers whose wills were proved in diocesan courts between 1825 and 1833, 40 signed their name with a mark.[5] In the Marsh, where old-style farmers persisted well into the century, a clergyman noted that their education 'has often been at the same school with their labourers'. One Marsh farmer sent his sons to school but refused to let his daughters go, since they needed only to milk, sew, cook,

---

[1] For the abandonment of the dairy, see Ivy Pinchbeck, *Women Workers and the Industrial Revolution*, 1930, pp. 8–16, 40–2.

[2] *Linc. Gaz.* 1 Feb. 1862; Ross to Monson, 9 July 1862, MON 25/13/10/14/101; C. Willett and Phyllis Cunnington, *Handbook of English Costume in the Nineteenth Century*, 1959, pp. 442, 446–7, 472.

[3] E. Peacock, *Glossary*, p. 258; Cooper, *Wise Saws*, i. 21; John Brown, *Literae Laureatae*, 1890, p. 7.

[4] There were many farmers' names in the annual 'Game List', appearing in local newspapers, of those taking out shooting licences. See also *P.P.* 1872, x, p. 53.

[5] Wills proved in the Prebendal Court of Corringham, the Stow Archdeaconry Court, the Lincoln Consistory Court, and the Court of the Dean and Chapter, L.A.O.

and bear children. Indeed, the farmers as a group, according to Henry Winn, a shrewd contemporary observer, were 'the least intelligent and informed group in society—all they know is country affairs; they can read, write, and do simple arithmetic but have little beyond these bare attainments; their mature studies are confined to the price-current in the county newspapers and Old Moore's Prophetic Almanack.'[1] Education, however, was taken much more seriously by the new-style farmers. Some employed governesses for their young children. Older sons attended local grammar schools; among the applicants for admission to the Horncastle Grammar School in 1855–7 were the sons of seven farmers, with holdings of from 110 to 610 acres; six of the pupils at Louth Grammar School in 1861 were sons of farmers whose holdings ranged from 57 to 900 acres.[2] Daughters probably attended the numerous private schools and academies in local market towns. Later in the century the most affluent farmers sent their children to boarding schools,[3] and a few farmers' sons have been noted at university. Much about this subject remains obscure, but the contrast between the old-style and the new-style farmers is clear, as is the growing gap between the farmers, now with access to educated culture, and the labouring poor. Education was added to property as a pillar of the new class.

As the farmers developed into a class they took new stances towards the other major groups in rural society. This involved a dramatic rupture of their ties with the labourers; it also altered more quietly their relations with the gentry. From their traditional subservience they shifted to co-operation, and when faced on occasion with gentry indifference, they gradually learned to assert their own social ideals and their own economic and political interests.

The strength of their new class ideals is best illustrated in the very highest stratum of farmers. They were men of capital, often owning considerable amounts of land; they included the dozen or so who were the sole occupiers of land in their parishes; with their wealth and position they felt free to trail an 'Esq.'

[1] *P.P.* 1867–8, xvii, p. 541; C. E. Heanley, *Toll of the Marshes*, 1929, pp. 46–7; Henry Winn, Diary, 22 Jan. 1845, L.A.O. For Winn, see the Appendix.

[2] Horncastle Grammar School records, T.P. 2/28, L.A.O. The Louth Grammar School students were identified in the 1861 Census, R.G. 9/2980, P.R.O.

[3] Information from Mrs. Gladys Sharpley of Louth.

after their name. Such men as Samuel Vessey of Halton Holegate, Robert Greetham of Stainfield, William Bartholomew of Goltho, Marshall Heanley of Croft, and Robert Martin of Asterby had more influence in local affairs than many a 'village squire'. They were at the very threshold of the gentry class: but they significantly resisted the temptation to launch themselves into the gentry, and continued to farm, remaining decisively in the farming class.[1] The middle-class gospel of work and of an active life prevailed over the traditional fascination with gentility and leisure.

Besides class values, new-style farmers also upheld class interests against the gentry. The 'Northern Farmer: Old Style', as in Tennyson's portrait, had traditionally been deferential to his squire:

> I hallus voated wi' Squoire an' choorch an' staate,
> An' i' the woost o' toimes I wur niver again the raate . . .
>
> Fur they knaws what I bean to Squoire sin fust a
> comm'd to the 'All
> I don moy duty by Squoire an' I done moy duty boy
> hall.[2]

But the new-style farmer, while usually following the gentry's political lead, had a larger financial stake of his own to be concerned with, and when aroused could act independently to protect it. In 1851–2 it was the angry farmers who took the initiative, when most of the gentry were apathetic or hostile, in demanding a second Tory candidate, Protestant and Protectionist, to stand in the 1852 election.[3] A generation later they emerged as political actors and not merely as voters or as a pressure group. Of 57 members elected in 1889 to the first Lindsey County Council, 11 were gentry, but 14 were farmers; and among the losers were Edward Heneage, the dominant landlord in the North Worlds, and Colonel Conway Gordon of Linwood, bottom of the poll at Market Rasen.[4] Farmers had far more in common with landlords than with labourers, but showed their

---

[1] See Holderness, 'Rural Society in South-east Lindsey', p. 347.

[2] *Poems*, pp. 1124–5.

[3] Olney, *Lincolnshire Politics*, pp. 126–7, 243. Still earlier, in the 1820s, farmers in several counties had acted independently of the gentry to petition Parliament for relief of the agricultural interest (Peter Fraser, 'Public Petitioning and Parliament before 1832', *History*, xlvi (1961), p. 206).

[4] *The Times*, 25 Jan. 1889, p. 8.

ability to turn their backs on landlord spokesmen for the 'agricultural interest' in order to defend their own class interests.

The new stance of farmers towards the landlords did not
usually involve opposition or hostility: both were capitalist
classes, whose interests usually coincided. The labourers, however, were not a capitalist class, and when new-style farmers
recast their relations with them they had to make a sweeping
repudiation of traditional pre-capitalist reciprocities that formerly
had bound the two groups together. Farmers sought to separate
themselves from the labourers and to reduce their relations with
them to the cash nexus.[1] Under the old system, farm servants
were lodged and boarded in the farmhouse; for better or worse
they were members of the farmer's family and household. But as
farmers' incomes rose, and their social aspirations, they and their
wives objected to the presence of half a dozen or more rough
working men in the house. So they were expelled from the farmhouse and either boarded out with a foreman or, more commonly,
hired as day labourers. The displacement of the farm servant
was noted in the 1830s; farm households of the old extended
variety, with seven or more farm servants in residence, were
recorded occasionally in the 1841 census, but by 1851 they had
virtually disappeared, though most of the larger farmers still
boarded the three indispensable servants to take care of the
horses. In the 1860s it was said that few had any farm servants in
the house.[2] Farmers thus had unilaterally abandoned long-term
contracts with servants involving multiple obligations and
replaced them with day hirings of labourers in which their own
responsibilities were reduced to the minimum.[3]

Many farmers regarded labourers as proletarians to be exploited
and did their best to maintain a docile and dependent pool of
cheap labour at their disposal, opposing allotments for labourers
and any education for labourers' children that went beyond bare

---

[1] In Dorset, similarly, the farmer 'takes strictly commercial views of his man and
cannot afford to waste a penny on sentimental considerations' (Hardy, 'Dorsetshire
Labourer', p. 182).

[2] Mingay and Chambers, *Agricultural Revolution*, p. 19; Hobsbawm and Rudé,
Captain Swing, pp. 43–6; *The Farmer's Magazine*, iii (1835), p. 212; *P.P.* 1867, xvi,
p. 22.

[3] It should be noted, however, that farmers tended to employ more labourers than
were strictly required—perhaps another gesture of conspicuous production—and
often kept older men in work despite declining strength (*Mkt Rasen W.M.*, 16 Nov.
1872).

literacy. If these views made economic sense, some of the farmers' other attitudes went beyond the conflict of economic interests to social animosity. In effect farmers regarded labourers as an alien and inferior race, with whom any spontaneous social contact could only be degrading. Farmers did not like to mix with labourers, and they did 'not like their children to mix with labourers' children', and kept them out of village schools. Of thirty-two children in the Church of England school at Gayton-le-Marsh, 1867–75, only two were from farming families; the church Sunday school at Fulletby attracted most labourers' children and some of farmers of up to 100 acres, but none from any of the larger farmers.[1]

New-style farmers went still further and suppressed the traditional agricultural festivities that had symbolized the mutual dependence of farmers and labourers and their common involvement in the fortunes of agriculture. The 'hopper feasts', for example, marking the completion of the sowing of wheat, whether in spring, or (as 'hopper-cake night') in the autumn, were moribund by the 1840s if not quite extinct.[2] Another such celebration was the clipping supper, held at the conclusion of sheep-shearing in June. Henry Winn recalled that in his youth in the 1820s 'almost every farmer in the village made a large quantity of frumenty on the morning they began to clip; and every child in the village was invited to partake of it'. Then another batch of better quality was made and taken round in buckets to every house in the village, and at night 'an excellent supper was provided for labourers and work people over which the master of the flock presided'. But 'now very few make frumenty for the children, and some make nothing extra at all for the occasion ... clipping suppers are now made chiefly for the farmers' friends and relations, not for the poor'.[3] Community had given way to class and family. The climax of the agricultural year was the harvest, which naturally had inspired the largest

[1] The Revd. Richard Parker of Well, A.T. Schools Questionnaire 1855, L.A.O.; Admissions Register, Gayton-le-Marsh Church of England School, School Records, L.A.O.; Winn, Teacher's Diary, pp. 236–7.

[2] Winn 2/29; Mabel Peacock, 'Folklore and Legends of Lincolnshire' (typescript in Folklore Society Library), pp. 44–5; Winn, Diary, 1 Nov. 1844.

[3] Winn, Diary, 20 June 1844. Sir Charles Anderson recalled frumenty as 'a capital mess of wheat creed, i.e., divested of its husk, boiled up with milk, currants, raisins and spice and which we used always to have at sheep-shearing' (And. 5/2/2, p. 33).

celebration. Earlier in the century the festivities began with the harvest home; even before the work was done, 'one youth would shout out (with others blowing horns)':

> 'I've rent my clothes and torn my skin
> To get my master's Harvest in.
> We have not thrown over, nor yet stuck fast
> And the load we are on is the last, the last . . . Hurrah.[1]

Then all would reply three times three every five minutes until the last load was in the yard; when the children climbed down from the load the farmer or one of his family got up and would 'scramble apples amongst them . . . the most diverting part of the ceremony'. The last load was decorated with boughs, and the day would end with a supper. But by 1844, according to Winn, farmers rarely allowed children on the harvest load, they no longer scrambled apples, and the supper, the high point of the festivities, had died out—'under the blighting influence of Class Respectability'.[2]

Having suppressed the harvest supper, however, the farmers later revived it, and from the late 1850s it rapidly became widespread.[3] Sometimes it was combined with the harvest festival of the parish church—itself a recent innovation—but usually it was given by the individual farmer. Sometimes it was for his labourers only, sometimes for their wives as well. (The suppers, like all such occasions, encouraged heavy drinking; in 1861 it was noted with surprise that after one such supper at Coates 'on the following morning every man was found busily engaged at his work, a rather unusual thing in some parts of this county after such a treat'.) Towards the end of the period the suppers came to resemble agricultural meetings of a more exalted kind, with 'loyal and patriotic toasts, songs, recitations, speeches' and 'the usual patriotic toasts, hymns, songs, and recitations'.[4] At one

---

[1] Winn, Diary, 11 Sept. 1844. A very similar text was collected at Wispington by the Revd. J. A. Penny: song no. 233, Percy Grainger collection, English Folk Dance and Song Society Library.

[2] Winn, Diary, 11 Sept. 1844; Winn 2/29, and 5/3, p. 63. Similarly Malcolmson, *Popular Recreations*, p. 164, notes the decline of harvest feasts in the first half of the nineteenth century and attributes it to 'the widening gaps between the social classes'.

[3] It was noted in 1861 that harvest suppers had become popular in the previous two or three years (*Linc. Gaz.*, 19 Oct. 1861).

[4] *Mkt Rasen W.M.*, 22 Oct. 1864; *Linc. Gaz.*, 7 Dec. 1861; *Hornc. News*, 22 Oct. 1870; *Mkt Rasen W.M.*, 27 Sept. 1873.

such supper the farmer invited a professional man from the local market town to take the chair. Even when reviving a local and communal festivity, the new-style farmer could not avoid reminding his labourers—by recitations, toasts, and so on—that his attachments and interests were national not local.

The chief providers of these feasts were the larger farmers— only they, at any rate, employed enough labourers to make such an affair grand enough to be worth noticing in a newspaper. The ten whose holdings can be traced had farms averaging 560 acres, ranging from 200 to 985. (There were three parishes—Welton, North Willingham, and Rand—in which all the farmers were said to have joined in giving a supper.) Most were in the Cliff region or not far from it, but the unevenness of the sources makes doubtful any conclusion about geographical distribution. The majority who gave suppers during the revival were men who entered their farms after 1851; this was indeed a revival, and not a survival of an old custom.

The transformation of the harvest supper well illustrates the contrast between the old- and the new-style farmer and between the old agrarian society and the new.[1] When the old-style farmer gave a harvest supper, it expressed his solidarity with his fellow workers and their common dependence upon the land. The transitional farmer, nervous about his 'Class Respectability', sought to avoid promiscuous contact with his inferiors by expelling farm servants from his farmhouse and by discontinuing the harvest supper and other agricultural feasts. After 1850 however the new-style farmer could take his class respectability for granted. He could also take for granted the dissolution of the social ties that had bound together farmer and labourer in the old village community—and he was well aware too of the mounting emigration from the villages and the diminishing supply of labour. When he gave a harvest supper, it was to fabricate for an evening a social harmony or solidarity which otherwise had ceased to exist; yet even a simulation of community might play on the labourers' vestigial longings for 'good masters' and dissuade them from migrating. Thus the older farmer and his

[1] The shearing supper described by Thomas Hardy in *Far from the Madding Crowd* (ch. 23) suggests an intermediate stage. The table was placed outside the house so that one end extended through a window to the parlour inside: 'Miss Everdene sat inside the window, facing down the table. She was thus at the head without mingling with the men.'

labourers constituted a community, and when he gave a supper it marked the natural climax of an ongoing way of life; the newer farmer and his labourers did *not* form a community, and when he gave a supper it conjured up an artificial, factitious community—a pseudo-*Gemeinschaft*.[1] If the farmer may be compared to a writer or artist, then the old-style farmer was, in Schiller's terms, 'naïve', aware of no rift between himself and his milieu, his dependants; the new-style farmer was by contrast 'sentimental', aware of the rift, and anxious to bridge it by a deliberate act of will. The one belonged to the age of community; the other, to the age of 'labour relations' and the manipulation of morale.

The tactics of manipulation were noticeable also in the response of farmers to labourers in the low point in the agricultural year. In the winter months, and particularly at Christmas, farmers made gifts of bread, flour, beef, mutton, and the like to their labourers and to the village poor.[2] These acts of beneficence became prominent in local newspapers around 1860, at about the same time as the revival of harvest suppers, and continued in an apparently increasing volume down to 1875. By then, after the rise of the labourers' trade unions, paternalism was no more than common prudence, but the appearance of paternalist charity simultaneously with the contrived harvest festivities suggests the presence of ulterior motives from the very beginning. Not only was it a reflection on the poverty of labourers in winter that bread and flour, the necessities of life, should have been appropriate gifts; it was also in the tradition of paternalism to keep wages so low that gifts of food should be necessary and that they should appear to come from the goodwill of the employer rather than from the labour of the worker, who would be unwilling to risk the loss of future favours. These were gifts, moreover, that could not be reciprocated in kind, but only by psychological submission: they tended to perpetuate, and symbolize, an unequal relationship of patronage and dependence. But though they appeared to be a prudent and inexpensive investment

[1] Pseudo-Gemeinschaft has been precisely defined by Robert K. Merton (*Mass Persuasion*, 1946, pp. 142, 144) as 'the feigning of personal concern with the other fellow in order to manipulate him better' and 'the mere pretence of common values in order to further private interests'.

[2] The poor generally received clothing from gentry benefactors and food from farmers.

in social control, they were a failure. The soaring emigration rate and the success of the unions showed that the discontents of the labourers could not be killed with kindness.

THE LABOURERS

England has no more important contributors to her greatness than the men who guide the plough.

G. F. Heneage, at the 1862 meeting of the Donington and Hainton Agricultural Society. (*Market Rasen Weekly Mail*, 29 Nov. 1862.)

The 'poor' were the majority in south Lindsey villages: craftsmen, small farmers, and above all the labourers.[1] Agrarian religious life, in simple quantitative terms, was predominantly the religious life of farm labourers and their families.

The largest and poorest of the three classes in agrarian society, they were also the most traditional in outlook and the last to emerge consciously as a class. With no land of their own, and working for wages, they formed an authentic proletariat; and lacking the franchise they were powerless in the political realm. They were the victims of the same agricultural improvement that enriched the farmers and landlords. Yet while the objective conditions of their lives were those of a working class, subjectively they were reluctant to abandon traditional values, and preserved a communal outlook in a class society. If being determines consciousness, it does not do so instantaneously. The decisive period of change came late for the labourers, in the second and third quarters of the nineteenth century. It was only as the farmers hardened into a class that the labourers began to come to terms with the new society. Gradually abandoning what were now disparaged as their 'roughness' and traditional ways—including traditional forms of protest—they acquired a new outlook, simultaneously more 'modern' and more proletarian, that was marked by greater individualism, self-discipline, solidarity, and readiness to organize in defence of common interests.

[1] Craftsmen and small tradesmen, who played an important role locally in Methodism, have not received the intensive study they deserve. Some at least enjoyed a superior economic position to that of labourers, but socially they were closer to the labourers than to the farmers. In a selected group of parish registers (see below p. 78, n. 1) the marriages of ninety sons of craftsmen were recorded, thirty-two marrying the daughters of other craftsmen, fifty-five the daughters of labourers.

The formation of the labourers' unions in the 1870s consolidated the growth of a dispirited landless peasantry into a mature working class.

Work

A survey of labouring life logically begins with the sphere of production, not only because it determined class relations, but also because it was fundamental for the labourers' whole way of life. Labourers, their wives and children all did work on the farm, and the structure and conditions of farm work under capitalist auspices affected them all, off the job as well as during the hours of work. Nowhere were the labourers more proletarian than when at work—yet in the interstices of the system there were vestiges of the more independent peasant ways of the past.

Before examining the labourers' work as employees, though, it is instructive to see them in their role as petty producers on their account, as cultivators of gardens and allotments. Potentially, these smallholdings might have enabled them to climb into the ranks of the small farmers, but in practice the dominant classes, fearful of creating an uncontrollable mass of independent producers, restricted the amount of land available to labourers. Gardens and allotments served if anything to stabilize the system, not to undermine it. Labourers valued their land, but it was not extensive enough to alter their proletarian status.

At the middle of the century in south Lindsey, gardens were 'universally attached to the cottages', labourers paying no additional rent for them. They were small plots, no more than a quarter of an acre, suitable for vegetables and potatoes, though some were mere flower gardens yielding 'moral benefits' along with the blossoms. Allotments were larger plots, ranging up to 5 acres, and were let separately from cottages. 'Frequently but not generally found' in Lincolnshire, they were most common on the estates of large landowners, especially resident ones, and least common in open parishes. Wheat and potatoes were the main crops, the wheat primarily for domestic consumption, the potatoes for feeding the pig or for market.[1] The yields were high, exceeding those obtained by capitalist farmers on their larger

---

[1] Clarke, *Farming of Lincolnshire*, p. 153; Winn, Diary, 29 May 1844; *P.P.* 1843, vii, pp. 214, 259; Colman, *European Agriculture*, i. 74; DuPré to Kennedy, 12 Aug. 1844, 3 ANC 7/23/45/40.

holdings; labourers at Willoughby, for example, got nearly two loads of hay per acre but farmers only half a load. Figures like these argued a case for spade husbandry and land reform, but the response of landlords was rather to demand high rents for allotments. At Nettleham in the 1870s labourers were paying the equivalent of £5 per acre, probably triple the rent paid by farmers.[1]

The immediate beneficiary of the potatoes grown on many an allotment was not the labourer but his pig—'that most useful and inestimable, yet much maligned animal', that Cobbett regarded as the embodiment of peasant prosperity. It was said that only a few lucky labourers had them in the 1820s, but in 1843 there was 'a fat pig in the house of every labouring man', and most 'cottagers', it was asserted, 'have a pig, which they do not sell, but kill, cure, and eat'. As Henry Winn noted, pigs were the 'poor man's savings banks'; a good one was worth £5 or more at a time when the total annual income of a day labourer might amount to £35, and pig clubs were formed to insure against untimely and expensive loss.[2] If later testimony from Kesteven can be believed, pigs were a source of recreation as well as sustenance: 'pigs were always a big topic of conversation in the village, and after the usual greeting it was quite normal to ask how the pigs were doing. . . . Such was the importance of pigs in village life that they were placed on a par with sermons.'[3] This intertwining of economic and non-economic concerns in a household setting was characteristic of the traditional pattern of work, but in the age of large-scale farming had become of marginal importance.

The next step in the ladder of peasant prosperity was the keeping of a cow, but cows were far less common, as few labourers had the 3 acres required to support one, nor the savings to buy one. The cow-keepers therefore were drawn from a slightly higher social stratum; one village cow club addressed itself specifically to the 'small farmer . . . and the industrious cottager'. It was argued that many labourers would have kept cows had they been able to afford them, but a labourer with a cow

---

[1] DuPré to Willoughby (copy), 26 Jan. 1848, 3 ANC 7/23/51/7; *Linc. Gaz.*, 2 Mar. 1872.

[2] Clarke, *Farming of Lincolnshire*, p. 157; News. Cutt., vol. B, pp. 127–8; *P.P.* 1843, xii, p. 271; 1861, xxi, Pt. 5, p. 9; Winn, Diary, 28 Sept. 1844.

[3] Fred Gresswell, *Bright Boots*, 1936, p. 71; see also Flora Thompson, *Lark Rise to Candleford*, 1945, p. 10, and M. K. Ashby, *Joseph Ashby of Tysoe*, 1961, p. 115.

threatened to become independent, and unavailable for farm work.[1]

It was this same threat, and fear, that led the large farmers to oppose the granting of allotments. A garden and a pig kept a labourer off the poor rates, but an allotment and a cow might divert him from his work for the farmers. In this spirit the farmers in vestry at Toynton St. Peter demanded that four small tenants on the Ancaster estate sell their cows and give up their privilege of grazing the lanes in summer.[2] It was clergymen who probably put the most pressure on landlords to grant allotments. After a lengthy campaign by the curate of Swaby the reluctant agents of the Ancaster estate granted 5 acres in the parish 'to keep him quiet', and the Revd. W. M. Pierce saw to it that 'almost every poor man in his parishes has an allotment of land': defying the farmers, he let 3 acres of his glebe at Fulletby to labourers and helped provide them with tools. Yet his successor discontinued the scheme, and in 1872 there were no allotments at all in Fulletby.[3] Thus a labourer's garden or allotment was a precarious holding, with none of the security of tenure generally enjoyed by peasants. A labourer was always a tenant, never the owner, of the cottage to which his garden was attached, and he was always subject to arbitrary eviction; the land he rented was his not by right but by the landlord's grace and favour. At best the labourer's holding was a barrier against destitution, not a stepping-stone to prosperity. When the labourers rose in protest in 1830 and the 1870s, their most urgent demand was for higher pay and a shorter working day; their desire for allotments or smallholdings was minor. Nor did landlords, of course, in granting allotments, have the slightest intention of resurrecting the 'bold peasantry' of yore: their purpose, as Henry Winn pointed out, was rather to 'make them more happy and contented in their station'.[4]

In the commercial agriculture of south Lindsey as well as in the labourer's household economy, men, women, and children all were expected to work. Labourers' children began farm work as early as the age of 4, and by the age of 10 both boys and girls were employed full time. The demand for child labour was

---

[1] *Stamf. Merc..* 23 June 1837; *P.P.* 1843, xii, p. 261.
[2] Tenants to Willoughby, 24 May 1850, 3 ANC 7/23/58/124.
[3] Forbes to Kennedy, 30 Dec. 1833, 3 ANC 7/23/2. 7/32; *Stamf. Merc.*, 9 Feb. 1838; Winn 2/29; News. Cutt., vol. B, pp. 20–1; *Linc. Gaz.*, 2 Mar. 1872.
[4] Winn, Diary, i. 16.

great and actually increased as agricultural technique advanced in the middle decades of the century. Children were employed in a great variety of tasks, most of which, like tending cattle and scaring birds, required an excessively long work week. Children usually had to work on Sunday, and boys aged 8 to 12 worked among the sheep in the turnip fields—a common job—seven days a week, even in winter.[1]

The organization of child labour took several forms. The most notorious was the public gang, a group of children and women hired full time by a ganger who sub-contracted work from farmers. But it was also the least common; public gangs were found only in the North Wolds, where labour of all kinds was scarce, and even there in no more than three places: Louth, Market Rasen, and Ludford. Private gangs—employed directly by a farmer who put one of his own labourers in charge—were found in labour-scarce Cliff parishes. The special features of the gang system were the regularity of employment and the exploitation of very young children: 'the faculty of making little children work is the peculiar art of the gangmaster, and the common objection of farmers to employing children themselves is the difficulty of getting any work out of them without a regular gangmaster.' And yet clergymen and others deprecated the 'immorality' and 'bad language' that were allowed by the laxity of the gangmaster's discipline. Elsewhere, in the central clay vale, for example, children accompanied their fathers in field work, singling turnips, and doing other chores.[2] However organized, child labour rendered attendance at day schools nearly impossible during the summer months and intermittent during the winter.

In the 1840s, if somewhat fragmentary evidence may be trusted, children did not work extensively in the fields, but by the 1860s the practice was widespread. The overseer of the poor at Reepham noted in 1867 that there were more children employed then in field work than there had been twenty years earlier— 'they didn't farm so well then'. Farmers liked child labour for its cheapness and were sorry to hire a man if a boy could do the job.[3]

[1] P.P. 1867–8, xvii, pp. 278. 299; 1867, xvi, pp. 2, 4; Winn, Teacher's Diary, 14 Feb. 1847; News. Cutt., vol. B, pp. 141–2, 155–6.

[2] P.P., 1867, xvi, pp. vi, 3, 16–17, 22; 1867–8, xvii, p. 73.

[3] P.P. 1867, xvi, p. 23; Larken to Monson, 5 Feb. 1855, MON 25/13/10/7/7. A farmer at Ludford paid a ganger (employing children) £1 per acre to pick ketlucks,

And they appear to have had few moral or religious scruples in laying down the conditions of work for children. At Swaby it was noted that 'some of the farmers make it compulsory [for] the boys to attend to their work during the greater part of the Lord's day, refusing otherwise to employ them during the week and this without additional wages'. Nor did they hesitate to play off the children against their fathers, and the fathers against the children. When they put pressure on labourers to allow their children to go out to work, the labourers could hardly refuse: they 'do not like to disobey the farmers, who employ them'.[1] Thus the increased demand for child labour spurred by agricultural 'progress' served to intensify the farmers' exploitation of the labouring class as a whole, simultaneously depressing the wages of the father and interfering with the education of the children.

At the age of 12, older children began a new stage in their working life. Girls had a fairly wide range of choice. Some remained at home to care for ageing parents, often trying their hand at dressmaking.[2] They were also in demand as workers in the fields. Farmers—and clergymen—wanted them to enter farm service, primarily as dairymaids. But the girls disliked this work, which was poorly paid and confining; 'the *most* educated wish to get some more refined employment'—domestic service—'the *ill* educated much prefer the activity of field work'.[3] The steady complaints from the 1840s that field work was causing a shortage of dairymaids suggest that the farmers had less power over labourers' daughters than over their sons. There were finally the many who left the countryside altogether to work in the towns.

For young men, the chief option was to join the ranks of the farm servants. Unmarried, living in the farmhouses, they were 'as distinct a class as bagsmen or couriers' and had a special place in agrarian society.[4] Despite being subjected to a severe work

---

a job that would have cost 30*s*. if adult labourers were employed (*P.P.* 1867, xvi, p. 20). See also Hardy, 'Dorsetshire Labourer', p. 185.

[1] The Revd. C. R. Cameron of Swaby, A.T. Schools Questionnaire 1855, L.A.O. Kaye to Monson, 31 Jan. 1855, MON 25/13/10/6.

[2] Of 103 single women aged 20 to 24 in the 1851 Census sample eighteen were dressmakers.

[3] *P.P.* 1867, xvi, p. 19; 1843, xii, p. 216.

[4] As noted by Sir Charles Anderson (*P.P.* 1861, xxi, Part 5, p. 10).

discipline, they were a wayward group, beyond the reach of organized religion, and indeed were notorious as bearers of traditional superstition and folklore.

Even after the expulsion of farm servants from the farmhouses and the conversion of servants into labourers, a good many 'indoor' servants remained, giving south Lindsey a high ratio of indoor to outdoor agricultural labourers. In the 1851 Census the ratio was 1 to 3, compared with 1 to 30 in counties like Essex and Wiltshire and 1 to 1·5 in the East Riding.[1] In south Lindsey at mid-century farm servants formed about 30 per cent of the unmarried male population aged 15 to 24; a further 12 per cent resided with foremen and 16 per cent were labourers living at home.[2] The farm servants proper were the majority and gave the lead for all the young unmarried labourers.

Like all servants they were engaged at the 'statutes', the hiring fairs held in the market towns. They were hired by the year and were paid only at the completion of their term of service. The typical farm servant, a 'horseman' or 'wagoner', cared for the horses, ploughed, and conveyed goods and produce to and from town and on the farm. Besides their wages—which on one farm in 1865 ranged from £7. 15s. od. to £16. 10s. od.—they received room and board.[3] They usually changed employers every year and rarely stayed more than two years with the same farmer.[4] In the 1851 Census sample only 16 per cent of the farm servants aged 15 to 24 were employed in their native parishes: on average they lived five miles from their place of birth. And it was said that they did not hesitate to run away from a master on slight provocation and 'remain in prison if committed rather than return to service'.[5] In any event their annual flitting made them the despair of the clergy: 'it is very difficult to get farm-lads together in time for preparation for an autumn confirmation. We get hold of them in winter and lose them again at Mayday uncon-

---

[1] Calculated from the 1851 Census. See also J. P. D. Dunbabin, 'The Incidence and Organization of Agricultural Trade Unionism in the 1870s', *Agri. Hist. Rev.* xvi (1968), p. 124.

[2] Derived from the Census sample.

[3] Farm records of John West of Dunholme, West 6, L.A.O.

[4] They were strict bargainers and would not alter their terms; Sir Charles Anderson said that he had known 'a good servant and a good master part for the sake of half a sovereign'. (*P.P.* 1861, xxi, Pt. 5, pp. 10–12.)

[5] According to the Revd. F. C. Massingberd of South Ormsby, in a letter in the *Lincolnshire Chronicle*, 24 Nov. 1855.

firmed.' And at a rural deanery meeting in 1872 'the difficulty of gaining influence over the farm servants was expressed on all hands'.[1] Although servants were the most traditional type of farm worker, their mobility and freedom from the influence of the dominant classes drew them closer to the free labourer of modern capitalism than to the traditional servant with personal ties to his master.

It was characteristic of the times that the discipline imposed upon the servants by their masters was exacting during the hours of work but loose at other times. They rose at three or half past, fed the horses at four, and did not reach the end of their duties until eight in the evening.[2] Female as well as male servants lived in the farmhouse and discipline after supper was lax. Servant girls fell from grace even in the presumably well-regulated households of squires and clergy; there were many cases of illegitimacy and a steady flow of maintenance orders from the magistrates.[3] And the census returns reveal a suspiciously large number of labourers' households which included an unmarried daughter around the age of 20 and a small child said to be a grandchild of the head of the family. The farmers' lack of supervision of their servants may well have reflected their general unwillingness to involve themselves in the lives of their inferiors.

This appears to have extended to their servants' religious lives. One aged labourer recalled that in his youth in the 1820s his master compelled him to attend church, but other evidence suggests that this was exceptional in later decades; in 1875 a clergyman noted that 'farm servants seldom dream of coming to church now, employers either not making it or not enforcing it as a condition of service'. And when servants did attend church, they did not sit with their masters but rather in separate pews specially designated for them. Even in church, masters and mistresses were 'too high to associate with them'.[4]

---

[1] Sotby, 1873 V.R.; Wraggoe Rural Deanery Minute Book, 19 Sept. 1872, Lincoln Cathedral Library.

[2] *Linc. Gaz.*, 22 Oct. 1859. An earlier quitting time, however, was reported by Colman in the previous decade (*European Agriculture*, i. 60).

[3] In Louth Union between 1857 and 1861, 57 of 105 women bearing illegitimate children were farmers' servants (*P.P.* 1867-8, xvii, p. 284).

[4] News. Cutt., vol. B, pp. 139-40; minutes of Conference of Archdeacons and Rural Deans, 21 July 1875, L.A.O. Winn, Diary, 17 May 1844.

The farm servants were thus a paradoxical group. As servants their work structure was of the most traditional type, yet their annual change of employer and their readiness to run away betray an urge for independence more characteristic of the modern proletarian.[1] At the same time they resisted the approaches of the churches and remained true to the traditional subculture of superstition.

The élite of the rural labouring class were the 'confined labourers'. Like farm servants, they were hired by the year, but they were usually married, and besides their wages always received a cottage, an allotment, coal, quantities of food, and sometimes still further benefits. Foremen were often confined labourers, as were shepherds. Their place in agrarian society and in the working class was ambiguous. They often lived apart from other labourers, yet their habit of changing places every year precluded the growth of sentimental ties between them and their employers.[2] Despite their dependence upon their masters and their vulnerability to eviction some of them rallied to the labourers' unions in 1872.[3] They were an élite among farm labourers, but at once a captive and a migratory élite, and they were not in a position to provide leadership, political or religious, for their less favoured but more independent brothers, the day labourers.

The ordinary day labourers constituted the majority of the work force. Their wages were the standard, urban as well as rural, for unskilled labour, and it was their conditions of work that best expressed the new dispensation of the capitalist economy and society. As Henry Winn observed, they were 'little else than machines for labour. . . . Many of their employers regard them in that light'.[4] A wider range of evidence about their work and working conditions does not contradict his view.

The labourer's day began early and lasted late. For many, about a quarter of those living in open parishes, it necessitated a journey

---

[1] Married labourers were mobile too. Only a quarter of those in the 1851 Census sample were residing in their native parish (and only a sixth of their wives) and a quarter (127 of 485) of labourers' children still living at home had been born outside the parish of current residence.

[2] *P.P.* 1867, xvi, p. 15.

[3] *Linc. Gaz.*, 24 Feb. 1872.

[4] Winn, Diary, 8 July 1844. Henry Colman's impressions, also from the 1840s, were very similar: 'Labour is considered merely as labour; human muscles and, sinews are regarded like the parts of any other implement' (*European Agriculture* i. 141).

to work in another parish. In winter, if the labourer had work at all, it began at sunrise and ended at sunset. In summer he awoke at five or half-past five, had breakfast, was at work by six, and worked without a break until noon. Lunch, consisting of cold bacon and bread, was eaten in a field, under a hedge, or in the stables—anywhere but in the farmhouse kitchen. After a short rest there was continuous work until six; and labourers were sometimes forced to work even longer without pay.[1] They worked six days a week—there is evidence of Sunday work as well—without a 'Saint Monday'; the only holidays were Good Friday and Christmas.

The actual work comprised a great variety of tasks, many of them demanding skill, nearly all of them strength and stamina. Over the long run the work was physically debilitating. In south Lindsey labourers often had to work 'on an empty belly' and were 'frequently wet to the skin through the entire day, and almost starved to death with the cold'.[2] Local dialect words like howelled, hot-ache, clamp'd expressed the discomfort and misery of working while dirty, wet, cold, hungry, and tired.

The terms of hire on which work was performed were far from uniform. Those for farm servants, confined labourers, and gangs have already been noted; those for day labourers could vary according to skill, season, and region. Some tasks were paid 'by the grate', i.e. on a piecework basis, notably harvest work, for which special rates were set and bargained over. Most of the variations, however, were tied to a basic daily or weekly rate which was standard throughout the area for most of the year. In 1800 the basic weekly rate was 11s. 6d.; between 1825 and 1850 it was usually about 12s. It then rose to 15s. as a surplus of labour gave way to a relative shortage. In 1872 the labourers' unions succeeded in increasing wages to 18s. and in 1874 they demanded 21s., but the farmers counter-attacked and reduced wages to 16s. 6d.[3] Yet even in the better-paid years after 1850 the labourers remained 'poor'.

---

[1] Clarke, *Farming of Lincolnshire*, p. 150; E. L. Jones, 'The Agricultural Labour Market in England, 1793–1872', *Economic History Review*, N.S. xvii (1964), pp. 324–6, 328. Rex Russell, *The 'Revolt of the Field' in Lincolnshire*, n.d. [1956], pp. 60, 76–7.

[2] Winn, Diary, 8 July 1844; Clarke, *Farming of Lincolnshire*, pp. 149–50; *Linc. Gaz.*, 24 Feb. 1872.

[3] Ibid., 2 Mar. and 10 Feb. 1872.

The Standard of Living

> The condition of the labourer is undoubtedly of a superior
> order as compared with what it is in most agricultural counties,
> but to say that it is 'good' is a matter which admits of hesita-
> tion; how the workmen exist in those counties where 7*s.* or 8*s.*
> is a common weekly wage . . . must for ever remain a mystery
> to many, when 9*s.*, 10*s.*, or 12*s.*, is here deemed a miserable
> pittance on which to feed, lodge, clothe, and warm six or
> seven individuals for seven days.
>
> J. A. Clarke, *On the Farming of Lincolnshire*, 1852, p. 159.

The standard of living question is as problematic for the village
as for the town labourer. Lincolnshire lay in the high-wage
district of rural England, and the Lincolnshire labourer was often
congratulated on his superior prosperity and comfort. Thomas
Cooper, the Chartist, for example, wrote that 'we never knew
what poverty was—we never saw it—in Lincolnshire. Nobody
knows what real poverty is in that happy country'.[1] But the
poverty of the labourers was real enough to them, particularly
when juxtaposed with the mounting affluence of the successful
high farmer. Their relative standard of living certainly declined;
whether it improved even in absolute terms is questionable.
J. A. Clarke, writing for an audience of farmers and landlords,
pointed out that money wages had hardly risen between 1800 and
1850, and concluded that 'after the lapse of half a century the
agricultural labourers of Lincolnshire are obtaining no better
livelihood in exchange for their toil than before'.[2] Whatever the
trend of real wages, the labourer was relatively worse off after
decades of agricultural prosperity than he was at the beginning,
since the farmers' income and standard of living had risen
swiftly and unequivocally.

The evidence for labourers' housing certainly suggests little
improvement. Throughout the period large families were packed
into small cottages. Many were in bad condition, even on the
large estates; they were 'a disgrace to common humanity' at
Willoughby, on the Ancaster estate, where the ordinary cottage
consisted of 'mud walls, cold damp mud floors, without a
chamber, generally, and where one is found, it is open to the

---

[1] Findlay to Kennedy, 13 May 1850, 3 ANC 7/23/58/90; Robert J. Conklin,
Thomas Cooper, 1935, p. 165.

[2] Clarke, *Farming of Lincolnshire*, p. 150.

roof'. They had low ceilings and a privy exposed to public gaze.[1] The Marsh, with its open parishes, seems to have had more than its share of poor cottages, which were inevitably overcrowded When they had only two rooms, one up and one down, the tenants insisted on 'lofty square Bedchambers and are never content with beds on the ground floor'; where there were two bedrooms, one was generally left empty in expectation of a 'chance lodger'.[2] The labourer would 'offer any available corner in his cottage to a relative, or even a stranger, for the purpose of making a little addition to his weekly earnings, or to accommodate a labourer, who would otherwise have to walk to and from his daily work'.[3] An extreme case of overcrowding occurred at Snarford, where a widowed labourer had in his cottage his father, five young children, an older unmarried daughter and her child, and an unmarried 'housekeeper' with three illegitimate children of her own; the thirteen people slept in four beds in a windowless bedroom twelve feet square and six feet high.[4] Such overcrowding was chronic when lodgers were present and children were young; when they were older and returned home from service for May Day, or for village feasts, or for Christmas, overcrowding was temporary, but, as clergy and others feared, even more likely to have immoral consequences.[5]

In the labourer's cottage there was no room of one's own, and scarcely any room, it would seem, for the 'private' or 'secret' prayer beloved by Methodists. A working man could probably find greater privacy in the fields or in a cowshed than in his own home. Yet the clergy found it possible to hold cottage services, and cottages proved to be congenial settings for the Methodists, with their taste for a hot, crowded, intense religious atmosphere. Crowded rooms and the lack of privacy were the domestic conditions of a communal society in which individualism was suspect.

The largest expense in the labourer's budget was food. Confined labourers and farm servants had meat daily and seem to

[1] DuPré to Willoughby, 24 Apr. 1848, 3 ANC 7/23/51/8; Findlay to Kennedy, 17 July 1858, 3 ANC 7/23/75/13.

[2] *P.P.* 1867–8, xvii, pp. 304–5.

[3] Kaye to Monson, 15 July 1858, MON 25/13/10/10/47.

[4] *Mkt Rasen W.M.*, 24 May 1862.

[5] The Revd. W. F. J. Kaye feared that a young housekeeper living with a small farmer ran a 'great risk of undue intimacy', but considered that immoral acts were 'rare' among the poor (Kaye to Monson, 15 July 1858, MON 25/13/10/10/47).

have been fed adequately. The ordinary day labourer, however, was worse off. He and his family subsisted chiefly on bread throughout the period, 'barley and black bread' earlier and wheat bread later, which was baked by their wives.[1] In the 1860s a labourer ate over two pounds of bread a day. Flour was the chief item of expenditure and might take up more than half the weekly wages. Several weeks' supply could come from the gleanings after harvest, and perhaps some from an allotment, but most had to be bought, and its price was critical for the cost of living. Labourers often had to buy their flour on credit, paying the miller twopence interest; in the end they paid more for their bread than the squire did for his.[2] With the bread they had butter, tea and sugar, and potatoes. A labourer with a garden or allotment was assured of a supply of potatoes if they were not all fed to a pig. The extent to which vegetables were grown and eaten is unfortunately obscure. Labourers who kept pigs had meat, though probably not enough to last the entire year, and those without pigs probably had meat infrequently.[3] In the 1870s they complained that they were paid too little to afford meat—which they would be given in the workhouse or in prison—and emigrants' letters printed in local and union newspapers invariably mentioned the low price of beef in Ontario or Iowa. There were also complaints of having too little for beer and tobacco. At best, then, the labourer's diet was sufficiently nutritious, if monotonous; at worst it was inadequate both in quantity and in quality.

The labourer's clothing was a part not only of his standard of living but also of his social status. During the century coarse homespun woollen was superseded by more fashionable styles, especially among female servants. By 1844 few of them were 'of the homespun school', and most aspired to wear fancy clothes; Henry Winn found it 'truly sickening to see the profusion of ribbonds and artificial flowers with which country girls were adorned'.[4] Around 1860 the fashion for crinolines reached into a

---

[1] News. Cutt., vol. B, pp. 127–8; Winn 2/29. Winn also recalled the 'good old days' of barley bread and barley pudding (Diary, 2 July 1844), and one of H. D. Rawnsley's informants in Somersby mentioned barley bread 'baäked on cowcassons' (*Memories of the Tennysons*, 2nd edn., 1912, p. 48).

[2] Clarke, *Farming of Lincolnshire*, p. 150; *Linc. Gaz.*, 2 Mar. 1872.

[3] *Linc. Gaz.*, 24 Feb. and 2 Mar. 1872. Winn noted that labourers who kept pigs exhausted their year's supply of bacon by the end of September (Diary, 20 Sept. 1844).

[4] Diary, 17 May 1844.

few labourers' cottages as well as higher in society. For men the standard and distinctive dress was the smock, which until they adopted trousers in the 1880s distinguished them unmistakably from their social superiors dressed in jackets and trousers. As in other parts of rural England the labourer usually had one smock to wear on work days, and another to wear on Sunday; hence Clarke's praise for 'the respectable appearance presented by Lincolnshire labourers on the Sunday', and the complaint by the incumbent of Willoughby about the backwardness of his parish, where 'the parents are dressed the same on the Sabbath as on the week day'.[1] The other item of clothing important to labourers and their families was boots. Around 1870 south Lindsey labourers spent an average of a shilling a week on boots: probably cheap and cheaply made boots, which wore out in a few months, for lack of the savings that would have enabled them to spend somewhat more for a sturdier and longer-lasting product.

A more comprehensive view of the labourers' standard of living emerges from a series of family budgets printed in local newspapers in the early 1870s, during the rise of the labourers' trade union movement. They very likely share a 'bias towards "respectability,"' in being reticent about expenditures on beer and tobacco, but their general outlines are plausible.[2] They show that the greatest single expenditure was for flour, ranging from less than a third to around half the weekly income. The only expenditure on meat was for bacon, in a family in which the wife worked; most of the bacon was intended for the head of the family. Other informants, including a 'dry Bread Eater', specifically mentioned their inability to buy meat. Two labourers also claimed to be unable to afford scholars' pence. Whatever the distortions of these budgets, no farmer or landlord denied their evidence that the margin for comfort in labouring life must have been narrow at best.

The labourers' last resort was public poor relief. Their fear of the workhouse was well justified, but the actual numbers there were kept low by the guardians' refusal to apply the workhouse

---

[1] Clarke, *Farming of Lincolnshire*, p. 157; DuPré to Kennedy, 12 Aug. 1844, 3 ANC 7/23/45/40. See also Anne Buck, 'The Countryman's Smock', *Folk Life*, i (1963). For labourers' boots, see Bourne, *Change in the Village*, p. 93.

[2] John Burnett, *A History of the Cost of Living*, 1969, p. 264. The budgets appeared in the *Linc. Gaz.*, 17 Feb., 2, 9, and 23 Mar. 1872; see also *P.P.* 1867-8, xvii, p. 297.

test with Chadwickian rigour. In most years the result of this policy was that the recipients of outdoor relief outnumbered the inmates of the workhouse by a ratio of ten to one.[1] In popular estimation outdoor relief was vastly superior to the workhouse; labourers regarded it not as a dole but as 'parish pay' which was theirs by right—a vestige of the traditional assumption that anyone unable to work had the right to be maintained.[2] There were, however, definite limits to official paternalism. Overseers commonly penalized members of friendly societies by deducting the value of club benefits from their 'parish pay'.[3] And husbands and wives were forced to separate in the workhouses. But the authorities' primary impulse seems to have been to offer outdoor relief. Work on the roads was another alternative to the workhouse, both for the able-bodied unemployed and for men incapable of normal work. As late as 1861 the parish overseers at Scampton paid an average of 12s. a week to men, not all of them able-bodied, for road work—at a time when farmers were paying 13s. 6d. to field workers. A similar scheme was reported at Bardney.[4] The workhouse was greatly feared but by the workings of the system seems not to have been an immediate threat to most labourers and their families.

What they found more difficult to avoid was seasonal distress, in the winter, arising from the seasonal cycle of agricultural work. In the harvest months, August and September, the demand for labur was at its height, with every available hand pressed into service; in some years the local supply was insufficient, and desperate agriculturists imported Irish labourers and talked of bringing in the army.[5] But in the winter months, December to February and sometimes beyond, agricultural work largely came to a standstill, and spells of bad weather often cancelled what little work was left. Since day labourers were paid only for days actually worked, rain and frost meant a loss of wages. It was precisely in the winter months that Methodist evangelism and

---

[1] Annual returns of the Poor Law Unions in *P.P.* In July 1862, for example, there were 408 receiving indoor relief and 4,632 receiving outdoor relief in the three most rural Unions in south Lindsey (*P.P.* 1862, xlviii, p. 165).

[2] Examples in *Mkt Rasen W.M.*, 2 Jan. 1876, and *Linc. Gaz.*, 7 June 1873.

[3] For example, at Normanby-by-Stow (*Linc. Gaz.*, 16 Mar. 1872).

[4] *Lincoln Journal*, 5 Jan. 1861; *Stamf. Merc.*, 28 Feb. 1851.

[5] Booth to Kennedy, 15 Aug. 1831, 3 ANC 7/23/48/8; Findlay to Kennedy, 8 Aug. 1848, 3 ANC 7/23/53/29; *P.P.* 1867, xvi, p. 6.

revivalism—helped too by the long hours of darkness—were at their height, when the need for warmth and consolation was greatest.

Over the period as a whole, distress was more acute in the early years, but the reaction to it—apart from the revolt of 1830—more concerted and significant at the end, in the upsurge of unionism in the 1870s. What came between these two great movements—isolated incidents of arson, mostly in the 1830s and 1840s—have not as yet yielded many of their secrets. Nevertheless the over-all chronology of unrest was much the same in south Lindsey as in the larger lowland zone of southern and eastern England.

In the great labourers' revolt of 1830 incidents of arson were reported in south Lindsey in a chain of parishes extending from Louth down the Middle Marsh and near-by Wolds districts to the Fen margins and southern Wolds.[1] There were complaints of low wages and unemployment, for which the importation of Irish labourers and the threshing machine were blamed. The threshing machines were the chief provocation and arson the response.

The next outbreak of protest, in the winter of 1834–5, was triggered by unemployment, falling wages, and the new Poor Law. As in 1830, south Lindsey labourers moved for the same reasons and at the same time as their brothers over much of eastern England. Three years later, in November 1837, two cases of arson were reported, but the next serious distress was in 1844–5. Incendiarism began at Scrivelsby in August, while the harvest was still in progress, and by December 'rewards for the discovery of incendiaries' were being offered at Spilsby. Distress returned at the same seasons in 1849–52, with a particularly bad winter in 1850–1, and again arson was the response. But in the more prosperous 1850s and 1860s arson ceased, and disaffection itself, in a more benign social climate, was barely visible.[2] Apart from the obvious correlation with distress, the meaning of protest between 1830 and 1850 remains to be clarified. It may be signi-

[1] Hobsbawm and Rudé, *Captain Swing*, Appendix III. Unfortunately Hobsbawm and Rudé underestimated the extent of the disturbances in Lincolnshire. See Rex Russell's review in *Agri. Hist. Rev.* xviii (1970), Part II, pp. 173–5.

[2] Booth to Kennedy, 12 Dec. 1834, 3 ANC 7/23/29/9: *Linc. Gaz.*, 2 Jan. 1835; *Stamf. Merc.*, 1 Dec. 1837; Winn, Diary, i. 81, 123; Findlay to Kennedy, 30 Aug. 1850, 3 ANC 7/23/59/51; Findlay to Kennedy, 7 March 1851, 3 ANC 7/23/60/52. See also Hobsbawm and Rudé, *Captain Swing*, ch. 15.

ficant though that incendiarism was noted particularly in the Middle Marsh, a region of early emigration.[1] While this was the period of maximum economic hardship and social tension between labourers and farmers, evidence suggest that incendiarism was not an expression of generalized outrage but a precise weapon directed at particular farmers.[2] Nevertheless, Henry Winn's contemporary diagnosis was probably close to the truth. The labourers, he said, asked for work but were denied it: 'they then frantically apply the . . . match to that abundance which . . . mocks their hungry stomachs and famishing families.'[3]

In the period that followed, the 1850s and 1860s, arson disappeared, emigration increased, and the labourers seemed to have been softened by the new atmosphere of social peace and tranquillity. Farmers and clergy were tempted to congratulate themselves on the success of their various community simulation exercises; and if the labourers still experienced seasons of hardship, these were now to be occasions for paternalism from above rather than for protest from below. In retrospect the labourers' silence in these years was deceptive, and the social harmonies superficial, but the dominant classes took these favourable signs at face value, and thus were all the more shocked when the unions erupted in 1872.

In bringing the labourers' protest to a climax, the unions not only employed new tactics but also revealed a new attitude towards distress.[4] If earlier protest can be formulated as a conjunctural response to a conjunctural stimulus, then the unions were a structural response to structural conditions. Labourers now reacted not against seasonal, temporary distress but against the inadequacy of employment and wages in 'normal' times. And unlike the sudden, furtive violence of earlier years, the unions were public, organized, non-violent, and permanent (though the

[1] Emigration was reported from Strubby (in the 1831 Census), from Alford (*Linc. Gaz.*, 14 Apr. 1840) and from Willoughby (3 ANC 7/23/59/56). Later the Amalgamated Labour League assisted many emigrants from the Alford area (*Labourer*, 16 Jan. and 3 July 1875).

[2] The target of arson at Great Steeping in 1850 was unpopular for paying lower wages than his landlord, who farmed in the same parish (Findlay to Kennedy, 9 Apr. 1850, 3 ANC 7/23/58/67).

[3] Winn, Diary, 3 Dec. 1844.

[4] See Russell, '*Revolt of the Field*'; J. P. D. Dunbabin, 'The "Revolt of the Field"': The Agricultural Labourers' Movement in the 1870s', *Past and Present*, no. 26 (1963); Hobsbawm and Rudé, *Captain Swing*, ch. 15.

farmers' opposition and sectarian conflicts led to their collapse within a decade). The great contrasts between the earlier forms of protest and the later suggest that the unions were more the product of a new situation than the fulfilment of an earlier potential. Perhaps the clue to the unions lies in the observation that if they were a climax to labourers' protest, they were a delayed climax: their origins lay not in a filiation of protest activities but in the wider changes in the labourers' life and outlook going forward in the period of the 'delay'. It was then, in the 1850s and 1860s, that the labourers appear to accelerate a process begun much earlier, abandoning the traditional culture of the poor and adopting a new class identity and class culture.

Towards Respectability

From the 1840s if not earlier, changes in the labourers' working conditions and standard of living were minor compared with the changes in their values and outlook. Their social 'being' had been established much earlier: it was now that their consciousness was transformed, becoming less traditional and 'communal', more modern and proletarian. This was particularly apparent in the acquisition of literacy and the growth of self-discipline.

In the course of the century illiteracy all but disappeared among south Lindsey labourers. The uses and consequences of literacy are unclear, but the fact itself was representative of the changes under way in labouring life.

Before 1850 Lincolnshire was among the more literate counties in England, though the labourers were of course the least literate group in society. In the county as a whole, 28 per cent of all bridegrooms in 1838–9 and 47 per cent of all brides signed the register with a mark; in 1853 the figures were 27 and 37 per cent, respectively. These figures, from the civil registers of marriage, were for persons of all classes. Figures for labourers have been calculated from a selection of parish registers and Wesleyan marriage registers.[1]

[1] *P.P.* 1840, xvii, p. 14; 1854–5, xv, p. 5. The parish registers used were those of Aisthorpe, Burton, South Carlton, Donington, Driby, South Ormsby, Panton, Rand, Reepham, Springthorpe Toft, and East Torrington; the Wesleyan marriage registers, those of Horncastle Wesleyan Chapel and of Wesley Chapel, Lincoln.

Percentages of Labourers and their Brides Signing Marriage Registers with

a mark

	Males	Females
1837–50	52	62
1851–75	33	29

It is obvious that literacy increased sharply for both sexes after 1850, but a more refined interpretation of the figures depends on two further considerations: the relation between being able to sign one's name and the general ability to write, and the relation between being able to write and the ability to read. It seems likely that the numbers signing registers corresponded fairly closely with the numbers able to write, and that a further 50 per cent of those signing with a mark were able to read.[1] It follows that before 1850 about 70 per cent of the labourers and less than 60 per cent of their wives were literate. After 1850 the great majority of both brides and grooms were literate.

The implications of these findings for religious practice are confusing. In the period of greatest religious excitement, before 1850, large minorities of both men and women were illiterate; after 1850, literacy increased and religious excitement decreased. Other evidence suggests that literacy and religious practice in rural England were inversely related.[2] But it remains an open question whether the religious revival contributed towards the final conquest of illiteracy or was undermined by it.

Behind the increase in literacy, a phenomenon of modernization, lay an increase in schooling, a phenomenon of class society. Education for the poor, particularly day schools, expanded slowly and painfully, inhibited by the apprehensions of the rich. Landlords were less than uniformly enthusiastic: 'the non-residence of some landed proprietors and the indifference of others is another cause of the difficulty,' noted one clergyman. The farmers, who in the past had gone to the same schools as the labourers, now gave their children a separate and elaborate education; and they opposed any education for the working class that went beyond bare literacy.[3] Too much education, it was feared, would

---

[1] R. K. Webb, 'Working Class Readers in Early Victorian England', *English Historical Review*, lxv (1950), p. 348; 'The Victorian Reading Public', in Boris Ford (ed.), *Pelican Guide to English Literature: From Dickens to Hardy*, 1958, p. 213.

[2] Rural counties ranking high in literacy generally ranked low in church attendance, and vice versa, in the Religious Census.

[3] The Revd. W. A. Ayton, Scampton, A.T. Schools Questionnaire 1855, L.A.O. P.P. 1843, xii, p. 218.

deplete the supply of labour. And the farmers' demand for child labour took children out of the classroom into the fields, further interfering with their education. By the 1860s children were thought to be leaving school earlier than in the past.[1] Attendance, irregular at the best of times, fell drastically in the summer months when the demand for child labour increased. Even Sunday schools were vulnerable, since farmers forced boys to work on Sundays. It remained for the clergy to support popular education, partly because they saw it as a weapon in the struggle with Methodism. Even their support was less than unanimous, but they carried a disproportionate part of the burden, in south Lindsey as else-where.[2] A still more disproportionate part of the burden was carried by the labourers themselves. For the day schools that were established by largesse from above were largely sustained by sacrifice from below. They were not free schools, but often drew the bulk of their income from the 'scholars' pence' paid by the children's parents. (The fear was expressed that free education would 'pauperize the vast majority of the population'.)[3] Thus parents whose child attended school paid twice—the school fees as well as the child's lost earnings. And what kind of education did their children receive for the money? Once the dominant classes overcame their fear of popular education they saw it as a mechanism of social control. Their hopes were more realistic than their fears: the historian of education in nineteenth-century Lindsey concludes that 'pupils learned attitudes and modest expectations rather than the three Rs. . . . The village schools, provided by their "betters", had been amazingly successful by 1870 in helping to stabilize rural society by reinforcing deference.'[4]

A second trend in labouring culture was the growth of self-discipline in outward behaviour. What had come to be deprecated as the labourers' 'roughness' was subjected to a multiple assault: from working people themselves, seeking self-control; from

[1] *P.P.* 1867–8, xvii, p. 86.

[2] Rex Russell, *A History of Schools and Education in Lindsey, Lincs., 1800–1902*, Pt. 3, 1966; J. S. Hurt, 'Landowners, Farmers, and Clergy and the Financing of Rural Education before 1870', *Journal of Educational Administration and History*, i (1968), pp. 7–8; Stone, 'Literacy and Education in England', p. 115.

[3] According to the Revd. Irvin Eller of Faldingworth, *P.P.* 1861, xxi, Pt. 5, p. 173; for the scholars' pence, see Russell, *A History of Schools and Education in Lindsey*, Pt. 1, 1965, p. 31.

[4] Russell, review of Hobsbawm and Rudé, *Captain Swing*, in *Agri. Hist. Rev.* xviii (1970), p. 174.

moralizing 'reformers', largely Evangelical; from a remote élite anxious to curb popular 'disturbances'; from the churches, in rare unanimity; and from the psychological impact of capitalist civilization, which was no less powerful in the countryside than in the towns. By the 1860s these forces of discipline—and repression—had largely triumphed: but it was an ambiguous triumph, as the 1870s would reveal.

The most vivid evidence both of the rough ways of the past and of the difficult transition to self-control is offered by the farm servants. Their outlook was the most traditional, the most conservative, in agrarian society. Close to nature—and particularly to the mysteries and lore of horses[1]—they were the bearers of tradition and superstition. Indeed they resisted the moralizers actively as well as passively. Not only did they rarely attend church themselves, but they jeered and insulted those who did. On Sunday afternoons and evenings it was their custom to congregate in the street and annoy and insult passers-by, particularly women on their way to chapel. They were the 'men and boys . . . too frequently seen loitering about on the Sabbath' at Ludford; the 'groups of ten to fifteen persons each, during the time of divine service who seemed to have met together for no other purpose than tumult' at Wragby; the 'parcel of louts or half-grown boys, who every Sunday assemble at the corner and insult every passer-by to the church' at West Rasen; the 'many groups of idlers [at Tealby] who congregate on a Sunday, particularly against the Primitives and other chapels, where they may be counted by dozens, and whose language at times is most disgusting'; and a similar 'mob of overgrown boys' at Dunholme.[2] In these skirmishes can be discerned not only a scorn and resentment at the moral pretensions of the religious, but also a protest: of the young against the old, the masculine against the feminine, the rough against the respectable, and of tradition against modernity. The 'loose habits' of this *most neglected class* were the despair of the moralizers.[3]

But this same 'class' also played an important part in the larger process by which labouring life became more orderly and

---

[1] See George Ewart Evans, *The Horse in the Furrow*, 1960.

[2] *Stamf. Merc.*, 3 June 1831, 29 Aug. 1851; *Mkt Rasen W.M.*, 10 Dec. 1870, 13 June 1857; *Linc. Gaz.*, 17 Sept. 1859.

[3] P.P. 1861, xxi, p. 10.

respectable. This was notable particularly in their conduct at the statute hiring fairs, one of the high points in the agrarian calendar. On Old May Day, 13 May, servants came to the towns to seek new employment for the coming year; on the following day, 'Pag-rag day', they left their old masters and returned home to visit their families; and at the 'May day market' they had their great annual holiday.

The statute fairs attracted domestic as well as farm servants, and all in great numbers. At Horncastle the street was 'crowded withe the females "standing" for "places"'. The young men and youths would '"stand" in the Bull ring and adjoining streets, where the masters would be looking round for suitable servants. . . . Young fellows who wished for a shepherd's place with a lock of wool in the hat girdle; and others who aspired to be wagoners with a knot of whipcord similarly exposed.' This was the 'slave market' attacked by the clergy and others as degrading but defended by the farmers on the grounds that they must see their servants before hiring them.[1]

On 'Pag-rag' day servants received from their masters the whole of their annual wages and generally went home to visit their parents, carrying their bundle of possessions with them. Families were reunited, the grown children crowding the available beds and dismaying the moralists.

The climax of the May pageant was the fair. At Louth thousands of villagers, chiefly servants, poured into the town to spend their wages and to have a holiday. Many came by railway; in 1867, 1,718 tickets were collected on the morning of the fair at Louth station. They came to pay the debts they had accumulated with tradesmen over the year.[2] But most of all they came for the excitement and amusement and for the crowds. Diversions were there in abundance:

Wandering players, extemporised theaters, cheap jacks, extraordinary giants or interesting dwarfs, the siege of Sebastopol, and the usual array of sights, combined with dancing booths to rob many of their money, and . . . their good names.[3]

---

[1] Winn 3/5, p. 7; *Lincs. Chronicle*, 24 Nov. 1855; *P.P.* 1861, xxi, Part 5, p. 11.

[2] *Louth Adv.*, 18 May 1867; a local newspaper noted that 'the tradesmen's turn comes with the May-day market, when Robin Readymoney and Caroline Cashdown pay up debts' (*Mkt Rasen W.M.*, 8 May 1875).

[3] James to Monson, 27 May 1862, MON 25/13/10/14/73.

At Horncastle the fair was held in the afternoon following the statutes. As Henry Winn recalled,

> It featured shows with wild animals, and various monstrosities . . . wax work shows, Merry Andrews, swing boats, shooting galleries, Punch and Judy. . . . The recruiting sergeant . . . with his fife and drum band parading the streets from Inn to Inn followed by crowds of admiring rustics, some with ribonds in their hats, their mothers and sweethearts in tears, beseeching them to beware of the enchanted shilling.

Army and navy recruiters were indeed regular visitors, and hasty decisions to enlist, aided by alcohol, must have been frequent. At night there was dancing till late hours as well as heavy drinking. Some farm servants managed to drink through their entire year's wages in the course of May week. Clergymen seldom failed to condemn the fairs for their encouragement to drunkenness and 'immorality'.[1]

Despite the fulminations of the moralists, however, labourers saw the fairs as 'their only holiday' and their best chance to meet members of the opposite sex. After 1850 the fairs gradually lost their hiring business to the new register offices, as female servants now could find jobs through the post, and by 1875 'the slave-market-like procedure is now all but extinct'.[2] Yet if the business side of May week declined, pleasure continued unabated. At the village statutes at Hainton, 1,500 attended annually in the 1860s, of whom only fifty came to seek work: the rest were there for a 'spree'. Yet much of the wildness and disorder that had formerly marked the fairs was on the wane. The 'light-fingered gentry' who had plagued earlier fairs were noticeably less active later, perhaps having moved on to more lucrative territory. The advent of police made a difference, but even more important was the growing sobriety and seriousness of behaviour among servants and labourers themselves. Better order was remarked upon at Louth in 1861; in 1870 it was reported that drunks were fewer and that by 8 p.m. most of the visitors were on their way

---

[1] 'Then and Now . . .', MS. booklet, p. 7, Winn 3/5; *Louth Adv.*, 21 May 1859; John Brown, *Neddy and Sally, or the Statutes Day, a Lincolnshire Tale*, 1841; P.P. 1867–8, xvii, p. 282.

[2] P.P. 1867–8, xvii, pp. 76, 282; Malcolmson, *Popular Recreations*, p. 54; *Louth Adv.*, 3 May 1862; *Mkt Rasen W.M.*, 8 May 1875. Servants stipulated in their new contracts that they should be free to visit other fairs that week even after they had been hired (*P.P.* 1861, xxi, pt. 5, p. 11, 1867–8, xvii, p. 282).

home.[1] What is remarkable is the rapid transformation in the behaviour of those who were largely untouched by institutional religion.

In the case of the village feasts the same forces of discipline were at work but in different proportions. Again the labourers' own capacity for order and decorum was evident, but even more important was repression by the dominant classes.

Although the village feast was often held on or near the day of the saint to whom the church was dedicated, it no longer had any religious connection and existed solely for pleasure. Unlike the statutes fair, its appeal was not just to servants but to the whole labouring population, and the amusements and entertainments reflected the social assumptions of labouring life. The dances, for example, favoured by labourers at a village feast included 'three, four, and six-handed reels', a 'set dance', and special dances for men, performed 'between two long churchwarden pipes'. It is significant that none of these dances, from Stixwould feast, were for couples: communal dances reflected a communal society in which the group was prior to the married couple. There was also wrestling at Stixwould, another survival from the older culture. The two opponents grasped each other's clothes near the chest with both hands, trying to pull each other down to their knees: 'the whole art consisted in giving the opponent as bad a kick as possible below the knee without being dragged down.'[2] It reflected a milieu of strength and effort, unlike middle-class culture with its taboos on physical contact.

The feasts were not free from disorder and violence. There was fighting—in which old scores were settled, sometimes fatally— and drunkenness. But the trend was towards sobriety and order. By 1874 it was noted at Tealby that 'country feasts ... are decidedly not so demonstrative as they were formerly, and though a fair muster of country cousins and visiting friends turned up on Sunday ... the anniversary was of a much quieter nature than some of former years.'[3]

This, however, was not good enough for the dominant classes, who objected to the feasts on principle. Feasts were independent

---

[1] *P.P.* 1867-8, xvii, p. 282; *Louth Adv.*, 21 May 1870.

[2] James Alpass Penny, *Folklore Round Horncastle*, 1915, pp. 15-16.

[3] News. Cutt., vol. B, pp. 11-12; *Stamf. Merc.*, 20 Nov. 1837; Winn, Diary, 10 July 1844; *Mkt Rasen W.M.*, 29 Aug. 1874.

of their control, and what was independent was threatening whether it took the form of innocent merriment or brutal fist-fights. It is significant that of the ten parishes for which references to feasts have been noted, all but one were in open parishes. In Stixwould, the one exceptional close parish, the feast was suppressed. Previous incumbents had been absentees; when a new parsonage was built, the incumbent was disturbed by the noise caused by the feast and had the squire suppress it.[1] Nor were feasts in an open parish safe from harassment. In 1835 the feast day at Bardney fell on a Sunday; the squire of Scrivelsby, Sir Henry Dymoke, a sabbatarian and magistrate, intervened, forbidding the sale of apples at the feast and afterwards directing a churchwarden to prosecute a 'Jinks'—a perambulating seller of gingerbread to children—for violating the Sabbath. This elicited a letter protest to Dymoke in a local newspaper. The feast, it said, was 'altogether quite a village concern'. There were 'no pickpockets, no thimble-men. . . . The poverty of the place protects it from the intrusion of vice, and hard labour—a thing you know very little about—secures it from any disposition to uproar.' Children, the writer went on, enjoyed their gingerbread and lollipops, men their pipes. 'There is a luxury in it, which gentlemen like you who have nothing to do but to visit and be visited, and who have nurseries at the other end of the house, can form no idea of.'[2] Nevertheless the gingerbread man was tried, convicted, and fined.

The feasts thus reflected labourers' culture in transition: the 'immaturity' of the adults in playing children's games,[3] their 'communal' dances, their disorder, their outgrowing of disorder, and the heavy-handed intolerance of their superiors, whose conception of social order left no room for independent popular entertainment, however innocuous.

The moralizers were less successful in repressing drink and the subculture of drink. It was the churches especially that fought this battle, for while disagreeing on temperance and teetotalism, they were unanimous in their hostility to the beerhouse, which was not only a den of iniquity but also a lowly but effective rival with its own set of attractions.

[1] Penny, *Folklore*, p. 15.
[2] *Linc. Gaz.*, 4 Sept. and 21 Aug. 1835.
[3] See below, p. 94.

On occasion the rivalry was direct, when the beerhouse opened —illegally—during the hours of divine worship.[1] But what mattered more was the underlying conflict between incompatible notions of life and conduct. Unfortunately it is difficult to reconstruct the ethos of the beerhouse, to recapture what Sir John Barleycorn meant to his disciples. Alcohol was the shortest road out of Hogsthorpe or Tetford as well as Manchester, but the accounts of the route that survive were written by those who disapproved of short cuts. To them the beerhouse was a veritable anthology of vice: 'drunkenness, gambling, quarrelling, swearing, indecent and profane jesting, obscene songs, rude and improper postures and anticks'—not to mention fighting and the plotting of crime.[2] Yet to labourers it had a positive appeal. It was a thoroughly working-class institution, a cottage opened by a labourer for his fellow labourers, and it offered them one of their few opportunities to escape the surveillance of the dominant classes. In a society under moralizing inhibitions it preserved something of the public frankness of the older society, providing an enclave in which sexual and aggressive impulses could be freely expressed. Yet even in the beerhouse the trend to self-restraint may have made itself felt. If evidence from Oxfordshire is representative, the atmosphere of the beerhouse in the 1880s was sedate, sociable and almost respectable.[3]

The only other working-class institution in the countryside, the friendly society, had a quite different set of social implications. Its members drank, but in moderation, and they conspicuously cultivated the virtues of self-help and self-discipline. At the same time the friendly society enabled them to satisfy their taste for ceremonial. Both its ethic and its ceremonial had religious overtones and at moments they brought it into conflict with the parish clergy, but the predominant note was one of cooperation. The friendly societies took pains to express their deference to the neighbourhood social élite as well as to endorse respectable morality.

In the villages of Victorian England as well as the towns friendly societies had the largest membership of any working men's organization. Trade unions were unknown in south Lindsey

---

[1] Examples in the Spilsby magistrates' Minute Books, Thimbleby 7/1, L.A.O.

[2] Winn, Diary, 16 May 1844.

[3] F. Thompson, *Lark Rise*, ch. 4.

before 1872, but friendly societies, drawing most of their membership from labourers and craftsmen, had flourished in many of
the larger villages and in the towns for a generation or
longer.[1] References to fifty-one friendly society branches have
been noted in over forty villages. The largest group were the
Foresters, with thirty-four Courts; the Odd Fellows, chiefly of
the Manchester Unity, had fourteen Lodges, and there were
three unattached societies.[2] Their actual catchment area was
greater than the numbers indicated, since a local branch
commonly took members from neighbouring villages as well
as its own. New branches multiplied most rapidly between
1837 and 1840, though others were being set up till the end of
the period.

The manifest purpose of the friendly societies was to provide
insurance benefits.[3] At 'Court Nelson' for example, the Foresters'
branch at Dunholme, membership was open to men aged 18 to
40. After one year of membership their monthly contribution of
1s. 3d. entitled them to sick benefits beginning at 10s. per week for
the first twelve months; at death, the member's survivor received
£10; on the death of the member's wife, he received £7, and on
the death of a second wife, £5.[4] Furthermore many branches
appointed a physician to care for ill members. The prudential
benefits of the societies, welcome as they undoubtedly were, were
not, however, more important than their moral atmosphere and
sociability.

They inculcated, and enforced, a code of responsible and
disciplined conduct. Drunkenness—the curse of the improving
labourer—strong language, and related misdemeanours were
punished by fines. And fighting or venereal disease disqualified
one from receiving sick benefits. A member also lost his benefits
if he was seen drunk or if he spent more than sixpence a day 'in

[1] Membership lists are lacking, but a hint of the social composition of a friendly
society survives in a list of trustees of the Dunholme branch of the Foresters:
they comprised seven labourers and five craftsmen (*Rule book*, F.S. 3/211/345,
P.R.O.).

[2] Figures derived from P.R.O. IND 25529, *Directory of the Ancient Order of Foresters'
Friendly Society, and Almanack, 1866–69*, and local newspapers.

[3] The nature of the link, if any, between friendly societies and the labourers' unions
is unclear, but it is noteworthy that local branches of the unions often established
sick and benefit societies: e.g. the Amalgamated Labour League branch at Southrey,
in Bardney parish (*Labour League Examiner*, 20 June 1874).

[4] F.S. 3/211/345, P.R.O.

ale or spiritous liquours'.[1] Thus the friendly society was an experiment in moderate drinking and in self-control.

The ritual calendar of the friendly society had its climax in the anniversary, usually held on a weekday late in May or early June. Members assembled in the morning, then proceeded round the village; in later years they often hired a brass band to lead the way. They ended their exercises at noon for a special service at the parish church, the parson pronouncing his blessing on collective self-help. Then followed a dinner, with the clergyman or some local superior farmer in the chair, and toasts, speeches, and drinking. Members then usually went on a second procession, to the houses of the clergyman, squire, and larger farmers, to solicit gifts for the society, while the band played. This was the most convincing way of expressing deference, but the massing even of respectable workers could easily have implied a threat as well. The procession would wander through neighbouring parishes and tap the funds of benefactors farther afield. Sometimes the celebration had a sequel the following day in a tea for members' wives, with dancing and drinking till late hours. Members marching in the processions were specially adorned for the occasion with 'sashes and horns'. Every society had its officers—a Foresters' Court included a Chief Ranger, Sub-chief Ranger, Treasurer, Secretary, Senior Woodward, Junior Woodward, and Beadle—who dressed up even more elaborately. The three chief officers of the Tealby Foresters in 1875 were dressed significantly as Robin Hood, Little John, and Friar Tuck, and rode grey chargers. (At the dinner they represented, respectively, Benevolence, Unity, and Concord.)[2] The whole village might be dressed up to welcome the procession as it went through: this was one of the most popular public occasions in village life, as well as one of the least religious.

More solemn was the procession to the grave of a deceased member. When one of the Foresters of Tealby died, in 1867, over thirty members met in the lodge room for a last tribute; 'near the residence of the deceased the members were drawn up in line on either side of the road' each bearing regalia and with staff in hand. Usually the members accompanied the body to the grave,

---

[1] *Laws of the Amicable Friendly Society of Wragby*, 1853, p. 7 (F.S. 1/402A/240, P.R.O.). Similar sanctions could be multiplied in the rulebooks of local branches.
[2] *Mkt Rasen W.M.*, 10 July 1875.

where, after the clergyman's rites, they would 'read their accustomed ceremony'—sometimes causing the clergyman some distress. In the 1860s the friendly society funeral was observed to be 'the largest ... which has taken place in the village for many years' or 'by far the largest ... ever witnessed in this village'.[1] These occasions marked at once the solidarity of the friendly society and the dissolution of the village community: it was an epoch in the history of the village when a death evoked an ampler tribute from a voluntary association than from the community itself. (The communal custom of singing the body to the grave disappeared in the course of the century.) Thus in both the funeral and the anniversary processions the friendly societies did more than proclaim their virtue and loyalty; they also demonstrated a corporate unity for which the precedent was the communal life of the traditional village and the only current parallel (apart from the unions at the end of the period) was the fellowship of the Methodist chapels. Like the chapels, the friendly societies reflected simultaneously the lingering desire for community and the irreversible dissolution of village society. They presented abridged versions of the community, limited to the upper strata of the labouring class, and recaptured something of the communal sense of the traditional village but without its coarseness.[2]

The question remains why these working men's organizations did not arouse the suspicions of the dominant classes. The fact that they lightened the burden of poor relief was a consideration, but more significant probably was the deference that the friendly societies consistently showed to their superiors. They named their lodges after the local gentry family, such as the 'Dalton' at Fillingham, sometimes, to underline the point, prefixing it with a 'Loyal'; when they begged contributions from the gentry and farmers they reverted to a comfortingly traditional relationship of paternalism and dependence; and they always chose the parish church for their anniversaries. Landlords, farmers, and clergy all were courted and all gave their blessing.

[1] *Mkt Rasen W.M.*, 21 Sept. 1867; *Linc. Gaz.*, 14 July 1860; Williamson to Kaye, 2 May 1839, Cor. B. 5/4/67/5; *Louth Adv.*, 6 Jan. 1866.

[2] Though the friendly societies had clear affinities with Methodism, which also fostered self-help and voluntary organization, their official religious links were exclusively with the Established Church. This was probably because they saw themselves as 'official' or communal organizations.

There were two central themes in the life of the friendly societies, self-control and ceremony, and the two were inter-twined. Friendly societies made a parade of virtue and virtue of a parade. The self-control was manifest in their attempt to regulate drinking and in their ability to assemble large numbers on their anniversaries and to parade, dine, and drink without disorder. After an anniversary of the Foresters at Donington, it was com-mented that 'so large a gathering without any drunkenness, quarrelling, or rioting, has scarce ever been known in the village'.[1] The self-control showed also in the prudence with which members laid money aside to insure against illness and to provide for funeral expenses. All this approach to virtue and respect-ability was simultaneously expressed and concealed by the regalia, the dressing-up, the bands, the parades, the officers of picturesque title. Villagers, as good practical Protestants, objected to ritualism in their churches but relished ritual when it was secular and held outdoors and above all when they performed it themselves. Apart from the special anniversary service friendly societies had remark-ably little connection with the churches. And their rules were secular in tone, making no reference to God or to Christianity. This was the Englishman's religious ideal—morality and ritualized conviviality and no theology.

By the 1860s the forces of discipline and repression had largely triumphed; yet for the churches, which had been zealous in the cause, the results were to prove ambiguous. The labourers had become more modern and moral, respectable, disciplined, yet not manifestly more Christian. Having given up some of their traditional spontaneity, they had learned the rules of capitalist social relations—and in the process had become perhaps less in need of direction from external agencies like the churches.

Conclusion

It was natural of the labouring poor to cling to the values and outlook of the older village community as long as they could, to reorient themselves to the new capitalist order only with reluctance. Yet the reorientation, when it came, was profound in its effect on the labourers' social and psychological outlook, for it involved the creation of what amounted to a new class

[1] *Louth Adv.*, 30 June 1860.

culture, growing out of the traditional culture but eventually superseding it. Literacy and self-discipline were only two of its elements, and a wider range of evidence needs to be explored to gain a sense of the process as a whole. The chronology of change as yet is no more than tentative, but it reveals a paradox which itself testifies to the autonomy of labouring life. In the second quarter of the century, the movement away from traditional attitudes appears to have been slight, despite the fact that this was the period of maximum pressure on traditional culture, from the farmers, with their nervous, aggressive tactics, and from the moralizing reformers, who were bearing down heavily on popular recreations. After 1850 the movement towards a new class identity and culture advanced more rapidly, despite the attempts of the dominant groups to block it, by perpetuating obsolete deferential and communal attitudes from the past. (It was characteristic of the period that cricket again was promoted as an all-class pastime, with a veritable mystique of class tolerance and harmony.)[1] In their external behaviour labourers did nothing to disrupt the era of good feeling: they practised an occasional conformity with the requirements of their superiors, taking part in the harvest suppers and thanksgivings laid on for them. But beneath the surface their class-consciousness was growing, however inconspicuously; calculated paternalism from above evoked an increasingly calculated deference from below.

The new culture was complex, a blend of the inherited way of life with necessary accommodations to capitalism and to the dominant social morality. Labourers were still constrained by the imperatives of poverty, which concentrated attention on making ends meet in the present and left little room for higher aspirations and sentiments. And, more than any other class, labourers had a strong preference for face-to-face social relations characteristic of the village milieu. This was offset, however, both by the move from 'disorder' to self-discipline, the diverse sources of which

[1] That cricket was an 'illusion of the age' as well as a game is apparent in a newspaper comment on a match in 1869 between Lord Monson's Burton Park Club and the Gentlemen's Servants Club: 'This match strikingly shows that cricket recognizes no distinctions of class; that it is, and ever has been, one of the principal agents in bringing the different grades of society into contact, and showing that God's mental and moral as well as His natural gifts, are bestowed alike upon the peasant and the peer. Some thirty, or even twenty years ago, this match would have been a social impossibility: but thanks to education, a liberal press . . .' (newspaper clipping in MON 24/IA/9).

have already been mentioned, and by a second modernizing tendency even more fundamental than the first. In the course of the century labourers conducted their own partial withdrawal from the 'crowd'—with its informality, intimacy, and also its immaturity—into a more privatized individual and family life, with a sharper division between adults and children and a more respectful and self-respectful formality in relations between adults. There was finally a primordial sense of occupational identity broadening into class solidarity. By 1870 the contours of this emergent culture were apparent. Along with Methodism, it was in this new class culture that the unions, the first great class organization, had their origins. They were the organizational conclusion to the growth, from a traditional labouring poor, of a modern working class.

It would be impossible to recount these social and cultural changes in any systematic fashion. Yet if one theme is to be selected, it is the decline of the 'crowd' and the complex rise of individualism. More comprehensive than the rest, it epitomizes the larger changes in labouring culture and can be traced in most aspects of village life.

For centuries the village had to a large extent been self-policing, responsible for maintaining its own internal order: hence, in the Middle Ages, the tithing men and the duty of the hue and cry. By the nineteenth century little remained of communal self-government, with the decay of manorial institutions and the rise of oligarchic vestries. But if the parish constable was not chosen by the community he was still a villager and not an outsider, and the community still exercised surveillance over the morals of its members, applying sanctions in the form of 'rough music', 'ran-tanning', or 'riding the stang'. When the unfaithful wife of a farm labourer at Bardney was discovered with her paramour, she 'met with a glorious serenade on tin cans and other like musical instruments with which the indignant matrons of the village expressed their disapproval'. At Sturton, a husband who beat his wife aroused the wrath of a band of youths who paraded the streets three nights with a tin pot, cows' horns, and guns; another beating led to more ran-tanning, until the demonstrations were stopped—significantly—by a policeman.[1] Thus the women of the

---

[1] *Linc. Gaz.*, 2 Mar. 1861 and 19 Feb. 1862. The youths at Sturton were probably farm servants, whom Sir Charles Anderson in the near-by parish of Lea identified as

village—almost certainly of the labouring class—took responsibility for their own kind, as the men did for theirs.

The village was a face-to-face society, whose members could hardly avoid knowing, even if they did not like one another. They kept the doors of their cottages unlocked, except at night and in the depth of winter. (In one Nottinghamshire village just across the Trent only the parson knocked before entering.)[1] Another sign of intimacy was that 'thou' and 'thee' were the usual second person pronouns: villagers were literally on an 'I–thou' basis with each other. And the pronouns were not the only sign of familiarity. Villagers customarily used nicknames instead of ordinary Christian names in conversation. Thomas Cooper recalled that 'old Lindsey folk made it a rule to shorten folks' names when they had to use them often'. Besides shortenings and alterations of names—'Cussitt' for Cusworth, 'Kiah' for Hezekiah, and 'Kucky' for Habakkuk—he mentions true nicknames: 'Cocky Davy', a tailor short in stature, and 'Tim Swallow-whistle', noted for his whistling. Two Mary Jacksons in the village of Fulletby were differentiated by the use of the nickname 'Hopping Polly' for the one who suffered from lameness. Henry Winn recalled that 'aged people and heads of families were spoken of as "Benny Bell" or "Billy Brooks" . . . Mister and Mistress were then sparingly used in common talk.'[2]

Labourers not only belonged to a community but also loved crowds and the physical sensation of crowdedness. Richard Hoggart's account of this in the twentieth-century urban working class is not without application, on a reduced scale, to nineteenth-century rural labourers: 'The sprawling and multitudinous and infinitely detailed character of working-class life, and the sense . . . of an immense uniformity, of always being part of a . . . seething crowd of people, all very similar even in the most important and individual matters.' This was the atmosphere at statute fairs—'one moving sea of heads'—and it was reproduced on a still smaller scale but with great intensity in Methodist

---

the chief suppliers of 'rough music' (*Lincoln Pocket Guide*, 1880, p. 18). See also E. P. Thompson, '"Rough Music": Le Charivari anglais', *Annales*, xxvii (1972).

[1] J. A. Penny, *More Folklore Round Horncastle*, 1922, p. 11; Cooper, *Wise Saws*, i. 185.

[2] Ibid. i. 1, 20, 38, 42, 61; Winn 3/5, pp. 4, 5. See also F. Thompson, *Lark Rise*, pp. 42–3, 90.

chapels, with their tightly packed congregations, places not for private meditation but for collective enthusiasms.[1]

The primacy of the community implied, demographically, the predominance of young people; and this perhaps was the reason for a certain childishness among adult labourers, particularly noticeable in their recreations. Ariès has described how adults of the upper classes, withdrawing from the 'crowd', reserved certain games and sports for their own exclusive use, abandoning the rest to children and to adults of the lower orders.[2] These games, though regarded as childish by the upper classes, continued to be played by adult labourers in south Lindsey, as elsewhere in rural England. In village feasts they jumped in sacks, climbed greasy poles, rolled wheelbarrows blindfold; as late as 1866, at a supper given by a farmer for his labourers, thirty of them jumped in sacks.[3] Farm labourers in Suffolk were known to play marbles, and in a Warwickshire village in the 1890s it was reported that 'on Sundays men and boys might be seen in their working clothes playing hop-scotch and leap-frog in front of the houses'.[4] The childish, degrading implications of such games were not lost on those (particularly Methodist ministers) who were striving to raise the labourers' dignity and self-respect. Those on the other hand who wished to keep them servile and weak actually encouraged them in such activities, particularly the most degrading of them all, fighting. After an evening of drinking at a village feast, according to Henry Winn, the labourers would emerge around midnight and 'perhaps a dozen pitched battles would be fought ... and the principal farmers in the village would be looking on and enjoying the fun'. Half the fun no doubt for these 'principal farmers' was the reinforcement of their sense of superiority and of their contempt for their labourers.[5]

The primacy of the community in traditional and working-class culture meant that other social units and loyalties were secondary. Perhaps some of the opposition to the early Methodists was provoked by the disruption they threatened to the unity

---

[1] R. Hoggart, *The Uses of Literacy*, 1957, p. 18; *Stamf. Merc.*, 25 May 1838.

[2] Ariès, *Centuries of Childhood*, pp. 89–92, 95–7.

[3] *Louth Adv.*, 27 Jan. 1866.

[4] George Ewart Evans, *Ask the Fellows Who Cut the Hay*, 1956, p. 215; M. K. Ashby, *Joseph Ashby of Tysoe*, pp. 150–1.

[5] Winn 3/6, sect. 2, p. 9. In a similar spirit American slave owners actively encouraged 'Sambo' qualities in their slaves (Stanley M. Elkins, *Slavery*, 1959, p. 131).

of the village. The public realm prevailed over the private and there was hardly a conception of individual privacy or of a unique spiritual life. In such a community, to be 'independent' was to be 'uncourteous, not given to oblige', and to be 'left to his sen' [himself] meant 'to do something foolish'.[1]

The pre-eminence of the community also implied a secondary role for the family. The priority of the group and of face-to-face encounters with neighbours combined with the inadequacies of housing to make labourers relatively more involved with outsiders and less with their own nuclear family.[2] This was reflected in the dances favoured by labourers and their wives at village feasts: they were dances not for couples but for larger groupings. Communal dances like reels reflected a communal society, while in the middle and upper classes, where psychological ties were weak with the community but strong between spouses, the nuclear couple was the unit on the dance floor, in dances like the waltz and polka.[3]

The continuing commitment to the life of the group, and the lesser emotional weight borne by the family, led squires and parsons and other persons of breeding and refinement to take a low view of labourers' family and personal life. They considered them callous and unfeeling, incapable of delicacy, sensitivity, romantic love and loyalty. The best examples are to be found outside south Lindsey. Thus one old woman in Worcestershire, speaking of the death of her sister, added: '"and there wor a worse job than that: the pig died all of a sudden, but it pleased the Lord to tak' 'im and they mun bow, they mun bow." Then the poor old lady brightened up, and said, ". . . the Lord's been pretty well on my side this winter for greens."' Similarly, a Norfolk woman told her parson, 'I reckon I've had a expense-hive family . . . they never seemed to die convenient. I had twins once, and they both died . . . and we had the club money for both of them, but then one died a fortnight after the other, and so

---

[1] E. Peacock, *Glossary*, pp. 142, 156.

[2] The dominant classes by contrast were idealizing privacy and domesticity; see Malcolmson, *Popular Recreations*, p. 156 and *passim*. Cf. a description of colliers' families by a character in a novel set in County Durham: '"People here haven't yet all got round to living really *private* married lives . . . Here they're not only married to one person, they're wedded to the whole community as well."' (David Bean, *The Big Meeting*, 1967, p. 103.)

[3] See Ariès, *Centuries of Childhood*, p. 78, and Frances Rust, *Dance in Society*, 1969, p. 123.

that took two funerals, and that come expense-hive.' To the parson it was 'very shocking . . . to hear the way in which the old people speak of their dead wives or husbands exactly as if they had been horses or dogs'. And when a woman in north Lindsey left her husband to run away with another man, one old woman commented, '"She were a varry foolish woman . . . she left a good Hoose and *three sides o' Bacon*!"'[1] It may be suggested that labouring family life was indeed callous in the ways pointed out by upper-class observers: when poverty was a constant concern, a threat if not a reality, higher and more delicate considerations had to be sacrificed. But the standards of the middle classes themselves need perhaps to be questioned; in particular, parsons and others crediting themselves with delicate sensibilities could never sufficiently deplore the labourers' gauche habit of remarrying after the death of a spouse—they noted with disapproval that the poor 'are *always* proud of having been married more than once'[2] and that friendly societies paid their members benefits on the death of a second wife. It remains to be demonstrated that middle-class ideals—not to mention practice—were more wholesome than those of the poor.[3] What is clear is the cleavage between the two classes and their moral ideals.

It was another feature of a society in which there was little privacy that sexual matters too were in the public realm. And for this reason perhaps popular sexual attitudes, if indirect evidence can be trusted, were not delicate but free of prudishness or shame or guilt. 'As happy as pigs in muck' in local speech meant 'having your fill of sensual pleasure'.[4] Folksongs treat sexuality as an obvious good, even if not the *summmum bonum*. In 'The Charming Bride', a Lindsey folksong, the singer knocks at a cottage door; a girl, living alone, sends him away, then invites him back: 'Then she came down and let me in, she kissed my cheeks, likewise my chin, and soon a game began; We spent that night in sweet content, next mornin' to the churuch [*sic*] we went, and she made

---

[1] S. Reynolds Hole, *Memories of Dean Hole*, 1893, p. 163; Augustus Jessopp, *Trials of a Country Parson*, 1890, pp. 46–7; Anderson to Wilberforce, 22 June 1857, Bodl. MSS. Wilberforce.

[2] Jessopp. *Trials*, p. 46.

[3] The poor law policy of separating husbands and wives in the workhouses makes its own commentary on complaints about the callousness of the poor.

[4] E. Peacock, *Glossary*, p. 174.

me a charming bride.'[1] This freedom about sexual matters—at the beerhouse, for example—was one of the chief targets of the moralizers.

It was consistent with the nature of communal society that 'bastardy is not looked upon as a disgrace in a woman, nor is any discredit thrown upon the offending man . . . the having had a child is not in the way of a woman's getting married afterwards, among the poor.'[2] Yet the pressures of poverty at the same time led labouring people to regard a large family with some dismay, or at least without enthusiasm. One reason women went to be churched after giving birth was to avoid having another child within the year: 'an bairns comes quick enif wi'cot encoregin' on 'em.' And a labourer was heard to say, after his wife gave birth to twins, that 'it would have been a kinder act if Heaven had been pleased to have taken them both away'.[3]

Many of the contrasts between traditional values as preserved by the labouring poor and middle- and upper-class values can be summarized in the contrast between public and private. The labourers' orientation towards the group weakened their commitment to the family, and if they were callous at home they still expected, with their tradition of mutual rights and responsibilities, good will in return from their superiors. The farmers by contrast were kind to their families but callous to their labourers, unsentimentally pursuing their own self-interest, exploiting not only their labourers' labour but also their communal, pre-class values and good will. Public and private thus received exactly opposite valuations in the village community and in class society. This gave an unmistakable asymmetry—apart from the gross inequalities in wealth and power—to relations between farmers and labourers.[4] As George Bourne noted in Kent, 'while the labouring people, on their side, betray little or no class feeling of hostility towards employers, the converse is not true.' And similarly with the

---

[1] Sung by W. Clark of Barrow (in north Lindsey) and collected by Percy Grainger in 1906 (song no. 261, Grainger Collection, English Folk Dance and Song Society Library).

[2] According to Col. Amcotts of Hackthorn, chief constable of the county (*P.P.* 1867–8, xvii, p. 287).

[3] M. Peacock, 'Folklore and Legends', pp. 64–5; Colman, *European Agriculture*, i. 65–6.

[4] This was expressed in the modes of address between farmers and labourers: farmers used 'thou' in speaking to labourers, but the latter used 'you' in reply. (Cooper, *Wise Saws*, i. 28 ff.)

labourers in Warwickshire, who inexplicably showed no rancour or resentment towards their superiors: "'Tis in their blood to expect fairness.'[1] From this disjuncture derives much of the pathos of the early decades of class society.

It also provides a clue to the labourers' self-image in this period. Colman and other observers agreed that labourers' outward appearance was that of tired, dejected, dispirited men; these impressions are confirmed by the evidence of local dialect, which though indirect, is suggestive and consistent.[2] The dialect words for farm labourer all significantly were pejorative: clod-hopper, joskin, bumpkin, chaw-bacon, whap-straw, Johnny-raw. And there were many variations on the themes of stupidity, idleness, awkwardness, foolishness:

awming	'lounging, moving, or acting in a foolish or lazy manner'
belking	'huge, clumsy . . . lounging about'
bladge	'a coarse, vulgar woman'
boof	'stupid'
cloddy	'awkward, ill-dressed man'
clot-head	'a foolish or stupid person'
cuttle-head	'stupid, foolish'
fassil	'to loiter, work lazily'
gawm	'to stare vacantly'
hakossing	'moving violently about, doing work idly whilst in an ill-humour'
gizzen	'to stare vacantly'
kelterment	'silly talk'
kilps	'a loose, disorderly, or otherwise good-for-nothing person'
jolter-head	'stupid'
lungious	'rough, violent, broad-built, strong, heavy'
moozles	'a slow person, a stupid sloven'
shamocking	'a slovenly, awkward gait'
skraum	'to throw oneself about awkwardly'
unheppen	'unskilful'
yawm	'to move about awkwardly'

[1] Bourne, *Change in the Village*, pp. 107–8; Ashby, *Joseph Ashby of Tysoe*, p. 53.

[2] The glossaries of local dialect include E. Peacock, *Glossary*; J. E. Brogden, *Provincial Words and Expressions Current in Lincolnshire*, 1866; J. Good, *A Glossary or Collection of Words . . . Current in East Lincolnshire*, 1900; E. Sutton, *North Lincolnshire Words*, 1881.

These, it should be noted, were not terms of upper-class snobbery but words used by labourers about each other. Many more of a similar kind could be cited, while words for dignity, respect, and responsibility were rare. It would seem that the proportion of pejorative and contemptuous expressions was much higher in the vocabulary that labourers commonly used for themselves and their activities than it was in the standard English used by and about middle-class speakers. As might be expected, it was the farm servants who expressed the self-depreciation of the working class most bluntly: they habitually addressed each other with the vulgar, discourteous 'yah'.[1] But it would appear that the class as a whole had to some extent internalized in its self-image the scorn and contempt felt for it by the upper classes.[2]

In the course of the century, much if not all of the older culture was altered. Not only was there the decline in violence and the growth of self-discipline, but labourers also began to react against the crowd itself, with a visceral aversion from its all-enveloping character. This was apparent in some verses from the 1860s on Horncastle fair:

> But little comfort there one meets,
> For all is bustle, jowt, and scrudge,
> In mucky, howry streets and lanes,
> Your ears are dinned, where'er you budge,
> Wi' little attramites o' bairns.[3]

The author went on to praise the quieter, less hectic entertainments at a fête at Scrivelsby in the park of the squire. A parallel reaction from the crowd and crowdedness of the early nineteenth century may be traced in Methodism. After 1850 Methodists began to build larger, more capacious chapels; the aim now was to provide room for everyone, which meant more than enough room. Earlier, the impression is of a crowd, a massed body attending services; later, it is of discrete individuals. Still later, Methodists would recoil from the 'loving cup' passed round at lovefeasts, fearing contagion from the germs of the crowd.

---

[1] Winn, Diary, 21 Oct. 1844.

[2] Hobsbawm and Rudé, *Captain Swing*, pp. 52–3.

[3] John Brown, 'The Rural Fete' (originally published in 1864), in *Literae Laureatae*, p. 56. 'Jowt, scrudge': jolting and squeezing; 'attramites o' bairns': dirty children (p. 56 n.).

At the same time, the autonomy and self-sufficiency of the community declined. 'Ran-tanning' and the village constable, which in their different ways had allowed the community to police itself with a minimum of outside intervention, were superseded by the police constable, who was paid from the rates and was responsible not to the village but to the county government. If the older society had regulated itself, class society now rejected mutual or communal responsibility and opted for a combination of individual self-discipline and police authority imposed from above.

The village's powers of entertaining itself also declined. The old church orchestras, playing in the west galleries of the parish churches, were disbanded by unsympathetic clergy,[1] while folk-singing entered a more gradual decline. One veteran folk-singer (from north Lindsey) early in the twentieth century considered folksong singing 'to have been destroyed by the habit of singing in church and chapel choirs, and waxes hot on this subject, and on the evils resultant upon singing to the accompaniment of the piano'.[2] Another cause may be suggested: the break-down of village society into classes destroyed the moral—and recreational—consensus in the absence of which folk-singers performed only for their own class, out of hearing of the upper classes.[3]

The advance of class attitudes and the retreat of communal ones affected other aspects of labouring culture. Class society drew a much sharper distinction between adult and child than communal society did, providing schools and special religious activities for children: in the course of the century labourers too accepted the distinction and began to regard children's games as inappropriate for grown men. At a fictionalized fête, the games set up for the labourers were still traditional; they included the 'jingling match' (men in blindfold trying to catch another man wearing bells) and throwing sticks at a pipe stuck in the mouth of a doll. The hero, a farm labourer, rejects such games: 'I thowt nowt on such bairnish tricks. . . . "How *men* could play!"

---

[1] See below pp. 145ff.

[2] Percy Grainger, 'The Impress of Personality in Traditional Singing', *Journal of the Folk-Song Society*, no. 12 (1908), pp. 164–6. It should be noted, however, that another of the folksingers interviewed by Grainger sang in the choir of his parish church for forty-five years.

[3] See below p. 334, n. 1.

thought I, "Why! . . . It's only fit for little boys."[1] The juvenile
and communal custom of using nicknames also declined. Adults
in the labouring class ceased to use nicknames for each other;
in the later part of the century 'every grown person is called Mr.
and Mrs., and would feel insulted if addressed in the former
fashion'.[2] This was due not only to the sharper distinction between
adult and child but also to the declining face-to-face intimacy in
the village—itself caused ultimately by the triumph of capitalist
individualism.

In 1870 the labourers' social position in some respects had
hardly changed. Thanks to emigration their wages had improved,
but farmers were circumventing this by actually heightening their
exploitation of child labour. If anything the dominant classes'
control over rural society was more secure and their tactics more
sophisticated in the 1860s than they had been a generation earlier.
When labourers' children were able to attend school they were
indoctrinated in deference and subordination; their parents were
exposed to all manner of manipulative flattery, with their lingering communal and deferential sentiments appealed to on every
possible occasion, harvest supper, gentry wedding, or cricket
match. But hungry as the labourers might have been for these
attentions in the 1830s, when they were not forthcoming, they
were largely unmoved by them in the 1860s. For in the meantime
they had become literate, disciplined in their conduct, and self-
respecting and self-reliant (even if more private in their mode of
social life). Their demands accordingly were not for more
charity, but for better wages and hours—and for dignity. No
longer had they any use for incendiarism, and while they were not
in a position to refuse charitable handouts, the paternalism they
respected most was the kind that paid higher wages. It was
therefore in the unions that the active protest of earlier decades
and the mature class culture of recent years alike had their
consummation. A modern, proletarian body of workers now had
an appropriate instrument to advance their cause: even if there
still were appeals to the farmers' goodwill, even if emigration had
to be the solution for many, even if their political emancipation
was delayed another decade. From the village poor had emerged

---

[1] Brown, *Literae Laureatae*, pp. 49–51.
[2] Winn 3/5, p. 5. See also F. Thompson, *Lark Rise*, p. 90, and Bourne, *Change in
the Village*, p. 97.

a labouring *class*, ready to face its exploiters and to claim its rightful place not only in the village but in the nation. It was in this spirit that Joseph Arch addressed the labourers in a speech at Market Rasen in 1874: 'The day is not far distant when you will be no longer called joskins and clodhoppers, but acknowledged as free citizens of the land.'[1]

[1] *Mkt Rasen W.M.*, 10 Oct. 1874.

III

THE CHURCH OF ENGLAND

IN the 1820s the Church of England was still pre-eminently a rural church. Its institutions worked best in rural settings and its ideal was a country parish—with a resident parson and squire and an obedient and devout people. A district like south Lindsey presented the Church with much that was congenial: small parishes, an agricultural economy, a rural society uncorroded by towns and industry. Yet despite these favourable conditions it found itself in difficulty. The Methodists, who were aggressive, expanding, and popular, had broken its monopoly and thrown it on the defensive: to be 'religious', in local parlance, was to be Methodist. The Anglican clergy, while enjoying considerable income and status, were often lax and lethargic when they were not absentee. Few resident gentry were available as allies. And not only had the religious community split, into Methodist and Anglican: the village social community presupposed by the Anglican ideal also was disintegrating, into a society of classes. How then were the clergy to stem the Methodist tide? And how could they reconstitute the religious community when the secular community was breaking apart?

Before the Church could even hope to accomplish these tasks it had to mobilize itself both organizationally and spiritually. The Whig administrative reforms of the 1830s enabled the Church to tighten its discipline and to redeploy its resources more effectively; and from within, the High, Low, and Broad Church movements quickened its spiritual life and restored clerical morale. It was, however, at the parish level that the battle was joined, and there strategy and tactics were determined not by politicians or theologians but by the parish clergy. Both their aims—to roll back Methodism and to preserve social stability—were to be accomplished by re-creating the parish as a worshipping community. The clergy were confident that their vigour and activity, contrasting with the neglect of their predecessors, would remove the grievances that had nourished Methodism and draw the discontented back to the parish church, where the entire village population would be united through participation in public ritual. Thus they tried to make baptism a public rather than a private ceremony, they urged everyone to participate in Communion, and they introduced the harvest thanksgiving. The plan, an experiment in social control with Durkheimian overtones, had only a limited success, for the 'communal' rites irritated 'class' sensibilities, and the Methodists in any event refused to surrender. The clergy therefore turned after 1860 in a somewhat different direction. Doubting their ability to conquer Methodism, they tried to sharpen the separate identity of Church people and Church principles. This plan succeeded, though in the process the Church contracted into a denomination. Thus throughout the century, it was Methodism which set the problems that the clergy attempted to solve, and in response to the Methodist Reformation they embarked, belatedly but resolutely, upon an Anglican Counter-Reformation.

ORGANIZATION

It was apparent to counter-reformers that the ecclesiastical machinery at their disposal was hardly adequate to the task. South Lindsey was part of the enormous diocese of Lincoln, the largest and least manageable in the country, and its size alone hampered attempts to initiate reform from above. In the Middle Ages it had extended from the Humber to the Thames, and in the early nineteenth century it still comprised the counties of Lincoln, Leicester, Bedford, and Huntingdon, nearly all of Buckinghamshire, and more than half of Hertfordshire, plus a few scattered parishes in other counties. Of its 1,248 parishes, the most of any diocese, half were outside the borders of Lincolnshire. These were transferred to other dioceses by the reforms of the 1830s, but at the same time Nottinghamshire was added, leaving a large diocese in which travel was not always easy even after the advent of the railways. Lincolnshire formed just two archdeaconries—Lincoln and Stow—both of which included parishes in south Lindsey. With 520 parishes the Lincoln archdeaconry alone was larger than all but six entire dioceses before the reforms of the 1830s. Thus at the archidiaconal as at the diocesan level, administrative resources were stretched thin.

In so large a diocese the bishop was necessarily a rather remote figure, particularly before the 1830s, when his chief residence was at Buckden in Huntingdonshire. After the reshaping of the diocese, a new palace was acquired for the bishop at Riseholme, north of Lincoln; though situated in the county it too was inconvenient as an administrative headquarters.[1] Between 1825 and 1875 four bishops occupied the see of Lincoln. The first, George Pelham, died in 1827 and left little impression on the diocese. His successor was John Kaye, Master of Christ's College, Cambridge, a mild academic and a cautious reformer as bishop. On his death in 1853 he was succeeded by John Jackson, a very moderate Evangelical, still more mild than Kaye, almost bland in manner, but successful as a reformer.[2] In the shiftings that followed the death of Archbishop Longley in 1868, Disraeli rewarded Jackson with London and appointed Christopher Wordsworth to Lincoln. Wordsworth, son of the Master of Trinity and nephew of the Poet Laureate, broke sharply with the ways of his two immediate predecessors. He was a lifelong polemicist against the Church of Rome, and in the letter in which Disraeli offered him the bishopric he extolled '"the shining example which you have set, that a true Protestant may be a sound Churchman"';[3] on coming to Lincoln he also directed his fire against Methodism. He combined, in a manner peculiarly Victorian and ecclesiastical, other-worldliness with pugnacity. After Wordsworth came Edward King; there could be no better illustration of the changing character of the episcopate than the contrast between Pretyman Tomline, who had preceded Pelham, and King. Tomline, first tutor then client of the younger Pitt, built an ecclesiastical empire, accumulating benefice after benefice for himself and his sons, pluralists many times over.[4] King, though a staunch Tory, was appointed by Gladstone; a bachelor,

---

[1] The choice of Riseholme reflected the wish of the Ecclesiastical Commissioners that bishops should 'consort on equal terms with the gentry' and that 'the most important thing about a bishop's residence was that it should be a fine gentleman's residence in good grounds' (G. F. A. Best, *Temporal Pillars*, 1964, p. 363).

[2] Alan M. G. Stephenson, *The First Lambeth Conference 1867*, 1967, p. 15. At the start of his episcopate he was regarded as pre-eminent among those Broad Churchmen who sought 'to win universal popularity' (*Edinburgh Review*, xcviii (1853), pp. 333-4).

[3] J. H. Overton and Elizabeth Wordsworth, *Christopher Wordsworth*, 1888, pp. 203-4.

[4] See G. F. A. Best, 'The Road to Hiram's Hospital', *Victorian Studies*, v (1961-2).

his saintly faith and Anglo-Catholicism gave him a greater influence on lay religious life than any of his predecessors.

Ranking below the bishop, but above the parish clergy, were the cathedral 'dignitaries': the establishment within the Establishment. Archdeacons, Dean and Chapter, Vicars-Choral,[1] and the lesser lights of Minster Yard formed a picturesque enclave; in the earlier years at least, their spiritual honours barely concealed a healthy appetite for the loaves and fishes of the Establishment. But beyond the cathedral precincts, their practical influence—fortunately perhaps for the Church—was severely limited. An exception ought to be made for the archdeacons, who held their own visitations, concerning themselves with church fabrics and petty disciplinary matters. On these issues they prodded and harried reluctant churchwardens, if a newspaper account can be trusted of H. V. Bayley conducting his visitation of the Archdeaconry of Stow:

His exhibition of ecclesiastical *hauteur*, his domineering, brow-beating manner of treating the churchwardens at his late visitation in the Cathedral, was exactly after the prevailing High-church fashion. . . . The churchwarden of Hackthorn was called up; he was threatened, interrogated, warned, jeered, and finally bullied into the assurance that the Archdeacon '*would have* the church roof repaired, and if the Churchwarden did not repair it, he (the Archdeacon) *would make him*.'

And to intimidate another recalcitrant churchwarden, Bayley 'commissioned the bold official Stonehouse, who looked as fierce as thunder and lightning . . . to go inspect the thatched church and compel the Churchwarden to repair it.'[2] Archidiaconal manners softened perceptibly in later years—there was nothing spiky in W. F. J. Kaye (son of the bishop), for example—though churchwardens continued to neglect their churches. But whether bellicose or unctuous, the archdeacon seems to have had little influence on religious, as distinguished from administrative, matters.

---

[1] Immortalized as 'Bawling Hett, and mumbling Jepson, Drunken Gray, and gambling Nelson' (*Linc. Gaz.*, 26 Nov. 1859). Nelson, however, was portrayed much more favourably by Samuel Bamford, the Radical, in his account of his year's imprisonment in Lincoln jail, 1820–1 (*Passages in the Life of a Radical*, 1844, ii. 171, 188–9, 193–4, 215). Recalling with gratitude the kindness and humanity with which he was treated by the local magistrates, he singled out Nelson for special praise.

[2] *Stamf. Merc.*, 22 June 1838. See also ed. N. S. Harding, *Bonney's Church Notes*, 1937, and W. B. Stonehouse, *A Stow Visitation*, ed. N. S. Harding, 1940.

What equipped the Church to work in rural society was not its bureaucracy—which hardly existed—but the parish system. Every inhabitant belonged to a parish and had a right to be baptized and married in its church, to attend its services, and to be buried in the churchyard. South Lindsey was divided into 239 ecclesiastical parishes, most of which coincided with civil parishes. Over a dozen were churchless, but of these only Aby had a large population. There were on average 224 churches open in the first half of the period, 225 in the second half.[1]

As the area of the average parish was only 1,700 acres, most of the churches were situated reasonably near the main centres of population in their parishes. In no more than about a dozen parishes was the church badly sited. At Willoughby, for example, most of the population was in the hamlet of Sloothby, two miles from the church. (The Wesleyans in the parish had chapels both at Willoughby and at Sloothby.) And the incumbent of Langton-by-Horncastle complained of 'this unfortunate feature in my parish, and in that of two or three others on each side of it, that they run down to the banks of the River Witham, and have a considerable amount of population located in that district. varying from four to seven or eight miles from their respective Parish Churches. ... How inefficient must be any attempts to maintain any pastoral connection with this portion of our Parishes.'[2] At Goulceby 'the present church ... is not only dilapidated, but inconveniently situated, being away from the people, whereas the Dissenting chapel is in the midst of the people.'[3] On the other hand there were churches favourably situated for residents of outlying hamlets in adjoining parishes. Markby church was crowded 'as it is adjacent to several villages and hamlets which are distant from their own churches or which have service only once a day'.[4] The churches in the adjoining parishes of Addlethorpe and Ingoldmells were only half a mile apart; in the early part of the period, services were held in each on alternate Sundays, equally convenient to inhabitants of both parishes. Marton and Gate Burton churches were another pair

---

[1] Middle Rasen Tupholme was closed and Langton St. Andrew opened in 1846; Riseholme was opened in 1851.

[2] Walter to Kaye, 30 May 1845, Cor. B. 5/4/118. This district, Langton St. Andrew, was the site of a church opened the following year; it later became Woodhall Spa.

[3] Dixon to Queen Anne's Bounty, 10 July 1872, Q.A.B. F.1930.

[4] Molson to Kaye, 1 July 1833, Cor. B. 5/4/115/9.

only half a mile apart; the vicar of Marton justified his practice of giving only a fortnightly second service on the grounds that his parishioners could go to Gate Burton in the afternoon if they wished: the afternoon service was held alternately in each church and 'the people of both Parishes prefer the plan'.[1] Possibly the same opportunities were open to the inhabitants of Scampton, Aisthorpe, and Brattleby, three small parishes in a line at the foot of the Cliff, each less than half a mile distant from its nearest neighbour. For most villagers, though, 'church' meant their parish church.

THE CHURCHES

By the 1820s many churches had fallen into disrepair, both internally and externally, and the reconstruction of church fabrics was one of the commonest aims of reformers.

The physical condition of many churches did not flatter the churchwardens and others responsible for their upkeep. Inspecting his archdeaconry in the 1840s, Stonehouse described Broxholme church as 'a small ruinous old building held together by the lead'. His colleague Bonney found Hameringham 'a miserable remnant of a church', Ashby Puerorum 'in a sad state'. Many churches were restored and rebuilt in the middle decades of the century, but in the 1870s there were still outstanding cases of neglect. Upton in 1876 was in 'so sad a state of ruin'; Hameringham was still miserable; Haltham, Tetford, and Mareham-on-the-Hill were 'lamentable'.[2]

Inside the churches too there were signs of neglect, even—so it seemed to reformers—of outright irreverence. The interior of Fillingham church was 'slovenly', the churchwardens having refused to act for twenty years. At Newton-by-Toft the archdeacon found 'the covering for the Table, brown, dirty and moth eaten'. Most offensive of all were the pews. Before the improvers and restorers went to work, about half the churches in the area were fitted mainly with pews, and about half with open seats. In some, like Cawkwell, there were 'open seats' for the

---

[1] Residents of Addlethorpe and Ingoldmells to Kaye, n.d. [?1835], Cor. B. 5/4/30/1; Marton, 1873 V.R.

[2] Stonehouse, *Stow Visitation*, p. 73; Bonney, *Church Notes*, pp. 161, 167; *Retf. News*, 23 May 1874 (for Upton); E. Trollope, 'The Churches of Horncastle and Other Parishes, Visited by the Society, on the 14th and 15th of June, 1876', Associated Architectural Societies, *Reports and Papers*, xiii (1876), pp. 168, 171, 174.

villagers and 'a large pew' for the non-resident owner or his tenant. Caenby was similar, with its 'abominable nuisance of a large high square pew belonging to Sir Charles Monck'.[1] The pews interfered with ritual functions, destroyed the communal, open character of the church interior, and symbolized private property and exclusiveness: everything about them infuriated reformers. In Belchford church there were 'two large pews abutting on the Communion rails, the division between them approaches the middle of the gate in the rails'. Archdeacon Stonehouse said of Scothern church that he 'never saw a place of worship so cram full of pews, so much so that there is no space reserved ... for Baptism'.[2] The conquest and command of the nave and chancel was a major aim of clerical reformers.

Country people, it was said, disliked attending a church 'where they have no seat',[3] and it seems likely that every family in a parish had or could have a sitting appropriated to it by the churchwarden. No rents had to be paid: these were 'appropriated free sittings'. With or without pews, the seating plan of the church accurately reflected the village social hierarchy, the 'influential inhabitants' having the best seats, persons of lesser consequence, the less desirable ones. The squire commanded a place of honour: whether in the chancel, or front and centre in the nave, or as at Burton and Hackthorn, in the west gallery, where, elevated above his tenants, he could monitor them during worship. At South Carlton, for which a seating plan survives, it is possible to retrace the social map of the entire village. The squire had a pew in the chancel; the incumbent's family sat in the front of the nave; immediately behind them was the largest farmer in the parish (with 615 acres); in the central part of the nave, on either side of the aisle, were the other farmers, the larger (with 320 and 200 acres) in front, the smaller behind; sharing seats near the back were a shopkeeper, shoemaker, school-master, and cottagers, with a special sitting reserved for 'servant maids'. There were also sittings in the north aisle; from front to rear, they were occupied by 'servant men', cottagers, a foreman, three labourers, two labourers and a shoemaker, two

[1] Hodge to Kaye, 6 May 1831, Cor. B. 5/4/123/5; Bonney, *Church Notes*, pp. 61, 149; Stonehouse, *Stow Visitation*, p. 71.

[2] Bonney, *Church Notes*, p. 147; Stonehouse, *Stow Visitation*, p. 71.

[3] Robert Gregory, *A Plea in Behalf of Small Parishes*, 1849, p. 9. Gregory, curate at Panton, was the future Dean of St. Paul's.

labourers, two more labourers with a pauper widow, a free sitting, and finally the vestry. Along the west wall of the church were free seats and in the chancel were the schoolchildren, sitting opposite Lord Monson's pew.[1] In churches without a choir—the majority at least until mid-century—the chancel was usually occupied by the squire, by the clergyman, or by Sunday scholars, and consequently was devoid of 'ecclesiological' symbolism. No evidence had been found in churches in the area in which seating was according to sex—men on one side, women on the other: that would have been appropriate in a more communal society in which class differences were less salient than they were in the nineteenth century. Even when clerical reformers tore down the pews, social stratification within the church remained, for every family still had its designated place according to its class position.

Until well after 1850 most churches in the area were unheated; they were cold physically if not spiritually. This may help explain not only the small church attendances in winter but also the appeal of Methodist chapels, which were generally heated, as well as being 'warm' in spirit. Churches rebuilt or restored from 1860 onwards were generally provided with a stove, though their effectiveness in the larger churches was probably not great, and few churches could be made as cosy as the average chapel.[2]

Churches were generally kept locked: 'With few exceptions our churches remain closed from Sunday to Sunday.' This was no less true of churches with High Church or Anglo-Catholic incumbents, like Springthorpe and East and West Torrington.[3] Anything like a Catholic church—perpetually open for prayer— was unthought of.

One of the most visible reforms carried out in the Victorian period was the repair, restoration, and rebuilding of the churches. The work was usually instigated by the clergyman; the church-

---

[1] Plan of Sittings, South Carlton parish records, L.A.O.

[2] Cold churches were still a problem as late as 1886 (Edward King, *Charge* . . . *at the Primary Visitation, October, 1886*, 1886, p. 58.

[3] William Nevins (rector of Miningsby), *The Clergy's Privilege and Duty of Daily Intercession*, 1847, p. 9; details about churches in *Free and Open Churches*, 1876, p. 29. The incumbent at Springthorpe was E. L. Blenkinsopp, a leading local figure in the English Church Union; and T. W. Mossman, at the Torringtons, was a member of the Order of Corporate Reunion, the Society of the Sacred Heart, and other advanced causes.

wardens and ratepayers were reluctant to incur the expense,
even where they did not positively prefer the old familiar church
and its furnishings. The incumbent of Springthorpe reported
that if he had not had

the greatest landowner in the place coming forward to give money and
countenance to it I should have had very great difficulty indeed in
getting the thing done at all. The people said, 'Oh, it has lasted our
father's time, it will last ours, and we think you had better let things
alone.'

Similarly, when the rector of a near-by parish wished to restore
the church, he was told at the vestry meeting, ''It has done for
our fathers, and it will do for us.'' When he reported the archi-
tect's opinion that the roof was unsafe, one parishioner retorted,
''If you will show me what is the most dangerous place in the
roof I will sit under it every Sunday.''[1] Money for the more
ambitious projects therefore came from other sources: the clergyman and his family and friends, landowners, and the Church
Building Society. Even so, the efforts of outsiders in such cases
were not uniformly appreciated by the parishioners. When
George Atkinson collected funds to restore the impressive
church at Stow, his parishioners criticized the motives of '''certain strangers . . . about to expend large sums . . . on works of
taste and antiquity, instead of substantial and necessary repairs'''.
They looked '''with jealousy upon a scheme for restoring a
cathedral character to their parish church, and thereby loading
their already groaning lands with a large increase of annual
expenditure'''.[2] Nevertheless, between 1840 and 1875 major
works were undertaken on 127 churches at a total expense of
£129,794. There was little activity until the late 1830s and early
1840s, when a number of completely new churches were built;
the next peak was around 1850, followed by another slack period
until 1857. The climax came in the 1860s, with an average of eight
major projects completed every year.[3] As in other fields of reform,
the main effort was made after the middle of the century. Earlier,

[1] *Church Union Gazette*, N.S. ii (1871), p. 119.

[2] *Lincs. Times*, 9 Apr. 1850. It should perhaps be noted, however, that Atkinson
had aroused much unpopularity in the parish before undertaking the restoration
of the church—which in the end was the solitary success of his ministry at Stow.

[3] See the *List of Churches, and Chapels, Built, Rebuilt, Restored, or Enlarged in the
Diocese of Lincoln since 1840*, 1873; White, *Directory*; Pevsner and Harris, *Buildings of
England: Lincolnshire*.

both the interior of the church and the exterior owed as much or more to the parishioners as to the clergy; after 1850 the clergyman took control over the church fabric as he did over every other aspect of church life. A respectable clergy now had respectable churches to officiate in. Yet despite or because of much effort to decorate churches according to the latest conceptions in ecclesiastical taste, parish churches remained more impressive, Methodist chapels perhaps more inviting.

PATRONAGE AND BENEFICES

Churches and parishes were provided with clergymen through the system of patronage, by which the owner of the advowson presented a clergyman to the living. The choice of incumbent, then, was in the hands not of the parishioners but of the patrons. Most were private and most were lay.

Patrons of South Lindsey Livings, 1825 and 1875
(Percentages)

	Private:		Oxford and	Ecclesiastical	The Crown
	clergy	*laymen*	*Cambridge colleges*	*dignitaries*	
1825	2·3%	61·9	3·7	20·4	11·6 (N=215)
1875	12·2	51·2	4·5	20·2	11·9 (N=201)

Among the ecclesiastical dignitaries the most important was the bishop, whose share of the total increased between 1825 and 1875 from 6·9 to 11·7 per cent. Yet in the early years at any rate this was a low proportion, compared with other dioceses; it meant that the bishop was unable to create many incumbents in his own image of churchmanship.[1] Since all the bishops, even the relatively Evangelical Jackson, were higher in churchmanship than the average lay patron, their lack of patronage and the predominance of lay patrons probably resulted in a body of clergy more Evangelical than would otherwise have been the case.

It was an area of poor livings. Rectories—not always well endowed themselves—were outnumbered by generally poorer

[1] Around 1835, 11·6 per cent of the advowsons in England and Wales belonged to the bishops of the respective dioceses (from table on p. 545 of Best, *Temporal Pillars*). Samuel Wilberforce, Bishop of Oxford, increased his share of the patronage in his diocese from 5 to 18 per cent between 1845 and 1859, as 'part of a deliberate policy ... to gain a more direct influence in the diocese' (Diana McClatchey, *Oxfordshire Clergy, 1777–1869*, 1960, p. 10).

livings—vicarages, discharged rectories and vicarages, and perpetual curacies. The clergyman who depended entirely upon his stipend was likely to be near the margin of genteel poverty.

Types of Benefice, 1856[1]

Donatives	5
Discharged rectories	18
Discharged vicarages	12
Vicarages	54
Perpetual curacies	24
Rectories	104
	217

Value of Livings, 1841 and 1872[2]

	£1–99	100–199	200–299	300–399	400–499	500–599	600–699	700–	Total
1841	60	59	37	29	16	9	1	2	213
1872	24	30	53	38	25	15	7	7	199

Earlier in the period, the majority of the livings were worth less than £200 a year (the median was £173); by the end of the period, nearly half were worth more than £300. Those deriving their income from the rents of land (received in exchange for tithe in the process of parliamentary enclosure) and those in which tithes were commuted in the 1840s both rose greatly in value after 1851 during the 'Golden Age' of English agriculture, while the small livings, poorly endowed with either glebe or rent-charge, were boosted by benefactions from their incumbents and by matching grants and augmentations from Queen Anne's Bounty and the Ecclesiastical Commissioners.[3] Here, too, if partly for different reasons, the major phase of Anglican reform only began after 1850.

The value of endowments had much to do with history but little to do with the needs of their respective parishes. It was not only the small parishes that paid small clerical incomes, but also some of the largest.

[1] Compiled from White, *Directory*, 1856.

[2] Compiled from *Clergy List*, 1841, and White, *Directory*, 1872.

[3] Lincolnshire was one of the classic areas of parliamentary enclosure—which was particularly important in the Cliff and Wolds districts of south Lindsey—and one in which the clergy benefited proportionately. It has been estimated that 16 per cent of the land subject to enclosure in the county was allotted in lieu of tithes, and an incumbent who received land in exchange for rectorial tithes might have several hundred acres and be among the largest landowners in the parish. See E. J. Evans, 'Some Reasons for the Growth of English Rural Anti-Clericalism *c.* 1750–*c.* 1830', *Past and Present*, no. 66 (1975), p. 96 and *passim*.

Large Parishes with Poor Livings, 1851

	Population	Income		Population	Income
Bardney	1,129	£60	Legbourne	461	£84
Barlings	352	55	Normanby	471	88
Baumber	371	37	Revesby	693	77
Hogsthorpe	790	95	Scamblesby	500	71
Huttoft	515	61	Stow	943	69
Ingham	514	50	Torksey	442	42

The figures in the table are only some of the more glaring examples. Even at the end of the period, after much had been done by way of augmentation, there remained undernourished livings at Barlings, Ingham, and Normanby. Yet it would be easy to exaggerate the 'beggarly state of the mass of the English clergy ... throughout the period of Queen Victoria's reign'.[1] The poorest clergy were the curates, yet even the worst-off, serving two parishes, had an income of £100 at the least—three times the average income of the farm labourer. A majority of incumbents were receiving at least £173, or about five times the income of their average parishioner. In view of the work involved—a few hours a week might suffice—the clergyman was generously rewarded. However, unless he enjoyed additional income from a private fortune or other sources, the clergyman was much less well off than a landlord, who might be receiving £2,000 or more a year. From the landlords, whose education was similar, he thus was separated by his inferior income, and from the farmers, whose income was similar, by his superior education, while from the labourers, the majority of his parishioners, he was doubly separated by income and education alike.

THE CLERGY

Jim wonder'd how it allus come,
In iv'ry village big or small,
The Parson's house, by some odd sum
Wos allus biggest of 'em all.

> J. Brown, 'Zeb. Gosling's Wedding
> Night' (1874), *Literae Laureatae*, p. 78.

The revival of the Church's fortunes, the rekindling of its piety and energy, depended primarily on the efforts of the clergy. With their education and rising incomes as well as their sacred

[1] C. K. Francis Brown, *A History of the English Clergy, 1800–1900*, 1953, p. 182.

function they won the respect due to gentlemen. At the same time, once the scandal of non-residence was corrected, a growing proportion of the parish clergy were men of zeal, increasingly militant in their churchmanship and eager to take the initiative in everything from the founding of Sunday schools to the reform of church music. But it is less clear whether there ever could have been enough clergymen of the type desired, zealous as well as gentlemanly, and, more fundamentally, whether they or any body of clergy could, unassisted, have stemmed the Methodist tide.

By the end of the period it would probably have been the parsonages that gave visitors to country parishes their first impression of the clergy. Large and substantial, they were the outward and visible sign less of the clergy's zeal than of their social position and of a certain affluence. For they were content no longer with the modest cottages of the past. The rector of Springthorpe considered it an excuse for non-residence that the parsonage in the parish had 'never been anything but a *very humble* Farmhouse'. Rand parsonage similarly was a 'stud and mud' edifice, its upper floor 'open to the thatch ... which no repairs can render a suitable residence for any persons above the rank of daily labourers'.[1]

The building of new parsonages was one of the successes of the reformers. In order to remove the excuse for non-residence, bishops began to require that a new incumbent, upon entering his living, should have a new house built, if the existing one was inadequate.[2] But there were other reasons for building: a poor benefice of £60 or £70 would not be helped much by an increase of £30, but 'a comfortable and roomy house at once presents a capability of procuring pupils and income'.[3] And room was needed for the parsons' increasing families, their servants, their dinner parties and for parish business—dining-rooms in new parsonages were larger than sitting-rooms.[4] And so important was the presence of the clergyman in the parish that the building of the parsonage generally took precedence over the restoration and rebuilding of the church. Of seventy-five parishes in which

[1] Case to Kaye, 23 June 1848, Cor. B. 5/4/62/14; Hale to Kaye, 28 Oct. 1829, Cor. B. 5/4/89/4.
[2] e.g. William Grice, rector of Tothill. (Grice to Q.A.B., 5 May 1851, Q.A.B. F.4692.)
[3] Bayley to Kaye, 1827, Cor. B. 5/4/140/1.
[4] Plans of parsonages in the files of the Church Commissioners.

the dates of both the restoration or rebuilding of the church and the building of the parsonage are known, the parsonage preceded the church in fifty-three, the church was first in fifteen, and in seven both were worked on simultaneously. At least one clergyman, A. M. Alington of Benniworth, 'felt it rather a reproach to himself that he had been obliged to build his own house before restoring the house of God.'[1] The new parsonage might cost anything between £700 and £1,400, and since parsons could not extract anything from their parishioners for such a purpose, they sought money elsewhere: from their friends, from Queen Anne's Bounty, and from their own private incomes. Precise dates are available for only a little over half the parsonages in the area, but they fall into approximately the same pattern as that of the churches: peak years around 1840 and 1850, and from 1855 to 1870. In most parishes the parsonage was situated near the church, at the centre of the village, but about a tenth were well outside the village in self-conscious isolation. Invariably sited with a southern exposure, the 'big house' represented not merely a social status but a whole style of life.

The primary purpose of the parsonage, and the parish system was to secure a resident clergyman: the whole pastoral effort of the church depended on the continuous presence of the clergy in their parishes. It was in Bishop Jackson's words 'the key-stone of our Church's system'.[2] Yet early in the period the key-stone was missing in most parishes. Absenteeism, not residence, was the rule. In 1830, more parishes were served by curates than by incumbents, and more by non-resident than by resident clergy.

Resident and Non-resident clergy[3]

Benefice served by	1830 No.	1830 %	1851 No.	1851 %	1875 No.	1875 %
Resident incumbent	54	25·1	101	48·3	153	76·9
Non-resident incumbent	50	23·3	45	21·5	30	15·1
Resident curate	30	14·0	30	14·4	13	6·5
Non-resident curate	81	37·7	33	15·8	3	1·5

Clergyman clustered in market towns—Louth was a notorious 'nest of rooks'—and sallied forth on Sunday morning to 'take their duty', absenting themselves from their parishes the remain-

[1] *Mkt Rasen W.M.*, 16 Oct. 1875.
[2] J. Jackson, *A Charge . . . at his Primary Visitation, in Oct. 1855*, 1855, p. 10.
[3] Calculated from diocesan specula, SPE 10 and 18, L.A.O.

ing six days of the week.[1] Considerable progress was made under Bishop Kaye—and the Plurality Act of 1838—yet even in 1851 nearly a third of the parishes were served by curates, and over a third by non-resident clergy. As much progress was to be made after 1850 as before. Whether it is to be attributed to a more rigorous conception of clerical behaviour or to the Whig legislation is an open question: Bishop Kaye gave most credit to the Whigs.[2] By 1875 non-residence had probably reached its minimum, for livings worth less than £100 were usually held in plurality.

The reduction in non-residence entailed fewer pluralities and more clergy in the area. The number of clergy serving local churches rose from 136 in 1830 to 154 in 1851 and 194 in 1875. This increase is even more impressive when the clergy residing in towns are omitted: in 1830 they numbered thirty-seven—more than a quarter of the total clergy—of whom only four had a living or curacy in the town; in 1851 there were thirteen, including three with town duty, and in 1875 the figures were respectively seven and three. The clergy actually living in country parishes therefore rose from 99 in 1830 to 141 in 1851 and 187 in 1875. The average number of persons per clergyman (excluding the clergy resident in the towns) dropped from 547 to 464 to 343. Less frequently did a clergyman have to serve more than one church on a Sunday.

The Decline of Plural Duty 1830–75

Number of clergymen serving	1830	1851	1875
one church	42	70	116
two churches	89	77	58
three churches	4	1	0

(Includes services taken by south Lindsey clergy in town churches and in north Lindsey.)

Very likely the number of clergymen serving three churches in 1830 is underestimated; Bishop Kaye himself recalled that when he entered the diocese in 1827 curates often held three curacies, and an illness would require one man to perform four or even five services on the same day. In 1852, though, he claimed that no curate 'now permanently serves three churches'.[3]

---

[1] Archdeacon Goddard noted with disapproval the 'ten or twelve clergymen residing in the town of Louth far from their flocks whom they visit only on Sunday' (Goddard to Kaye, 30 Mar. 1827, Cor. B. 5/4/140/7).

[2] J. Kaye, Works, n.d., vii. 416.

[3] ibid. vii. 417.

One consequence of the decline in non-residence was a change in the status of curates. Early in the period most curates were stipendiary curates, hired to substitute for absentee incumbents. Long engagements of twenty years or more were not uncommon: Matthewman Manduell was curate in the rich living of Tetford for over forty years, and R. A. Lafargue was curate of Snarford and Friesthorpe for thirty-three years, never holding a living of his own. At the opposite extreme from these 'perpetual' curacies there were short-term hirings, some lasting a year or more, others a single Sunday. One veteran of short-term duty claimed to have officiated in over thirty churches in the Alford neighbourhood; another complained that 'the most itinerant Parsons in England are the unbeneficed Clergy of the establishment'.[1] In time, however, stipendiary curates gave way to assistant curates. By the end of the period there were at least twenty assistant curates in the area, generally younger men serving a sort of apprenticeship to resident incumbents.

Whether resident or not, incumbents generally did not change livings very often. In the fifty-year period under study, 130 of 210 livings had three incumbents or fewer, while only thirty-seven had five incumbents or more. Incumbencies of thirty and forty years were not unusual. This contrasted with the pattern in Methodism, where under the rule of itinerancy ministers changed circuits every three years if not more frequently, and constant variety and novelty were the result. In an age in which sermons were regarded as a superior form of entertainment, the stability of the Anglican ministry, which carried dangers of stagnation and monotony, may well have been a disadvantage.

The resident clergy were not spread evenly over the countryside, and the regional variations, as measured by the ratio of laity to clergy, were considerable.

Complete precision in calculating regional figures is impossible, since parsons living in one region might serve parishes in another, but the general pattern is probably accurate enough. The South Wolds, with their small parishes and attractive villages, had consistently the most favourable ratio of laity to clergy, followed

---

[1] Quarmby to Kaye, 22 Aug. 1831, Cor. B. 5/4/114/9; John Wray (vicar of Bardney), *A Voice from the Church*, 1835, p. 42. Between 1827 and 1858 the small parish of Biscathorpe was served by a succession of eleven non-resident curates who came from seven different parishes in the neighbourhood.

by the Cliff, the Middle Marsh (surprisingly), and the Central vale. As expected, the Outer Marsh, with its open parishes, flat terrain, and unhealthy atmosphere, had the worst figures, apart from 1830, when the North Wolds clergy were deserting their flocks for the more urbane atmosphere of Louth. The ratio in the Till basin also was consistently unfavourable. There were relatively twice as many clergy in the South Wolds as in the Outer Marsh, and presumably twice as much effective clerical influence over the laity. Yet despite the regional variation, the over-all trend was uniform. In every region there were more clergymen at work in 1851 than in 1830, and more in 1875 than in 1851; and in every region the ratio of clergymen to population improved in the two successive periods. The Establishment reacted to its early Victorian crisis with impressive vigour.

Ratio of Population to Clergy, by Region[1]

| | 1830 | | | 1851 | | 1875 | |
	Number of Clergy	Population per Clergyman	Clergy	Population per Clergyman	Clergy	Population per Clergyman
Till basin	8	695	12	579	15	453
Cliff	9	554	13	452	17	343
Central vale	23	454	28	464	36	368
Fen margin	6	665	9	522	10	436
South Wolds	23	411	30	329	39	238
North Wolds	8	985	17	575	24	390
Middle Marsh	11	613	19	453	30	287
Outer Marsh	6	809	8	808	13	525
South Lindsey	94	575	134	473	184	349

By 1875 the parish system had reached its zenith. With few exceptions there was a resident clergyman in every parish whose population was large enough to justify one, as well as in many a parish of smaller population but with a substantial benefice.

Since 1830 the number of parishes with resident clergymen more than doubled, from a little over a third to three-quarters of the total. Even the ill-favoured Outer Marsh had it share.[2]

[1] Clergymen serving south Lindsey parishes but residing in towns or in north Lindsey have been excluded.

[2] At the middle of the century the important village of Hogsthorpe had its first resident incumbent since the Reformation (White, *Directory*, 1856, p. 502).

Parishes with Resident and Non-Resident Clergymen, 1830 and 1875

1830

	Resident incumbents	Resident curates	Total resident clergy	No resident clergyman
Till basin	6	1	7	9
Cliff	2	5	7	13
Central vale	14	6	20	25
Fen margin	4	1	5	5
South Wolds	12	6	18	31
North Wolds	4	4	8	25
Middle Marsh	5	5	10	23
Outer Marsh	3	3	6	9
	50	31	81	140

1875

	Resident incumbents	Resident curates	Total resident clergy	No resident clergyman
Till basin	12	1	13	3
Cliff	14	2	16	5
Central vale	32	3	35	10
Fen margin	7	0	7	3
South Wolds	32	4	36	13
North Wolds	22	1	23	11
Middle Marsh	25	0	25	8
Outer Marsh	7	5	12	3
	151	16	167	57

At its peak efficiency, then, the Church had a full-time professional in virtually every village of any consequence. In the course of a generation, legislative and administrative action had produced striking reforms; everything, it seemed, that could be accomplished by such methods had demonstrably been accomplished: more clergy, more resident incumbent clergy, spacious new parsonage houses, bigger incomes, old churches restored and new ones built. Yet the object of the reforms was not merely administrative tidiness but pastoral effectiveness. Whatever the virtues of the Establishment in its national aspect, its success or failure as a church depended upon the qualities of the clergy in their parishes.

In one respect, at least, they were well suited to the demands of Anglican reform and revival: they were predominantly a young and middle-aged clergy whose vigour was not reduced by the infirmities of age. Of 153 clergymen serving south Lindsey parishes in 1851, only twelve were 65 and older; more than a fifth were under 35, and three-fifths were between 35 and 54.[1] And they were to a surprising degree a celibate clergy. Of 142 whose marital status can be determined, forty-six were single, eighty-seven were married, and nine widowed. The proportion of bachelors was higher among the clergy than in the general male population for every age group; there were many unmarried clergymen besides the younger men in their late twenties and thirties waiting for a living to fall vacant before taking on the responsibilities of marriage. This large minority, often living in rented lodgings, needs to be recalled along with the traditional married clergyman and the family life of the parsonage.

Most of the clergy had been to university, at least 137 of the 153. There were eighty-eight Cambridge graduates, forty-five from Oxford, and four from Trinity College, Dublin. The predominance of Cambridge men, which was much greater locally than in the church as a whole, may have given an Evangelical cast to the clergy.[2] The fact that only seven had read for honours probably reflects more on the unreformed state of the universities than the intellectual capacity of the pass men.

In politics the clergy were overwhelmingly Conservative. Whigs and Tories usually divided the parliamentary representation of north Lincolnshire but in the second quarter of the century, when religious issues aroused as much controversy as parliamentary reform and protection, the clergy proved consistent supporters of the Tory and Conservative candidates.[3] In 1835, for example, sixty-four parsons gave fifty-seven votes to the Tory candidate, twenty to the Whig, and only six to the Radical sitting member, who to be sure was known for his anti-clericalism as well as his enthusiastic support of church reform. Six years later religious issues were no less important. 'Civil and religious liberty' was one of the watchwords of Lord Worsley, the sitting Whig member and eldest son of Lord Yarborough, the Whig chieftain in the county; the phrase succinctly expressed his approval of the Whig church reforms and his family's friendly feelings towards Methodism. He received only eleven clerical votes, compared

---

[1] Data from the 1851 Census enumerators' books, J. A. and J. A. Venn. *Alumni Cantabrigienses*, and Foster, *Alumni Oxonienses*.

[2] Between 1834 and 1853, 4,903 Cambridge graduates were ordained deacon, and 4,264 from Oxford (Brown, *History of the English Clergy*, p. 250).

[3] Poll books for the 1835, 1841, and 1852 elections.

with eighty-one and seventy-five for the two Tory candidates. In 1852 the sitting Whig member, whose Protectionist and anti-Maynooth sentiments had seemed lukewarm at best, received only twenty-six votes, while the two Tory candidates, campaigning on a platform of 'Protestantism and Protection', received eighty-seven and sixty-six. The clergy—more Tory even than the landlords—were probably the most partisan block of voters in the electorate.

They were also dividing into church parties. Just as the parliamentary parties were reviving, so the High, Low and Broad Church parties arose to claim the loyalty of the 'old-fashioned country parson' whose rather indeterminate churchmanship was likely to be 'Evangelical if anything'.[1] Curiously, it is more difficult to identify the clergy's churchmanship than their political allegiances. Compared with political parties, church parties were more numerous—no fewer than nine were detected by W. J. Conybeare in 1853—more ambiguous, and less well documented. Before 1850 the church parties are hard to delineate; the proportions of the 'high and dry' and of the 'low and slow' persuasions remain unknown. Nevertheless the trend after 1850 is clear even if the estimate of the strengths of the various parties is tentative. Between 1851 and 1875 the number of clergy who left evidence of their churchmanship rose from 90 to 160, an unambiguous sign of 'politicization'.[2]

Church Parties, 1851 and 1875

	Evange-lical	Moderate Evange-lical	Central	Moderate High Church	Advanced High Church	Total
			Numbers			
1851	29	12	4	33	12	90
1875	56	18	26	23	37	160
			Percentages			
1851	33	13	4	37	13	100
1875	35	11	16	14	23	100

[1] A comment on Joseph Spence of East Keal in an Evangelical periodical, quoted by Walker, *Tales*, p. 5.

[2] 'Church Parties', *Edinburgh Review*, xcviii (1853). At the middle of the century, the chief indicators of High Churchmanship were the S.P.G. and the Additional Curates Society; the more numerous Evangelical organizations included the Church Missionary Society, the Church Pastoral Aid Society, the British and Foreign Bible Society, the London Society for Promoting Christianity Amongst the Jews, the Lord's Day Observance Society, the Evangelical Alliance, and the Cambridge University Prayer Union.

At mid-century the clergy were chiefly divided between Evangelicals and moderate High Churchmen; Ritualists and other
advanced High Churchmen were a small minority. By the end
of the period the picture was more complicated. The 'centre'—
its content perhaps differing little from the moderate High
Churchmanship of 1851—was now stronger, and High Churchmen were more sharply differentiated into moderate and advanced
parties. The question of ritual had become much more pressing,
but it did not divide the clergy into two monolithic camps. The
'ritualists' were not necessarily Anglo-Catholic in doctrine, while
their opponents included not only the Evangelicals but also a
good many 'central' and moderate High Churchmen, particularly
of the older generation.[1] The most likely estimate of a tangled
situation is that despite the advent of a flamboyant ritualist
party, the Evangelicals suffered no loss in relative strength
after 1850 and the central churchmen positively gained. At
any rate the growth of partisan sentiment and affiliation is
unmistakable.

Compared with their personal views on disputed ritual and
theological issues, the clergy's collective status in society was far
less complex: they were gentlemen, whatever their churchmanship. A radical like Edward Steere might deplore this but could
not deny it.[2] But when parsons further elevated themselves by
adding gentlemanly personal qualities to the status of office,
ambiguities of sentiment and role crept in.[3] If there was tension
between the code of the landed gentleman and Christian ideals,
the combination of clergyman and gentleman was all the more
problematic. The self-conscious F. C. Massingberd found it
'difficult always to keep up the thought and wish, in society, to
be taken for a *clergyman* and nothing else. Apt to desire to be taken

[1] There were thirty-seven local clergymen singing the Remonstrance against the
Purchas judgement and the Declaration of the Three Deans, which favoured ritualism, but 101 signed the Address to the Prelates against the Eastward Position and
Vestments.
[2] R. M. Heanley, *Memoir of Edward Steere*, 1890, p. 95.
[3] The ambiguities were of course shared by their parishioners, who tended to
regard the clergy's gentlemanly status as more fundamental than their clerical
function. An old woman in the parish of Sausthorpe had been asked by the incumbent (T. P. Dale, the Ritualist martyr) to remember him in her prayers; she mentioned this to his wife, adding, '"And I doos, mum, I doos. I saäys every night,
Mr. Daäles is a gentleman, I saäys"' (H. P. Dale, *Life and Letters of Thomas Pelham
Dale*, 1894, ii. 107).

also for a *gentleman*. How much more dignified as well as humble, the opposite course.' He had his dual identity in mind again on another occasion, reproaching himself for harshness towards his wife: '*Oaths* too, in the mouth of a Presbyter of Christ's Church! And how little like a *gentleman*.'[1] The two roles, parson and clergyman, did not sit easily together. A gentleman, with a university education and a taste for leisure, lived a private life and did not mix spontaneously with his inferiors, with whom he did not pretend to have much in common. A clergyman, however, was expected to be out among his parishioners, sharing their concerns, winning their trust, praising, admonishing, guiding them. Only a few of the more conscientious and self-aware clergymen spoke of the tension between the two roles, but it affected them all. Reconciling the two roles may not have been difficult for those who possessed neither the income of a real gentleman nor the calling and zeal of a real minister. It was easy for the clergy to remain in the genteel world at a distance from the labouring poor who were the majority in their parishes. Few, at any rate, went local to the extent of Joseph Spence of East Keal 'who always spoke in the local dialect', his 'vulgar idiom and plain way of preaching' contrasting with the educated accents of his brethren.[2] And few would have desired, or deserved, the compliment received by Edward Steere from one of his parishioners at Skegness: '*a downright shirt sleeve man, and a real Bible parson*.'[3]

It was perhaps natural for gentlemen-priests to avoid undue exertion in the discharge of their clerical duties. Some kept their pastoral work to a minimum; even in 1870, one of them recalled, 'many of the clergy had ... too little work'.[4] F. C. Massingberd, more energetic than most, sighed, 'Oh for some engrossing occupation!' and added his own commentary: 'Alas what a wish for a Priest who has two churches, and near 400 souls lying six

[1] Journal, 5 Aug. 1842, Mass. 8/1; 4 Aug. 1847, Mass. 8/2. Contributing towards Massingberd's awareness of these tensions was the fact that he not only was one of the most self-reflective and conscientious clergymen in the area but also held one of the best livings: worth upwards of £800 a year, it gave him the income of a small squire.

[2] Walker, *Tales*, p. 2; Bogie to Kaye, 15 Aug. 1839, Cor. B. 5/4/75/3.

[3] Heanley, *Memoir*, p. 49. Steere used occasional dialect words in sermons; e.g. *Notes of Sermons*, 2nd ser., ed. R. M. Heanley, 1886, p. 127.

[4] Heanley, *Memoir*, p. 93; Overton and Wordsworth, *Christopher Wordsworth*, p. 228. Overton was incumbent of Legbourne, 1860–83.

miles scattered!!!'[1] In the void left by unperformed pastoralia lay the temptation of a life of leisure. 'Our real danger', said John Carr of Brattleby to his colleagues, was 'becoming enamoured of a peaceable and retired life, and of literary tastes'. Bishop Jackson, speaking of the dangers inherent in an established church, noted more comprehensively that its clergy tended to become

mere gentlemen and men of literature, or farmers, perhaps, or sportsmen; whose tastes and sphere of action seem to lie, not in pleading for God with souls publicly and from house to house, but in the library, the drawing-room, and the garden, if not in the ball-room, at the card-table, and in the hunting-field.

Such activities, he continued, emasculated their ministry, not only with the 'religious ... but even more so with the keen men of the world, who, though not religious nor loving religion, know well enough what religion ought to make those who believe its truths'.[2]

The library tempted more clergymen then than now; the card-table, an installation at the 'Tory news-room' in Lincoln, was reported to be popular with the 'cathedral grandees'. The hunting-field too had its clerical contingent: William Tower of South Willingham was 'a fox-hunting Divine and nothing else ... all the week in a green coat'.[3] And parsons played many an innings on the cricket pitch, at the Burton Park Club and elsewhere.[4] They seem also to have done their share of entertaining, despite the shortage of congenial society; Egremont Richardson of Belchford was remembered as a 'bon vivant ... popular among his clerical brethren'—'like several others, [he] gave an annual clerical dinner', while Massingberd, forever ambivalent, asked himself 'whether we could not manage to give up giving dinner

---

[1] Massingberd, Journal, 28 Feb. 1839, Mass. 8/1.

[2] J. Carr, The Duties of the Parochial Clergy, 1842, p. 12; J. Jackson, Rest Before Labour, 1859, p. 7.

[3] Stamf. Merc., 20 Apr. 1838: Goddard to Kaye, June 1827, Cor. B. 5/4/140/15. For Tower see also Cooper, Wise Saws, ii. 125. His neighbour, the curate of Brattleby in the 1830s, was another unabashed devotee of hunting and shooting (Hill, Victorian Lincoln, pp. 173-4).

[4] Burton Park Cricket Club records, MON 24/IA/1, 2, 9, 10. There were often four clergymen on the Burton Park side in the early 1850s, but by 1870 they had largely disappeared.

parties altogether'.[1] The Marshland clergy surprised the curate of Strubby in 1843 with some less conventional pastimes:

The clergy here being the only resident gentlemen in the country, employ themselves entirely in their gardens, and are very different in their habits from many of the Northamptonshire clergy. The villages here are so very *thinly* populated and yet so many Baptists (who are most bigoted against the church, and will not even *receive clergymen* into their houses) that there is but very little weekly duty in most parishes about. When I was visiting at Mr. Allott's, a Mr. Vyner (a neighbouring clergyman and a magistrate...) asked me if I was fond of retirement and country amusements, for, (he added) 'the clergy in this neighbourhood would not exist, if they could *not garden* and *do their own carpentering*,' and a few days ago Mr. Allott (who is also a magistrate) went to *brew* for a brother clergyman, who was not well skilled in that art!... The clergy here do everything they can for one another, and are not nearly so high and lofty as *many* we have been accustomed to.[2]

Gardening indeed must have occupied many an otherwise idle clerical hour. At the annual show of the Louth Floral and Horticultural Society in 1839, clergymen took eighteen of twenty-nine prizes for fruit and twenty out of thirty for vegetables. And the successor to the fox-hunting parson at Willingham-by-Stow was 'an enthusiastic grower of hollyhocks and gladioli, taking prizes for them all over England. The hollyhocks used to have great bonnets over them to protect them from the sun'.[3] Good husbandry, said Lancelot Andrewes, is good divinity: but good horticulture? The image of a clergyman cultivating his garden suggests a lack not only of zeal and energy but also of congenial social peers in the village. The clergy's income put them on the same level as the farmers, but their education aligned them with the gentry.[4] Lacking company in the village they may have found it easiest to retreat into a privatized style of life and to remain cut off from their parishioners except on Sundays. This may well have

---

[1] J. Conway Walter, *Records, Historical and Antiquarian, of Parishes Round Horncastle*, 1904, p. 24; Massingberd, Journal, 24 Sept. 1846, Mass. 8/2.

[2] William Layng to unknown recipient, 13 Nov. 1843, Misc. Dep. 165/4/1, L.A.O. John Allott, mentioned in the letter, was rector of Maltby-le-Marsh.

[3] *Stamf. Merc.*, 2 Aug. 1839; Lord Hawke, *Recollections and Reminiscences*, 1924, p. 16.

[4] When a (rich) local farmer proposed marriage in 1846 to one of the daughters of the incumbent of Wainfleet, the first response of the clerical household was one of consternation (G. H. Cholmeley, *Letters and Papers of the Cholmeleys from Wainfleet 1813–1853* (Lincoln Record Society, vol. lix, 1964, p. 83).

been the fate particularly of the poorer clergy in squireless parishes; the revival of rural deanery meetings after 1850 offered them the prospect of sociability as well as discussions of professional matters. Perhaps too the peculiar social isolation of the clergy led them to assert and magnify their authority in their own domain—in the churches themselves.

RITES AND SACRAMENTS

Most of the clergy in south Lindsey were not ardent Ritualists at any time between 1825 and 1875. They were content with the modest place allotted to the rites and sacraments by the Prayer Book and by Anglican tradition. But if not Ritualists they did increasingly give greater emphasis to ritual, particularly after 1850. They hoped to make it the focus and expression of a reconstituted community of worshippers, in which all villagers, labourers as well as squires, should take part. It was in this spirit that they attempted to suppress private or familial performances of the sacraments and to make them public and communal. And increasingly they regarded ritual behaviour, notably attendance at Communion, as the test and badge of Anglican commitment. But at every stage they came into conflict with the prejudice and preference of laymen in a class-divided society in which privacy and convenience ranked above church law and communal sentiment.

The rules in the Prayer Book governing the administration of baptism stated that

The Curates of every Parish shall often admonish the people, that they defer not the Baptism of their children longer than the first or second Sunday next after their birth, or other Holy-day falling between, unless upon a great and reasonable cause . . . . And also they shall warn them, that without like great cause and necessity they procure not their children to be baptized at home in their houses.

Baptism was intended to be a public rite, performed during the regular service in the presence of the congregation. For every boy to be baptized there were to be two godfathers and one godmother, and for every girl, two godmothers and one godfather. Practice, however, deviated noticeably from this ideal. Baptism was usually delayed a month or more after birth—except for weak and sickly babies who were baptized as soon as possible. A more serious and very common deviant practice was that of baptizing without sponsors.[1] At Bucknall, where the custom prevailed, parents said '"they cannot afford the expense of treating the sponsors."' Or, if they agreed to have sponsors, they asked that the rite be performed on a weekday: '"Oh! we will not have it on a Sunday. How are the gossips to enjoy themselves after the christening?"'[2] To insist that the sponsors be communicants, and to perform baptism as prescribed during morning or afternoon services, sometimes provoked opposition. Still worse was the indiscriminate practice of private baptism. It drew an attack from Archdeacon Bayley in 1826 but was still common more than thirty years later.[3] It was requested whether the child was ill or well, and especially by Methodists, who objected to the rule requiring godparents. 'To accommodate them [Methodists] as far as I can,' one clergyman wrote, 'I have been obliged not to look very strictly to the letter of the rubrick, respecting the *sickness* of an infant, before I name in private houses.'[4] So great was the disparity between the rubrical and sacramental ideal and the actual mundane practice of 'naming' that Bishop Jackson felt justified in complaining that baptism had become a mere 'civil ceremony or superstitious charm . . . perhaps no ordinance of the Church has been allowed to degenerate into an unreal form so much as the Sacrament of Holy Baptism'.[5]

The social meaning of baptism was evidently shaped less by religious considerations than by attitudes towards the community and the family, the public realm and the private. In six parishes with resident clergymen during the first half of the period, the majority of the children were baptized on weekdays—almost certainly privately—while the majority of the labourers' children received Sunday baptisms—which were more likely to be public.[6]

---

[1] Deprecated by Bishop Jackson in his primary visitation (*Charge*, 1855, p. 24).

[2] White to Kaye, 8 Jan. 1834, Cor. B. 5/4/10/1; Winston to Kaye, 31 July 1850, Cor. B. 5/4/70/1. 'Gossips' (derived from 'god-sibs') was the vernacular term for godparents.

[3] Wimberley to Kaye, 25 Jan. 1849, Cor. B. 5/4/14/3; H. V. Bayley, *Charge Delivered to the Clergy of the Archdeaconry of Stow*, 1826, p. 16; J. Jackson, *Charge*, 1858, p. 20.

[4] Winston to Kaye, 31 July 1850, Cor. B. 5/4/70/1; Otter to Kaye, 3 Dec. /1832/, Cor. B. 5/4/89/3; Smith to Kaye, 12 Feb 1834, Cor. B. 5/4/83/7. The use of the vulgar word 'name' is remarkable in a clergyman.

[5] *Charge*, 1855, p. 24. For the rather limited superstitious uses of baptism, see below p. 272.

[6] The parishes were Faldingworth, Fillingham, Horsington, Panton, South Ormsby, and Driby.

Farmers, gentry, and clergy, for whom membership in the local community was secondary to their class and family loyalties, preferred private baptism, withdrawn from the village congregation; baptism in these classes was more likely to be, as Bishop Jackson complained, 'a family festival with very few religious associations indeed'.[1] Among the labourers, however, class and family were still secondary to community, and baptism was still a public, communal event. But as their outlook shifted from community to class they too demanded private celebrations.

For years the bishops had urged that baptism be performed publicly, during the afternoon service, and by the end of the period they had won a considerable, though not total, victory. Of 207 churches for which returns were made to visitation inquiries in 1873, public baptism as the rubric required was practised in 129; this was done 'not always' or 'occasionally' in twenty-three; in twenty-six parishes children were baptized after public services were over, usually in the afternoon; and in twenty-five others it was noted only that baptisms were not performed at the recommended time. Nevertheless popular resistance had defeated the attempted reform in several parishes. The vicar of Edlington 'found the public administration of Baptism in the church to stand in the way of children being brought to that Holy Sacrament, so I open the church whenever it is wished, by all classes'. At Donington 'the people are not agreeable to the change of customs of 100 years'; the rector of Kettlethorpe 'tried Baptism during service some years ago and . . . the people objected to it very strongly and stayed away'. Indeed at South Willingham 'farmers and others have come to my church *because* Baptism has been administered during service at their own'.[2] Yet if the visitation returns are accurate, baptism in a majority of churches was again a congregational, public rite. Parish baptismal registers show an increase in Sunday administrations after 1850. The worshipping community had temporarily been reconstituted. But in over a third of the parishes the modern, non-congregational practice was already established: baptism in the church on Sunday afternoon following the regular service (or on a weekday) with only the family present. This practice had its origins not in the neo-congregationalism advocated by the bishops but in the

[1] Jackson, *Charge*, 1855, p. 24.
[2] 1873 V.R., Clergy.

earlier custom of private, domestic baptism which had survived in a large minority of parishes; it corresponded with the assumptions of a society in which class and family now overshadowed community.

In these same circumstances an attempt was made to revive public catechizing. Thought to have been all but universal in the eighteenth century, it had evidently fallen into disuse by the second quarter of the nineteenth. But its reintroduction was urged upon the parish clergy by successive bishops, beginning with Kaye, who saw it as a weapon against the alarming religious ignorance of the young.[1]

In practice the attempted revival was an almost total failure: the visitation returns of 1873 show that public catechism was held in only nineteen churches out of 207. Wherever it was introduced it was resisted. The incumbent of Minting reported that 'although tickets and rewards are given at Church only two or three can be induced to remain for catechizing'. When the vicar of Sotby tried it, the congregation regarded it as an 'innovation' and 'absented themselves from church, so it was given up'. C. A. Wilkinson at South Willingham 'tried catechizing again and again in the church and upon failure have given it up'.[2] The source of the difficulty appears to have been the same as in the case of baptism: the rubric specified that catechism was to take place in the presence of the congregation, during the evening service. Even Archdeacon Stonehouse conceded that in its rubrical position, after the second Lesson, it was 'a disagreeable interruption of the service'. A further clue was supplied by the vicar of Hogsthorpe, who believed that *public* catechizing is *out of date*'.[3] It was out of date in presupposing a genuinely 'mixed' congregation of adults and children: in the new society, however, the division was sharper not only between classes but also between age groups, and adults disliked having the service interrupted for a childish activity. Catechism survived by migrating to the day and Sunday schools, which respected the growing differentiation between youth and adults and between instruction and worship and began to institutionalize a distinct youth subculture.

[1] Bayley, *Charge*, p. 17; Kaye, *Works*, vii. 343; Jackson, *Charge*, 1855, pp. 15–16. Bishop Wordsworth recommended catechizing in his Primary Visitation (*Horne. News*, 29 Oct. 1870).

[2] Minting, Sotby, and South Willingham, 1879 V.R.

[3] Stonehouse to Kaye, 19 Apr. (?), Cor. B. 5/4/85/1; Hogsthorpe, 1873 V.R.

Public catechism ignored the new social realities, and the Church was powerless to synthesize a worshipping community from the increasingly differentiated segments of the wider village society.

In the case of confirmation, a strategy that worked with rather than against the prevailing social currents produced happier results. The objective was not to reintroduce the rite but to suppress the disorder and even wildness that accompanied it, both within the church and outside it. Clerical reformers were appalled by early Victorian confirmations, an untamed survival of the old 'rough' society. After the confirmation at Alford in 1837, for example, it was reported that many of the young people went straight from the church to the public houses, where the attractions included 'lewd women' and dancing as well as drink; the clergy 'were obliged to call in the assistance of the constables' and it was 'not the first time such profanation of a solemn rite has occurred'.[1] Three years later there were similar scenes at Lincoln and at Louth, where

a great number of the rural youth of both sexes afterwards filled the various public houses in the town, and presently showed by their manners and behaviour that their recent training had left them as barbarous and unchristian as the 'untaught savage brood'.

And at Gainsborough 'many of them appeared to have been confirmed in wickedness instead of godliness, from their riotous, bacchanalian, and pugilistic proceedings ere they left the town in the evening'.[2]

Reform proceeded on two levels: the young gradually disciplined themselves, and the clergy imposed stricter control from above. Bishop Kaye had already improved security inside the churches by decreeing

the Principal Door *only* of the Church to be open for admission. . . . The Candidates to be conveniently seated in the pews: the Males on one side of the Middle Aisle, the Females on the opposite side; keeping their tickets open in their hands, to be delivered when required. . . . Wandsmen to be placed at the Door, and in and about the Churchyard, to prevent noise. The clergy of the several parishes to remain near the pews in which the children are seated, for the purpose of overlooking them.

[1] Hildyard to Kaye, 17 Aug. [1837], Cor. B. 5/4/30/3.
[2] *Linc. Gaz.*, 16 June ,11 and 25 Aug. 1840.

Further reforms were instituted by Jackson. In 1855 he raised the standard age for candidates from 14 to 15; and he began to hold confirmations in village churches on a large scale, covering a third of the parishes in the diocese every year. Previously the bishop had held confirmations only every three years, in conjunction with his visitation of the diocese, and had largely confined them to town churches.[1] Even before the new measures had gone into effect the bishop was pleased to report that confirmation was 'no longer a mere day of childish amusement'. In 1864, after raising the minimum age, he noted that candidates were fewer in number but better behaved. Outside the churches, however, the decline in confirmation revels probably owed less to controls from above than to that growing self-restraint from below that was equally noticeable in the conduct of farm and domestic servants at village feasts and statute fairs.

The clergy's larger aim, rebuilding the congregation, required that as many young people as possible should be confirmed, but in this they appear to have had only mixed results. Unfortunately the data are unsatisfactory except at the very end of the period, and complicating matters further is the fact that there were always some older people among the candidates—perhaps seeking the episcopal cure for rheumatism.[2] Of the fourteen males from Panton confirmed between 1857 and 1863, four were over 21 (they ranged from 22 to 45); of the twenty females confirmed, six were over 21 (ranging from 22 to 37).[3] Within the 'normal' ages, 15 to 17 were the most frequent, accounting for over half the total. In the area as a whole, girl candidates outnumbered boys considerably, despite the fact that boys outnumbered girls in the relevant age group. The girl candidates confirmed at seven rural churches (local centres for perhaps a dozen parishes in each neighbourhood) in 1846 outnumbered the boys 524 to 408; in 1848, 408 to 294; and in 1851, 356 to 289. Only about four boys

---

[1] Notes for the 1840 Confirmations, 'Confirmations 1835–51', Lincoln diocesan records V.VII, L.A.O. Jackson, *Charge*, 1855, p. 27. Kaye, however, had also set fourteen as the minimum age and in 1846, 1848, and 1851 had held confirmations in village churches ('Confirmation Papers 1839–52', Lincoln diocesan records; Mass. 9/62).

[2] See below, p. 273.

[3] Lists of confirmees at end of baptismal register, Panton parish registers. It should be noted, however, that Panton was served in this period by an incumbent and curates of unusual energy.

were confirmed for every five girls. Now in 1851 it can be estimated that in the 15–19 age group males outnumbered females
by a ratio of five to four; if *all* the females in this age group were
confirmed, the ratio of four male to five female confirmees would
mean that no more than 64 per cent of the males were confirmed;
if half the females were confirmed, less than a third of the males
were, and so on. More precise estimates are possible for the 1873
confirmation. The totals can be set against the estimated numbers
in the 15–19 age group for each sex.[1] The 984 male candidates in
1873 were 30 per cent of the estimated 3,293 males in the age
group; the 1,403 female candidates were 52 per cent of the
estimated 2,725 females. But since the candidates included older
persons as well, the true percentages for this age group are lower.
Most farm servants and unmarried day labourers were evidently
beyond the reach of the clergy, and a good many dairymaids and
domestic servants as well. Class variations in the rate of confirmation are impossible to determine, but the figures do indicate
a significant divergence between the early religious careers of
young men and those of young women.

Parsons agreed in blaming the circumstances of the farm servants for the general shortage of confirmees. At Ranby it was
reported that young people generally went into service before
the age of confirmation; at Haugham the population was 'scattered
and often changing—it is difficult to find candidates for Confirmation as often there are none'. Sometimes the timing of confirmation was criticized:

I much regret that May the 15th or 17th should be appointed for the
Confirmation at Spilsby. Your Lordship is aware that servants leave
their places on the 14th; that there follows a time of dissipation when
people are not accessible and the roads not passable in consequence of
the drunkenness, swearing and loose conduct that prevails. The
candidates in the country chiefly consist of servants; the females will be
engaged in 'May day cleaning' during most of the previous month and
will not be allowed to attend to the clergyman's instruction. Or if they
should, they would pass out of my hands, and possibly go to homes
where the Confirmation was over.

---

[1] 1846 and 1848 figures in 'Confirmation Papers 1839–52', Lincoln diocesan
records, L.A.O.; 1851 figures in 'Confirmations North Lincs. 1851', Mass. 9/62;
the estimate of the age structure in the early 1870s is based on the composite age
structure of eight of the most rural Registrar's Sub-districts in south Lindsey in
the 1871 Census.

And in parishes where Methodists were strong, their disapproval of confirmation—whatever their willingness to be baptized, married, and buried according to the Prayer Book—would be likely to reduce the number of candidates.[1]

The motives of the candidates were not strikingly spiritual even after the riotous festivities of earlier decades had subsided. Confirmation, an old gamekeeper noted, was 'for young lads and lassies who want a holiday at Horncastle', and they could still expect a treat at the end of the day. An old woman in the Saus-thorpe neighbourhood recalled that 'There wasn't mooch fooss about confarming in my time. But there, I saays to my lad, you go to the confarmin', and Mr. Daales [the clergyman] "ull maake it oop to tha".'[2] The incumbent of Sixhills and South Willingham claimed that 'many young people got confirmed two or even three times, as they changed parishes, for . . . "the lark of the thing" and the meetings and teas and presents'. When he announced that there would be no feast or rewards, 'none of the villagers reported themselves in either parish'. A low turnout was also obtained by one of the few parsons who conscientiously discouraged anyone coming to confirmation who was not well prepared.[3]

Indeed the customary teas and treats associated with the rite must have held a far greater appeal to most young people than its purely religious purpose, which was after all to prepare them to make their first Communion.[4] Many confirmees never became communicants at all. This was especially true of young male confirmees. Of thirteen male confirmees at Panton in 1854 and 1857, only four subsequently communicated; of seventeen female confirmees, thirteen became communicants, a significant divergence. If this pattern was general, then relatively fewer boys than girls were confirmed, and of those few, relatively fewer again became communicants. A further scrap of evidence comes from South Ormsby, where six girls, recently confirmed, made their

---

[1] Ranby, Haugham, and Ashby-by-Partney, 1873 V.R. Bogie to Kaye, 3 Aug. 1848, Cor. B. 5/4/106/19.

[2] Penny, More Folklore, p. 38; Dale, Life and Letters of Thomas Pelham Dale, ii. 107.

[3] The incumbent of Newton-on-Trent, 1873 V.R.

[4] R. D. B. Rawnsley of Halton Holegate warned that no one should be confirmed who did not intend to become a communicant (Sermons Preached in Country Churches, 2nd ser., 1867, p. 329). Bishop Kaye, however, did not consider confirmation a prerequisite for communion (Works, vi. 215).

first Communion in 1857: none, however, went back a second time. It would appear that these farm labourers' children shared the assumption of contemporary urban working-class teenagers: 'that the process of becoming an adult is roughly collateral with the cessation of religious practice'.[1] There were in all likelihood very few who agreed with the clergy that confirmation inaugurated their adult religious practice; it was rather the end of the Sunday school era, celebrated with appropriate festivities, and the beginning of a long period, continuing through the years of domestic and farm service until marriage and beyond, in which formal religious practice was at low ebb.

Like confirmation, the Anglican marriage ceremony deserves attention less for its religious content than for its social ambience. Most parsons did not take the Anglo-Catholic position that it was a sacrament, and did not ascribe to it much religious value; for them, as for their parishioners, it was a civil rite performed within church walls.

Most villagers, including most Methodists, preferred to be married in the parish church.[2] This was in spite of the practice followed by certain clergymen of taking the whole of the marriage fees at the first posting of banns, thus doubling the cost of a wedding for a man and woman living in different parishes. Illegal in itself, the practice tended to encourage couples to be married by the Registrar or by Methodist ministers, whose fees were lower.[3] The standard fees to the clergyman and parish clerk were 10s. 6d. or 11s.—the best part of a week's wages for a farm labourer. But against the cheapness of a non-Anglican marriage had to be set its inconvenience, since it was performed in a town chapel (few village chapels were licensed until the end of the century) or by the Assistant Registrar in the embarrassing precincts of the Union workhouse.

There was still a trace of religious influence in the reluctance of parsons to perform marriages during Lent. Of a total of 821

[1] Lists of communicants, South Ormsby and Driby parish records; David Martin, 'Interpreting the Figures', in Michael Perry (ed.), *Crisis for Confirmation*, 1967, p. 111.
[2] In 1871 there were 787 marriages in the four most rural registration districts in south Lindsey: 74·1 per cent were performed in parish churches and only 6·6 per cent in Registry Offices (Registrar-General, *34th Annual Report*, 1873, pp. 18–19).
[3] Jackson, *Charge*, 1861, p. 33. In his next visitation charge he threatened proceedings against these clerical profiteers (*Charge*, 1864, p. 18). See also Watkin to Jackson, 13 Feb. 1856, Cor. B. 5/4/57/1.

weddings in sample parishes, only forty-nine, or 6 per cent, occurred during Lent—the expected figure, if marriages had been spread evenly through the year, being about 11 per cent. The most popular month for marriage was May, especially for farm servants, who took the opportunity to marry after leaving their previous employment. Between 1838 and 1850 Lincolnshire had the highest percentage of marriages in the second quarter (April to June) of any English county.[1] Tuesday and Thursday were the favourite days for weddings, Friday, Saturday, and Sunday the least common: perhaps another trace of religious or superstitious influence. In all of these respects there was little variation from one class to another, but that was not the case in the choice between marriage by banns and marriage by licence. About half the farmers and most gentry and clergy and their children were married by licence, while marriage by banns was the rule for the great majority of labourers and craftsmen. The upper classes shrank from the publication of banns, which not only exposed their matrimonial intentions to public view—and to villagers' comment on the sexual consequences—but also submitted them to a kind of public consent, as though anything a mere labourer might say could block them. In practice the upper classes did not begrudge paying the additional fees to ensure privacy: their whole mode of social life, with its family and class dimensions, was premised upon the withdrawal of 'private' affairs from the local village community.[2] The majority of villagers, however, had their banns 'axed' before the congregation, and the sense that communal approval, far from being unwelcome, was actively being sought, is unmistakable. Local dialect suggests that the banns were not a mere form of words—on the first time of asking they were 'axed up' and on the third time they were 'axed out'—and an unofficial custom enabled the congregation to affirm the match as emphatically as possible. Ordinarily the couple were absent from church on the third

---

[1] Registrar -General, *Thirteenth Annual Report*, 1854, p. v.

[2] F. C. Massingberd was among the critics of the upper-class practice of marrying by licence (*Lectures on the Prayer Book*, 1864, p. 132). Cf. Tennyson's play, 'The Promise of May', in which the gentlemanly villain asks the woman who wants to marry him, 'When shall your parish-parson bawl our banns/ Before your gaping clowns?' and she replies, 'Not in our church—I think I scarce could hold my head up there. Is there no other way?' He suggests marriage by licence. (*Poems and Plays*, 1965, p. 731.)

publication; after the banns were 'axed out', the parish clerk would say, 'God speed them well', to which the people would reply, 'Amen'.[1] Here again was the contrast between the private family realm of the classes and the public realm of the masses.

Some of these same themes reappear in the social context of Holy Communion, but with important shifts in emphasis. For this was no mere rite, but 'the sacrament' *par excellence*, and it was a vision of what Communion might be—the religious expression of the whole community, with every adult villager taking part—that guided the clergy in their effort to re-create the village congregation. Since the clergy came to regard it as the test of church membership, it provides a test of the success of the whole clerical reform enterprise.

Clerical views of the sacrament naturally varied widely, but the predominance of Evangelical and moderate churchmen in the area ensured that extreme claims for it were rare for most of the period. 'I attach no superstitious virtue to the Holy Sacrament,' said R. D. B. Rawnsley, 'I do not say that a man cannot be saved without it.' Most clergymen probably shared his view that it was a 'memorial of your Lord's sacrifice . . . the Atonement'. F. B. Hurcomb's response was more personal: 'Our heart swells with grateful emotions and affectionate love'; but not more sacramental: 'It is valued like the precious relic of a departed friend.'[2]

Despite their moderate views of its intrinsic religious character, the clergy saw new value in it as an index of Church commitment, particularly when the battle with Methodism sharpened after 1850. To clergy of all shades of churchmanship, regular Communion became the badge of Church membership, identifying the genuine Christians and separating churchmen from Methodists: 'Only communicants have any real claim to be called Christians . . . full members of the Church.' The right to administer Holy Communion likewise distinguished the clergymen from Methodist preachers and others of lesser authority. (Laymen, however, could administer the sacrament of baptism.) By the 1880s a 'backward or neglected' parish was defined by Bishop King as one with a low percentage of communicants.[3] This

---

[1] Winn 5/5, p. 58; Brogden, *Provincial Words and Expressions*, p. 16.

[2] R. D. B. Rawnsley, 'The Feast Refused', in Edmund Fowle (ed.), *Plain Preaching*, 1873, p. 42; R. D. B. Rawnsley, *Christian Exhortation*, 1871, pp. 165, 268; F. B. Hurcomb, *Sermons*, 1877, p. 109.

[3] Steere, *Notes of Sermons*, ii. 51–2; King, *Charge*, 1886, p. 86.

increasing emphasis on communion was an impressive shift in clerical opinion, but in drawing the Church further away from the Methodists on the one side and from 'popular Protestantism' on the other, they risked alienating the great majority of their own parishioners.

It was essential to this conception of Holy Communion that the sacrament be celebrated frequently. But throughout the first half of the century and well into the second half, three or four celebrations a year were standard; if by 1873 a monthly celebration was the most common frequency, a majority still celebrated less often.[1]

Annual Number of Celebrations of Holy Communion
1858 and 1873

	3 and 4 times	*5 to 11 times*	*12 and above*
1858	134 parishes	57	17
1873	49	68	88

Like other reforms, more frequent celebration was a post-1850 phenomenon: the largest increase in the diocese as a whole took place in the early 1860s.[2] Quarterly celebration still had its adherents, chiefly among the older clergy, at the end of the period; it was the younger men, representing all the various church parties, who were the innovators. Indeed the gradual but general advent of a more elaborate ritual owed less to the small band of Ritualists than to the moderate and Evangelical majority who abhorred Ritualist 'excesses'.

To celebrate Communion more often was one thing, to increase the number of lay communicants and the frequency with which they communicated was another, more important and more difficult. The Prayer Book laid down the rule that 'every Parishioner shall communicate at the least three times in the year, of which Easter to be one', but it seems clear that most villagers were not meeting even this minimum requirement. Samuel Martin of Snarford deplored 'that very common ... neglect which is so visible among us'; at Halton Holegate, later in the period, Holy Communion was 'greatly neglected amongst us. Many who come both to Morning and Evening Prayer go away, as a matter of course, when the Holy Communion is administered'. In Steere's parish it was common to say, 'Oh, I never com-

---

[1] 1858 V.R. (churchwardens); 1873 V.R.
[2] Jackson, *Charge*, 1864, p. 12.

municate.'[1] Villagers absented themselves from the Communion table because, they said, they felt unworthy, lacking in moral perfection. A characteristic clerical reply was that of William Nevins (a High Churchman): reception was not dependent upon 'the qualification of the receiver', and former sins were 'no bar to present mercies'; indeed, anyone could receive the sacrament 'until excommunication has actually been pronounced'.[2] Only from the older part of the congregation did communicants come forth in satisfactory numbers: Steere's communicants were 'a few oldish people', but he wanted to see 'a whole congregation of communicants'. His exhortation was, 'Let us *all* meet at Easter at the Lord's table, not old communicants only'.[3]

The average numbers of communicants at the end of the period were stated by the parish clergy in their returns to the 1873 visitation inquiries; from these figures have been computed the median percentages of communicants in parishes within given ranges of population.

Average Number of Communicants as Percentage
of Parish Population: 1873

Population	Median percentage
1–99	12·0
100–199	6·0
200–299	4·4
300–399	3·9
400–499	3·0
500–599	2·6
600–	2·4

These were remarkably low figures, even when allowance is made for the fact that the total number communicating in a parish over a year was greater than the average per celebration, and that they could make their canonical three communions and no more. What was soon to become the target figure for communicants—10 per cent of the population—was reached only in the smallest parishes of less than 100 persons, whose combined population was only 6 per cent of the total in south Lindsey in 1871. Even on the most generous estimate, the great majority of adults—perhaps 80 per cent or more—

[1] Samuel Martin, *Family Sermons*, 1838, p. 14; Rawnsley, *Christian Exhortation*, pp. 260–1; Steere, *Notes of Sermons*, i. 118.
[2] Nevins, *Scriptural Doctrine*, pp. 5, 22.
[3] Steere, *Notes of Sermons*, i. 123.

were non-communicants; those meeting their obligation of three communions a year must have been a tiny minority.[1]

The influence of the size of population on the level of communicants is clear; there was also regional influence. Regional comparisons (between groups of parishes of the same population) indicate that the upland regions tended to be above the medians and the lowland regions below, with the Southern Wolds and Cliff on the one hand and the Central vale and Outer Marsh on the other forming the sharpest contrast.

For more precise information about communicants it is necessary to turn to the parishes of South Ormsby, Driby, and Panton, for which lists of communicants have survived.[2] Unfortunately these were untypical in important respects: all were small, close parishes, none had a Methodist chapel, and all (Driby was united with South Ormsby and the churchless parish of Calceby to form a single benefice) had energetic incumbents during the relevant periods. These incumbents (and their curates) were, moreover, as moderate High Churchmen, somewhat more inclined to ritual than the majority of their clerical contemporaries. The conclusions reached must in some respects be considered highly tentative, subject to the discovery and analysis of further lists for other parishes.

The evidence from all three parishes agrees on the influence of age on Communion. Young people rarely appeared at the altar rails, and servants—farm and domestic, male and female—almost never. In the better part of a ten-year period at Ormsby, the only servants to receive Communion were both older than the average, a farmer's housekeeper and a governess. Six girls, recently confirmed, made their first Communion at Ormsby in 1857 but did not go back a second time.

Among the labourers, those in their fifties—beyond the age of child-rearing—were far more likely to be at least occasional communicants.[3] Although the number of farmers in these parishes

---

[1] In 1886 Bishop King considered that in an 'average' country parish a tenth of the total population might reasonably be expected to be on the communicants' roll; in smaller parishes the proportion might reach a fifth or even a third, while in backward or neglected parishes it was a fortieth or less (*Charge*, 1886, pp. 75, 92).

[2] The predominance of older people among the communicants suggests that the prospect of receiving alms may have been one of their motives.

[3] The lists are among the parish records.

Communicants and non-Communicants: Labourers, Cottagers, and Servants

	age	Males		Females	
		Communi-cants	*Non-com-municants*	*Communi-cants*	*Non-com-municants*
Driby,	50 & over	6	1	4	1
1861	25–49	2	7	2	3
	15–24	0	13	1	8
South	50–	8	6	5	7
Ormsby,	25–49	5	18	5	20
1861	15–24	0	27	0	25
Panton,	50–	2	2	3	0
1857–	25–49	1	11	2	6
1860	15–24	0	10	0	8

was too small to be of much significance, they too tended to be more frequent communicants in their later years.

The influence of class and occupation was as strong as that of age. The few farmers in these parishes were fairly regular communicants; it is probable that farmers generally were more frequent than their labourers, though less so than the gentry. Unfortunately there were too few craftsmen in these parishes to yield even a tentative pattern. Among the labourers, the majority of the population in the three parishes, there were few communicants except in the oldest age group.

The evidence on the differences between men and women reveals contradictory tendencies. (Only labourers and their wives will be considered.) At Panton, labourers' wives were, as expected, more frequent communicants than their husbands. But at Driby from 1853 to 1859 the pattern was startlingly different. There were eight labouring couples living in the parish through the entire period covered by the lists; in seven of these, the husband communicated considerably more often than his wife. Out of a possible thirty-five Communions, the seven husbands averaged 20·3, their wives only 5·3. In the larger and adjoining parish of Ormsby, with a population of 261 in 1861, compared with seventy-nine in Driby, seventeen labouring families resided continuously throughout the period; in six, neither partner was recorded at any of the fifty-six celebrations; in eight, the husband communicated more often (averaging 9·9) than his wife (averaging 1·8); in three, the wife communicated more often than her husband. The evidence from Ormsby is less decisive than that from Driby, but points in the same direction.

Even in the three farming families at Ormsby the husbands communicated more often than their wives: the respective averages were 22·7 and 17·7. On general principles—women generally being more partial to religious ceremony, men to preaching—the women might have been expected to outnumber the men. If the unexpected pattern at Ormsby and Driby was not merely a freak or the result of the personal influence of F. C. Massingberd, it may possibly have represented a survival of an older tradition in which the husband was not only the head of the family at home, but also its 'official representative' in the community—and at church. In this connection, it is notable that in 1861, eight of the thirteen labourers who communicated at all did so the canonical three times, but of the ten labourers' wives who communicated, only one did so. It was as though the public, canonical obligation lay on the men, while the wives appeared at the altar rails by personal choice—a communal responsibility for the men, an individual decision for the women.[1] Whether or not this is borne out by subsequent research, there is one further aspect of the male and female patterns worth mentioning. It is a remarkable fact that husband and wife did not show exactly the *same* pattern more often. (The only couples with this pattern were those in which neither partner was a communicant.) In labouring families, the disparity between husband and wife was usually considerable, whoever was the more frequent. This suggests that the labourer and his wife led independent religious lives. But if the tiny sample at Ormsby was typical, that was not the case with farmers. The difference between the average for the farmers and that for their wives was much smaller than it was for the labourers; it suggests that the farmer and his wife were more likely to act as a religious unit, presumably because they were more likely to form an intense emotional and psychological unit.

The influence of Methodism can also be traced. In compiling a speculum of his parishioners in 1855, Massingberd indicated that five of the Ormsby labourers were Methodists.[2] Four of the group

---

[1] There was also of course the practical consideration that the wives might have to stay at home with young children, but in the ages of child-rearing neither husbands nor wives communicated very often.

[2] 'Ormsby cum Ketsby, Calceby and Driby Parochial Book, 1855', Mass. 8/5. The nearest chapels, one Wesleyan and the other Wesleyan Reform, were at Whitepit, a hamlet in the adjoining parish of Swaby, a mile and a half from Ormsby.

proved to be the four most frequent communicants of all the labourers, ranging from eight to twenty-two Communions. Their wives were all communicants too, though not among the most frequent. Methodism evidently did not discourage and may well have encouraged Communion at the parish church. Even in this secluded parish, blessed by a resident squire and a conscientious, well-paid resident incumbent, the most potent religious stimulus in the lives of the farm labourers was Methodism.

Thus the clergy failed to realize their larger aspirations for Communion in village society. Most villagers were nothing like frequent communicants, and even where conditions were favourable, in parishes like Panton and Ormsby and Driby, clerical initiatives found a response only in highly specific subgroups—with regard to class, age, and sex—who formed a small minority of the village population.

THE SUNDAY SERVICE

Holy Communion was for the élite; for the ordinary churchgoer, Morning and Evening Prayer were the standard services, and it was they that most fully represented Anglican worship.

They were long services. The morning service consisted not only of Morning Prayer, but also of the Litany and about half the Communion service, down as far as the prayer for the Church Militant, and lasted anywhere from seventy or eighty minutes to an hour and three quarters. Evening Prayer—which was almost always held in the afternoon—was shorter, but could last an hour and a quarter. Nevertheless it was claimed that 'the poor, generally speaking, are never tired, however long the services may be'.[1]

While much of the service was taken up with prayers, canticles, and lessons from the Bible,[2] its centrepiece was the sermon—despite the absence in the Prayer Book of any mention of a sermon in Morning or Evening Prayer. Of the more than half a million sermons preached from local pulpits between 1825 and 1875 only a few have survived, but if they were at all representative they indicate that sermons tended to be long by contemporary

[1] Gregory, *Plea*, p. 11; see also Jackson, *Charge*, 1855, p. 22.
[2] At least two local parsons added their own commentary after reading the Lessons (Walker, *Tales*, p. 3).

standards. An Evangelical curate in the 1830s who timed some of his sermons recorded preaching forty-five minutes on one occasion, nearly an hour on another.[1] Of the various modes of preaching it is remarkable how many clergymen chose to preach extemporaneously. The practice was by no means confined to Evangelicals; the young High Churchman F. C. Massingberd noted in his diary in 1831 that he had 'not completely written a sermon for many months past, preaching sometimes partly and often wholly extempore'.[2] Indeed the fluency of extemporaneous speakers and preachers of all denominations was one of the wonders of the age. Preaching from notes or from prepared texts were the other alternatives, and many clergymen, like Rashdall and Massingberd, probably used all three methods at different times. Sermons preached from notes (like those of Edward Steere) were practically extemporaneous, but written ones drew criticism for their 'flowery language' and 'absurd delivery',[3] and Bishop Jackson warned specifically aginst 'theological essays' pitched over the heads of the majority of an average congregation.[4] The 'rigid and formal' style of written sermons was probably developed furthest by William Mason of Bilsby, whose sermons resembled or caricatured those of the Methodists in their mechanical construction: a text, its 'division', a conclusion, and an 'application', with clearly marked sections and subsections.[5] Another danger of written sermons was their ease of verbatim repetition, particularly during a long incumbency.[6] Far more is known about the 'production' of sermons than about their 'consumption', and the taste of the villagers can only be surmised, but very likely it was close to that of Henry Winn: he preferred sermons 'illustrating Scripture history', which had

[1] John Rashdall, Diary, 7 Oct. 1833 and 2 Feb. 1834, L.A.O. Misc. Don. 125.

[2] Diary, 13 Sept. 1831, Mass. 8/1.

[3] Rashdall's comment on a sermon he heard at Skendleby (Diary, 27 Apr. 1834).

[4] *Charge*, 1855, p. 123. Perhaps it was sermons of this kind that prompted the comments of Tennyson's 'Northern Farmer: Old Style': 'An' I hallus com'd to 's choorch An' 'eerd 'um a bummin' awaäy loike a buzzard clock ower my 'eäd, An' I niver know'd whot a meänd, but I thowt a 'ad summut to saäy'.

[5] W. Mason, *Sermons Preached in the Parish Church, Bilsby*, 1858.

[6] Joseph Spence of East Keal used the sermons that his father had preached in the same parish (Walker, *Tales*, p. 4); Arthur Wright of Gunby and Welton-le-Marsh wrote his own and re-used them repeatedly, each time recording the date and place on the first page of the sermon (MS. sermons in possession of Mr. Terence Leach, Dunholme, Lincoln).

'something rich and striking in them, which is sure to take better with the generality of hearers, than dry doctrinal subjects, over which 'tis more than ten to one, but half the congregation fall asleep'.[1]

Only in church was there a possibility of falling asleep; and perhaps not only during the sermon. For the Anglican service as a whole was conducted in a manner calculated not indeed to be soporific, but to preserve serenity and decorum. The negative aim was to avoid disturbing displays of emotion, the positive aim, decent, modest uplift. There was thus a distinctive tone and style to Anglican worship, and, since its implicit virtues of order and restraint were also social virtues, a distinctive social atmosphere. Just as the seating plan in the church recapitulated the external social hierarchy, so the tone of worship echoed certain secular values. Indeed the social manner of worship was more significant than the theological matter. This was only underlined by the contrast with Methodism. Chapel services were not only noisy, expressive, and egalitarian, they were also the setting for the 'linear' events of repentance and conversion: they challenged the 'cyclical' nature of Anglican services as well as their decorum. In an age of religious excitement and of denominational rivalry the Church's subdued and orderly devotions put it at a certain disadvantage; it was not a Methodist who asked, 'When did you ivver hear a man cry out for mercy in a church?'[2]

Yet if villagers did not cry out, neither did they always comport themselves in church as the clergy would have wished. They were reluctant to kneel for prayers, and altogether there was something casual and unreverent in their church manners. One parson was moved in the late 1860s to issue a set of instructions for them almost as if they were children:

Do not loiter or gossip on the road . . . when you have come to your accustomed seat, kneel down in private prayer . . . join in a reverent and *audible* voice in *all* those portions of the Service which belong to the

---

[1] Jackson, *Charge*, 1855, p. 23; Winn 1/1, p. 100. More to popular taste was a sermon by a Marshland clergyman on Zaccheus the Publican, in which he drew a contrast between 'the *shortness* of Zaccheus' stature, and the *height* of his impudence, and the *length* of his exactions'. It had a warm response. '"Dang it", said the churchwarden . . . "our parson hit the nail on the head today". "Blow me", responded the overseer, "don't I wish I had that *little chap's* head here, and my fist was the hammer!"' (*Stamf. Merc.*, 26 Dec. 1851).

[2] Quoted by H. D. Rawnsley, *Memories of the Tennysons*, p. 42.

congregation. Offer up all your prayers on your knees—not in a half sitting position, which is unseemly. Do not loiter on the way home.[1]

If the causes and cultural meaning of villagers' church manners can as yet hardly even be guessed at, their consequences involved a further instance of the thwarting of the clerical will by popular resistance.

The struggle was renewed on still another front in the dispute over the offertory. At the beginning of the period, according to Massingberd, there was no offertory in most churches, not even at Holy Communion, though the Prayer Book ordered a collection of alms for the poor every Sunday, whether Communion was celebrated or not.[2] The revival of the offertory therefore became part of the programme of clerical reformers. It was a difficult operation: Bishop Jackson had to assure his clergy that it was not Romish, but he had also to warn them of the greater difficulty caused by lay opposition to the practice. In the well-regulated parish of South Ormsby, F. C. Massingberd found it hard to introduce the custom even on days when the sacrament was celebrated. In many parishes it was impossible to make collections for any purpose.[3] Farmers, having already paid tithe or tithe rent-charge or rent for the glebe, as well as church rates, considered themselves sufficiently taxed by the Church. And the poor looked to the Church for benefits, not for further demands on their meagre wages. It was paradoxical that the clergy should ask the laymen for more money when the differential between their income and their average parishioners' had never been greater.

The one feature of Anglican worship that proved more amenable to clerical reformers was its music; the very thoroughness of their reforms had social as well as musical consequences. At the beginning of the period, church music consisted of metrical

---

[1] Arthur Garfit, Dunholme and neighbourhood Parish Magazine, Sept. 1868, collection of Mr. Terence Leach. Other local clergy to complain of the popular refusal to kneel were R. D. B. Rawnsley (*Sermons*, p. 193) and Massingberd (*Lectures*, p. 148).

[2] F. C. Massingberd, *A Real Diocesan Synod as the Remedy for Present Difficulties*, 1868, p. 20.

[3] Jackson, *Charge*, 1861, p. 30, and *Charge*, 1858, pp. 30-1; Massingberd, *A Real Diocesan Synod*, p. 20; A. T. Schools Questionnaire, 1855, L.A.O.

versions of the psalms, either 'the quaint and ancient doggerels of Sternhold and Hopkins' or 'the less poetical even if more modern psalms of Tate and Brady'.[1] Each line was first read out by the parish clerk (for the benefit of the illiterate) and then sung —ideally by the whole congregation, but all too often by the parish clerk alone—to the accompaniment of the band of instrumentalists perched in the west gallery. It was later recalled

at the giving of each hymn, how Sampson, the village blacksmith, would clear up and give a general signal for all to make ready; how first fiddle would pass round the rosin; how a little time was devoted to screwing up and sounding; after about ten minutes passed in the above operations, and some half-dozen slaps with the pitch-fork against the pulpit to find the key-note, away went the choir at a snail's gallop![2]

A 'Village Parson in the District' recalled 'with a shudder the village singing in the good old times':

How the parish clerk used to give out (murdering the Queen's English in every word he spoke) four dreary verses from Tate and Brady; how the premonitory scrape on the fiddle used to warn us of the coming storm; how the discordant notes of viol, trombone, clarionet, sackbut, psaltery, dulcimer, and all kinds of music, the nasal twangs of the untrained rustics would make still more hideous a tune hideous at the best; how the most absurd—not to say, blasphemous—ideas would be suggested by the senseless division of words; how we would hail with delight the conclusion of the last verse, and ... relapse into dumb despair as, according to immemorial usage, the verse was repeated with redoubled energy.[3]

Beginning in the 1840s the clergy embarked upon an ambitious reform programme intended to suppress the bands in the west gallery and replace them with choirs in the chancel; they also demoted the parish clerks and installed barrel organs (replacing them later with harmoniums). The final stroke was to introduce hymns, in an effort to encourage congregational singing. (Older High Churchmen like Archdeacon Bonney had dismissed hymns as mere human creations, not found in the Bible, and debarred them from Anglican worship.)[4] In principle the new music was

[1] *Louth Adv.*, 28 Nov. 1863.
[2] *Mkt Rasen W.M.*, 18 Nov. 1865.
[3] *Louth Adv.*, 18 Apr. 1863.
[4] H. K. Bonney, 'Sacred Music and Psalmody Considered', in *Practical Sermons* by 'Dignitaries and Other Clergymen of the United Church of England and Ireland', 1846, p. 23.

more beautiful, more varied, and more congregational than the old, but in practice results were mixed. The unmelodic clerk was often replaced not by a hearty congregational chorus but by a choir that provoked what was no more than a new version of the old complaint: 'How miserably is our service misrepresented by a duet between the clergyman and the choir, one, perhaps both, not reading or singing very devoutly.' Congregations simply refused to sing; and so the best that could be said for the changes was that 'if village singing is not yet a treat, it is at any rate no longer a nuisance'.[1]

This modest improvement in church music was not accomplished without social disruption. It affected not only the bands but also the parish clerks, whose decline, which had begun as long ago as the Civil Wars, now entered its final stages. Yet their role was not limited to music; it was their duty 'to take charge of the Church . . . to ring the Bell on a Sunday . . . to set out the Books or place the cushions for either the reading desk, the altar, or the pulpit . . . to unlock the church doors, or to see that they are safely locked, after the different services.'[2] For this they were paid £1 to £5 a year (£2 gave a freehold voting qualification) plus fees for assisting with marriages, churchings, and burials. When the clergyman was resident, he could usually appoint his own parish clerk, but when non-resident, the choice was made by the vestry, i.e. the farmers. In the latter case, parish clerks were frequently elected primarily 'with a regard to parochial economy. . . . Poverty is made the chief qualification.'[3] Indeed in 1851 most were labourers in their later years.[4]

The parish clerks had survived the first round of musical reform—they had mastered the barrel organ—but the advent of the harmonium and the organ made them all but obsolete.[5] With

---

[1] Steere, *Notes of Sermons*, iii. 41; *Louth Adv.*, 18 Apr. 1863. Local evidence thus supports the conclusions of Owen Chadwick, *The Victorian Church*, Part I, 1966, p. 520.

[2] Hobart to Kaye, 19 Feb. 1844, Cor. B. 5/4/117/7. This was at Nocton in Kesteven but applies as well to south Lindsey.

[3] Field Flowers, *A Plan for Increasing the Usefulness of Parish Clerks in Small Country Villages*, 1829, pp. 4–5. (Flowers was incumbent of Tealby.) The same point was made by a curate at Saxilby: Stockdale to Kaye, 21 Apr. [?1834], Cor. B. 5/4/114/9.

[4] Of thirty-two parish clerks identified in the 1851 Census, twenty-three were labourers and four were cottagers; half were over 60 and a further quarter were in their 50s.

[5] P. H. Ditchfield, *The Parish Clerk*, 1907, pp. 61–2.

few exceptions—Henry Winn held his post at Fulletby for seventy-six years until his death in 1914—they were a disappearing race by the late 1860s.[1] Nevertheless, the musical reasons for their decline were perhaps not the only ones. The traditional parish clerks, irredeemably plebeian and rustic, could hardly rise up to the polished and dignified tone that new-style clergy desired in church services; and they preserved a certain measure of control over the pattern of worship, an independence from clerical direction—attested in many an anecdote—that was incompatible with clerical sovereignty. Thus while their departure was justified by musical reasons it was not unwelcome to the clergy on other grounds.

The parish clerks' musical colleagues, the west gallery instrumentalists, met a similar fate, and for similar reasons. Reformers criticized their musical shortcomings and introduced the harmoniums and organs that seemed to make them obsolete. But as in the case of the parish clerks there were non-musical considerations as well. The west gallery bands were if anything even more independent of clerical control: they were 'petty tyrants in matters musical ... feared and respected by parson and people alike'.[2] Their position depended upon their own technical ability—and once they started playing, they could not easily be stopped. Clergymen asserting their control over every other aspect of church life were bound to be irritated by the autonomy of the orchestras and unlikely to shed many tears for them. The departure of the orchestras and the parish clerks upset the traditional balance between parson and congregation: the parson was now what he had not been before, sole and unchallenged master in the church. For the organists who succeeded the parish clerks and village bands—chiefly wives and daughters of parsons, squires, and farmers—were much less independent than their predecessors and far more likely to be subservient to the clergyman.

The second great innovation in church music, besides the organ, was the choir. It was intended to magnify the role of the congregation in worship, but its practical results were less clear. The many parishes with small populations could not recruit enough singers to form a choir at all; while the choirs that did

---

[1] *Retf. News*, 12 Dec. 1868. Winn's extraordinary span in office is recorded in the inscription on his gravestone in Fulletby churchyard.
[2] K. H. Macdermott, *The Old Church Gallery Minstrels*, 1948, p. 1.

exist were very largely composed of women, and thus increased the role of women rather than that of the congregation as a whole. A local newspaper noted in 1867 that there were 'few men in the country choirs of Lincolnshire', and detailed evidence supports this conclusion.[1] At a choir festival at Holton Beckering in 1864 tenors were scarce and basses totally absent, and at a Festival of Parochial Choirs in 1869, attended mostly by country choirs, there were 448 'Melodists' or sopranos, 197 altos, 77 tenors, and 118 basses—more than three female singers to every male. Ten south Lindsey parishes were represented at the Festival, their choirs totalling 137 members, 3·5 per cent of their combined population of 3,947. In an 'average' parish of 395 people, there would have been only one tenor, two basses, three altos, and eight sopranos. At another festival in 1870 four parishes from the Till basin region were represented; the choirs, which formed 3·3 per cent of the total population of the parishes, contained sixty-two women and only fourteen men.[2] The sexual imbalance is made still more impressive when it is recalled that men formed a majority of the adult village population.

Whether the changes in church music resulted in real improvement is not easy to determine: the singing congregation seems no more in evidence at the end of the period than at the beginning. There had been, however, important changes in the *social* structure of Anglican worship. As a consequence of the replacement of parish clerks and west gallery bands by organists and choirs, there was a shift from the group apparently composed entirely of males[3] to one predominantly female. (This closely paralleled the replacement of farm by domestic servants in the households of new-style farmers, who, like the clergy, were also seeking a more genteel style of life.) This was at the same time a shift from a group drawn from the ranks of labourers and craftsmen to one with a larger representation from the higher social ranks. And the clergy also shifted the balance decisively away from their congregations to themselves. Whatever the wishes of the villagers, Anglican services became more dignified, more feminine, and more clerical.

[1] *Mkt Rasen W.M.*, 5 Oct. 1867.
[2] ibid., 11 June 1864; *Lincs. Chronicle*, 25 June 1869; *Retf. News*, 18 June 1870.
[3] Though women could hold the office of parish clerk, no instances of this have come to light in south Lindsey. The west gallery also was a male preserve.

They also became more numerous. In the first half of the century, when the average clergyman served more than one parish, most churches had only a single service on Sunday. After 1850 the decline in pluralism and non-residence made possible a second service.

Frequency of Services in Parish Churches.

	Monthly	fort- nightly	One per Sunday	One and two alter- nately	Two per Sunday	Three per Sunday	Two on summer Sundays One on winter Sundays
1830	1	12	199	1	7	0	0
1851	0	1	170	3	45	0	3
1873	0	0	85	8	121	3	4

If south Lindsey was like the rest of the diocese, the second service was adopted on a large scale in the middle 1850s, at the urging of Bishop Jackson.[1]

The second service, it was argued, would allow those who were prevented by domestic duties from attending the morning service—servants, mothers with infants—to attend in the afternoon. Yet even if no one came, a second service was urged for the sake of the parson's self-respect—a single service had 'the appearance of a reluctant discharge of an irksome task'.[2] The most serious argument was that the absence of a second service in the past had encouraged the growth of Methodism and that its introduction would help draw Methodists back into the chuch.[3]

The experiment, which was more appropriate in towns than in villages, was only moderately successful. At West Keal, H. J. Ingilby 'really was tired of preaching to empty pews on one part of the day. The people of my parish will not attend twice'. At Kettlethorpe, it worked well from March to November, but during the winter, the 'way to the church being very wet, I have found that more people on the average have attended (for the

---

[1] Specula, SPE 10 and 18, Diocesan records; Jackson, *Charge*, 1855, p. 11; *Charge*, 1858, p. 6.

[2] Gregory, *Plea*, p. 8. John Carr of Brattleby employed an assistant curate to take the afternoon service, for he 'had a strong presentiment that if he ever preached twice one Sunday he should die'—which proved true when the curate's illness forced him to take both services (*Lincoln Journal*, 22 Jan. 1861). On the morning of the fatal day, he wrote the registration of his own death (Hill, *Victorian Lincoln*, p. 174, n. 1).

[3] Kaye, *Works*, vii. 255; Gregory, *Plea*, p. 12.

three winter months) with one service than when I had two'. The introduction of the second service at South Ormsby meant that 'a very good congregation has been divided into two rather scanty ones'.[1] The second service, which generally began at 2 or 2.30 p.m., would undoubtedly have been still less successful if it had been offered in the evening—the prime time for the Methodists. Whether from prudence or from love of ease, the parsons conceded the evening service without a fight.

If church-going had ever been automatic and unanimous, it was no longer, and church attendance was affected by a variety of social circumstances. Attendances were higher in summer than in winter; one parson put them highest in summer and autumn, lowest in spring, intermediate in winter.[2] The reasons for this probably include the cold weather and the discomfort of unheated churches in winter, but it is odd that the major phase of the liturgical year, from Advent to Trinity Sunday, should have been the period of lowest attendance. At any time of year the afternoon service was generally better attended than the morning service. On the Sunday of the Religious Census (30 March 1851), adults attending church in the morning were 12·5 per cent of the total population of their parishes, compared with 20·7 per cent in the afternoon.[3] In the twenty-nine churches offering two services there were adult congregations of 1,259 in the morning but 2,343 in the afternoon. Those for whom church attendance was a social obligation were content to attend one service only.

The farmers ... with their families, very commonly make a point of attending the single service; they look upon it as necessary for keeping up their respectability, as giving a countenance to religion, as paying a compliment to their clergyman, as setting a good example to the poorer portion of the parish ... as proving their churchmanship.[4]

Farmers seem to have preferred the morning service; at Willoughby it was well attended by 'all the respectable farmers and their families in the neighbourhood, but the prayers in the afternoon are entirely neglected'.[5] It may be inferred that the after-

---

[1] Ingilby to Kaye, 17 July 1830, Cor. B. 5/4/125/7; Atkinson to Kaye, 19 June 1850, Cor. B. 5/4/9/7; Massingberd to Kaye, 10 June 1833, Cor. B. 5/4/84/3.
[2] Comments by incumbents of Goulceby, Scremby and Welton-le-Wold in the Religious Census, H.O. 129/429/1, 430/1 and 431/1, P.R.O.
[3] Calculated from the original returns, H.O. 129/428–32, 434, P.R.O.
[4] Gregory, *Plea*, p. 8.
[5] DuPré to Kaye, 12 Feb. 1832, Cor. B. 5/4/7/1.

noon service was attended by a higher proportion of the poor than the morning service; labourers, after six days of work, may well have enjoyed a late lie-in on the day of rest, and would have preferred the afternoon service. The disparity between morning and afternoon attendances suggests that many poorer people attended church fortnightly at best, perhaps only monthly.

Still another factor tending to reduce attendance, especially in the afternoon, was the need to attend to farm animals. On Census Sunday several clergymen explained small attendances by pointing out that it was 'the very height of the lambing season' and that 'the sheep require attendance day and night'.[1] The regions with the highest populations of farm animals were the Marshes, and it was there that the demands of animals interfered most with church attendance. At Addlethorpe and Ingoldmells, in the Outer Marsh, the houses were 'widely scattered, and principally occupied by graziers or shepherds, who from situation or requisite attention to the sheep and cattle are very rarely able to attend at church more than once on a Sunday'. The afternoon service was the one most affected: afternoon congregations (16·9 per cent of the population) in Outer Marsh churches on Census Sunday were only slightly larger than morning ones (15 per cent). At Mumby the morning congregation was 'almost always the larger one' and the rector of Willoughby noted with regret that 'the farmers in these marshy districts consider the Sunday afternoon, after they have been at church in the morning, as their own; and they invariably visit either their friends, or their distant stock.'[2] And boys hired by farmers in these regions to 'tent' cattle worked all day Sunday and never got to church at all.

Further analysis of church attendance is based on the original returns of the Religious Census of 1851, to which several references have already been made. As a source it is both indispensable and seriously flawed. Some of the returns (considering now those of the Church of England only) are clearly estimates—rounded figures—and clearly too high. More serious, many are missing, the clergymen apparently forgetful of their duties in a

---

[1] Entries for High Toynton and Swaby, H.O. 129/429/2 and 431/1.

[2] Residents of Addlethorpe and Ingoldmells to Kaye, n.d. [?1835], Cor. B. 5/4/30/1; entry for Mumby, H.O. 129/430/2; DuPré to Kaye, 15 Feb. 1832, Cor. B. 5/4/7/1.

state church; a few actually refused the information.[1] For over a quarter of the churches the return either gave no figures for attendance on Census Sunday or was omitted altogether. In some cases there was a failure to distinguish between the general (adult) congregation and Sunday scholars. And unfortunately no attempt was made to collect information on the sex composition of church attendants.

Still, it yields much of substance. Perhaps the least problematic finding is the pattern of services. There were morning services in ninety-five parishes, afternoon services in ninety-three, and evening services in two parishes. Most churches only offered a single service: sixty-four in the monring and the same number in the afternoon; there were morning and afternoon services in twenty-nine parishes, morning and evening services in two.

Figures for church attendance survive for churches in parishes whose total population was 43,871, or just over two-thirds the population of the whole area in 1851. Total adult attendances amounted to 9,472, which was 21·6 per cent of the total population, or about a third of the estimated adult population aged 15 and over.

As has been mentioned, congregations were larger in the afternoon than in the morning; this was true in every region (though the difference was small in the Outer Marsh), in every parish type, and in parishes of every level of population.

The level of attendance was strongly related to the size of population: a much higher percentage of the population attended church in small parishes than in large.[2]

Size of population	Morning	Afternoon
1–199	22·2%	34·5%
200–599	12·9	20·3
600–	7·4	13·7

And it was in the very smallest parishes, with populations under 100, that the levels of attendance were highest.[3] The differential

[1] The rector of Scampton considered the questions 'unnecessarily inquisitorial' (H.O. 129/428/3).

[2] This was also the case in rural Leicestershire, where the general level of church attendance seems to have been considerably higher (David Thompson, 'The Churches and Society in Leicestershire, 1851–1881', unpublished Ph.D. thesis, University of Cambridge, 1969, p. 58).

[3] Morning attendances were 29·2 per cent of the population, afternoon attendances 41·8 per cent.

between large and small parishes is only slightly reduced by the fact that there were relatively more children in open parishes.

When attendance is analysed according to parish type, the results are as 'theory' would predict: the more open the parish, the lower the level of attendance.

Parish Type and Church Attendance as a Percentage of Total Population

Parish Type	Morning	Afternoon
A	18·6	26·1
B	15·9	25·2
C	8·1	16·4
D	9·4	18·2

But close parishes were generally smaller in population than open parishes: how much of the variation should be attributed to the open–close distinction and how much to the difference in size? If the figures for open parishes are compared with those for close parishes in the same population range,[1] the tentative conclusion is that attendance was affected more by the size of population than by parish type: but from a different perspective it is clear that the size of population itself was highly correlated with parish type.

Church attendance was also higher in parishes with resident squires than in squireless parishes of the same size, both in the morning and in the afternoon (in churches with only one service). This was especially true of the morning service. In seven of nine squires' parishes enjoying two services, attendances were above average in the morning but below average in the afternoon. It would seem that when respectability was a prime motive for attending church, one attendance on a Sunday sufficed, and that preferably in the morning.

Regional comparisons unfortunately are difficult to make because so many returns are lacking, and only comparisons between groups of parishes of the same level of population are meaningful. Most of the regional figures do not deviate strikingly from the general averages; and the deviations that do occur are not consistently in the same direction for the same region. On the basis of rather imperfect evidence it would

[1] Figures were available for morning congregations in eleven parishes whose population was between 300 and 399 and in twelve parishes in the 400–499 group, and for afternoon congregations of fifteen parishes in the 400–499 group.

appear that regional influence *per se* was not of great importance, though it would require better data and formal statistical methods to reach more than a tentative conclusion. This is not, however, to say that there were no differences from region to region; regions varied considerably in the proportions of their population in small parishes and large parishes, and they consequently varied in their over-all level of church attendance. The South Wolds, for example, where a high proportion lived in small parishes, had a higher level of church attendance than the Outer Marsh, where most lived in large open parishes.

Throughout the discussion, the figures for attendance have been those of adult congregations. In small parishes, too small to maintain a separate Sunday school, the figures for the 'general' congregation probably included some children. Sunday schools in the middle of the century still taught secular as well as religious subjects, and attendance at Sunday school therefore cannot be considered a purely religious act.[1] In any event, Sunday scholars raised the percentage of the total population attending church in the morning from 12·5 to 19·4, and in the afternoon from 20·7 to 26·8—not enough to alter significantly the general pattern.

The final impression is one of a low to middling level of church attendance. On the most favourable calculation—that in churches and Sunday schools with two services the congregations were completely different—total attendances amounted to about 31 per cent of total population, though the number of attendants was of course somewhat lower. The insoluble problem of 'twicers' can be avoided by excluding the thirty-one churches in which there were two services—by counting (adult) attendances, then, only at churches offering a single service. This calculation yields the result that 16·4 per cent of the population attended churches open in the morning, 23·9 per cent in the afternoon; or about 27 per cent of the adult population in the morning and about 38 per cent in the afternoon. These are clearly far from indicating majority practice—the majority, at least, did not attend weekly. Those who could attend only in the afternoon may have been regular fortnightly attendants at churches where the single service alternated between morning and afternoon, but even if

[1] David Thompson, 'The 1851 Religious Census: Problems and Possibilities', *Victorian Studies*, ii (1967), p. 90.

everyone who was absent in the morning appeared regularly in the afternoon, they could have attended no more frequently than once a month. If 30 March 1851 was anything like a typical Sunday, church attendance was customary for a large minority of the village population, but not a majority.

About the motives that led people to attend—or not to attend—church, little is known, or perhaps can be known. For farmers, church attendance was essential in 'keeping up their respectability', but labourers' motives are less clear. Large congregations on Good Friday are explained by the farmers' custom of giving their men a paid holiday, on the understanding that they attended church that afternoon: in one village at least, for some labourers it was the only time they went to church, and one old labourer on the Ancaster estate was said never to go to church except on Good Friday and other days 'when he is paid'.[1] Perhaps a more common motive among the poor was to show their respect for the parson, a 'deferential type of attendance which often was coupled with attendance at chapel in the evening. As Edward Steere, curate at Skegness, was told by one of his parishioners, '"We comes to church in the morning to please you, Sir, and goes to chapel at night to save our souls"'.[2] In general it was 'but too true that by far the greater proportion of the poorer people who come to church, in places where there is only one service, go regularly to the meeting-house as well'.[3] Indeed it was a commonplace that most who attended church also attended chapel; those who attended either exclusively were a small minority. In any event three types of motive for church attendance can be identified, corresponding to the three times of day in which services were held. In the morning service the characteristic attendant was the squire or farmer anxious to keep up his respectability; in the afternoon it was the poorer people, showing their respect for the parson; the rare evening services were for the few who were poor and pious but not Methodist. Local evidence therefore supports Abraham Hume's view of the morning service as the 'service of necessity', the afternoon as the 'service

---

[1] This was at Scremby (H. W. Haxby, Diary, 26 Mar. 1869 and 7 Apr. 1871, L. A. O. Thimbleby 4/11); Findlay to Kennedy, 8 Feb. 1859, 3 ANC 7/23/76/29.

[2] Heanley, *Memoir*, p. 49. Helen Dale observed that in the Sausthorpe neighbourhood in the South Wolds 'the church was attended on occasions to soothe the squire or parson' (*Life and Letters of Thomas Pelham Dale*, ii. 106).

[3] Gregory, *Plea*, p. 13.

of convenience', and the evening service as the 'service of devotion'.[1]

THE HARVEST THANKSGIVING

If the clergy's larger aim had been to rebuild their congregations, they appear on the whole not to have had the results they might have hoped for. Villagers were largely unresponsive to their efforts and appeals, and the numbers of regular attenders and of communicants showed no substantial increase. Their one success came not in the traditional Prayer Book services but in a nineteenth-century innovation: the harvest thanksgiving. Adopted locally around 1860, it spread fast in the following decade and proved universally popular—with all varieties of churchmanship and with clergy and laity alike.[2] What is significant is not merely that it became popular, but the sources and contexts of its popularity, social as well as religious.

At its least elaborate, it was simply a special designation for the regular Sunday service, but usually it achieved a higher degree of ceremonial and was a separate service in its own right. Held on a weekday, it almost always began with a procession, with clergy, Sunday scholars, and villagers all taking part. The church having been decorated with harvest motifs, there was a morning service, often including a celebration of Holy Communion. The collection was devoted to a worthy cause like the County Hospital or the Lancashire cotton workers during the cotton famine or the wounded in the Franco–Prussian War. In the afternoon, the parson joined the squire (if there was one in the parish) and the farmers in providing a dinner for the labourers and working lads; the toasts struck the predominant note of paternalism—and of deference. Women and children received a tea, sometimes a more substantial 'knife and fork tea'. There were games and then perhaps another service. In the evening there was sometimes dancing; a more modern touch appeared at Gayton-le-Marsh in 1868, when the entertainment consisted of a magic lantern and lecture. The day's events concluded with 'God Save the Queen'. This combination of ritual and recreation in a communal setting—

---

[1] A. Hume, quoted by W. S. F. Pickering, 'The 1851 Religious Census—a Useless Experiment?', *British Journal of Sociology*, xviii (1967), p. 390.

[2] Down to 1875 at least it was, however, still a recognizably clerical affair, initiated and shaped from above. Its declension from thanksgiving to festival, and its emergence as the supreme popular religious holiday, were later developments.

'Merrie England' was the later term for it—had an immediate impact. After the first harvest thanksgiving at Rand, the old clerk, who had lived in the parish sixty years, confirmed that '"never in his time had there been such a grand do-ment"'.[1]

Among the clergy the earliest advocates of the service were High Churchmen. But it was also taken up by Evangelicals—just as frequent Communion was, and in much the same period. By 1870 Evangelicals like Field Flowers of Tealby and Edmund Haskins of Stow had introduced it in their parishes: to be sure without the intoning or the 'fully choral' service favoured by their High Church brethren.[2] The Evangelical style was apparent at Fulletby in 1870, where 'the decorations in the church were simple and effective, without any admixture of ecclesiastical symbolism'.[3]

The acceptability of the harvest thanksgiving to all shades of churchmanship may have owed something to the fact that its predominant symbolism, whether ecclesiastical or not, had so little to do with Christianity. Church decorations intimated at best a secondary role for the orthodox faith; at Little Steeping in 1859 there was on the altar 'a sheaf of wheat, the first cut in the neighbourhood, with a cross of bright flowers pinned on it' and 'a wreath of ivy with seeds growing out of it went round the bottom of the Altar on the floor'. And at Rand in 1863 the procession of clergy and choir to the church was headed by a labourer bearing not a cross or a banner but 'a sheaf of the finest wheat'.[4] If the script of the church service was orthodox, the props and decorations were heretical: they expressed the divine creativity not so much of God as of Nature. It would be inaccurate to call this secularization, for this was still a religious act engaging religious feelings; it was, however, religious in a pagan and not a Christian sense.

As a religious phenomenon the harvest thanksgiving reflected contemporary concerns only to the extent that it was part of a larger growth in moderate ritualism. It was rather as a social phenomenon that it belonged to a particular time and place.

[1] *Louth Adv.*, 12 Sept. 1868; *Mkt Rasen W.M.*, 26 Sept. 1863.

[2] *Mkt Rasen W.M.*, 10 Sept. 1870; *Retf. News*, 26 Sept. 1868.

[3] *Hornc. News*, 24 Sept. 1870.

[4] Edward to Ann Steere, 8 Aug. 1859, in David Neave, 'Letters of Edward Steere', *Lincolnshire History and Archaeology*, no. 2 (1967), p. 69; *Mkt Rasen W.M.*, 26 Sept. 1863.

Harvest thanksgivings were orderly and peaceful—like other public occasions after 1860 such as friendly society anniversaries, and statute fairs, but unlike the old harvest homes. Not only were the new celebrations marked by 'loyalty and temperance', they also began in the parish church (as did friendly society anniversaries)—'while in former times the idea would have found no favour'.[1] Another contrast with the past was that the harvest thanksgiving was organized—either by the parson alone or with the assistance of squire and farmers—rather than 'spontaneous'. And while the harvest home had been a purely local affair, the harvest service (like the farmers' revived harvest suppers) tended to connect villagers with the larger society: the collection during the service was devoted to some outside cause, and the 'loyal toasts' and 'patriotic songs' at the dinner fostered a civic or national rather than parochial consciousness. But what above all marked the harvest thanksgiving as a phenomenon of the 1860s was its close association with the revived harvest suppers of the 'era of good feeling': both sprang from the same desire to express and create a social harmony after the unmediated conflicts of the previous decades.

The introduction of the harvest thanksgiving in the 1860s thus situates itself in two distinct contexts, one long-term and religious, the other short-term and social. By giving ritual expression to the sense of the creative powers of Nature it filled a gap in the Church's rites and festivals that had lasted since the Reformation. Yet while meeting an age-old need of an agricultural people it also responded to a particular social conjuncture. The mood of the 1860s was set in large measure by the return of agricultural prosperity in the 'Golden Age', which encouraged new-style farmers to take a more relaxed if more manipulative approach to class relations. It is not difficult to see the harvest thanksgiving as a response to the same mood and moment: a parallel and complement to the harvest supper, with confident new-style clergy in association with the farmers. In both the thanksgiving and the supper, class divisions were overlaid by a willed appearance of communal solidarity. But while the supper did little else, and did not survive the passing of prosperity (and the advent of the unions), this was only secondary and temporary in the thanksgiving, which by articulating villagers' pagan senti-

[1] *Hornc. News*, 24 Sept. 1870; *Louth Adv.*, 8 Aug. 1863.

ments towards Nature found the basis for a more enduring popularity.

PASTORALIA

If the clergyman's primary role was to perform rites and services, no one denied the importance of his pastoral duty. But the nature of that duty, and of the clerical authority that lay behind it, was unclear. Did the parson merely lead and guide his flock, or did he exercise spiritual authority over them? Was he a shepherd —or a director of souls? The question had apparently been answered by the Reformation, which rejected the Roman Catholic sacrament of penance and severely weakened the discipline of the confessional and of public penitence. Yet as long as ecclesiastical and secular courts enforced the Church's moral code, the parish priest could still consider it his duty to name sinners and turn them over to the courts: this indeed was integral to the pastoral theology of a George Herbert. But when it too declined, pastoral authority was diminished, for lack of either ecclesiastical or secular means of enforcement.

By the nineteenth century the clergy's rising incomes and status (and to some extent their magistracies) partly compensated for the loss of coercive pastoral authority, but they were no less aware that that authority no longer was theirs, and a minority actually envisioned recovering it. This did not include many Evangelicals: Archdeacon Kaye assured churchwardens that the Church had no desire to revive the old 'presentments of persons violating the laws of our holy religion'. Yet even his father, the bishop, while granting that the Church 'assumes to itself no dominion over the consciences of men', nevertheless recognized that since the sixteenth century it had felt 'the want of a penitential discipline'; and he went on to urge the revival of excommunication without temporal penalty, in order to end the confusion regarding the propriety of a church burial for notorious sinners.[1] High Churchmen and Anglo-Catholics went further. Keble and others sought to revive private confession in order to penetrate the souls of their rustic parishioners; Bishop King regretted that

---

[1] W. F. J. Kaye, *Sermon ... at the Visitation in May, 1859*, 1859, p. 6; J. Kaye, *Works*, vi. 151, and vii. 317–19. Edward Steere (*Notes of Sermons*, ii. 51) urged the revival of excommunication for the more precise purpose of refusing 'sinners' the sacrament.

'we have no discipline to enforce the rule of Communion three times a year on all our parishioners'.[1] Other High Churchmen hoped to separate the sheep from the goats by compiling a list—and posting it on the church door—of those who communicated the mandatory three times a year and attended church at least one Sunday in three. But this was a lost cause, the hopes unrealistic. As one shrewd villager observed, 'The fact is she [the Church] has not the authority to enforce the old discipline, and this she well knows.'[2] Indeed Anglican discipline was much inferior to that of the Methodists, though the parsons perversely accused the Methodists of lawlessness. The Wesleyan circuit superintendent had—and used—the power to remove a member's name from the books by a stroke of the pen, a power no bishop or parson could rival. In gaining wealth and status the clergy also gained new social influence over the laity; but influence did not satisfy them, for it was a poor substitute for the authority which their predecessors had enjoyed and which they found it impossible to recapture.

Lacking the means of spiritual and legal coercion, the clergy looked instinctively to the possessors of social and economic power: the landlords. An example from the parish of Torksey shows how natural it was for the clergy to invoke the temporal arm. The curate, troubled by the advances made by the Primitive Methodists, asked the principal landowner, Lord Brownlow, to buy up a few cottages not already in his hands which were used by the Primitive Methodists as a place of worship and Sunday school: 'It would facilitate materially the getting rid of that sect, and by that means the putting an end to the only existing Sunday school.' Nevertheless the alliance between parson and squire was not automatic. The chief resident owner at South Reston became a Wesleyan local preacher and threw his influence against the Church; the chief landlord of Donington, the non-resident owner of a third of the parish, 'does not contribute 6d. to any charitable purpose connected with the parish'. The owner of the parish of Kirkstead and patron of the donative even refused to pay the clergyman a stipend. Local magnates declined to contribute towards the salary of the schoolmaster of Low Toynton, arguing that they had no land in the parish. But within his parish a resident

[1] King, *Charge*, 1886, p. 92.
[2] Winn, Diary, 25 Feb. 1846, Winn 1/1.

squire generally considered himself master and he would seldom
be resisted by the parson, nor by the archdeacon or the bishop.
When the desecration of the churchyard at Well was brought to
their attention, they felt powerless: 'Mr. Dashwood does as he
pleases there from time immemorial.'[1]

The power of the landlord was particularly felt when he came
into conflict with the Church over financial matters. At Tathwell,
where the incumbent of over fifty years was a relation of the
squire (and a sufferer from 'mental debility'), 'from neglect, or
ignorance, if not from deference to family Interests and Connections, a very inadequate Consideration had been taken from the
Tithes'. The interests of the Church evidently were subordinated
to those of the family. The Church was again the loser in the
commutation of tithes at Broxholme: 'the patron of the living
being the sole proprietor, it is reasonable to suppose that he would
have the best of the bargain with the Rector.'[2]

Parsons and squires did work together, but any particular
alliance was vulnerable to disruption when the squire died or
sold out. As the incumbent of Manby complained, 'nearly the
whole of this parish, owing to the death of my valued friend Mr.
Welfitt, has been lately divided and sold in lots and been bought
by Dissenters, many of whom never enter the church'. The sale
of half the parish of Driby around 1868 was disastrous for the
Church interest: it was now 'owned and occupied by non-residents, who take no interest in Church matters in the parish,
give no subscriptions to Church objects, usually engage Non-
conformist foremen and labourers, and change them so frequently that it is very difficult indeed to obtain any influence
over them, while as far as they were able they have got rid of the
Church people who were in the parish before'.[3]

In most parishes, though, the absence of a resident squire
compelled the clergy reluctantly to adopt different strategies.
The incumbent of Willoughby spoke for many in complaining

[1] Torksey: Allcroft to Kaye, 2 May 1848, Cor. B. 5/4/85/1; South Reston: Harrison to Kaye, 9 Jan. 1837, Cor. B. 5/4/90/4; Donington: Mossman to Kaye, 18 Oct.
1850, Cor. B. 5/4/14/2; Kirkstead: Robinson to Kaye, 19 Jan. 1844, Cor. B.
5/4/19/12; Low Toynton: Kennedy to Kaye, 12 Apr. 1852, Cor. B. 5/4/105/8;
Well: Goddard to Kaye, Report on Spring 1830 Visitation, Cor. B. 5/15.
[2] Waite to Kaye, 20 July 1841, Cor. B. 5/4/56/2; Penny to Tithe Commissioners,
4 Feb. 1840, I.R. 18/4799.
[3] Manby, 1873 V.R. Driby, 1866 V.R.

that there was 'not one inhabitant here beyond the rank of farmer; no resident gentleman who by his property, influence and charity, could assist and cooperate with me in promoting the spiritual and temporal welfare of my parishioners'.[1] Country parsons had come to expect in their parishes the social equivalent of Protection, and were ill at ease in conditions of free trade.

Lacking the means of coercion, whether ecclesiastical or secular, they had to rely upon their own powers of influence and persuasion. Yet the pastoral role was in principle a broad one, as they were continually being reminded. Bishop Jackson pointed out, in his primary visitation, that

The key-stone of our Church's system is the residence of the parochial Clergy. That each Parish should have its own pastor, authorized to preach the word of God in the Parish Church, to whom is committed the cure and government of the souls of the Parishioners, who is to live among them and with them, to visit them in their homes as well as to minister to them in public, and thus to be familiar with their individual characters, wants and trials, and enabled to adapt his instructions, warning and encouragement to each—this is the ideal.

Active pastoral care, Archdeacon Bayley noted more concisely, should extend from 'the cradle to the grave'.[2]

The chief instrument of pastoral care was house-to-house visiting, which ranked second in importance only to preaching. Yet the repeated exhortations from bishops and others suggest that many of the clergy were neglecting their pastoral duty: one local parson specifically reminded his colleagues that it was important to visit even 'the humblest . . . though the usages of society may make this at first somewhat difficult'.[3] The accepted object of pastoral visitation, particularly in the first half of the century, was to promote the 'spiritual and temporal welfare' of the parishioners, with as much emphasis on the 'temporal' as on the 'spiritual'. Whatever else he did, a clergyman visiting a poor family was expected to promote their temporal welfare by leaving them some money. If John Rashdall was typical, clergymen in the 1830s were leaving half a crown in an ordinary visit—more than a

[1] DuPré to Kaye, 23 Sept. 1851, Cor. B. 5/4/152.
[2] Jackson, *Charge*, 1855, p. 10; Bayley, *Charge*, p. 28.
[3] J. B. Smith, *The Consistency and Faithfulness of Ministerial Character*, 1840, pp. 14–15. Parsons were urged not to wait to be sent for by the sick, but to get there ahead of the Methodists (Bayley, *Charge*, p. 27).

farm labourer received from a full day's work.[1] Indeed the
temporal benefits of pastoral visitation may well have been more
highly appreciated than the spiritual: at Ormsby and Driby, F. C.
Massingberd found that his 'visits among the poor (at Driby
especially) seem to be productive only of discontent with their
Parish, and perhaps hypocrisy towards me'. He questioned
whether it might be more expedient 'to confine oneself to education, visitation of the sick, and attention to their bodily comforts,
leaving religion to sermons and books'.[2]

The clergy indeed were recognized targets for the needy and
the importunate, like the struggling freeholders at Mumby who
'think every charity is due from the vicar'.[3] A more general view
of the Church as a source of 'temporal welfare' was expounded
by an inmate in the Kirton House of Correction (in north Lindsey), in a letter to his wife:

It is all very good for the Methodistical rascals to give the kids some
toggery, but by all means get under the wings of the Cormorants of
Mother Church—who are wide awake and will deal more bounteously
with you—as they are more adept at fleecing the natives.

He advised her to send their son 'to the largest house in the
parish, as it is sure to be a parson's, and get his maw filled'.
Finally, thinking of the distribution of alms to the poor, he
hoped that 'the ensuing *Easter* will be of profit to you'.[4] This
attitude could not have surprised the clergy: their liberality had
practically encouraged it. Indeed there was a kind of contract
between the clergy and the poor: the right of the poor to receive
exacted the duty of the clergy to give—a duty inherent in the
office and not a matter of personal choice. And the benefits were
not limited to charity. The demand for private baptism, particularly in the first half of the century, rested on the popular
view that the clergy should be not only in but at the service of
their parishioners. The assumption was, as one parson wrote
indignantly, 'that any parishioner can *claim the attendance of the
Clergyman at whatever hour he chooses, and demand his Services*'.[5] By
the middle of the century this was evidently a lay rather than a

[1] Rashdall, Diary, 30 Nov. 1833 and 19 Jan. 1834, Misc. Don. 125, L.A.O.
[2] Mass. 8/1, 30 Jan. 1827.
[3] Mumby, A.T. Schools Questionnaire 1855, L.A.O.
[4] Quoted in Anderson to Wilberforce, 20 Oct. 1856, Bodl. MSS. Wilberforce.
[5] Sutton to Kaye, 27 Nov. 1848, Cor. B. 5/4/115/11.

clerical view, and it seems particularly doubtful whether the older clergy's readiness to comply with lay demands was shared by the more elevated new-style clergy. But there was little essential change in the lay view, that the clergy existed to provide benefits —ritual services as well as material charity—and not to impose duties.[1]

If the clergy began now to make heavier religious demands on the laity, they by no means repudiated their charitable duties. Indeed, in an era of sharpening conflict with Methodism, the longer purses of the clergy were recognized as one of the Church's special advantages, and Bishop Kaye often reminded them that whenever they gave money to the poor or spent it with village tradesmen they were advancing the interest of the Church. The trouble with pluralism and non-residence was that parishes were served by curates, who lacked the income to exert much influence in them, while a resident incumbent, with the full value of the living at his disposal, could make a correspondingly deeper impact. By and large the clergy appear not to have shirked their charitable duty, particularly during the winter months, when gifts were needed most. Probably the most liberal was the incumbent of Mareham-le-Fen, who maintained the poor in his large parish from his own resources: there was 'no need for any relieving officer to come to the village with the half-crown and a loaf'.[2] The most calculated use of Anglican money was to bribe children to leave Methodist Sunday schools: but the most common result of the stream of half-crowns was to enhance the personal popularity of the benefactor rather than to cultivate loyalty to the Church.[3]

Next to visiting, the most important pastoral instrument was the school. If the older generation in a village was lost to Methodism, a clergyman might still get a grip on the children. Until mid-century and beyond, this was done primarily by means of the Sunday school. In 1851 there were more children in the Church's Sunday schools than in day schools in every Registration District in Lindsey. In the Spilsby district, for example, the most rural in the area, there were 1,292 pupils in the day schools but 2,227

[1] See A. W. Smith, 'Popular Religion', Past and Present, no. 40 (1968), p. 182.
[2] Linc. Gaz., 25 Jan. 1862.
[3] For Methodist fears of Sunday school bribery, see below p. 214. An example of popularity earned by generosity was that of C. F. Moore of Belleau (Stamf. Merc., 4 Oct. 1839).

in Sunday schools.[1] The attraction of the Sunday schools was not only that they permitted work on weekdays, but that they were free, while the day schools charged 'scholars' pence'. And many girls who were unable to attend day school were enrolled in Sunday schools; in the Spilsby registration district in 1851 boys greatly outnumbered girls in the day schools, 2,630 to 1,562, but the margin was much smaller in the Sunday schools, 2,359 to 2,308.

Similar figures were revealed by the Lincoln Diocesan Board of Education's inquiry in 1855.[2] In parishes whose combined population in 1851 was over four-fifths that of the whole area, there were, on an average Sunday, 2,403 boys and 2,384 girls in the Anglican Sunday schools; they formed about half the estimated eligible population in their parishes. A comparison of these figures with those of church attendance indicates that many adults who did not attend church must have sent their children to Sunday school; the Church of England was closer to being a majority institution among children aged 5 to 12 than in any other segment of the population.

The subjects taught in Sunday schools included reading and writing as well as religion, and the precise balance between secular and religious subjects is not easy to determine, but it probably shifted to the latter after 1850 as day schools attracted more pupils.

The overwhelming majority of day schools in the area were connected with the Church of England—only nine parishes are noted to have had Methodist day schools. Depending for their effectiveness on the support, material as well as spiritual, of the clergyman, the church day schools were credited with 'silently putting into the hands of the church' an 'enormous leverage'.[3] Whatever their success in instilling deferential social attitudes, their religious results were unimpressive. The inspectors' reports indicate that the pupils' attainments in scriptural knowledge were mixed, that they often memorized the Catechism without understanding it and rarely were taught private prayers. Of the many educated in church schools, few went on to be confirmed,

[1] P.P. 1852–3, xc, p. 161.
[2] A.T. Schools Questionnaire 1855, L.A.O.
[3] Rex C. Russell, *A History of Schools and Education in Lindsey, Lincolnshire, 1800–1902*, Part 4, 1967, p. 76; George Jeans, Report on Church of England Schools in Calcewaith Rural Deanery, 1861, 1861–2 Inspectors, A.T. Schools L.A.O.

and still fewer became regular communicants. With every advantage of money and trained personnel, the Established Church was unable to induce many children to abandon the faith of their Methodist fathers.

THE RESPONSE TO METHODISM

The strength of Methodism in south Lindsey was unmistakable and the clergy were in no doubt that it was their most serious problem. 'All religion seems to be among Methodists in this country', observed F. C. Massingberd; T. W. Mossman was 'struck with the enormous preponderance of Methodistic feeling and language. . . . Methodism is the religion, such as it is, of the great mass of the Lincolnshire poor'. When the clergy described the state of their parishes it was Methodism that dominated their accounts. In Lusby the majority of B. D. Bogie's parishioners were 'either actual Dissenters . . . or constant attendants at the Methodist chapel'; Skendleby was 'full of Dissenters ready to find ground of complaint ; the population of South Willingham consisted 'almost entirely of Wesleyan Methodists .[1] There were Methodist churchwardens and parish clerks. The unhappy rector of Donington, a parish of 485 souls, deplored the fact that there was 'not a single person whom I can designate a member of the Church of England'.[2]

What then was to be done about Methodism? The question could not be ignored. By 1858 even ordination candidates were given tips on the 'treatment of dissenters'.[3] In the absence of a common strategy, individual attitudes and tactics varied widely, from co-operation to competition to persecution.

Some Evangelicals were positively friendly to Dissent. B. D. Bogie of Lusby indeed claimed that 'the greatest part of the *Church of Christ* in Britain was to be found not among the

---

[1] Massingberd, Diary, 19 Mar. 1826, Mass. 8/1; T. W. Mossman, 'The Church in Lincolnshire', *Union Review*, iii (1865), p. 262; Bogie to Kaye, 15 Aug. 1839, Cor. B. 5/4/75/3; Cheales to Kaye, 10 Apr. (?), Cor. B. 5/4/104/25; Wynter to Kaye, 30 June 1832, Cor. B. 5/4/21/5.

[2] 1873 V.R. One churchwarden was a Methodist local preacher, the other a Swedenborgian. In another parish the parson was rebuked by the parish clerk for having evening service, 'because then he could not attend "the means"' (of grace, i.e. Methodist services). Conference of Rural Deans, 15 July 1873, Minute Book of Conferences 1873–7, diocesan records, L.A.O.

[3] Edward to Jane Steere, 7 May 1858, Neave, 'Letters', p. 66.

members of the established churches, but among the Dissenters; and those few in the Church of England were due to 'the leaven of godliness from the Methodists and Dissenters'.[1] Field Flowers of Tealby accepted invitations to speak at Wesleyan missionary meetings and joined his Wesleyan colleagues at meetings for the British and Foreign Bible Society.[2] 'Brotherly love was said in 1875 to exist at Hogsthorpe, where the vicar called upon the Wesleyan minister at his manse. At Torksey and at Mareham-le-Fen Wesleyan and church Sunday scholars celebrated their anniversaries together.[3] At the funeral of a Wesleyan local preacher at Minting, the incumbent cheerfully granted permission to the mourners to sing hymns both in church and at the grave, and even offered to give them out himself.[4] The curate at Swaby probably spoke for many when he noted that 'the Wesleyans have a strong party, and deprive me of a part of the congregation in *one* service (the afternoon) but I endeavour to avoid all irritation, and so we jog on together, as friendly as possible'. At Bardney, in 1851, co-operation reached the point where the Sunday scholars attended the Wesleyan chapel one Sunday, the parish church the next; and at Ingham, the schoolroom was administered by nine trustees: three churchmen, three Wesleyans, and three Primitive Methodists.[5] A good many parsons, if not actually friendly towards Methodists, at least blunted the sharp edge of rubrics in order to avoid antagonizing their Methodist parishioners.

Majority Anglican opinion, however, took a much harsher line. According to William Nevins, Methodists were guilty of the 'awful sin of schism'.[6] And in 1873 Bishop Wordsworth issued a 'Pastoral to the Wesleyan Methodists in the Diocese of Lincoln' in which he recalled to them the fate of Korah, and pronounced

[1] B. D. Bogie, *The Crisis*, 1836, p. 11. His wife rented a sitting in the Wesleyan chapel at Old Bolingbroke (Seat-rent book, Spilsby C.R.).

[2] *Mkt Rasen W.M.*, 28 Jan. 1860, 23 Mar. 1867. Flowers also initiated the building of a chapel at Bleasby Moor, in his other parish of Legsby, which appears to have been intended for joint use with the Wesleyan Reformers (*Mkt Rasen W.M.*, June–Oct. 1858, *passim*).

[3] *East Lincs. Times*, 23 Oct. 1875; *Linc. Gaz.*, 12 July 1862; *Stamf. Merc.*, 13 July 1838. *Hornc. News*, 14 May 1870.

[4] ibid., 14 May 1870. Edward Steere showed the same consideration at the funeral of a Methodist in his parish of Skegness (Neave, 'Letters', p. 70).

[5] Cromwell to Kaye, 11 July 1844, Cor. B. 5/4/92/1; Bardney, Religious Census, H.O. 129/428/1, P.R.O. Ingham, A.T. Schools Questionnaire 1855, L.A.O.

[6] Nevins, *The Clergy's Privilege and Duty*, p. 11.

'wilful schism' a 'deadly sin and a tremendous evil, both for time and eternity'.[1] Schism was not their only failing. They were condemned for 'fanaticism'—as Roman Catholics were for 'superstition'—and for doctrinal errors as well, particularly their view of the Holy Spirit. The clergy allowed that it had played a vital role in the early history of Christianity, but now that the religion was 'established . . . it requires no such extraordinary influence of the Holy Spirit'; indeed, 'the pretensions to similar effects of divine visitations in later [times] are at once unwarranted and delusive'.[2] Tithes and compulsory church rates thus demoted the Third Person of the Trinity. The Holy Spirit was conceded to be a 'comforter' and to have the ability 'to teach and to remind us of our duty to God and man', but the clergy could not bring themselves to admit that it could sanctify.[3]

Another favourite target of Anglican critics was the spontaneous emotionalism of Methodist services. F. C. Massingberd hoped 'by degrees to inoculate' his Methodist parishioners 'with a preference for the calm dignity of our service in comparison of the wild excitement which John Wesley has bequeathed them'. The object of preaching was to maintain 'the calm, serious, and sober dignity and devotion of real Christianity', not 'to stir up the passionate feelings of the heart'.[4] Methodist revivals, in the opinion of Bishop Kaye, were 'mere animal excitement'. And, in a discussion of home missions, his son, the Archdeacon of Lincoln, 'urged his brethren to be very, very careful of making mere feeling the standard of the working of God's spirit'.[5] Carrying the attack still further into the Methodist camp, churchmen denigrated the Methodists' appreciation of good sermons: 'prayer, not preaching, is the first object of public worship.' They condemned, too, the '"itching ears"' of laymen who sought

---

[1] Christopher Wordsworth, *A Pastoral to the Wesleyan Methodists in the Diocese of Lincoln*, 1873, pp. 6, 11. The Pastoral shattered the *modus vivendi* that had been established in many parishes and 'filled the minds of many of the clergy with dismay' (Overton and Wordsworth, *Christopher Wordsworth*, p. 242). Overton, incumbent at Legbourne, was in a position to know the reactions of the parish clergy.

[2] Martin, *Family Sermons*, p. 144.

[3] R. D. B. Rawnsley, *Sermons*, p. 50; Arthur Wright, MS. sermon on Ps. 51:11–19, collection of Mr. Terence Leach.

[4] Massingberd to Kaye, 2 May 1838, Cor. B. 5/4/84/3; Smith, *Consistency and Faithfulness*, p. 22.

[5] J. Kaye, *Works*, vii. 373; Conference of Archdeacons and Rural Deans, 15 July 1873, 'Conference of Rural Deans 1873–77' minute book, Lincoln diocesan records.

novelty and variety in their preachers.[1] Yet they sensed that villagers were attracted not only by Methodist sermons, but also by their prayers, especially extemporary prayers. Edward Steere warned that 'the love of extempore prayers is no sign of spirituality', and Bishop Wordsworth favourably contrasted the state Church's set forms of prayer with the Methodists' '*extemporaneous effusion*'. Extemporary prayers, especially among the Primitive Methodists, were deplored for allowing 'large scope for the demonstration of excited feelings'.[2] Only a secondary appeal was made to theological argument and to biblical texts; it was rather a question of class culture: the clergy judged Methodism not so much by the canons of the Church as by the canons of genteel and middle-class manners, and found it guilty not merely of heresy but of the worse sin of vulgarity.

Clergy taking a hard line on Methodism could choose from a variety of specific tactics. Perhaps the commonest was straight denunciation from the pulpit: 'palavering the Church of England and bulragging the dissenters'.[3] High Churchmen manifested their displeasure at Dissent as they had done since the early days of the Oxford movement, by crossing themselves when they passed a conventicle; locally, a Primitive Methodist camp meeting prompted a passing clergyman to stop his ears with his fingers— their delicacy protected from the elements by black kid gloves. Occasionally clergymen adopted a more active policy not easily distinguished from bullying. The incumbent at Burgh-on-Bain threatened three of his parishioners with a prosecution for disturbing the peace: they had stopped by the side of the road to listen to the singing from a Wesleyan service in a nearby cottage. One parson refused to baptize the children of Methodists, but more common was the reluctance or refusal to bury Methodists.[4] Possibly the chief Methodist-baiter was William Molson of Hogsthorpe. After 'forgetting' to appear at the church to bury a Methodist, he was asked whether he disliked burying dissenters;

[1] Jackson, *Charge*, 1855, p. 15; Gregory, *Plea*, p. 12.

[2] Steere, *Notes of Sermons*, iii. 276; Christopher Wordsworth, *Miscellanies: Literary and Religious*, 1879, ii. 121; E. L. Blenkinsopp, 'Catholic and Protestant', in ed. Orby Shipley, *Studies in Modern Problems by Various Writers*, 1874, p. 26.

[3] This description of local Anglican sermons appears in a letter from 'One of the People', adapting a phrase of Bishop Selwyn's (*Linc. Gaz.*, 1 Oct. 1859).

[4] *Stamf. Merc.*, 23 Feb. 1838, 3 May 1839; *Linc. Gaz.*, 8 June 1861; *Mkt Rasen W.M.*, 16 June 1872. Refusal to bury was a tactic appealing to High Churchmen and Evangelicals alike.

he answered, '"I should like to bury them all."' To a mother whose child had received a Primitive Methodist baptism he said '"What a pity that such a lovely child should not have a Christian name."' And when a site between the Wesleyan and Primitive Methodist chapels was proposed for a new parsonage, he declared that 'he would not live in it, as he would be crucified between *two thieves*'.[1] The clergy had, finally, ample scope for 'active intolerance and whimsical restrictions' in operating the village day schools.[2]

A less bellicose strategy, more congenial to mainstream clerical reformers, was to exploit as fully as possible the standard instruments of pastoral ministry—charity, visiting, Sunday and day schools; without resorting to bullying, the advocates of this strategy sought to defeat Methodism in fair and open competition. They succeeded to the extent of checking the further advance of Methodism, but they failed in their maximum aim of driving it back. They do appear, however, to have accomplished more than the practitioners of simple counter-aggression.

There was a third set of approaches that emphasized the similarities between the Church and Methodism instead of the differences. Clergymen new to the area and to their parishes often assumed that once the scandal of non-residence was corrected the Methodists would come streaming back. Bishop Wordsworth added the argument that Wesley had never intended to set up an independent Church, and that the Wesleyans now had no reason for a separate existence. In this spirit Wesley's essay 'On Constant Communion' was reprinted in a parish magazine.[3] Though there were few institutional similarities between the two churches, a High Churchman drew attention to the fact that the Methodist class meeting was 'one side of the confessional under another name'.[4] A more promising strategy was to fight fire with fire: to adopt from Methodism its own special features. What was needed most was to widen the scope for lay activity, the lack of which was acknowledged by Bishop Jackson to be 'one of our Church's

---

[1] George Shaw, *Life of Rev. Parkinson Milson*, 1893, pp. 135–6.

[2] As at Scothern (*Linc. Gaz.*, 10 Aug. 1861). It is notable, however, that twenty clergymen and others declared their support for a conscience clause in day schools in 1870 (*Mkt Rasen W.M.*, 30 Apr. 1870).

[3] Wordsworth, *Pastoral*, p. 5; Dunholme and neighbourhood Parish Magazine, Feb. and March 1868 (Leach collection).

[4] *Retf. News*, 12 Dec. 1868.

great errors'. He returned to the theme in his 1861 visitation: 'We not only assert to ourselves rightly the functions which belong to the Clergy, but we practically hold too much of a monopoly of those which are equally competent to lay believers'. Sunday schools he particularly urged as an outlet 'for those of our parishioners—young men and women especially—who feel the duty of doing good'. But there was no enthusiasm for the proposal that the bishops should 'authorize a body of *lay*-preachers' to meet Dissent 'with its own most potent weapon', and the development of responsible work for laymen in country parishes never went very far.[1]

This exclusive reliance upon the clergy was symptomatic of the Anglican campaign against Methodism and helps to explain its limited success: while it contended with Methodist zeal it was at the same time undermined by difficulties from within, some of the clergy's own making, others inherent in the nature of the Establishment. The clergy's experiment in ritualism, which further alienated and alarmed the Methodists, was launched at a time when hopes of drawing them back into the Church had not yet been abandoned. More serious were the Church's institutional rigidities. The individual clergyman was at a disadvantage in competing with 'a widely extended organization of Dissenting Ministers' (and local preachers) in a society in which 'people run after strange preachers ... Dissent takes advantage of this and supplies them accordingly. The Church, at least in the country, does not.'[2] Worst of all were the clergy's own misperceptions of Methodism. Their assumption that the mere reform of old abuses would lead the Methodists to abandon their chapels betrayed an ignorance of the vitality of Methodist communities. Many clergy also refused to admit that Methodism was a *religious* movement, with its own theology and spirituality. A typical attitude was that of the parson who desired 'someone of experience and high Church principles to carry out the arduous task of instructing the ignorant and mistaken people'.[3] And in insisting that only the poor went to chapel, in overlooking the many farmers in Methodism, the clergy underestimated its economic and social as well as its religious strength. Inspired by these almost wilful

---

[1] Jackson, *Charge*, 1855, p. 35; *Charge*, 1861, p. 22; Sotby, 1873 V.R.
[2] Sotby, 1873 V.R.
[3] Winston to Kaye, 20 June 1850, Cor. B. 5/4/70.

misunderstandings, the clergy's hectoring and bullying tactics proved ineffective, even counter-productive. At the end of the century the problem was still the same, and Bishop King was exceptional among Anglicans in discerning the religious reality of Methodism and the futility of mere counter-aggression:

There is so much to be done with our dear religious dissenting Lincoln-shire people. They need to be taught and shepherded lovingly—but not driven, and led by example and sympathy, as well as by teaching. . . . Our great problem is to transplant Lincolnshire piety (which dissent has caught) on to Church lines.[1]

SOCIAL ATTITUDES

No doubt it is always dangerous to infer a group's subjective outlook directly from its objective actions and social position, but in the case of the clergy the evidence of their public activity is consistent and suggestive. Not only did their economic position rest ultimately on the fortunes of agriculture, but they associated themselves with landlords and farmers (whatever the complica-tions of relationships with particular individuals) in the joint project of reconciling agricultural capitalism with social stability. They played their part in the agricultural and ploughing societies, they had long been prominent in the moralizing repression of popular recreations, and their conservatism was emphatic. This pattern of activities implies a conservative social outlook different from that of the farmers or landlords; what can be recovered of their social attitudes from their sermons confirms and complicates the impression of a distinctive variety of conservatism with its own internal tensions.[2]

Like the other dominant groups, the clergy affirmed the ideal of a hierarchical and unequal society. This was subtly qualified however, by the more egalitarian ideal implicit in the reforms they attempted to bring about in public worship. They wished their congregations to become worshipping communities, every member of which was equal before God and equally a partaker of the Sacrament. The congregational ideal did not contradict the larger conservative ideal: indeed it was intended to reinforce it.

[1] King to Larken, 1903, Larken VI/14, L.A.O.
[2] An exceptional figure, outside the conservative consensus, was E. R. Larken, rector of Burton, who was a member of the Leeds Redemption Society and supported other communitarian projects. See J. F. C. Harrison, *Social Reform in Victorian Leeds*, 1954.

But its stress on community put it at odds with the class divisions that conservatives wanted to maintain, and it is significant that later thinkers would draw very different social conclusions from similar religious premises.

In their economic and social teachings the clergy encouraged paternalism in the rich and acceptance and resignation in the poor. It was the duty of the rich to be charitable to the poor and to give generously to the clergy the means with which to build churches and schools. There were still traces of the old view that wealth was dangerous to faith and morals: R. D. B. Rawnsley spoke often of 'dangerous wealth', and Edward Steere observed that 'a retired businessman is very seldom happy . . . If having riches is dangerous, longing for them is worse'.[1] Poverty on the other hand was a positive good: it stimulated virtues like 'industry' and 'fidelity to an employer' as well as 'kindness'. 'The fear of the workhouse', Steere concluded, was 'a real help to a good life.'[2] The poor were warned not to compare their condition with that of others in society; it was their duty rather to be content with their lot and to obey 'those put in authority over them'.[3] Resigned contentment was particularly timely, as Steere pointed out, during Lent. When everyone had an obligation to fast, some were 'so poor, so afflicted, they cannot fast. It is for them to cultivate a quiet, contented spirit, to make a voluntary fast of what they have not, and cannot expect to have'. The value of religious faith was underlined by R. D. B. Rawnsley: 'The knowledge that we shall rise again . . . consoles us for any hardship in our lot now.'[4]

The clergy's ideal was conservative, but it was no simple consecration of the *status quo*—nor of an idealized recent past. They identified with Old England—sometime before Catholic Emancipation and the Whigs—yet rejected its rough 'crowd' scene, its popular recreations, and its unfitting church music. Its communal character they wished to preserve only in its ritualized remnant, public worship. They were no less ambivalent towards the agricultural capitalism that dominated contemporary

[1] R. D. B. Rawnsley, 'The Feast Refused', p. 46; Steere, *Notes of Sermons*, ii. 306–7.

[2] John Penrose, *Fifty-Four Sermons*, 1851, pp. 262–3; Steere, *Notes of Sermons*, ii. 306.

[3] J. Kaye, *Works*, vi. 350; C. Wordsworth, *Miscellanies*, iii. 404–5.

[4] Steere, *Notes of Sermons*, i. 190; Rawnsley, *Christian Exhortation*, p. 127.

rural society. Economically they were its beneficiaries, politically they upheld the 'agricultural interest', but temperamentally they were quite out of sympathy with its hard calculating rationalism, with the cash nexus, and with the spirited improvers' faith in progress. Their own view of the future by contrast was static and non-progressive: it hardly allowed even for ameliorations or mitigations, short of the Second Coming. Their social ideal was equally static: a stable hierarchy with fixed social categories and watertight parish boundaries. Geographical mobility was as antipathetic as social. The practice of attending church in another parish created 'a great breach in the parochial system' and bred a disturbing taste for novelty.[1] It was wrong to compare one's person with the clergy of other parishes: wrong to compare any aspect of one's condition with that of anyone else. A profound contentment with one's lot was the clergy's aim; it had the incidental virtue of removing the need for excited feeling, suggestive of Methodism. A final feature of the clergy's conservatism was the important role they assigned to themselves as guarantors of the social peace. A close parish writ large—unequal and immobile, softened only by paternalism and by Anglican moderate ritualism —was the clerical image of the good society.

CONCLUSION

For the Church of England the nineteenth century in south Lindsey was less a 'Golden Age' than a time of troubles, of which Methodism was only the largest. Locally as well as nationally the critical period came early, in the 1830s, when the evils of pluralism and non-residence at last came under attack, when new incumbents were alarmed by the aggression of the Methodists—and by the indifference and ignorance of the rest, and when class divisions were deepening; the menace of the Whig reforms, coming after the Tories' betrayal of Church interests in Catholic Emancipation, only added to the sense of crisis. It was in these same years of danger that the Church responded with its strategy for reform and recovery. The strategy, inevitably, was a clerical one—not least because what appeared to be the prime cause of the Church's difficulties, the non-residence of the clergy, was now being corrected. After decades, even centuries of neglect, parishes were being 'worked' by a new band of energetic, resident parsons: who

[1] Gregory, *Plea*, p. 9.

could predict what they might not accomplish? And to a large extent they rose to the challenge. Well paid and well housed, they took command of their parishes and set out to revitalize them: regardless of churchmanship, they did more pastoral work, they held more services, including more celebrations of Holy Communion, and they remodelled public worship. Everything they could have done, unassisted, they apparently had done, and by their efforts the Church survived its crisis and began to face its Methodist rivals on something like even terms.

There were, however, serious limitations to the clerical strategy. Reform from above, by the impatient bishops and archdeacons, was slowed by the Church's own decentralizing system of private patronage and by the parson's freehold. A reform as essential as the full enforcement of residence was one of many that were delayed until after the middle of the century, long after the rise of Methodism and the emergence of class divisions. And there was always a substantial minority who while residing in their parishes were content to live as gentlemen of leisure, doing their Sunday duty and little else. More serious still was the fact that the clergy as a body had become gentlemen, with the appropriate education and income; whether or not they were gentlemen of leisure, their status made them remote from the great majority of their parishioners. Even a new-style farmer might lack the education and polish to consort with them as equals, and they were separated from the labourers by a social and cultural gulf that was virtually unbridgeable. There was a common view 'that the church was for the "quality"';[1] furthermore, the clergy were too deeply implicated in agricultural capitalism and in the moralizing repression of popular recreations to win the affection of the victims of these forces.[2] There was thus a contradiction between means and ends in the clerical strategy: in helping to elevate the secular status of the clergy, it tended to reduce rather than increase their religious influence.[3] Its final limitation was its total

[1] And that the chapel was for the poor (Dale, *Life and Letters of Thomas Pelham Dale*, ii. 106).

[2] Throughout the English countryside it was the clerical magistrates who had been 'the leaders . . . in that crusade "for the Reformation of the Manners of the Lower Orders" which swept the county Benches between 1786 and 1800'. E. Moir, *The Justice of the Peace*, pp. 107–8.

[3] There were in any event definite limits to the effectiveness of clerical influence that was purely personal, as is apparent in the case of Bishop King and Anglo-Catholicism. He was greatly loved and esteemed, but he did not shake the instinctive

renunciation of any active role for the laity—apart from landlord influence and church choirs and perhaps Sunday schools—at a time when 'lay agency' was one of Methodism's most powerful attractions.[1]

Even without these weaknesses the Church was perhaps unlikely to cut seriously into Methodist strength or to foster a communal spirit in congregations splitting apart irreversibly into classes. The results of the clerical reforms consequently were mixed. The rites and sacraments were made public and communal, but they aroused little enthusiasm when they did not provoke outright opposition. The Methodists proved highly resistant to the various tactics employed by the clergy; by the 1860s the Anglican counter-offensive had checked the Methodists' advance but had not rolled them back. The clergy achieved greater —though temporary—success in their secular aims. The social message they proclaimed to the poor—the virtues of resignation and obedience—appear to have had some effect before the rise of the unions; the clergy helped to stabilize society even if they did not christianize it.

By the 1870s these failures or limited successes had become apparent, and their impact on the clergy was as far-reaching as that of the original challenge of the 1830s. Once they recognized that some of their major aims would have to be abandoned, they could not avoid reconsidering their strategy—and indeed their whole conception of the role of the Church in country parishes. Older assumptions were particularly undermined by the failure of their tactics against the Methodists, who now clearly were there to stay, a permanent disruption (as the clergy saw them) of the unity and integrity of the parish. It was all the more vexing that instead of withdrawing into their chapels they continued to attend church as well—as did the many non-Methodist 'floaters'— and to be married and buried according to the rites of the Church. Though villagers were at ease in this ambiguous situation, the

---

Protestantism of the majority: one Lincolnshire woman remarked that he was '"a nice-spoken gentleman, but a bit gay for a gospel minister"' (Walker, *Tales*, p. 10).

[1] Even in the 1870s the Visitation Returns indicate that in many parishes the only lay assistants were the wife and daughters of the parson, who complacently described them as doing all that was necessary. The role of the clergy wives (extolled by Elizabeth Pierce, wife of the incumbent of West Ashby, in *Village Pencillings*, 1842, pp. 70–1) deserves further study.

more militant clergy (particularly the High Churchmen) chose increasingly to sharpen rather than blur the lines between Churchmen and Methodism; their growing alarm at the clamour (national rather than local) for disestablishment only furthered this tendency. If the clergy in the past had ministered to the entire population of their parish, promoting their 'spiritual and temporal welfare', they now began to concentrate on the loyalists—the 'church people'—and on the cultivation of 'church feeling'. By the 1870s they had formulated a new conception of the model layman, identified by his 'church tone' or 'church feeling' or 'church principles'. The operative term often added to these phrases was 'distinct': it was aimed not so much at 'distinct' Methodists as at the larger mass who indistinctly attended both church and chapel.[1] The ideal parishioner was defined not by his creed or his spirituality—in which he was perhaps likely to be outshone by the Methodists—but by his behaviour, his institutional loyalty. He was a regular communicant as well as attendant, and above all he never strayed into chapel. Thus after the disappointments of the original reform programme there emerged a narrower conception of the parson's role, a less comprehensive and more partisan notion of the Church in divided country parishes, and an 'institutional' model of the lay churchman: the Church was narrowing, and being narrowed, into something approaching a denomination.

What then were the effects of the clerical reforms on the religious life of the laity? Until more is known about the pre-Victorian situation the answer must remain tentative. But it is clear that the Church largely failed to overcome class divisions and differences: farmers and labourers went their separate ways through baptism, Sunday school, confirmation, marriage, Sunday services, and Communion. The clergy's largest single accomplishment was to alter the balance between the sexes in public worship, expanding the role of women while reducing that of men. Whatever the earlier pattern was, females now showed a higher propensity for religious practice than males at every age beginning in childhood. Girls appear to have been apter learners than boys in Sunday school and were more likely to be confirmed and

---

[1] The clergy's trust in 'church feeling' was already apparent in the 1873 Visitation Returns. It had the same sharp edge in Leicestershire, where the 'floaters' were again the target (D. Thompson, 'Churches and Society', p. 314).

to receive their first Communion.[1] And as religious practice increasingly was governed by personal inclination, women may have become more frequent communicants than men. At most the clergy assisted, but did not originate, the larger process by which religion became a women's domain. Their role was similar with regard to another shift in the social bases of religion, the growing differentiation of the religious life of children from that of adults. This had its origins in the growing social differentiation between children and adults, a phenomenon of class society. The Sunday schools, a religious innovation that accorded with the changed social reality, prospered: the revival of public catechism, which attempted to reverse social change, failed. There was no popular echo to the clergy's emphasis on Communion, and few villagers conformed with the clerical ideal of the mature religious career— its beginnings in confirmation and first Communion, and un- interrupted progress thereafter. The actual pattern was closer to the modern one, with peaks in childhood and old age and a deep trough in young adulthood, corresponding with the social cir- cumstances of servants and young married couples. The harvest thanksgiving won a place in village religious life, but it repre- sented a clerical concession to popular paganism rather than a deepening of popular Christianity. Popular assumptions about the Church were unshaken by clerical teachings. That church and chapel were equal in validity if distinct in function, that the church was the forum of respectability and deference, and the chapel the arena for the saving of souls—these continued to be articles of the village faith.

Popular attitudes towards individual clergymen do not lend themselves to generalization; personal qualities varied, as did the readiness to promote parishioners' temporal welfare. Scattered evidence in local newspapers suggests, however, that curates may have been more likely to win popular esteem than incumbents. When parishioners presented farewell gifts to clergymen leaving for another parish, the silver salvers went disproportionately often to curates. But there was also an important undercurrent of anti-clericalism, and not only among the gentry. A villager recalled that the young Alfred Tennyson, son of a local pluralist,

[1] The superior Sunday school attainments of the girls, including the memorization of verses from the Bible, and the indiscipline of the boys, are frequently noted in Henry Winn's diary as a Sunday school teacher at Fulletby (Winn 1/2).

'"would have liked to get up a [Methodist] meeting hissen, for the church parsons were such hypocrites. . . . He was quite a religious young man was Mr. Halfred . . . least ways would have been if he had been dragged up by the Wesleyans."[1] His brother Frederick justified his low opinion of the clergy in terms that would not have upset many educated people in the early 1830s:

If I said that I believed there were very few just men in the church, I alluded to the notoriously profligate lives of many of the Bishops and Clergy. . . . At the time of their introduction to the sacred Office they must either have been extremely ignorant of its responsibility, or influenced by no other motive but the hope of concealing the Loaves and Fishes of the Establishment under the cloke of their hypocrisy.[2]

Henry Winn, a parish clerk and church Sunday school teacher, considered that the clergy were more interested in 'secular honours and emoluments' than in 'securing the veneration and obedience of the people from a principle of esteem and love'. The reputation of the clergy for piety is reflected in the remarks of one of Winn's fellow villagers, a farm bailiff and Wesleyan class leader (admittedly thought to be 'a very bigoted Methodist'): when he was ill, his parish clergyman, William Pierce, 'attended him so well that he gained his confidence. . . . He said he was not aware there was so much religion in a church parson.'[3]

It is a final clue to the failures of the Church in south Lindsey that that farm bailiff's observation could be reversed and lose none of its truth: the clergy were not aware there was so much religion in the people. They held in fact a low opinion of their parishioners' ability to lead a serious religious life, even of their ability to assist the clergy in the work of the parish: one incumbent informed the bishop that it was 'absurd to suppose there can be Parochial Councils, Church Helpers, Lay Agents, District Visitors in a small poor parish, where there is only one person who keeps a servant'. It was the clergy's contempt for rustic spirituality that Bishop King urged them to abandon when he

---

[1] H. D. Rawnsley, *Memories of the Tennysons*, p. 42.
[2] Frederick to George Tennyson, 10 Sept. 1831, H 91/83, 2 T. d'E., L.A.O.
[3] Winn 5/3, p. 103.

summoned them to a higher conception of pastoral work; Lincolnshire villagers, he said, might yet become 'models of what English Agricultural poor can be, when they have been made intelligent members of the Church. We do not know yet what spiritual capacity and beauty there is in our people.'[1]

[1] Langton-by-Horncastle, 1873 V.R. King, *Charge*, 1886, p. 85.

IV

WESLEYAN METHODISM

WHAT the clergy had still to discover in 1886—the 'spiritual capacity' of the people—was what the Methodists had known for more than a century, and Methodism consequently dominated the religious life of south Lindsey. The very word 'religious', in local parlance, was synonymous with 'Methodist'. To be 'a "religious" man or woman . . . means simply to be a "joined member" of one of the Methodist sects . . . Negatively, a religious person must not be exclusively a member of the Church of England, whatever else he may be.'[1] In virtually every parish with a population of 250 or more there was at least one chapel, or Methodist services in some secular building, or access to a chapel in an adjoining parish. And not only had Methodism established itself in chapels and congregations but also in popular culture. According to one clergyman, 'anyone would be struck with the enormous preponderance of Methodistic feeling and language'. He could 'never recollect to have been in a dwelling, however poor, in which one or more copies of Wesley's Hymns were not to be found', while he only found copies of the Book of Common Prayer in one cottage out of four—despite the fact that the Prayer Book was given away by the clergy and the Wesleyan Hymnal had to be bought.[2] The Methodists held their strength throughout the period and beyond: in 1886, Bishop King summed up the results of his first visitation returns as 'Dissent! Dissent! Dissent!'[3]

The Wesleyans were by far the most important branch of Methodism in the area, even after the secession of the Wesleyan Reformers around 1851; the Primitive Methodists were in numerical terms little more than an auxiliary. The Wesleyans' pre-eminence in local Methodism was recognized in the dialect: if to be 'religious' was to be a Methodist, then to be a 'Methodist' was

---

[1] Mossman, 'The Church in Lincolnshire', p. 263. By the same token, anyone who took religion seriously whatever his denomination would be called a 'Methodist'. See similarly Barrie Trinder, *The Industrial Revolution in Shropshire*, 1973, p. 273.

[2] Mossman, 'The Church in Lincolnshire', p. 262.

[3] King to Bramley, 1886, quoted by Owen Chadwick, *Edward King*, 1968, p. 21.

to be a Wesleyan. 'They're Methodisses or Ranters, toner' (the one or the other).[1]

The Wesleyans were not recent arrivals in the area, but had been active in both towns and villages long before 1825. John Wesley himself had visited societies at Tealby, Raithby-by-Spilsby, Mumby, Trusthorpe, Newton-on-Trent, and Hainton, as well as the towns. Around 1790 the presence of Methodists was noted by clergymen in at least seventy-five parishes.[2] Gainsborough had become the head of a separate circuit as early as 1777; Horncastle followed in 1786, Louth in 1800, Lincoln in 1802, Spilsby in 1803, Alford and Market Rasen in 1814; the map of the circuits thus was virtually complete a decade before the beginning of the period under study—there remained only Wainfleet to separate from Boston in 1840 and Bardney from Horncastle in 1867. Finally, besides the institutional framework, there was a nucleus of 'hereditary Wesleyans'—Wesleyan by long family tradition—who were the backbone of the cause in many villages.

In 1825, then, Wesleyan Methodism in south Lindsey had a long history behind it and was solidly established. At the same time it was still true to its revivalistic origins, with no lack of exuberance, conversions, and other phenomena of 'religion of the heart'. Eventually its revivalism gave way to tranquil denominationalism, but it evolved slowly—the process was not complete till the end of the century—and for long periods its charismatic and its bureaucratic elements existed side by side without conflict.

Between 1825 and 1875 its history divides clearly into a phase of growth down to the middle of the century and a subsequent phase of relative stagnation or decline.[3] The turning-point was the Wesleyan Reform movement around 1850, which in the Lincoln, Louth, and Market Rasen circuits culminated in disastrous secessions; over half the rural membership in these circuits was lost, never to be regained. Before 1850 membership had grown faster than the total population, but afterwards it barely kept pace, and the stagnation occurred in all the local circuits, not just those affected by the Reform movement. After 1850 there were also changes in the internal character of Wesleyan Methodism.

---

[1] E. Peacock, *Glossary*, p. 257. In this chapter I follow the contemporary practice of using 'Methodism' to refer to Wesleyan Methodism.

[2] Speculum, 1788–92, SPE 4, Diocesan records.

[3] It therefore paralleled national trends. See Robert Currie, *Methodism Divided*, 1968, pp. 91–2.

Threatened by the Anglican resurgence it backed away from the Establishment and moved closer to Dissent. And as the rigour and revivalism of older Methodism waned, entertainment and secular values took their place, accelerating the evolution of Methodism into a denomination.

MINISTERS AND SERVICES

Throughout the period the organization of Wesleyan Methodism changed little. Wesleyan Methodism as a whole was not a church but a 'connection'. The basic unit, the 'society', comprised the members of a single congregation with their own place of worship. Societies were grouped in circuits, each with a town at its head; a circuit comprised one or more town societies and a dozen or more societies in the surrounding villages.

For most of the period there were only seven circuits in south Lindsey, and they were among the larger ones in the connection, being regarded by ministers as 'very extensive,' 'wide and laborious', and 'unwieldy'. The Louth circuit in 1851 had forty-nine 'preaching places' (including those in north Lindsey and in the town of Louth); the Lincoln circuit, the next largest, still had thirty-nine ten years later.[1] The remoter villages in these large circuits therefore lay at inconvenient distances from the ministers, who were stationed in the towns at the centres of the circuits, and the lack of ministerial oversight was made worse after 1850 when the Anglican clergy came in large numbers to reside in their parishes. But apart from the formation of Bardney circuit in 1867 —a circuit not with a town but an overgrown village at its head— proposals to counter the Anglican threat by creating rural subcircuits were never carried out. The ministers remained in the towns while the majority of Wesleyans were still in the villages.

Still, much depended upon ministerial effort. Indeed, in classic Wesleyan ecclesiastical polity, which prevailed in the first half of the century and beyond, the 'pastoral office' was elevated far above mere 'lay agency', and its powers and privileges derived from an

[1] Hickson to Bunting, 31 Mar. 1837, Hindson to Kneeling, 11 July 1860, Wesleyan ministers' correspondence (henceforth Wes. min. corr.), M.A.R.C. Thornley Smith, *A Christian Mother: Memoirs of Mrs. Thornley Smith*, 1885, p. 73; circuit plans, Louth C.R. and M.A.R.C.

exalted, almost ultramontane conception of ministerial authority.[1] In practice, the local lay notables of the Wesleyan societies and circuits held considerable countervailing power and formed a body of permanent officials whose position in the local community curtailed the power of the transient ministers. But if curtailed, that power was still impressive; and in a crisis much depended on the individual minister. When the Reformers at the middle of the century challenged the 'Popery' of Bunting, the 'tyranny' of Conference and of the itinerant ministers, the outcome varied from circuit to circuit according to the character of their respective ministers. In the Gainsborough circuit, the ministers' 'conciliatory manner' pacified the rebels; but when James Loutit, 'a high-toned Conference man', was appointed superintendent of the Louth circuit, the conflict was fought to the bitter end.[2]

Their ministerial duties imposed a heavy workload on them: a constant round of week-night prayer meetings in the villages as well as the Sunday services and pastoral visiting. Indeed they worked a good deal harder than their clerical counterparts. (Their retirement and insurance fund was significantly called the Worn-Out Ministers' and Widows' Fund.) Yet there were ambiguities in their position which recall those of the clergy. When they made pastoral visits, the poorer members of their flocks looked to them for the same largesse they could expect from the parish clergy. The poor, one minister recalled, 'fancy we are *gentlemen*' dressed in 'decent black clothes and white neckcloths . . . We talk and pray with them, and leave *no silver* . . . But if we have no private property, how can we relieve them?'[3] Lacking the resources of the clergy, they were tempted in their visiting to concentrate on the more 'influential' portion of the membership.[4] Overworked as they were, and underpaid, the preachers who

---

[1] See the chapter on the 'Pastoral Office' in John C. Bowmer, 'Church and Ministry in Wesleyan Methodism, from the death of Wesley to the death of Bunting', unpublished Ph.D. thesis, Leeds University, 1967.

[2] *Lincs. Times*, 20 Aug. 1850; *Stamf. Merc.*, 1 Aug. 1851.

[3] James Kendall, *Remarks on Pastoral Visiting among the Wesleyans*, 1852, p. 10.

[4] Thomas Cooper, disenchanted with Wesleyan Methodism as he had known it in the Gainsborough and Lincoln circuits, scorned the '"gentleman preachers"' who had 'an ever-watchful regard to their own importance when they make a pastoral visit . . . They have an almost intuitive perception of the strict necessity of making frequent calls in certain directions, while they perceive with equal clearness that a large part of their flock may be neglected with impunity' (*Stamf. Merc.*, 27 Apr. 1838).

called for repentance and conversion made their own pretensions to respectability.

Conversion was indeed the explicit and primary aim of ministers and preachers in Methodist services, but it was not the sole and exhaustive one. While uppermost in the Sunday services, it was only in the background during class meetings and other occasions reserved for members; and it yielded to still other interests in the secondary growth of missionary meetings and chapel and Sunday school anniversaries. The special Methodist religious ethos is suggested in the phrase 'means of grace' which they gave to their central services. It implied that the 'means' above all served the 'ends' of the participants, and that their experience of divine grace was direct and personal: in the Church's 'divine service' and public worship', by contrast, collective, 'external' worship took precedence over the individual religious quest. The contrast between Methodist and Anglican approaches to prayer—one of many— had similar implications. In the church there was 'common prayer', led by the parson, according to 'set forms', but in the chapel prayer was invariably extemporaneous, and it was offered by ordinary members and local preachers as well as by ministers, and to be 'mighty in prayer' was a distinction open to any Methodist. Yet as long as ministers were known as 'itinerant preachers' and chapels as 'preaching houses', the sermon remained the centrepiece of the Wesleyan service.

Ministers ordinarily preached extemporaneously, sometimes with notes, 'very rarely . . . from a full manuscript';[1] it is not clear what the usual policy was among local preachers. Thomas Cooper recalled that in the Gainsborough circuit around 1830 few even made notes before preaching, though the best individual preacher memorized his in advance. The extraordinarily successful Charles Richardson preached from notes; Joseph Bush, later a minister and President of Conference, perhaps significantly wrote his out in full. Yet the majority probably relied on 'spontaneous combustion'.[2] Whatever strategy they followed, their sermons gener-

---

[1] James Kendall, *Eccentricity*, 1859, pp. 101–2.

[2] Thomas Cooper, *Life of Thomas Cooper*, 4th edn., 1873, p. 89; John E. Coulson, *The Peasant Preacher*, 2nd edn., 1866, p. 80; Arthur Hoyle, *Joseph Bush: A Memorial*, 1907, p. 23. Even a warning to local preachers against extemporaneous sermons nevertheless urged them always to 'leave your hearts open . . . to the assistances of the Holy Spirit! Calculate upon them and never hesitate to follow them' (Samuel Tindall, *The Means of Obtaining Materials for the Pulpit*, 1849, p. 33).

ally took their structure from the technique of 'dividing' the text. The result was at least outwardly clear, with three distinct sections, each developing the line of thought inspired by the text. Those that were written out might achieve the 'technical regularity', prized by connoisseurs. Most of the local preachers, especially those from village societies, must have had a rustic, popular character, well suited to their congregations. Among the local preachers recalled by Henry Lunn was a 'steam threshing machine man': when he warmed to his subject, 'his arms moved from side to side, as he moved when he was putting the sheaves of corn into the machine'. Another 'local' in the Horncastle area preached before he could read properly—his wife read the Bible lessons to him until he knew them by heart—but 'his transparent zeal and earnestness roused his hearers'.[1]

Unfortunately the content of sermons—so many of which were extemporaneous—remains obscure, as does in particular the frequency with which preachers invoked the terrors of hell-fire. In two surviving sermons by Charles Richardson the themes were probably common, the literary polish uncommon. In the first, dating from perhaps the early 1830s, the terrors of hell were not minimized:

Suppose that Christ appears in person, and stands before you; every eye would be fixed. O! See the Man of Sorrows.' He left the courts above to suffer for you sinners. Remember what you have read of His sufferings and death in the Gospels. Now, He takes off the hatches and uncovers the pit; you may smell the stench and smoke, hear the heart-rending cries and groans coming from the burning gulf, and as you see lost souls agonizing in horrible distress, you perhaps feel just ready to drop into it. But the loving Saviour speaks to thee, and pointing to his head crowned with thorns, he speaks again, and says, I suffered this to save thee from hell. . . . Then he opens heaven, and shows the glory of the place, and . . . . he says, 'only forsake thy sins, and saints and angels shall be thy companions, crowns and glory shall be thine' . . . pointing to the crown of thorns upon His head, with tears and entreaties [he] beseeches you to be reconciled to God. Oh! who can bear it? Who can withstand?[2]

In his last sermon, preached in 1864, he struck a more positive note unveiling the glories of heaven:

[1] Henry S. Lunn, *Chapters from My Life*, 1918, pp. 12–13.
[2] Coulson, *Peasant Preacher*, p. 366.

There the sun is risen to set no more . . . the darkness of sin shall no more pervade the land; the darkness of Providence shall no more perplex the thoughts; the darkness of hell shall no more alarm the fears; the darkness of the grave shall no more conceal our friends . . . we shall for ever bask in the beams of the Sun of Righteousness . . . a land of permanent rest, where pure enjoyment reigns, and where there is no more toil, or suffering, or danger, or want; no more persecution for the sake of the cross, no more buffeting against the storms of life. There our labours end . . . a land of constant peace. No national convulsions, no domestic quarrels, no conflicting passions are there. All are the subjects of one king; all are children of one family, all are sanctified by one spirit . . . a land of unmingled pleasure. . . . Not one streaming eye shall there be seen; not a single groan shall ever be heard . . . every eye sparkling with joy; every heart dancing with gladness . . . a land of glorious liberty . . . free men, living in the privileges of a blessed emancipation, from the tyranny of Satan, from the dominion of sin, from the fear of a house not made with hands; a country of captive exiles for a land of noble freedom, where all are priests and kings . . . a land of abundant supplies . . . no famine there . . . bread enough and to spare. There a poor despised Lazarus doffs his tattered garments, and is adorned with the best robes; none are parched with thirst, for the rock rolls living streams amongst them; none faint with weakness, for the new wine of the kingdom revives them. This is a land of corn and wine . . . a land of perfect holiness. God, angels, and saints are holy, and none can be allowed to enter the country where they dwell, but those 'who have washed their robes, and made them white in the blood of the Lamb', and kept them clean. A guilty conscience, impure affections, a stubborn will, and disordered passions, exclude from paradise. 'Except ye be converted.'[1]

If Richardson's sermons had a higher literary polish than most, they nevertheless were representative, not only in their themes but also in their constant aim—to make conversions. Indeed it was this aim that gave Methodist sermons their character as 'performative utterances'. Because the preacher began with a purpose rather than a theme, his text, if he used one, became a kind of script; he employed the advocate's arts of tone, rhetoric, and gesture; the result was a performance, an almost theatrical occasion, an entertainment. The congregation for their part were participants rather than onlookers, actively responding and contributing to the event; and over the years they became exacting

[1] ibid., pp. 368–9.

critics of sermons and preachers. In these favourable conditions ministers and local preachers developed an enormous variety of techniques and styles. Thomas Cooper recalled that when he was a local preacher in the Lincoln and Gainsborough circuits he strove to make his sermons 'worth listening to . . . They contained passages of euphony, of pathetic appeal, of picturesque description, and power of argument and declamation'.[1] On the other hand there were miscarriages, such as the sermon by a local preacher (a small farmer) that Henry Winn heard at Fulletby: 'a crude mass of unconnected ideas and uncouth phrases, delivered in a tone loud, boisterous, and peculiarly disagreeable, which a labouring man as we returned home together not unaptly compared to a "long rawming shout".' On another occasion Winn commented that a sermon on the text 'And there shall be no night there' was 'not very luminous' and that the preacher 'lost the thread of his discourse and appeared very much confused'.[2] Yet the best preachers commanded an elaborate technique, if perhaps artificial by contemporary standards. Charles Garrett was said to have had complete mastery of whispers, tears, and gestures. Taking off one's coat in the pulpit was a favourite gimmick, though deplored by practitioners of a more austere mode of delivery.[3] Another device was to break off preaching and lead the congregation in a hymn. Thomas Cooper recalled doing so in one sermon when 'shouts of praise from believers . . . overpowered my voice'; for Charles Richardson it succeeded only in increasing the excitement—he would then resume preaching 'amidst expressions of holy emotions and devout praise'. On one occasion, when he was preaching on the kingdom of God, 'describing the excellency and glory of Christ as a king, his audience became very much impressed, and many voices gave loud expression to adoring joy and exultation, when Mr. Richardson suddenly exclaimed "Let us crown Him!" and immediately sang out in his own rich and ringing tones: "All hail the power of Jesus' name!" . . . The whole of the congregation arose upon their feet, and with deep emotion and grand effect, joined in the hymnal coronation of their Lord, swelling the chorus, "Crown Him! Crown Him! Lord of all!"'[4]

[1] Cooper, Life, p. 91.

[2] Winn, Diary, 23 Mar. 1845 and 22 Mar. 1846, Winn 1/1.

[3] James W. Broadbent, The People's Life of Charles Garrett, n.d., p. 4; James Kendall, Ministerial Popularity, 1847, pp. 30–1.

[4] Cooper, Life, p. 90; Coulson, Peasant Preacher, pp. 348–9.

The responses aroused by the sermons were spontaneous, uninhibited, fervent. The congregation for the early sermon of Charles Richardson quoted above were typically 'unable to control their feelings' and 'began to sob and weep aloud in every direction.[1] Accounts of sermons—and not only those written by the preachers—abound with the cries and shouts of the congregations. The noise was greatest in the village chapels, at least after 1850, when town congregations sought greater restraint and decorum in their services; by the end of the period the excitement aroused in the villages by a special missionary preacher would shock the more respectable town congregations.[2] Still less sympathetic were some of the ministers. James Kendall took particular exception to stamping and to pounding with the hands; others were ambivalent, distinguishing between 'animal excitement' and 'feeling'; for Thomas Hodson the people in the Louth circuit were 'rather too noisy . . . but as good is done I put up with the noise.'[3] The boisterous style thus came under criticism not only from the clergy outside Methodism but also from its own ministers and town chapels, and in the end it would decline even in its rural strongholds.

Among the noisemakers were likely to be persons beginning the process of conversion. Those who were 'wounded' by the sermon went forward to the 'penitents' form' or 'pew' reserved for them in the front of the chapel; there they were attended to by the minister, the local preacher, or by specialist 'prayer leaders'. The prayer meeting after the evening service was a common setting for the final stages in the process, and the meeting might last late into the night. On one such occasion, after a sermon by Charles Richardson,

Both praying men and praying women laboured with all their might, and seemed as if inspired from on high, while numbers of broken-hearted sinners were sighing and groaning and crying aloud for mercy, twenty together; and six or seven persons praying aloud at the same time. We did our best to keep order, and had had three rows of benches set, the penitents on one side and the praying people on the other. . . . The people crowded the penitent bench till we were

---

[1] Coulson, *Peasant Preacher*, p. 60.

[2] See the extracts from a journal kept in 1874–5 in *Methodist Recorder*, XXXIX (1898), no. 2044, pp. 92–3.

[3] Kendall, *Ministerial Popularity*, p. 67; William Hurt, 'Eminent Piety', in *Sermons by Wesleyan-Methodist Ministers*, 1851, p. 208; Hodson to Arthur, 15 Jan. 1844, Wes. min. corr., M.A.R.C.

obliged to tell them they must wait, and when some found pardon, we took them away to make room for others. . . . I left the place all on fire.

Henry Winn recalled the eagerness of a recent convert to have his mother follow his example; during a prayer meeting he got her to the penitents' form and 'in a fit of enthusiasm he roared out, "Go to the rigg, brother Fletcher, and stick to it Mother."'[1]

Those who were converted and became members of the Connection also joined a class and were expected to attend the weekly class meetings. Among Methodist institutions the class meeting had a high place: it was exclusively for members and indeed was the test of membership. The classes usually met on Sunday; there were hymns and prayers, but the main purpose was to enable members to speak of their religious experience of the previous week, to confess to each other and encourage each other. The class leaders exercised a pastoral oversight over their members and were perhaps the most important lay officials in Methodism. Yet national evidence suggests that by the 1860s many members were beginning to find the class meeting unhelpful and boring and that their children were repelled by it.[2] The conflict always latent in Methodism between class and congregation, between the inner core of members and the larger mass of hearers, became explicit. Eventually the congregation triumphed and the class meeting atrophied, surviving only in name. Local evidence is regrettably scarce; but a passing comment by Richardson's biographer suggests that some discontent was being felt with class meetings around the middle of the century: he thought it noteworthy that as many as thirty of the forty members of Richardson's class were often present. It is likely that the decay of the class meeting occurred first in town societies, where Methodists and their children were more sophisticated and self-conscious than their country cousins, but the local chronology is obscure.[3]

The sacrament of the Lord's Supper was by contrast 'not . . . the

---

[1] Coulson, *Peasant Preacher*, p. 100; Winn 5/5, p. 63.

[2] T. Hughes, *The Condition of Membership in the Christian Church*, 2nd edn., 1873, p. 84; Thornley Smith, *The Youth of Methodism*, 1859, p. 102; Joseph Willis, *The Class and the Congregation*, 1869. See also Currie, *Methodism Divided*, pp. 125–9, and Henry D. Rack, 'The Decline of the Class-Meeting and the Problem of Church-Membership in Nineteenth-Century Wesleyanism', *Proceedings of the Wesley Historical Society*, xxxix (1973).

[3] Coulson, *Peasant Preacher*, p. 41; Lunn, *Chapters*, p. 18, mentions that class meetings were still active in Horncastle in 1877.

test, but the *seal and token* of Church membership'.[1] It was for members only, but they appear to have been reluctant participants when it was celebrated in their own village chapels. Some continued to take Communion in the parish church;[2] others—chiefly farmers, presumably—received the sacrament in a town chapel.[3] In Wesleyan chapels it was always administered by a minister, not by a local preacher, and it belonged to the urban, ministerial, 'high church' side of Methodism.

The children of the Wesleyans were surprisingly poorly provided for. Wesleyan Sunday schools were greatly outnumbered by the church schools. In the Alford circuit in 1837 the majority of societies had no Sunday school; in the Lincoln circuit, a few years later, only six of eighteen societies in south Lindsey had Sunday schools.[4] The Religious Census recorded them in 45 societies out of 121. They may have become more numerous in the second half of the period—in the Bardney circuit, seven of nine societies in 1876 had Sunday schools and three-quarters of the chapels (in 1870) in the Alford circuit—partly because of the more bellicose attitude of the Established Church. In 1862 there was a complaint that 'the influence of Rural Clergy is in some places diminishing the number of our Scholars, inducements of a pecuniary and charitable kind being employed to secure their attendance at the Church Schools'; one Sunday school in the Spilsby circuit had to be given up, the children "'having been bribed away to the established church."'[5] Another reason for the expansion of Sunday schools may have been the decline in emotional conversions and the subsequent need to recruit new members more systematically. At the same time, the differing emphasis on Sunday schools reflects a wider contrast between the Established Church and Wesleyan Methodism: churchmen could afford to sacrifice the adult generation and concentrate on children, but the voluntary church (if forced to choose) had to make certain of its adult supporters before recruiting young people.

[1] *Watchman*, 4 Jan. 1865.

[2] F. J. Jobson, *A Mother's Portrait*, 1855, p. 100; Lunn, *Chapters*, p. 242.

[3] Many country members were reported to attend Spilsby chapel (*Watchman*, 31 May 1865).

[4] Note on 'Sunday Schools', Jan. 1837, Alford C.R.; note dated June 1842, Circuit Schedule Book 1838–46, Lincoln C.R.

[5] Circuit Schedule Book 1876, Bardney C.R. *Horne. News*, 16 July 1870; District Committee meetings, 21–3 May 1862 and 27–9 May 1863, Lincoln District minute book, M.A.R.C.

Revivalist methods, however, were less conspicuous among the Wesleyans than might be expected, less so than among the Primitive Methodists. Revivals there certainly were: one in 1826 that lasted ten nights, including a lovefeast and evening service that continued till 3 a.m. As late as 1862 a revival broke out at Kirkstead, with prayer meetings not only in the chapel, 'but in almost every house in the neighbourhood'. And still later, in 1865, a revival was reported at Ulceby at the time of the building of the first chapel in the parish.[1] But the Wesleyans seem not to have planned revivals with the same forethought and calculation as the Primitive Methodists; in particular, they had no counterpart to the protracted meeting, at least as a regular institution.[2] They too were subject to the cycle of enthusiasm and apathy, but less so than the Primitives. There was probably a solid nucleus of 'hereditary' Methodists in most Wesleyan societies which gave them a stability lacking in the younger sect.

SOCIAL COMPOSITION

It is apparent that Wesleyan chapels attracted large congregations, in which all occupations and classes were represented in some degree; but a more precise analysis of the social composition involves both conceptual and empirical difficulties. Who in the first place were the 'Wesleyans'? There were the members, of course; there were also adherents or hearers, regularly attending Wesleyan services—often renting seats in the chapels—but not becoming members. There were also the many villagers who regularly attended both church and chapel without a definite preference for either. Still others attended irregularly or casually, perhaps limiting themselves to the anniversaries and other festivities. In an ordinary congregation, then, could be found many degrees of commitment, and while information survives for office-holders, and in a few chapels, for seat-renters, the ordinary members, not to mention adherents and casual attenders, remain obscure. It is therefore useful to begin by establishing the size of Wesleyan congregations, comparing Wesleyan and Anglican attendances reported in the Religious Census.

[1] Coulson, *Peasant Preacher*, pp. 37, 40; *Linc. Gaz.*, 15 Mar. 1862; *Watchman*, 5 Apr. 1865.
[2] See below pp. 226–7.

It is noteworthy that Wesleyan congregations were generally larger than those in the parish churches, despite the disruptive effects of the Reform movement. To be sure, of twenty-eight parishes where the Wesleyan service and the Anglican service were held at the same time, the Anglican congregation was larger in sixteen. (In one parish the combined Wesleyan and Wesleyan Reform congregations exceeded the Anglican.) But total attendances were greater in the Wesleyan chapel than in the parish church in fifty parishes, while the reverse was true in only twenty-one. And in a further six parishes the combined Wesleyan and Wesleyan Reform or Primitive Methodist or Independent congregations exceeded the church congregation. If only the best-attended services at church and chapel are considered, the Wesleyan exceeded the Anglican in fifty-one parishes out of seventy-eight. The Wesleyans attracted not only the religious élite of the area, but also its masses: it was more catholic, paradoxically, than the Establishment. The attendance figures alone suggest that large numbers of labourers must have been present at Wesleyan services.

Wesleyan congregations, which included substantial numbers of labourers, probably reflected fairly closely the social composition of the general population. But labourers were under-represented among the office-holders—the easiest group to identify—who were drawn disproportionately from farmers, craftsmen, and shopkeepers.

Occupations of Wesleyan Lay Office-Holders[1]

	Farmers		Craftsmen, shopkeepers		Labourers		Total
	N	%	N	%	N	%	N
Stewards, 1851	58	58	35	35	8	8	101
Class leaders, 1851	29	37	27	34	23	29	79
Local preachers, 1861	37	33	55	49	20	18	112

Over half the society stewards making returns to the Religious Census were farmers, of whom nearly two-thirds had holdings of more than a hundred acres; men of substance were not out of place in this office, with its responsibility for financial affairs, and society stewards were often the 'chief supporters' of the cause in

---

[1] Circuit plans, the principal source, are unfortunately not available in complete sets, and not all of the office-holders could be identified in the Census; labourers therefore are probably under-represented in the table.

their village. Class leaders were more evenly distributed among occupational groups, and labourers were relatively more numerous here, though still under-represented. There was further variation among the local preachers. Almost half of those identified from circuit plans of 1861 were craftsmen and shopkeepers, including thirteen grocers and ten shoemakers, but only two butchers. (Shoemakers were well represented among all three groups of officials, but only the local preachers included many grocers.) Farmers were thus particularly prominent among the stewards and craftsmen among the local preachers; labourers made their best showing among the class leaders, though even there they were outnumbered by other occupations. Only six women were noted, five class leaders and one steward.

Since no class books for the area have survived, it is impossible to determine the balance among the ordinary members. But where membership figures are available, it is at least possible to calculate what percentage of the total population were Wesleyans. In the Connection as a whole, 10 per cent was considered a good average; down to 1851 this was reached locally in the Louth circuit and approached in Lincoln, Market Rasen, and Spilsby. It would appear that the Wesleyans in this period kept pace with and even grew faster than the expanding general population.

Wesleyan Membership as a Percentage of Total Population

circuit	1831	1841	1851	1852	1854	1871
Lincoln	4·5		7·9	3·9		4·1
Louth	8·6		10·1		4·7	5·1
Market Rasen		8·2	7·8	4·5		5·8
Spilsby			7·6			7·8

But after 1850 their performance was less impressive. In the Spilsby circuit, which was spared the Reform disruption, the percentage of members in the whole population hardly varied between 1851 and 1871. And apart from Market Rasen, the circuits affected by the Reform movement did not recover their losses. It should be noted that these percentages are calculated against the total population in the various circuits; percentages in parishes with Wesleyan societies were of course higher. And the percentage of the adult population—those aged 15 and over—was still higher, by about 50 per cent. By whatever calculation, these were high proportions by national standards; when 'hearers' or adherents are counted, the Wesleyan presence becomes even more imposing.

For there was a large body of Wesleyan adherents, attracted by the services but unwilling for various reasons to submit to the discipline or expense of membership. This was no less true of other Methodist and Dissenting denominations, locally and nationally, and as a result, attendance at their places of worship was consistently greater than the number of members. In 1851, sixty-two Wesleyan societies in south Lindsey had a total membership of 1,957, but the total attendance at the best-attended service in each was 4,584; assuming that every member attended, there were in the average congregation four non-members for every three members. Exactly the same ratio is yielded by six chapels for which figures are available in the late 1860s. A social analysis of Wesleyan Methodism must therefore address itself to the congregation as well as the class, the adherents as well as the members.

The subject comes into sharper focus in a few chapels for which seat-rent books survive, listing the names of those who were willing to pay for the privilege of a reserved seat in chapel. Those renting seats consistently outnumbered the members. In Nettleham chapel in 1872, sixty-eight persons rented seats, but there were only twenty-eight members in the society. At Fenton chapel in 1851, fifty-nine persons rented a total of ninety seats, but there were only thirty members.[1] Ten years later there were still fifty-nine persons renting seats but only thirty-four members. It would appear that many of the adherents were quite firm and faithful in their less-than-total commitment. Examining the Wesleyan seat-renters in greater detail in the chapels at Fenton, Upton, and Horsington reveals the influence both of occupation and of geographical distance. At the chapel at Fenton, in Kettlethorpe parish,[2] half the farmers of the parish, more than half the craftsmen, and about a third of the labouring families rented seats in 1851.

[1] Seat-rent books for Nettleham and Fenton chapels; Circuit Schedule Book, Lincoln C.R.

[2] About half the population of the parish (541 in 1851, 486 in 1861) lived in Fenton township half a mile from the church at Kettlethorpe; most of the remainder lived at the hamlet of Laughterton, a mile from the chapel at Fenton and three-quarters of a mile from the church.

Occupation and Place of Residence of Seat-Renters in Fenton Chapel, 1851

	Fenton township		Laughterton hamlet		Kettlethorpe hamlet		Kettlethorpe parish	
	renters	total	renters	total	renters	total	renters	total
Farmers	4	8	2	6	2	3	8	17
Craftsmen, shopkeepers	16	24	1	6	0	0	17	30
Labourers	13	28	7	27	1	4	21	59
Total	33	60	10	39	3	7	46	106

In Fenton over half the families rented seats, but only a quarter of those in Laughterton, a mile from the chapel. Ten years later about half the families in each of the three occupational groups rented seats—a rising proportion of labourers—including two of the six farmers with more than 300 acres. The effect of distance again was apparent: thirty-three of the fifty-nine families at Fenton were renters, but only twelve of thirty-eight families at Laughterton a mile away. (Three of seven families at Kettlethorpe near the church had seats in chapel.) Similar conclusions emerge from an analysis of Upton chapel in 1851.[1] (The chapel was in Upton township; the parish contained a second township at Kexby half a mile away.) Of the nineteen farming families in Upton township, nine rented seats, as did six of eight craftsmen's families, but only five out of twenty labouring families. Very few Kexbyites of any occupational group appear among the renters: the Primitive Methodist chapel in Kexby was presumably more convenient. Evidence survives also for the chapel at Horsington around 1840.[2] Of the twenty farmers in the parish (mostly under 100 acres) half rented seats in the chapel, as did half the thirteen craftsmen's families, but only six of thirty-two labourers' families. Twenty years later the chapel was enlarged; the list of contributors shows that half the farmers' families contributed, seven of thirteen craftsmen's families, but only eight of forty-one labourers' families. The evidence just surveyed is too scanty to support anything like a sweeping conclusion, but a common pattern emerges. Farmers were well represented in every case, and there is little reason to suppose that larger farmers preferred the services of the parish church: at Upton, notably, the six largest farmers (with farms ranging from 100 to 270 acres) all had seats in chapel.[3]

[1] Upton Chapel Seat Book, Gainsborough C.R.
[2] Horsington Chapel Book, Bardney C.R.
[3] And at Horsington in 1860 five of the eight farmers with holdings of 100 acres

Relatively more craftsmen, shopkeepers, and other members of the rural lower middle class rented seats than any other group. Labourers rented the least often—but there were always free seats for the poor. Finally, those living at a distance from the chapel were less likely to rent a seat or pew in it; and farmers and craftsmen were more likely than labourers to walk (or ride) to a seat in a distant chapel.

Of all the groups in local society, the gentry undoubtedly were the least friendly to Methodism, yet they were by no means uniformly hostile. There had been a Methodist squire at Raithby-by-Spilsby early in the century;[1] Hynman Allenby, a small owner at Legbourne, was a Wesleyan local preacher; and Weston Cracroft-Amcotts of Hackthorn is known to have 'confided to his diary that he was really a dissenter, but that he wanted to live with his own social class and among gentlemen'.[2] Some landlords, however, were unfriendly and refused to sell them land for a chapel. Even the Monsons, Whigs after 1841, refused a site to their Wesleyan tenants in South Carlton, and despite Weston Cracroft-Amcotts's sympathies with the Methodists he did not allow them one until 1869, after they had met for decades in a private house.[3] But an unfriendly landlord was not necessarily fatal to the cause: besides meeting in a house they sometimes could build a chapel just across the boundary in an adjoining parish.[4] In any event some of the largest landowners in the district were positively friendly to Methodism, above all Lord Yarborough in north Lindsey, who may well have had some influence on his fellow Whigs in the south. The Heneages, for example, the principal

---

or more contributed to the chapel fund, but only five of the thirteen with less than 100 acres.

[1] Robert Carr Brackenbury, who died in 1818. (See Terence R. Leach, 'The Methodist Squire of Raithby', *Journal of the Lincolnshire Methodist History Society*, i (1970), and Mary Smith, *Raithby Hall*, 1859.) Brackenbury's widow, also a Methodist, kept Methodist tenants on the estate, notably at Lusby, down to her death in 1847.

[2] F. Hill, *Victorian Lincoln*, p. 180, citing his Diary, 29 Sept. 1851.

[3] Petition from the Wesleyans of South Carlton to Monson, n.d. [probably c. 1880], MON 23/2/5a–6; *Mkt Rasen W.M.*, 12 June 1869.

[4] The Wesleyans of Hatton had no hope of building a chapel in the parish, which was owned by the arch-Tory Colonel Sibthorp, but obtained land for one just across the parish boundary in Minting; the Wesleyans of Snarford, blocked by the (Roman Catholic) owners, the Tichborne family, built instead in neighbouring Welton; the situation was the same in Muckton, where the opposition of the Lister family led the Wesleyans to build in Little Cawthorpe.

resident landlords in the North Wolds, allowed chapels in three
of the four parishes on the estate.[1] And such was the strength of
Methodism that strict Tories like the Chaplins and the Stanhopes
had to respect it. When James Banks Stanhope stood for Parliament in 1852 he brought one of his Wesleyan tenant farmers with
him to election meetings—there was a chapel in his home parish of
Revesby; once elected he did not neglect his duty of contributing
to Wesleyan funds.[2] Even the more bellicose Tory landowners had
Wesleyan tenants, prompted perhaps by a latent anti-clericalism
to tolerate, if not positively to encourage, the Wesleyan interest in
their parishes.

Methodism was of course much stronger among the farmers,
who were the backbone of many a village society. As the evidence
for the seat-renters suggested, the appeal of Methodism was not
limited to the smaller farmers: some of the largest in the area
were members. When the Alford circuit undertook to pay off its
chapel debts, seven of the eleven large contributors of 50 and 100
guineas were farmers; one farmed 164 acres of rich grassland in
the Marsh; two more had 200 acres each; there was a farmer of
480 acres, another of 724, and an owner of 2,000 acres who
occupied a farm of 200. At Great Carlton in the Louth circuit
two principal farmers, Roger Sharpley, farming 1,406 acres, and
John Foster, with 396, both were Wesleyans. Men of their means
and influence could do much for chapel, circuit, and connection:
a single large farmer might contribute the site for a chapel and
much of the money as well. As officials, farmers tended to be
society stewards and class leaders, though there was no shortage
of local preachers. Unofficially, they provided 'preachers' homes'
for the ministers when they came out to the village chapels for
weeknight services; the ministers recalled their 'profuse hospitality':

The friends in the country places were exceedingly kind to us. Many
were wealthy farmers, and they not only found us first-rate accommoda-
tion both for man and beast, when we visited them, but supplied us
very generously with Christmas cheer in that interesting and joyful

---

[1] There was also a Roman Catholic chapel in the home parish of Hainton: the
Heneages were traditionally Roman Catholic, though two successive heads of the
family in the first half of the century were Church of England.

[2] He gave £3 to the relief fund for chapel debts in the Alford circuit in 1858 (list
of contributors, Alford C.R.).

season, which lasted very often four or five weeks, and consisted of pork sausages, pork-pies, etc.[1]

At the 'family altar' Methodist farmers brought their children and other dependants into the fold. The household of Francis Riggall, farming 355 acres at Dexthorpe, was representative: when the children were present, his wife 'would pray for each by name', and though he did not specifically hire Methodist servants, they all became Methodists under his influence. William Riggall, a farmer of 175 acres at Tetford, a class leader and 'liberal supporter' of Wesleyan interests, 'commanded his household after him'.[2] A Wesleyan farmer would also hire Wesleyan labourers. When the parish of Ruckland was rented to a Methodist farmer (the whole parish was one farm), the Anglican incumbent assumed that he would employ Methodist labourers. Such farmers would bring in suitable labourers to work in the parish if there were none there already. A labourer who showed promise as a local preacher or who simply was a faithful Methodist might find work with one Methodist farmer after another. Charles Richardson worked as a thresher for three successive Wesleyan farmers, serving the last of them as a kind of domestic chaplain, leading the family devotions. When he set up his own business as a woolwinder, 'many of the farmers who employed him were religious men'.[3] Indeed, farmers could patronize Wesleyan craftsmen and shopkeepers in the villages and Wesleyan merchants in the towns. Louth was particularly important in this respect and the dominant figure in the town society, John Booth Sharpley, was a corn merchant. Finally, a farmer could seek to apprentice his sons to Wesleyan craftsmen. For those who wished to be part of it, there was a wide-ranging network of co-religionists who reinforced religious ties with economic interest, social intercourse, and kinship.

This network also included labourers and others lower in the social scale, and Methodism thus tended to bring together those who in secular society were divided by class lines. Farmers and labourers met on equal terms in class meetings and farmers

[1] Joseph Whitehead, *The Evangelist and Pastor*, 1879, p. 91; see also John H. Beech, *Outer Life of a Methodist Preacher*, 1884, p. 92.

[2] Joseph Bush, *Elizabeth Riggall: A Memorial*, 1793, pp. 32, 39; *Wesleyan Methodist Magazine*, cii (1879), pp. 559-60.

[3] Coulson, *Peasant Preacher*, pp. 12-13, 65.

listened to sermons preached by labourers and craftsmen; all of this implied a suspension of the class divisions deepening in the wider society. Methodism thus served to retard the emergence of the farming class.

Too little is known about the social position of artisans and shopkeepers to allow a full interpretation of their allegiance to Methodism, but there is little doubt at least that they were more consistently Wesleyan than any other occupational group. And it is clear that they were in a position to benefit economically from the patronage of farmers and other Wesleyan customers, though evidence is lacking to show that this was a motive for joining. Some Anglicans claimed, without offering evidence, that Wesleyan shopkeepers put pressure on their customers—many of whom were in debt to them over long periods—to attend chapel. In fact the direction of influence may have been precisely the reverse. At Bardney, for example, it was noted that 'so many attend *both* [church and chapel] especially Shopkeepers for the sake of custom'. In a market town like Spilsby it was expected that churchmen would take their business to churchmen, and that Methodists would take theirs to fellow Methodists: 'their trade', the Ancaster estate agent noted, 'is mostly with that party'.[1] As so often in the nineteenth century, religion was a public commitment that determined a person's social identity. Finally, the high proportion of craftsmen and shopkeepers in the ranks of local preachers suggests a possible implicit protest against the ecclesiastical and social establishments, the claiming of a place in the social sun.

The scarcity of precise information on membership is especially frustrating in the case of the labourers. They appear to have rented seats in chapel less often than craftsmen or labourers, yet it cannot be inferred from that fact that they were less likely to attend services in chapel or to be members. On general principles—the well-attested observation that the working classes are less inclined to join voluntary organizations than the higher classes—a lower level of membership would be expected. But that would not preclude a high level of attendance, with a proportionately higher level of adherents. Labourers could find in Wesleyan Methodism much that suited their tastes—sermons without frills, spontaneity

---

[1] Bardney, 1886 V.R. Findlay to Kennedy, 29 Apr. 1851, 3 ANC 7/23/60/71, and 9 Mar. 1858, 3 ANC 7/23/74/48.

and informality. For some it provided a whole way of life, the means to occupy and improve virtually every spare hour. Indeed it probably appealed most to the respectable labourer or to the rough labourer bent on improving himself, for it consistently promoted 'modern' attitudes towards life and work. It condemned the childishness of adults who still played juvenile games;[1] indirectly it reacted against the roughness of the older society. If it was slow to commit itself to the cause of total abstinence, its round of tea meetings featured 'the cup that cheers but not inebriates', and the setting for a respectable form of sociability. Those who became local preachers might acquire unrivalled experience in public speaking. Methodism tended to de-parochial-ize villagers, unlike the Establishment, which sought to confine them within their parishes physically and mentally. Every Wesleyan was brought in contact with local preachers from other villages, and from the town, and with the succession of itinerant ministers. The system promoted circuit-mindedness, and beyond that, connection-mindedness. And missionary enterprise—the missionary anniversary was one of the principal 'special services' in the calendar, and often justified the invitation to a special minister from outside the circuit—took villagers still further into the wider world. (It might also be noted that about a tenth of the ministers in south Lindsey circuits in the course of the period had had previous experience in overseas missions.) Above all, Method-ism acknowledged the infinite worth of the labourer's soul and his practical worth as an active member of his society. In Methodism, labourers were not just part of the anonymous mass of the poor, but class leaders, local preachers, or perhaps just converted persons. Thus they were recognized as individual souls before they were recognized as individuals. The sense of personal worth and the sense of the seriousness of life gained from Methodism in religious matters would eventually pass over into secular life.

Yet Methodism could also exert an influence on labourers that was the reverse of modern. When they indulged in late-night lovefeasts and revival meetings, work discipline was undermined; the inter-class fellowship within Methodism perpetuated a sem-blance of the traditional village community, delaying the advent of modern class solidarity. And when Methodists created their

[1] *Mkt Rasen W.M.*, 1 Oct. 1859.

economic networks they reversed the modern tendency to differentiate the economic from other realms.

For all classes, Methodism constituted a community within the dissolving wider community. This function was conservative, but in differing degrees for different groups. It was probably least so for artisans and shopkeepers, who found in Methodism a way of asserting themselves against the social and religious establishment. For the farmers, it preserved something of a traditional communal outlook and retarded the growth of class consciousness. It also did so for the labourers, but at the same time it awakened the sense of individual identity and of the transcendent worth of the soul which previously had been dormant or repressed, and it replaced traditional village ways with a more individual and responsible conception of conduct.

SOME SOCIAL CONSEQUENCES

The general social consequences of Methodism, like its effects upon particular classes, were ambiguous, with 'traditional' and 'modern' influences at work simultaneously. A good example is its effects on relations between town and countryside. While its predominant effect was to bring villagers into closer contact with the towns and to expose them to urban influence, it also kept town Methodists in touch with the chapel life of the villages. Local preachers from the villages preached in town chapels, and town preachers came out to village chapels. Villagers attended services in the towns, and town 'friends' flocked to special services in the country.[1] And there were familial and financial links between town and country members.

In most of these exchanges, though, the initiating impulse and greater vigour came from the towns. In many villages, Methodism was first planted by 'missionaries' from the towns: the Wesleyans of Louth had '"followed the example of the Saviour Himself, who preached in the villages of Galilee as well as in the cities"'.[2] It was a Horncastle man who formed a class at near-by High Toynton and led it for thirty-five years; and another from the same town

[1] Many visitors were present at one of the great events in local Methodism in the second quarter of the century—the lovefeast on New Year's Day in Horncastle chapel, known as the 'Horncastle glory' (Benjamin Gregory, *Life of Frederick James Jobson, D.D.*, 1884, p. 19).

[2] *Louth Times*, 31 Jan. 1880. I owe this reference to Dr. R. J. Olney.

who for many years led a class meeting at West Ashby.[1] The flow
of preachers was also predominantly from town to village, as was
the flow of visitors to special services. Thus a missionary meeting
at Heapham in 1872 attracted visitors from Lincoln, Gainsborough, and Brigg in north Lindsey, and in 1860, when the
Saxilby chapel was reopened, special trains were chartered to
carry visitors from Lincoln.[2] Town laymen often presided at
missionary and Sunday school anniversaries in country chapels,
but rarely if ever was it the other way around. A large proportion
of the trustees of village chapels were townsmen; in six chapels in
the Bardney circuit in the 1860s, thirty-one of seventy-three
trustees lived in towns.[3] By the end of the period, there were complaints of a lack of 'Methodistic aggression in the rural district'
and of an unwillingness among country members to contribute
their proper share towards circuit funds; it was felt that the
village societies had become too dependent upon the town societies.[4] That dependence also appeared in the social and economic
links between town and country Methodists. There was of course
interdependence as well, notably between farmers and tradesmen;
in fact certain families prominent in south Lindsey Methodism
like the Sharpleys and the Riggalls had dual branches, with
merchants and tradesmen in the towns and farmers in the countryside. Nevertheless the long-term economic as well as demographic
drift was from village to town, and the economic attraction
of Methodist farmers could not rival that of urban counterparts.
Methodist tradesmen appear to have taken special pains to employ
Methodist apprentices and assistants: thus J. Morton and Son,
ironmongers at Louth, advertised in *The Watchman*, a Wesleyan
newspaper, for 'an Assistant. A Wesleyan preferred'.[5] Henry
Lunn, 'Wholesale and Family Grocer' at Horncastle, who had
earlier advertised in the same paper for a Wesleyan assistant, well
illustrates the workings of the family and economic network in
urban Methodism. He had come to Horncastle to set himself up in

[1] *Wesleyan Methodist Magazine*, lxxviii (1855), p. 185; xci (1878), pp. 757–8; cv
(1882), pp. 171–3.
[2] *Retf. News*, 15 June 1872; *Linc. Gaz.*, 30 June 1860. So great was the town members' appetite for entertainment that an event as unmomentous as a Sunday school
anniversary the following year also justified a chartered train (*Linc. Gaz.*, 23 Mar.
1861).
[3] List of chapel trustees in Circuit schedule book 1867–90, Bardney C.R.
[4] *Methodist*, 5 Feb. 1874.
[5] *Watchman*, 13 Dec. 1861.

business under the guidance of his uncle, Mark Holdsworth, a
Wesleyan chemist and druggist. His son was active both in the
family business and in local Wesleyan affairs before embarking on
his career.[1] And one of Holdsworth's apprentices, Joseph Bush,
son of a Wesleyan small farmer in a near-by village, became first
a local preacher and later a minister and eventually Chairman of
Conference. Similarly, a Methodist father would try to place a son
as an apprentice with a Methodist craftsman: Christopher Cole, a
grocer and draper of Skendleby, advertised in *The Watchman* for a
place for his son, 'a respectable youth', with a joiner and builder—
'a pious family will be preferred'.[2] In these affairs the predominant
influence was the town. Thus both the formal institutions of
Methodism and its informal networks broke down parochialism
in the countryside and brought the villagers into the urban
world.

As a voluntary organization Methodism also fostered in its
members a new outlook, individual as well as collective, towards
money. To some degree this was inevitable in a church without
endowments, but in Methodism finances sometimes attracted
more attention even than the figures of membership. Thus the
ministers of the Spilsby circuit noted in a quarterly report on the
state of the circuit that there was first of all 'financial prosperity',
as well as 'good and attentive congregations, and a deepened
spirituality among the societies'.[3] Methodism collected money for
numerous funds: chapels, worn-out ministers, and especially for
foreign missions. Despite the high degree of 'lay agency', most of
the trouble of managing these funds devolved upon the ministers.
Some won special reputations as good 'business men', but 'some
studious men', James Kendall complained, '*hate* this everlasting
pounds, shillings, and pence work'.[4] Missionary funds were
especially time-consuming; guest preachers had to be arranged for
anniversaries at every society in the circuit. Indeed, one element
in the cult of preachers was financial: a popular preacher would
attract large congregations and large collections. No secret was
made of this when the well-known James Everett was invited in
1845 to preach at a chapel reopening: 'Our friends at Scamblesby

---

[1] He was a controversial Wesleyan medical missionary in India, a promoter of
ecumenical conferences, and founder of the travel agency.
[2] Lunn, *Chapters*, p. 4; Hoyle, *Joseph Bush*, p. 20; *Watchman*, 6 June 1855.
[3] *Watchman*, 29 Mar. 1865.
[4] Kendall, *Remarks*, p. 9.

very earnestly solicit the favour of your services to reopen their Chapel. ... They have been at considerable expense in the enlargement and are anxious to make the reopening as productive as possible.' An unpopular minister would threaten not only the spiritual health of a circuit but also its financial prosperity: a leading layman in the Alford circuit urged Dr. Bunting not to appoint a certain minister to the circuit, for if he did, 'the *cause must sink*, and the *funds decline*'.[1] The most important financial concern was chapel debts. Chapels were inevitably built to accommodate not only the members and current hearers, but also, in a speculative spirit, the expanded congregation of a more prosperous future; the resulting debt could cause anxiety for decades. So great was the burden in the Alford circuit that a special fund-raising campaign was launched in 1858 to pay it off; the Spilsby circuit followed a decade later.[2] The final clearing of a debt was a time for jubilation: when, only two years after the chapel was built, the Hackthorn society announced the happy news, 'the effect produced will not soon be forgotten. All the people began to *shout* praises and thanksgiving to the Most High, who had so prospered his people.'[3]

Even without chapels to pay for, the calls on Methodist purses were unremitting. Besides paying seat-rent, a Methodist was expected to contribute to circuit funds—a penny a week in class meeting and a shilling a quarter at the renewal of the ticket of membership—and to connectional funds like the Worn-Out Ministers' and Widows' Fund, each with its appointed time of collection in the denominational calendar. In the churches, by contrast, the clergy found it difficult to extract any voluntary contributions at all, and landlords probably took as much in impropriated tithes as they gave to church funds. Rarely did they match the level of giving set by affluent Wesleyan farmers, exemplary benefactors of chapel, circuit, and connectional funds. The less affluent Methodists and adherents were no less generous; the trio of anniversaries—chapel, Sunday school, and missionary —were great money-makers as well as popular festivals. It is remarkable that the Wesleyan Missionary Society, the most

[1] Crookes to Everett, 22 June 1845, and Abbott to Bunting, 29 July 1840, Wes. min. corr., M.A.R.C.

[2] Alford Circuit Relief Fund 1858, Alford C.R. Notebook for 'Scheme for the extinction of Chapel Debts', Spilsby C.R.

[3] *Mkt Rasen W.M.*, 1 July 1871.

remote of these causes, held if anything a greater appeal than any of the others.[1] Methodism thus affected attitudes towards money by requiring regular contributions, by eliciting gifts and commitment to distant causes, and by drawing its members into large projects like the building of chapels which involved the repayment of debts over extended periods.

Methodism was even more rigorous in its moral demands, particularly on the local preachers, who were subject to an exacting collective self-discipline. In their quarterly meetings they devoted much time to the consideration of complaints about individual preachers and to imposing suitable punishment. Missing an appointment without arranging a substitute was the most common misdemeanour: but the less frequent ones perhaps reveal more about the Methodist social and moral ethos. A local preacher in the Alford circuit who was guilty of the 'sin of intemperance' was not only dropped from the plan but expelled from membership.[2] For the lesser indiscretion of having 'married out of the Lord' (condemned by the connectional rules) a preacher in 1849 was 'expostulated with'; two decades later one was told that he 'must withdraw' from the cricket club he had joined.[3] Failure in business was regarded as destroying a preacher's credibility. A grocer and draper of Huttoft, having settled with his creditors for eight shillings in the pound, was removed from the plan; in the Bardney circuit, 'Messrs. Dobson and Waterman, having failed in business, have sent in their plans'.[4] To be a Methodist, and presumably a fervent one, did not automatically bring success in one's calling. Discipline over ordinary members, though formidable in theory, was less strict in practice. In earlier Methodism women were expected to dress plainly, without ostentation, but by the second quarter of the century few if any traces of this code survived. Around 1860 the fashion for crinolines conquered Methodist women as well as more worldly ones,

[1] Lunn (*Chapters*, pp. 8–9) recalls a labourer in the early 1850s who donated sixpence from his weekly earnings of fifteen shillings to the Missionary Society.

[2] Local preachers' minute book, Alford circuit, 22 Dec. 1859. The circuit plan, issued quarterly, listed all the chapels and 'preaching places' in the circuit and indicated for each the names of the preachers appointed for every service that quarter; it also listed the ministers and (in order of seniority) the local preachers—hence, to be 'dropped from the plan'.

[3] Local preachers' minute books, Alford circuit, 29 Mar. 1849; Spilsby circuit, 23 Sept. 1869.

[4] Minute books, Alford circuit, 24 Sept. 1858; Bardney circuit, 27 Dec. 1869.

and at Wragby chapel it was reported that they were finding difficulty in fitting them through the doors of their pews.[1] Sabbatarian laws proved more hardy. Henry Winn recalled that the Methodists of his youth, in the 1820s, would clean their shoes on Sunday but not grease them, since that benefited the leather, and that men who had not shaved before midnight on Saturday 'would wear the beard of another week sooner than infringe upon the Sabbath'.[2] The sabbatarian code appears to have relaxed somewhat in later years, but the chronology is obscure. The appeal of temperance, by contrast, grew considerably from the 1830s to the 1870s, though it never became as strong among the Wesleyans as among the Primitive Methodists. As late as the 1850s stewards would offer ministers a glass of port after their sermon. Locally, Wesleyans seem to have shown some sympathy with the movement at its outset: in 1838, total abstinence meetings were held in Wesleyan chapels at Withern, Hogsthorpe, and Willoughby. But the last of these was interrupted, significantly, by a 'little drop' man—a Wesleyan local preacher. One of his fellow preachers, at a temperance meeting two years later, 'dealt out some hard hits at his brethren and religious professors generally, because many of them hesitated to give the pledge and assist the cause'.[3] By 1875 it was estimated that two-thirds of the Primitive Methodist ministers in the area but only half of the Wesleyan ministers were teetotallers.[4] And throughout the period the membership included innkeepers and brewers. The Wesleyans brought the temperance cause to more people than any other denomination, but did so less wholeheartedly and compellingly than the Primitive Methodists or the separate temperance organizations.

If ambivalent about temperance, Wesleyans eagerly promoted the larger ideal of self-improvement; and their enthusiasm for it reflects the growing influence of secular and middle-class values in Methodism in the second half of the century. The newer teaching tended to displace religious concerns even if it did not eliminate them. When a Wesleyan minister condemned the labourers' custom of playing children's games, he said that

[1] *Mkt Rasen W.M.*, 24 Sept. 1859.
[2] Winn 3/1, p. 16.
[3] *Stamf. Merc.*, 5 Jan. and 25 May 1838; *Linc. Gaz.*, 27 Oct. 1840.
[4] *Retf. News*, 11 Dec. 1875. See also Brian Harrison, *Drink and the Victorians*, 1971, pp. 179–81, 311.

jumping in sacks 'and eight or ten other fooleries were equally out of character with the manifest march of mind which distinguishes the nineteenth century, and awfully inconsistent with the Christian religion, which consists of "Righteousness, peace, and joy in the Holy Ghost"'.[1] Placing the march of mind before the Holy Ghost was a sign of the times: Thomas Hughes devoted an entire book to the theme, extolling the pursuit of knowledge to the neglect of matters like sin and repentance.[2] Other ministers in the area preached the full Victorian gospel of self-help and character-building. A representative work in this genre was William Unsworth's *Self-Culture and Self-Reliance*, appearing in 1861; its content is accurately reflected in its subtitle, *The Poor Man's Help to Elevation on Earth and in Heaven*. Rejecting the 'doctrine of innate ideas' (and ignoring the doctrine of Original Sin), he offered to poor young men—young women were apparently denied the prospect of self-help—the chance to rise 'to comfort, respectability, and intelligence'. It was 'no disgrace to be poor'—indeed poverty stimulated effort, and most great men had 'risen from the middle and lower classes'. Yet the hard-working, self-improving young man was not encouraged to put economic goals first; making the most of his talents was above all required 'on moral grounds, from a conviction of duty to God, himself, and his fellows'.[3] The moral imperative took precedence over the economic, and the goal was not so much the making of money as the remaking of the self, an impressive and sufficient accomplishment in itself.

Rewards in the after-life, like monetary rewards, were not forgotten, but they were not a central motivation. Though the ideal of self-culture was in some sense religious it was ceasing to be distinctively Christian; the emphasis had shifted from soul-making to self-making. The new ethic was discussed further by Joseph Bailey in *Life's Crowning Ornament, or Excellence of Character and How to Acquire It*. The virtues he admired were openness, generosity, decision, and diligence; they were to be acquired by 'self-culture', whose 'fixed principles' included the care 'never to

[1] *Mkt Rasen W.M.*, 1 Oct. 1859. Ironically the warning was directed against a fete at Bayons Manor, Tealby, the seat of Charles Tennyson d'Eyncourt—a Radical M.P. for Lambeth and a generous supporter of village schools and mechanics' institutes, with an almost visionary faith in the march of mind.

[2] T. Hughes, *Mental Furniture*, 1857.

[3] W. Unsworth, *Self-Culture and Self-Reliance*, 1861, pp. 3, 12, 17.

lose one moment of time', daily Bible reading, and 'the habit of persevering prayer'. 'Character,' the author concluded, was 'the only thing you can take with you into eternity.'[1] If he gave his message a slightly more Christian colouring, he and his fellow ministers advocated an essentially secular ethic of self-realization; and unlike the clergy with their static social ideal, they all welcomed social mobility at least as an indirect consequence of their teaching. Whether they made many converts is an open question; like orthodoxy on the one hand and certain items of pagan folklore on the other, these social superstitions were probably 'accepted' more frequently than they were acted upon.

The political influence of Methodism is less easy to trace than might be expected. Membership lists are lacking, and the poll books, which say nothing about the unfranchised, record only outward behaviour and not beliefs and convictions. And there were no contested elections after 1852 to elicit political choices. In the 1841 election, sixty-two Wesleyan electors have been identified; twenty-seven plumped for Lord Worsley, the Whig, while twenty-five voted for the Conservatives Christopher and Cust. Altogether Worsley received thirty-seven votes, Christopher thirty-three, and Cust twenty-seven. In 1852, 118 Wesleyans have been identified; forty-three plumped for Cholmeley, the Whig, while fifty-one gave two votes to the Tories Christopher and Stanhope. Altogether Cholmeley received sixty-four votes, Christopher and Stanhope sixty-three each. Thus 36 per cent of the Wesleyans plumped for Cholmeley and 43 per cent gave two votes to the Tories; the comparable percentages for the Lindsey electorate as a whole were 34 and 45.[2] If there was a Whig or Liberal tendency among the Wesleyans, it was slight at best. Wesleyan farmers renting land from Tory landowners generally voted Tory like the other tenants; those renting from Liberal landowners likewise conformed to the wishes of their landlords. Perhaps the effect of Methodism on political attitudes and beliefs, as distinguished from voting behaviour, was greater—and it may well have increased in the second half of the century—but at present it is impossible to measure.

[1] J. Bailey, *Life's Crowning Ornament*, 1871, pp. 14–18, 23, 25, 27.
[2] Poll books for North Lincolnshire, 1841 and 1852; Olney, *Lincolnshire Politics*, p. 134.

RELIGION AS ENTERTAINMENT

More important than any of Methodism's external effects on secular life were the ways in which its internal religious activities met secular needs. Wesleyan acts of worship—not to mention its 'special services'—provided chapel-goers not only with the means of grace but also with the means of entertainment. In a society lacking public forms of diversion, Wesleyan Methodism offered a respectable counter-attraction to the beerhouse and village feast on the one hand and a more enjoyable alternative to the parish church on the other.

One of the keys to the success of Methodism was that it was attuned to what as early as the 1830s had been identified as 'the real spirit of the age . . . the prevailing thirst for religious novelty and variety'.[1] This was unlikely to be satisfied in the parish church, where villagers might have to endure the sermons of the same clergyman during a long Victorian incumbency, and were warned not to seek relief elsewhere. In Methodism, however, there was novelty and variety in abundance. Later in the century it was recalled that 'when intercourse was limited, and openings for any sort of administrative and spirit-stirring service were few, the little Methodist chapel, and the Circuit, and the Conference, and the visits of the famous preachers, and the perpetual freshening of the itinerancy, lifted the people above the common lethargies.'[2] Above all it was sermons that moved—and entertained—congregations, and the leading preachers inevitably became Methodist folk heroes: 'In the absence of all other excitements, eloquence was the supreme delight . . . preachers were the major stars.'[3] Methodists had 'a strange sense of ownership in their preachers', the best of whom, with their powerful, sometimes idiosyncratic performances, became the objects of a virtual cult.[4] Since a popular preacher appearing at a missionary anniversary or other special service could be counted on to attract a large crowd—and elicit large contributions—the 'major stars', not to mention a local star like Charles Richardson, were in constant demand. Over-

---

[1] This was the view of Thomas Cooper, as a local correspondent of the *Stamf. Merc.*, 28 Dec. 1837.

[2] Hoyle, *Joseph Bush*, p. 15.

[3] W. J. Dawson, *Autobiography of a Mind*, 1925, p. 48. This recollection of Methodist life in St. Albans applies to south Lindsey as well.

[4] Lunn, *Chapters*, p. 267.

worked, some of them all but preached themselves to death, but the popular thirst for eloquence could never be completely satisfied.

It was after 1850, in the special services, that Methodists went furthest in providing villagers with entertainment. Inevitably this was at the expense of a blurring of religious content; the anniversaries owed to Methodism their theme and occasion and auspices, but not their meaning, or a large part of their attraction. A star preacher was indispensable, to assure a large attendance: when Punshon, one of the famous Wesleyan preachers, appeared at Horncastle for a bazaar and service, an 'immense crowd' was attracted and a barely credible £444 raised for circuit funds.[1] But the entertainment value of sermon and preacher was now being exploited in a setting quite different from the 'means of grace'. Not only was the anniversary held out of doors, in some farmer's field. There was also the insistent fund-raising, the tea-meetings, and above all the vast crowd; a chapel anniversary at Hackthorne, with a population of 248, was reported to have drawn 400 to the tea-meeting and 500 to the evening service.[2] By its sheer numbers an anniversary took on the character of a popular social festival, with respectable concourse and temperate conviviality as prime attractions. These were very real attractions to villagers whose traditional fairs and feasts had come under attack from parsons and magistrates; but they were attractions that presupposed specific, and temporary, social conditions. Like the Anglican harvest thanksgiving, the anniversaries reflected the post-1850 mood: the economic prosperity, the relaxation of class tensions, the sober and orderly behaviour of crowds; they also depended on the cult of preachers and on the continuing scarcity of respectable means of secular entertainment. With the passing of these conditions the anniversary-festivals dwindled into mere anniversaries, even if chapel-goers never lost their taste for a good sermon.

RELATIONS WITH THE CHURCH OF ENGLAND

Of all the Methodist and Dissenting groups the Wesleyans were the closest to the Church of England. While they rejected Anglican organization and found its piety wanting, they supported the

---

[1] P. Featherstone, *Reminiscences of a Long Life*, 1905, p. 42.
[2] *Mkt Rasen W.M.*, 23 July 1870.

principle of establishment and did not consider themselves full-
fledged Dissenters; many Wesleyans worshipped regularly in
their parish church. At the same time, however, they were the
Church's principal local rivals. They professed friendly respect for
the Church, but their numbers and zeal threatened it, and the
peaceful coexistence they offered was inevitably rejected by the
increasingly militant Anglicans. The advent of ritualism only
sealed their growing alienation, and by 1875 they were more
independent and critical of the Church than ever before in their
history.

Their respect for the Church was genuine. Wesleyan services
in south Lindsey were often scheduled so as to avoid a direct
conflict with those in the parish church, and members and
adherents alike often attended both church and chapel on the
same day. A staunch Wesleyan like John Rushby, a farmer at
Toynton St. Peter, left £150 to the Wesleyan day school, but was
'no bigot' and was 'not infrequently a worshipper at his parish
church'.[1] Even at the end of the period there were many parishes
like Spridlington: the Wesleyan chapel in the village was rarely
open at the same time as the parish church, 'the Wesleyans leaving
their place of worship sufficiently early to go straight to morning
service at the parish church. . . . After afternoon service in the
church a united family of Church and Dissent meet in the Wesleyan chapel, where they worship in a less formal but not less hearty
manner.'[2] Relations between Wesleyans and churchmen in the
Horncastle area were said to be free of conflict and hostility in the
1860s. Where parsons were friendly and content with the *status
quo*, Wesleyans showed no hostility.[3]

But increasing numbers of the parish clergy were unhappy with
the *status quo* and hoped to repulse the Methodist challenge. If the
Methodists directed their 'aggression' at the lukewarm and the
indifferent, the parsons were eager most of all to recapture those
lost to Methodism, and the Anglican counter-attack that gained
momentum after 1850 poisoned relations between the two
churches. The energetic and affluent new clergy alarmed Methodists particularly by taking aim at their Sunday schools—on which

[1] *Linc. Gaz.*, 4 Dec. 1875.
[2] ibid., 27 May 1871. The church in Spridlington appropriately was 'devoid of
ritualistic excesses', and the sermons, 'though not extempore', were 'free, flexible,
and full of truth'.
[3] Lunn, *Chapters*, pp. 2–3 and *passim*.

they were now increasingly reliant—luring children with bribes into the church schools or insisting that day scholars in church schools should attend church on Sunday. A threat of this kind led the Wesleyans at Scamblesby to set up their own day school out of sheer self-defence.[1] The more general threat posed by an active resident clergy could not be ignored: as early as 1865 it was recognized that the great size of the Methodist circuits made it 'impossible to bestow on our societies and congregations in the villages that pastoral oversight which is indispensable to the preservation of Methodism in such localities'.[2] Two years later the formation of the completely rural Bardney circuit brought more ministers to the villages, but the 'Home Mission Circuits' that would have served the same purpose were never established.[3] Wesleyans were dismayed to find themselves on the defensive in country parishes, and their outlook was far less optimistic in 1870 than it had been only ten or fifteen years earlier; the Anglican resurgence affected it more deeply than the Wesleyan Reform disruption at the middle of the century.

The spread of ritualism was even more disturbing. Ministers in the Lincoln District feared in 1873 that the interests of Methodism were 'seriously affected by the great activity of the Ritualistic section of the Church of England'; one of the ministers in the Gainsborough circuit lectured in the same year on the theme, 'The teaching of the Ritualists opposed to the doctrines of the Church of England and in harmony with the doctrines of Popery'.[4] Methodists still felt themselves to be close enough to the Church of England to act as keepers of its Protestant conscience, but they also feared the attractions of ritualism among their own congregations.

The climax of the Anglican counter-attack was Bishop Wordsworth's *Pastoral* to the Wesleyans in 1873; their replies indicate a reluctant but growing alienation from the Establishment. William Hudson, minister at Lincoln, called it 'an astounding manifesto. It must indeed rouse to hostility many who have hitherto lived in peace with the Bishop and his Church'. He regretted that Wesleyans were no longer able to ignore the

[1] *Louth Adv.*, 23 Feb. 1867.

[2] *Watchman*, 31 May 1865.

[3] Minutes of May 1873 meeting, Hull District minute book, M.A.R.C.

[4] *Retf. News*, 15 Mar. 1873; committee meeting, 27 May 1873, Lincoln District minute book, M.A.R.C.

Church of England and concentrate on their own work.[1] They rejected Wordsworth's contention that John Wesley was a good High Churchman and that he would have wished to stay within the Anglican Church; and they repudiated Anglican doctrines of apostolic succession, schism, and confirmation, among others. But their heaviest fire was directed at the Ritualists and Romanizers within the Church of England. 'Whilst every shade of doctrine from sapless rationalism on the one hand, to semi-popery on the other, is now taught from the pulpits of the Church of England, the Wesleyan pulpit retains its evangelical purity . . . its old Protestant ring.'[2] The bishop was told that his invitation to the Wesleyans to return to the Church was '100 years too late', and that he would be better employed purging the 'Popish follies' from his own churches.[3] Now it was the Church that was showing aggression: through no desire of their own, the Wesleyans reluctantly abandoned the role of loyal opposition and took a more independent stance, closer to Dissent, though without becoming as radical as the Primitive and Free Methodists.

In the last analysis, Anglican–Wesleyan relations were marked by a basic asymmetry. Wesleyans respected the Church, but to many of the clergy the very existence of Methodism in country parishes was unnatural and objectionable. At most, Wesleyans hoped to become the Church of the majority, but Anglicans hoped to extinguish Methodism and Dissent altogether. It was improper for a strict churchman to attend Methodist services, but it involved no breach of connectional discipline for a Methodist to worship in the parish church, to receive its sacraments, to serve it as parish clerk or churchwarden. At the local level relations depended almost entirely on the attitude of the individual clergyman. When he was friendly to the Methodists, they were friendly in return, and when he was hostile they were as well.[4] In 1875 many of the clergy were still tolerant of Methodism, but the tendency of the Anglican revival was to turn clerical attitudes from friendship to mere tolerance and from tolerance to hostility; the

---

[1] W. Hudson, *An Answer to Bishop Wordsworth's Pastoral*, 2nd edn., 1873, p. 3.

[2] W. Lindley, *A Reply to the Bishop of Lincoln's Pastoral*, 4th edn., 1873, p. 10.

[3] Wesleyan Ministers in the Gainsborough Circuit (T. S. Gregory, D. Jones, H. T. Brumwell), *Two Letters to the Bishop of Lincoln*, 1873, pp. 6–7.

[4] The same conclusion was reached by T. H. S. Escott, *England: Its People, Polity, and Pursuits*, 1879, i. 41.

Wesleyans were repelled from the Church with which their ties had been close for generations.

CONCLUSION

It is not surprising that a religious movement whose offerings and appeal were so broad and diverse should contain potentialities or tendencies which, complementary at an earlier stage, eventually came into opposition. On the one hand was a rigorous conception of the spiritual life and of moral conduct, involving conversion, the responsibility of membership, self-exposure in the class meeting, and subjection to Wesleyan discipline. On the other hand was the popular desire for entertainment, which was gratified in the Sunday service and in the special services. Of course the two tendencies converged as well as diverged. Sermons and singing appealed to all, revivalism yielded excitement as well as conversion, anniversaries commemorated as well as entertained. But by 1875 the divergence was apparent. If the class meeting was still viable, revivalism had declined, discipline relaxed, and 'special service' extravaganzas multiplied. Despite the Anglican challenge, Wesleyan rigour had given way to entertainment.

It was before undergoing this transformation that Wesleyan Methodism exerted its greatest appeal—during the previous seventy-five years, when traditional social relations were breaking down and traditional values were being undermined. For those who were reluctant to give up the sociability of the old village community, Methodism created a new, artificial community. Farmers and labourers could unite in the same congregation and in the same class meeting when they were being separated from each other in the wider society. The Methodist class denied, temporarily at least, social class. More generally, Methodism, with its structured community and ethical values, provided a new way of life and internal discipline for villagers 'who had previously little need of such . . . who had been controlled by community regulation, by agrarian values'.[1] Methodism thus had its maximum appeal in the period of transition between community and class— it is perhaps not accidental that the Methodist meanings of 'class', 'society', 'brothers', and 'friends' had their greatest currency in this period. This was also the period between the decline or suppression of the traditional recreations and the advent of

[1] Bryan Wilson, *Religion in Secular Society*, 1966, p. 25.

modern mass leisure, when Methodism was in a unique position to satisfy the popular desire for respectable entertainment. Before 1850, Methodist rigour and Methodist entertainment were in simultaneous demand. After 1850, as class relations eased and class cultures took shape, the need for rigour diminished; a generation later, Methodist entertainment would face serious secular competition. Thus the classic period of Wesleyanism coincided with a specific phase in the history of agrarian society, when large numbers of farmers, craftsmen, and labourers, reluctant to accept class separation and conflict, sought new forms for the older communal modes of social relations and new values with which to orient themselves in the new society.

The social origins of Wesleyan Methodism are therefore as complicated, and for some of the same reasons, as its specifically religious character. Its social consequences, simultaneously 'modern' and 'archaic', are no less so. Methodism preserved communal values, delaying the advent of classes and suspending class consciousness where it did exist, yet it also fostered an individualism and self-consciousness that were alien to the older society. It extended the villagers' awareness to the wider environment, urban, national, and international—but confined it within a Methodist framework of circuit, connection, and missionary society. Similarly ambiguous was the role of Methodism in instilling a new work ethic. If it was affecting anyone, it ought to have been the local preachers—who also were being initiated into chapel financial matters—yet a number of them were dropped because of their business failures. And the work ethic was so tenuous for a Charles Richardson that he worked only half the year in order to be free to go on preaching tours.[1] On balance Methodism served predominantly to further the cause of the modern, but not consistently and not always consciously.

The most important social consequence of Wesleyan Methodism was perhaps neither archaic nor modern. In creating an ethical community within the community and an extensive social network beyond it, Methodism gave its followers a distinct social as well as religious identity. To be a Methodist was to have Methodist friends, employers, customers, relations, masters, and

---

[1] John Kent, review of E. P. Thompson, *The Making of the English Working Class* in *Proceedings of the Wesley Historical Society*, xxxiv (1964), p. 188; Coulson, *Peasant Preacher*, pp. 50, 70.

servants; it was to have a distinct place, to take a certain stance in the world. At times rural society was divided more sharply by religion than by social class, and the principal responsibility for this lay with Wesleyan Methodism. In this respect it created a characteristically Victorian situation, in which religion was the key to social identity. The transition to the modern situaton occurred when growing class consciousness, growing concern for respectability, and the growing self-consciousness—indirectly fostered by Methodism itself—made impossible, particularly among the middle classes, the self-exposure required by the class meeting and revival meeting. They also made religion a matter of individual concern, belonging to the private rather than to the public sphere. The final ambiguity or irony about Methodism is that it helped to create the self-consciousness that undermined its own institutions. Its evolution from sect to denomination to that extent was self-generated, independent of the wider society.

V

PRIMITIVE METHODISM

I feel religion to be a blessed reality. It has not all been noise.
Robert Fawcit of Hogsthorpe, on his deathbed, 1855.
(*Primitive Methodist Magazine*, 1855, p. 699.)

THE Primitive Methodists, as they themselves would have
admitted, played no more than a secondary role in south
Lindsey, never rivalling the resources and membership of the
Church of England and the Wesleyan Methodists, the older and
larger groups that dominated the local religious scene. Yet their
role was nevertheless a distinctive one. For while the other
groups were large and heterogeneous—their followers formed a
cross-section both of rural society and of rural religiosity—Primitive Methodism was not only small but also homogeneous. The
'Ranters', as they were called, were poor—most were farm
labourers—and they were fervent. Moreover, although the various
branches of Methodism resist easy classification as sect, church,
order, cult, or denomination, Primitive Methodism in south
Lindsey presented many of the features of what sociologists of
religion have called a conversionist sect: missionary evangelism,
membership by conversion experience, strong internal discipline,
lay activity in organization, and spontaneity in worship.[1] Given
these characteristics, and its particular social base, Primitive
Methodism in south Lindsey invites analysis on two levels, as a
sect, a specific form of religious organization, and as the expression of the lower orders in rural society.

Like other sects of its type, it underwent a rapid internal
evolution that transformed its original character within two
generations. Beginning as a conversionist sect, it proceeded to lose
much of its original intensity and fervour, and by the 1870s had
taken on the characteristics of a denomination. Three stages in
this evolution can be identified: a 'heroic age' of missionary
expansion from 1820 to 1840, then two decades of revivalism and

[1] See especially Bryan Wilson (ed.), *Patterns of Sectarianism*, 1967.

consolidation, and after 1860 a third period of slackening energies, introversion, and denominationalism. Since other branches of Methodism underwent a similar transformation, it is probably to be explained less by external factors—though it can be linked with changes in the wider society—than by the internal dynamics of the sect itself.

Nevertheless, there can be no question of ignoring the sect's social composition, particularly since no other religious group in the area had a higher proportion of farm labourers. Primitive Methodism attracted farmers and craftsmen too, but it is from the farm labourers that it derived not merely its financial difficulties but also its style and tone—its directness, emotionalism, and spontaneity. By the same token, no other religious group left a deeper imprint upon its working-class members.

It should be kept in mind, though, that while Primitive Methodism was in an important sense a working-class sect, it attracted fewer farm labourers than its rivals, the parish churches and the Wesleyan chapels. An indirect indication of its subordinate position can be gained from the 1851 Religious Census, which shows that it had only forty-three places of worship in the area, compared with 124 for the Wesleyans and over 200 for the Church of England; thirty-eight of the forty-three faced direct competition from the Wesleyans as well as from the parish churches, and in nearly every case the Primitive Methodist attendance on Census Sunday was the smallest of the three. Since the majority of farm labourers were not Primitive Methodists, and since farmers and craftsmen played key roles in the sect, it is best to approach it less as the vehicle of a distinct social group than as a sect, a distinct type of religious organization, with its own internal structure and dynamics.

CIRCUITS AND PREACHERS

The machinery of Primitive Methodism was similar to that of the parent Wesleyan body but was more democratic and decentralized, favouring the laity where Wesleyanism favoured the ministers and giving authority to the circuit and district while the Wesleyan system was dominated by Conference.[1] Nevertheless in

---

[1] After the secession and expulsion of the Wesleyan Reformers the loyalist Wesleyans were popularly known as 'Conference Methodists'.

both was to be found the same proliferation of offices, officials, and meetings, and a strong family resemblance remained.

But the social bases of the two connections differed widely, and the poverty of the Primitive Methodists left its mark. Over long periods many congregations worshipped in cottages and barns rather than in chapels they could not afford. On Census Sunday, 1851, twenty-five congregations met in chapels, but a large minority, eighteen, met in other premises. Neither the building nor the financing of a chapel was an easy matter, and ministers specialized as 'chapel-builders' or as 'debt-reducers'.[1] The debts incurred in building a chapel often proved to be heavy burdens, and fund-raising continued for many years to pay them off. Within the chapels most of the sittings were rented—as in other branches of Methodism—and the rents were the societies' largest source of income. For Primitive Methodists, spiritual and financial prosperity were inseparable—and in an unintended way chapel-building may indeed have drained their spiritual as well as their financial resources.

While the most obvious unit of organization was the village or town society with its place of worship, it was crucial for Primitive Methodism as for the other branches of Methodism that these local units should be linked and co-ordinated in circuits. In the early decades, Primitive Methodist circuits enjoyed a high degree of autonomy, and probably in no other branch of Methodism was circuit organization as important. Ministers and local preachers circulated from chapel to chapel; 'country friends' attended special services in town chapels and the 'town friends' returned the favour; and prosperous laymen not only supported their own society but spread their bounty over an entire circuit.[2] Thus small village societies were not condemned to struggle alone, and the most was made of meagre resources. After the middle of the century the circuits yielded their independent powers to the districts, the next higher level of organization, but the local bias persisted.

The role of the ministers is less clear. Compared with their Wesleyan counterparts they were less well educated, less powerful, and more obscure; few left autobiographies. For most of the

---

[1] H. B. Kendall, *Origin and History of the Primitive Methodist Church*, n.d., ii. 455.
[2] Notably William Byron and John Maltby, large farmers in the Louth circuit. (Kendall, *Origin and History*, i. 452–3; *P.M.M.* 1864, pp. 296–303; 1873, pp. 747–50.)

period they were confined to the same district, and they had less opportunity than the more mobile Wesleyan ministers of winning a national reputation. And they were less sharply distinguished from their local preachers—they continued to be 'brothers' and 'itinerant preachers' when their Wesleyan counterparts had become 'reverend' and 'ministers'. Nor were they set apart in economic terms. In the Gainsborough circuit in 1852, for example, the superintendent minister received a total income of £62.12s. od. and the second minister only £36—about as much as a farm labourer. Steady increases brought their basic stipends in 1873 to £80 and £64 respectively,[1] rather above the earnings of the farm labourer, a sign of a more differentiated ministry. But for most of the period the minister was *primus inter pares* among the body of preachers and not an authoritative superior.

The work of a minister in a country circuit was formidable. On Sunday he usually had to journey to one or more village chapels and preach two or even three sermons. Still more demanding were the weeknight services in the villages. On four or even five nights a week the minister led services in different village chapels; this involved walking (at least until the 1850s) to the village in the afternoon, receiving hospitality at the home of one of the members, conducting the service, and walking back to the town late at night.

Of course they did not undertake the entire Sunday preaching duty single-handed. The majority of Sunday services were in fact conducted by local preachers. In four sample quarters less than a quarter of the total of 1,248 Sunday services were taken by ministers.[2] In village chapels they conducted less than a fifth of the services, the remainder being taken by the local preachers.

For ministers and 'locals' alike preaching was clearly their main work, and it was as preachers that they were known and ranked—in Primitive Methodist parlance the average preachers were 'acceptable,' the better ones were 'useful', and the best were 'popular'. Their aim was to save souls, and their message was stripped to essentials. They preached the 'three R's: ruin, repentance, and redemption'; the appropriate style was 'plain, pithy,

---

[1] Quarterly account book, Gainsborough C.R.

[2] This analysis is based on four circuit plans: Lincoln circuit, Apr.–June 1831; Louth, Jan.–Apr. 1839; Alford, Apr.–July 1860; Gainsborough, Jan.–Apr. 1874. The first is in Central Chapel, Lincoln; the second and third are in Hartley–Victoria College, Manchester; the fourth is in Gainsborough C.R.

pointed, and practical'. Conversions were the aim, as many and as quickly as possible. It was said of one exemplary minister that in his preaching 'he was proverbially a "just now" man, whether in reference to pardon or purity'.[1] At their best they preached with 'liberty' or with 'power' or with 'unction'; and since no great social or educational distance separated them from their congregations, they freely entered into the enthusiasm and excitement often kindled by their sermons. Yet amidst the uproar they never lost count of the number of penitents seeking pardon, the number converted, the number receiving 'entire sanctification'—and the amount of money collected. It was in this spirit that John Stamp looked back in 1839 over his three years as minister in the Louth circuit:

We have built 16 chapels, enlarged one, bought another, and fitted up a large room; and have had an increase of 25 local preachers and 416 members; and our last quarter's income was £65 more than the first . . . I have walked more than 10,000 miles, have preached upwards of 1,500 sermons, and have visited near 6,000 families.[2]

In Methodism, it was axiomatic that the workings of the spirit could be caught and set down in black and white. The apparatus of circuits, offices, record-keeping, and money-collecting, the diligence of the ministers—all served not to deaden the spirit of the faithful but to raise it to new peaks: such at least was the official assumption. In the long run, however, energy was diverted from the spiritual ends to the proliferating bureaucratic means.

THE 'MEANS OF GRACE' AND THE 'SPECIAL SERVICES'

The Primitive Methodists stood out among the organized religious groups of the area for their single-minded commitment to evangelism and revivalism. This appeal for souls was issued through what they and other Methodists called the 'means of grace'—'forms of worship' reflects a different religious setting and is not an exact equivalent. There were also 'special services'—principally the chapel, missionary, and Sunday school annivesaries—which be-

---

[1] Charles Kendall, *The Christian Minister in Earnest*, 1854, p. 41. This was a reference to Atkinson Smith, born at Scotter in north Lindsey and minister at Gains-borough 1844–5.
[2] *P.M.M.* 1839, pp. 418–19.

came prominent after 1850 and, as in Wesleyan Methodism, developed into popular festivals. Together they were remarkable for their number and variety.

The most familiar service was the Sunday afternoon or evening 'preaching service'. With extemporary prayers, hymns, and readings from scripture as well as the sermon, it too aimed at coversions. Its effectiveness was increased after 1840 by the introduction of the 'penitents' form', a pew at the front of the chapel reserved for 'seekers after pardon', on whom the congregation could direct their prayers and moral pressure. A composite picture of a Sunday service would reveal a hot, crowded chapel, a collective mood subject to swift change from tension to excitement to exultation, and—a good deal of noise, from the spontaneous shouts and cries of the congregation. One minister wrote in his diary after such a service, 'Legbourne. Many people. Flashing, thrilling, and transforming glory.' Another service was described as 'a very, *very* mighty time; two persons fell to the floor during the sermon; in fact, the whole congregation was broken down. One obtained liberty.'[1] The phenomena of 'enthusiasm' were consistently reported in Sunday services from the earliest missions in the 1820s down to the 1850s, when they began to be eclipsed by decorum, respectability, and 'worship'.

For the élite the prayer meetings were the most cherished means of grace. Often held on Sunday evenings after the last public service, they featured extemporaneous prayers both by prayer leaders (designated specially for these services) and by ordinary members; altogether they encouraged the fullest expression of lay piety. 'Prayer meetings both in chapel and cottage' were the 'delight' of Mrs Ann Oliver of Belchford; another member 'never attended ... a prayer meeting without praying [out loud]'. Probably the same was true of many of the most committed members.[2]

When a person was converted, and became a member of the Primitive Methodist Connection, he also joined one of the classes in his local society, a village society usually comprising from one to three classes. Regular attendance at the weekly class meeting

[1] Shaw, *Life of Rev. Parkinson Milson*, p. 136; C. Kendall, *Christian Minister*, p. 48.
[2] *P.M.M.* 1835, p. 439; 1881, p. 185; see also G. M. Morris, 'Primitive Methodism in Nottinghamshire 1815–1932', unpublished Ph.D. thesis, Nottingham University, 1967, pp. 123–4.

was a condition of continuing membership, and the class meeting ranked in esteem above most of the other means of grace. As in other branches of Methodism, the class leader would ask the members of his class in turn what the state of their soul was and what edifying experience from the previous week they could relate, and they answered more or less freely, in an atmosphere of spontaneous testimony and mutual confession. There were also the usual hymns and extemporary prayers. Outside the meeting, the class leader had a pastoral responsibility for his members, and often attended on them when they were ill or dying. In Wesleyan Methodism the class meeting began to decline from perhaps the 1860s, when fears for its future were expressed, but in local Primitive Methodism it seems to have still been thriving in the 1870s, if matter-of-fact references in obituaries are any indication.[1]

After 1840 the chief specialized instrument of revivalism was the protracted meeting, a series of consecutive nightly meetings in a particular chapel, lasting one week or two or even longer, with a different preacher or preachers every night. It was usually held in December or January, when agricultural work was lightest, and nights were long and cold. Protracted meetings were characteristic of the second stage in the evolution of Primitive Methodism, the 1840s and 1850s, when the aim was not only to make new converts but also to rekindle the lukewarm piety of existing members. Like the camp meeting a generation earlier, the protracted meeting was adopted from America, where it was a feature of the new revivalism that had arisen after 1800.[2] In both countries it marked a transformation in the theory and practice of revivalism: once regarded as an unpredictable act of God, a revival was now consciously planned and carried out by acts of men. Even so, protracted meetings could get out of control and protract themselves beyond their scheduled limits. An early example in Springthorpe, in 1845, lasted fifty-eight days and yielded at least twelve conversions—in a village whose population was a little over two hundred; at Donington a protracted meeting that began on 23 November 1856 lasted until the following 10 January, and yielded nearly twenty conversions.[3] The conversions were encouraged by

---

[1] e.g. *P.M.M.* 1874, p. 180.

[2] John Kent, 'American Revivalism and England in the Nineteenth Century', in *Papers Presented to the Past and Present Conference on Popular Religion 7 July 1966*, p. 14.

[3] *P.M.M.* 1846, pp. 309–10; 1857, p. 170.

the use of the penitents' form, another element in the new calculated approach to revivalism.

The most distinctive of the means of grace was the camp meeting—it had been the determination of Bourne and Clowes, the founders of the connection, to hold camp meetings that led to their expulsion from the Wesleyans and the founding of the Primitive Methodist Connection. The camp meeting, usually held on a Sunday in summer, began in the morning; a wagon was drawn into a country lane, with one or more ministers and several local preachers present. There was singing, prayer, a sermon, an exhortation, then a break for dinner. In the afternoon a procession went round the village singing hymns, returning to hear short sermons from the preachers. At a camp meeting at Tetford in June 1837, eight preachers spoke for ten minutes each; they alternated with more hymns and prayers—at one point two or three praying parties formed and prayed out loud simultaneously. Ending at five the meeting was followed by a lovefeast in the evening.[1] Despite the notoriety of the camp meeting, it was at most an occasional event and could not have been the principal evangelistic technique even in the 1820s. By the 1850s a single camp meeting was regularly scheduled for each village society every year.

Lovefeasts were as popular in Primitive Methodism as in other branches of Methodism, and were probably held much more frequently than the somewhat comparable ceremony of the Lord's Supper. Descended from the 'agape' of primitive Christianity, they featured the quasi-sacramental breaking of bread in common and the drinking of water from a common loving-cup, but the chief events were the spiritual testimonies offered by members.[2] Although they were intended to confirm the faith of existing members, conversions sometimes took place, in scenes of great excitement. At a lovefeast in Tetford in 1837

The Spirit of God went through the congregation like fire. The speaking was with great liberty; and, behold, a shaking, and a cry for mercy; and after a long and hard struggle, the Lord converted five souls. And at a late hour we returned home, weary in body, but rejoicing in spirit.[3]

---

[1] P.M.M. 1838, p. 70; see also Henry Winn's eyewitness account of a camp meeting at Fulletby in 1844 (Diary, 22 Sept. 1844).
[2] Frank Baker, Methodism and the Love-Feast, 1957, pp. 15, 25.
[3] P.M.M. 1838, p. 70.

Lovefeasts were often held in the evening after camp meetings, which indeed they probably surpassed as a 'popular "religious entertainment"'. Yet the very features that made them popular in the early years—the communal cup and the self-revealing personal testimonies—would later tell against them in an age of hygiene and reticence.

The place of the sacrament of the Lord's Supper—always referred to by Primitive Methodists as 'the sacrament'—is not easy to determine. In the Horncastle circuit between 1839 and 1842 sacraments were regularly scheduled for every society in the last quarter of the year; an average village society could expect one celebration per year at most.[1] References to the sacrament were equally rare in obituaries and in reports of circuit activity, and it may be conjectured that it did not have a high status. It appears to have been associated with ministers and with town chapels: in the villages, by contrast, lovefeasts, usually conducted by local

*The Lord's Supper and the Lovefeast in Town and Village Chapels**

| | towns | | villages | |
	ministers	local preachers	ministers	local preachers
Lord's Supper	4	0	12	4
Lovefeast	7	0	12	35

* These figures are calculated from the four circuit plans cited above, p. 223, n. 2.

preachers, were preferred, and the ethos was more 'Protestant' and communal.

The link between the means of grace and the special services is provided by the Sunday school. In the first generation of Primitive Methodism, when the evangelistic appeal was to adults, Sunday schools were rare in south Lindsey. In 1840 only one was reported in the three circuits of Lincoln, Horncastle, and Louth,[2] while the Religious Census noted only three in forty-three places of worship. More appeared after 1851, as the outward evangelistic impulse weakened and was turned inward, children becoming for the first time a source of new converts. With its evangelical role and its operating expenses the Sunday school called forth the Sunday school anniversary, one of the most important of the special services.

[1] Quarterly Meeting minute book, Horncastle C.R.
[2] *P.M.M.* 1840, p. 348.

The special services, taking the form of anniversaries, were the most popular events in the Primitive Methodist calendar. Piety, though not absent, mattered less than the festivities, the fellowship, and the fund-raising. Special preachers might be invited, and the occasions attracted fellow villagers as well as 'friends' from other parts of the circuit.

The Sunday school anniversary was held in the spring—often on Good Friday—at the end of the school year. It began with the scholars walking in procession round the village, carrying banners, singing hymns, and begging contributions from householders. In the afternoon they recited pieces in the chapel,[1] sang hymns, and then retired for games. Later they sat down to a treat of tea and plumcake while the adults held a public tea meeting, with special addresses. The anniversary was completed on the following Sunday with special sermons and collections in the chapel. Altogether the Sunday school anniversary symbolized the new direction taken by Primitive Methodists after 1850. Not only were they concentrating on their children but also asking their fellow villagers for their pennies instead of their souls, and thereby accommodating themselves to village life.

The missionary anniversary was similar in format, extending over two days and featuring a tea-meeting with a public address, but it lacked a communal dimension. Instead there seems to have been a certain competition among the collectors to see who had collected the most money during the previous year. The poverty of the Primitive Methodists ensured that this anniversary did not rival the munificence on display at its Wesleyan counterpart.

The chapel anniversary reflected the sect's poverty in a different way. The debts that a society incurred in building a chapel weighed heavily, and the chapel anniversary was intended not only to celebrate and commemorate the opening of the chapel but also to raise money to pay off the debts.[2] When they were finally liquidated—that was the time to celebrate. Like the other special services the chapel anniversary became widespread only after 1850 when the displacement of energy from spiritual ends to

[1] Which were 'often quite unsuitable, and occasionally positively ridiculous' in the Louth circuit in 1862 (Shaw, *Life of Rev. Parkinson Milson*, p. 139).
[2] This was the explicit policy in the Market Rasen circuit in the 1860s (Quarter Day Minute Book, C.R.).

organizational means was changing the character of Primitive Methodism.

When fully elaborated the means of grace and the special services constituted a distinct liturgical year. It comprised a weekly cycle of Sunday services, prayer meetings, and class meetings; a fortnightly cycle of weeknight services; and a variety of annual events: the missionary anniversary, the protracted meeting in December or January, the Sunday school anniversary in spring, the camp meeting and the lovefeast in summer, the chapel anniversary, usually in the second half of the year, and perhaps 'the sacrament' in the autumn. This calendar was in some respects more Methodist than Christian, for the traditional Christian holidays, with the possible exception of Christmas, were either neglected or subordinated to specifically Methodist festivals. Good Friday was remembered only because it was so often annexed for Sunday school anniversaries, and no particular attention seems to have been given to Easter, the climax of the traditional year. Primitive Methodism thus created its own version of sacred time, an alternative to the orthodox calendar still observed in the parish churches. On another level, this was also an alternative to the unrespectable leisure activities of the rural populace: hymns, Sunday school, and tea meetings competed with folksongs, beer drinking and village feasts. The anniversaries, which multiplied after 1850, have a further significance, for they mark a new stage in the sect's inner evolution and a new stance towards the 'world'. Now relaxing their evangelistic effort, Primitive Methodists offered entertainment rather than admonishment, raised money rather than elevating souls, and celebrated themselves and their own accomplishments—now that the heroic age was past.

SPIRITUALITY

It was all but taken for granted that members were regular attendants at the 'social means of grace', at class meetings and chapel services. But Primitive Methodism also attempted to give direction to the inner religious life: a member was expected to seek a progressive deepening of his religious experience and faith, to have a spiritual career. The principal stages of the career—conversion, 'entire sanctification', a pious and edifying death—

were defined in Methodist terms, but much of the content came from the members themselves and their milieu.

Form and content were fused in at least one respect. Primitive Methodism was a 'religion of the heart'. This was what Methodism demanded and what villagers were happy to supply—and vice versa. They wanted religion to be 'experimental'. As one woman put it, she 'did not wish to *skim* on the outside of religion but to dive into the full ocean of His love'.[1] More specifically, they often dwelt on the pleasure and satisfaction they obtained from religious experience, and described it in imagery that suggests erotic experience as well; in accounts of revivals and conversions, a pattern of tension, climax, and release is unmistakable.[2] Primitive Methodism heightened anxiety and guilt, but the weight of the evidence—admittedly from 'official' sources—suggests that it gave members more pleasure than pain, more pardon than guilt, more liberty than repression. Indeed it can be suggested that the 'pardon' offered to labourers by Primitive Methodism was for a guilt and unworthiness that had been induced in them not by the preachers but by the dominant social classes, quite outside the religious sphere. And when the Anglican Church all but condemned the expression of feeling, Primitive Methodists gloried in it.

Feeling, however, was not the sole reality. Primitive Methodists affirmed unhesitatingly the objective existence of supernatural phenomena—God, angels, Satan, heaven, hell, miracles. As late as 1867 a minister saw fit to condemn the belief in witchcraft,[3] and Primitive Methodists shared with fellow villagers a vivid sense of the malice of Satan. 'Satan has been harassing me much, but I have overcome' was the theme of more than one Primitive Methodist deathbed. Most members came from the social strata in which 'superstition' was rife, and they brought everyday assumptions about supernatural forces and phenomena with them from the cottage to the chapel.[4] And it should not be supposed that wealth-

---

[1] *P.M.M.* 1841, p. 270.

[2] And in Charles Kendall's account of his fellow minister from Lindsey, Atkinson Smith: 'No sooner did Mr. Smith taste the sweets of pardoning mercy, than he panted for additional holiness and fuller joys. He pressed forward into the possession of entire sanctification.' (*Christian Minister in Earnest*, 1854, p. 12.)

[3] *Louth Adv.*, 22 June 1867.

[4] This, along with the persecution with which the sect was threatened, may help to explain why the doctrine of special providences appealed so strongly to Primitive

ier members had a different outlook. An incident reported in the *Primitive Methodist Magazine* suggests otherwise: after the death of Mary Roe of Willingham-by-Stow, her class leader—'a person living independent'—and his wife told the minister that 'Mary had paid them two visits since her death, and the last time with just enough light to dispel the gloomy darkness from the room, when she spoke to them, and, amongst other things, said she was happy'. And John Maltby—a large farmer and leading layman in the Louth circuit and a national officer in the Connection—'had a strong opinion that the spirits of his departed friends were all about him, descending to join him in his worship, while he attempted to rise up to theirs.'[1] That witches and Satan and disembodied spirits intervened in human life—beliefs of this kind were embedded in village culture, and Primitive Methodism accommodated them more easily than any other organized religious group.

Yet if Primitive Methodist spirituality was nourished by the traditional culture, it grew within a specifically Methodist framework. Conversion, the crucial first step in the spiritual career, had no antecedents in the traditional culture. Indeed the whole process of conversion came to be described in a highly conventional vocabulary, and it is difficult to determine the relation between the stylized accounts in denominational sources and the reality experienced by unliterary villagers. Yet if the terms were used in a conventional and prescribed manner, they were not intrinsically obscure. Conversion was ordinarily referred to as 'finding liberty' and 'receiving pardon', and the sources give little reason to doubt that it involved sin and guilt and that it was far more than an act of will. In all these accounts conversion was a process rather than an event, and often a rough and turbulent one. The 'sinners' began by being 'wounded', often 'trembling' and 'crying'; then, as 'penitents', they would 'cry for mercy' as they 'struggled for liberty'. The final stage did not necessarily come at once—it was often reported that 'several persons were in distress, but did not obtain a sense of pardon'—or even in a chapel. One member, Matthew

Methodists, both locally and nationally. The *Magazine* included among its obituaries and other features a 'Providence Department', with accounts of the 'Deliverance of a Sabbath Scholar' and the 'Preservation of a Gospel Minister' and a stream of other 'Remarkable Interpositions' of Divine Providence.

[1] *P.M.M.* 1834, p. 121; 1864, p. 299.

Keyworth of Corringham, 'in the most intense agony of soul . . . rolled on the stable floor' and finally received pardon while praying in his bedroom. And a woman who after converting had backslid was recovered for the faith when a minister prayed with her and 'God made her happy'.[1]

Conversion was only the beginning of a Primitive Methodist's spiritual career. Particularly in the early decades, he was expected to 'grow in grace', to strive for holiness—even for 'purity' or 'perfection'. The highest and rarest stage was that of 'entire sanctification'; it was advocated only by a minority of the ministers, but by those few, like Atkinson Smith, with great energy: 'Get wholly sanctified, get it in connection with other blessings, or get it instantaneously, or get it progressively, but do get it: "Be ye holy."'[2] In practice, however, it was an extremely infrequent accomplishment; in nearly a hundred obituaries of local members in the denominational magazine, it was mentioned only once.[3] But it nevertheless was representative of the spirituality of the early years; the religious aspirations of the poor were highest when their social position was most depressed and when the 'saints' were most persecuted. The broader Methodist ideal of holiness, free of melodrama, had a greater attraction and popular influence.

In public worship Methodist ideals are less apparent than the voices of the villagers. In all the services it was the laymen who dominated, preaching, praying, singing, shouting. It was their testimony and prayers that formed the larger part of prayer meetings and lovefeasts, not to mention class meetings, and even when a minister was in the pulpit their exclamations and interjections mattered as much as the sermon. Chapel services, uncouth and undignified, scandalized those who valued decency and good order. In 1868 an unsympathetic outsider could still complain of the 'vain, foolish, noisy and disgraceful ebullitions of excitement in which pleasure seekers love to indulge . . . the thudding and thumping of hundreds of boots and shoes till every fibre in the floor shivers as with an electric shock'—and of such comments

[1] ibid. 1855, pp. 755–6; W. Lidgett and W. Keyworth, *Life of the Late Matthew Keyworth*, 1890, p. 6; Shaw, *Life of Rev. Parkinson Milson*, p. 142.

[2] C. Kendall, *Christian Minister*, p. 72.

[3] *P.M.M.* 1868, p. 171. Its rarity is confirmed by samples of the first fifty obituaries printed in the *Magazine* in 1830 and in 1850: it was cited in only three cases out of the total of 100.

from the congregation as '"Isn't that a cutter. . . . First class . . . Well done, old ——!"'[1] But doubts had already arisen from within. As early as 1855 an official obituary said of one member that 'in the public means of grace he was at times carried beyond the bounds of decorum. But those who knew him excused his very loud responses'.[2] The village poor had gained their voices in the chapels just as they were being silenced in the churches, but the vulgarity, once a virtue, at length became an embarrassment, and spontaneity yielded to decorum in the chapels as in the wider society.

For all the boisterousness of the public services, where piety might be measured in decibels, private prayer was not neglected. The same Robert Fawcit whose responses were 'very loud' also loved 'secret prayer', and for another member it was 'the weapon with which to beat the powers of darkness'.[3] Religion for the poor was becoming—perhaps for the first time—a private as well as a congregational affair, a matter of personal inclination as well as public obligation.

This tendency was taken still further in the 'conversion' of family and home to religious purposes. Partly this was a matter of necessity: before the great wave of chapel building in the late 1830s, services were held elsewhere—in barns and granaries but most often in cottages. At Withcall, over 2,000 services were held in the cottage of John Evison, a farm labourer.[4] And in every society one or more families would volunteer to give hospitality to visiting ministers and local preachers; in these 'preachers' homes' the preachers formed part of a kind of religious extended family, and sons of these families, inspired by the visitors, often went forth to become preachers themselves. The head of such a family might well be the 'chief supporter' of the society in the village; and in societies depending on the leadership and support of a particular family—'family causes', as distinguished from 'village causes'—the chief supporter would come from the same family, generation after generation.

Yet even in the 'village causes' the family as a unit was being claimed for religion. Early converts to Primitive Methodism often

---

[1] *Retf. News*, 29 Aug. 1868.
[2] *P.M.M.* 1855, p. 699.
[3] ibid. 1866, pp. 309–10.
[4] *Louth Adv.*, 20 Mar. 1875.

had to endure disapproval and opposition from their families, and had joined as individuals, but in later years the family itself emerged as a religious unit.[1] The few Primitive Methodist farmers in the area gathered family and servants for prayers twice a day, and the custom spread to poorer members as well. At the 'family altar'—Primitive Methodists deprecated altars in churches —families were united and children converted. One father prayed four times a day for the conversion of his children and another prayed 'hard and long' for his. Children began to be converted before reaching adolescence.[2] A boy preacher appeared, beginning to preach at the age of 12, and child 'saints'. Mary Hill, daughter of the chief supporter of the Springthorpe society, was converted in 1853 at the early age of 9 years and 4 months; when she died, a little over a year later, her spiritual career was commemorated on her gravestone in Springthorpe churchyard:

> Though young in years I prayed to God above,
> Full sixteen months my heart enjoyed his love,
> He saw me fit a fadeless crown to wear
> And took me hence from this vain world of care.

Evangelism shifted its aim from outsiders to insiders, from adults to children, from the ungodly to the immature. This may well have been an inevitable 'second generation' phenomenon; in any case, family religion meant children's religion, taming and domes-ticating the spontaneous adult fervour of the previous generation.

Holy living was incomplete without holy dying, and Primitive Methodists were as concerned with death as anyone was in a century in which it was an obsessive presence, not banished to the periphery of consciousness. Death struck infants and children and persons in the prime of life as well as the aged, and it was dealt with consciously and elaborately in ways ranging from super-stition to mourning etiquette to theology. In Primitive Methodism it was a central concern that for a time rivalled even conversion in importance. And as with conversion, a set of conventions arose to guide the believer on his deathbed.[3]

[1] For examples of persecution see *P.M.M.* 1822, pp. 205–7; 1861, p. 373.

[2] ibid. 1858, p. 380; 1861, p. 19; 1864. pp. 298–9; Lidgett and Keyworth, *Life*, p. 13.

[3] The following section is based on about 100 obituaries of south Lindsey members in the *Primitive Methodist Magazine*.

The deathbed was ideally to be a scene of triumph, exemplary for the survivors. It was recongized that the last illness could be painful, yet however great their 'afflictions', members were expected to be 'patient', and not to allow their faith to be 'clouded'. At these times they were likely to be visited by class leaders and ministers, who comforted them, inquired about their spiritual state—and took care to record their last faithful words.

These deathbed statements, preserved in obituaries in the denominational magazine, display in varied imagery three major themes: triumph over affliction and temptation, joyous entry into heaven, and sheer exaltation. Some members were content to say that they were 'happy', or that they were thankful that they 'had not religion to seek'. Some quoted hymns, testifying to their pervasiveness in Methodist life. But most drew upon a stock of biblical and regal imagery. Those who were confident were 'on the Rock'. For others, 'the chariots are coming'; 'I am bound for the kingdom'; 'I am in Jordan above the waves'; 'My title's clear to an inheritance, a crown, and a kingdom.' They struggled with Satan and triumphed, thanks often to the blood of Jesus. 'Satan had been trying to harass her, but it was no use, he had no power . she was washed in the blood—not merely sprinkled but washed.' 'I am sanctified, washed, cleansed in the blood of the Lamb.' They were to go to Jesus. 'I want to go to Jesus, I love Him.' 'Jesus is mine, and I am his . . . . Lord help me! Come Jesus and fetch me.' It is Jesus right through.' 'Jesus can make a dying bed soft as downy pillows are.' When no longer able to speak, they waved a hand 'in token of victory'.

After the funeral of a departed member, a minister would 'improve his death', that is, preach a funeral sermon, either in the chapel or in the Wesleyan chapel if their own was too small. These services often resulted in conversions.

For some Primitive Methodists the final earthly memorial was an obituary in the connectional magazine. Indeed a large portion of the *Primitive Methodist Magazine* was devoted to obituaries, the proportion being greatest in the sect's early years. The obituary was sketchy about secular biographical details, rarely mentioning the person's occupation, but it always presented the date and circumstances of conversion, and lauded his piety and services to Primitive Methodism, and—so great was the obsession with death—described his deathbed scene and recorded his last pious aspirations. Often in fact the account of the death took up most of the obituary. But from the 1860s the deathbed scenes began to be treated in a less explicit or more perfunctory manner. The crumbling of the conventions may be seen in the account that appeared in 1875 of the death of Mrs. Elizabeth Footit of Withcall: 'When the last messenger came, she was seated in an armchair, and while she was engaged in wiping the perspiration from her brow, she exchanged mortality for life.'[1] Once death ceased to be exemplary, it could not long remain triumphant, and so at length became merely embarrassing—a process by no means complete in the 1870s but representative of the slow dissolution of the whole pattern of Primitive Methodist spirituality.

SOCIAL BASES

Compared with the dominant Anglicans and Wesleyans, the Primitive Methodists were numerically very small, and consequently their regional and local distribution was uneven. While the Wesleyans formed societies in every parish from which they were not excluded by the irresistible hostility of a resident squire or by the minuteness of the population, the Primitive Methodists owed much to unpredictable individual enterprise. Nevertheless, the social and geographical pattern of Primitive Methodist congregations was not wholly arbitrary, and it is possible at least to identify the types of parish in which they were more likely to establish themselves. And while evidence about individuals is scarce, there is enough to yield a tentative notion of the sect's occupational structure.

The geographical distribution in south Lindsey at mid-century can be plotted from the Religious Census. The forty-three Primitive Methodist places of worship were concentrated in three areas: (1) the Till basin and Cliff; (2) the large villages of the south-western Wolds; and (3) the Marsh. The first of these areas was adjacent to the Scotter district, a rural stronghold of revivalism,[2]

---

[1] *P.M.M.* 1875. p. 567.

[2] Scotter, in north Lindsey, was no more than a large village, but it was in a state of continuous revivalistic excitement, and from it was launched a 'wide evangelistic movement' that eventually created nearly a dozen separate circuits; the important Conference of 1829 was held there—the only time it was held in a village—and Kendall testifies to its 'former, almost diocesan, importance' (*Origins and History*, i. 434).

and both the others were near towns with flourishing societies: to that extent the pattern was determined by accessibility to pre-existing sources of missionary zeal.[1]

The distribution with respect to parish type shows that most societies were established in open parishes with large populations. Yet the over-all weakness of the sect is apparent in the fact that in a majority of open parishes, where conditions were least unfavourable, there was no society. In close parishes societies were extremely rare. (And in parishes with resident squires they were

Primitive Methodism and Parish Type in 1851

	Parish type				
	A	*B*	*C*	*D*	*totals*
Parishes with Primitive Methodist services	9	3	11	18	41
All parishes	130	27	34	46	237

even less likely to appear than the Wesleyans.) A similar calculation for the Lincoln and Horncastle area shows that the parishes in which they ever held services at any time in the period 1821 to 1851 were chiefly those with the larger populations.[2]

Primitive Methodism in the Lincoln and
Horncastle Area, 1821–51

	Population in 1831		
	−149	150–299	300–
Parishes with Primitive Methodist services	8	15	18
Parishes without Primitive Methodist services	40	22	7

Open parishes with large populations were more hospitable to Primitive Methodism than close parishes with small populations. But the pattern of strong and weak societies is less clear. When Primitive Methodists did gain a foothold in a small parish they sometimes flourished there while societies in large parishes were minuscule. There were nine parishes in south Lindsey with populations in 1851 of 800 and over: Primitive Methodists held services in six of these, but three were tiny congregations. Of the nine parishes in which they had the largest attendance of any place of worship in the Religious Census, seven had populations of less than 400. A similar pattern holds true at the local level. In the

---

[1] It was also affected by the fact that the Wesleyans had established themselves in the area first; rarely did the Primitives have a parish all to themselves, but they may have found growing space in parishes in which the Wesleyans were flourishing less than usual. Relations were generally friendly between the two groups.

[2] Based on circuit plans of 1821 and 1831; Quarterly Meeting Minute Book, Horncastle C.R., and the Religious Census.

Horncastle circuit in 1841 there were only ten village societies out of a potential thirty or forty; the five largest villages had the four lowest percentages of membership and the five smallest had the four highest percentages.

As with the Wesleyans, the social composition of the membership is elusive, but more is known about the local preachers and other office-holders. A total of fifty-eight local preachers have been identified from circuit plans and other sources spanning the whole period. Over half were farm labourers, who were therefore in the same proportion among the local preachers as they were in the general population; farmers, however, were under-represented and craftsmen and others were over-represented. It is remarkable that labourers (and cottagers) were also well represented among 'chief supporters'. At the same time, farmers were more prominent

Occupations of Chief Supporters

Farm labourers	11	Shoemakers	1
Farmers	10	Cattle jobbers	1
Cottagers	4	Millers	1
Blacksmiths	2	Veterinarians	1
Wheelwrights	2	Grocers and drapers	2
			35

Local Preachers and Chief Supporters

	Local Preachers		Chief Supporters	
	N	%	N	%
Farmers	10	17	10	29
Craftsmen, etc.	18	32	10	29
Labourers	30	51	15	42
Total	58	100	35	100

in this group than they were among the local preachers; as in Wesleyan Methodism, the organizers and officials tended to come from a higher social level than the preachers.

The social composition of the membership is much less clear. An indirect indication may be obtained from baptismal registers

Occupations of Fathers of Children Receiving Primitive Methodist Baptism in the Gainsborough, Horncastle, and Louth Circuits, 1844–75

	Farmer	Labourer	Craftsman, etc.	Illegitimate	Total
Number	28	317	68	28	441
Per cent	6·3	72·0	15·4	6·3	100

for the years 1844 to 1875 surviving for the Gainsborough, Horncastle, and Louth circuits.[1]

It should be noted, however, that over half the baptisms were performed in only five parishes; moreover, since local Primitive Methodists do not appear to have valued baptism either as a sacrament or as a mark of piety, Primitive Methodist baptism is not necessarily a sign of membership. If these figures say anything about the membership as a whole, it is that labourers were the great majority, a conclusion that is consistent with qualitative evidence.

Some further indirect evidence for the social composition of the membership may be obtained from aggregate membership figures for four village societies in the Gainsborough circuit, 1851–72.[2] Trial members were added to the books overwhelmingly in the first quarter of the year, and new members in the second quarter, while members were dropped from the books evenly throughout the year. These figures not only testify to the importance of protracted meetings but also suggest that farm servants did not often become members, for otherwise there would have been many more members lost in the second quarter, since farm servants usually left their places in May. New members were probably attracted from the more stable ranks of the married.

The record of baptisms in the chapel at Springthorpe affords some final indirect evidence. This was admittedly a quite untypical situation: the Primitive Methodist chapel was the only dissenting place of worship in the parish, and the incumbent for much of the period was an outspoken Anglo-Catholic. It is significant as an extreme case, showing how far the sect could advance in favourable conditions. Between 1844 and 1875 about 11 per cent of the population (which ranged between 200 and 300) were members—perhaps double that proportion of the adult population. About 30 per cent of all baptisms performed in the parish in this period for children living in the parish were performed by Primitive Methodists. The proportion was virtually the same for the children of each of the major occupational groups and for those of unmarried mothers. In a number of families there were 'mixed' baptisms, some children receiving an Anglican, others a Primitive Methodist

[1] In the circuit records, L.A.O.
[2] Figures from the Quarterly Account Book, C.R.

baptism; the numbers of 'mixed' children may then be compared with the total number of children baptized in each occupational group.[1]

'*Mixed' Baptisms and Total Baptisms, by Father's Occupation, in Springthorpe, 1844–75*

	'*Mixed' baptisms*	*Total baptisms*	*Percentage*
Farmer	17	37	45·9
Craftsman	20	51	39·2
Labourer	91	152	59·9
Total	128	240	53·3

Farmers and craftsmen were somewhat more likely to have all their children baptized in the same place, whether church or chapel, while labourers were more likely to have one or two of their children baptized in the chapel, though like the other groups they had most of them (60 per cent) baptized in the church. It would appear that farmers and craftsmen perhaps made a more definite and exclusive commitment to one church or the other; labourers had a weaker institutional commitment and were more likely to 'shop around' or to be guided by mere convenience.

Through most of the nineteenth century, Methodist members were outnumbered in the chapels by 'adherents' and others who attended but did not join. It is possible to compare the membership of six societies in 1851 with the attendance recorded in the Religious Census. The total population of the six parishes was 3,660, the total membership 136, and the attendance (at the best-attended service only from each society) was 436. Even if all the members attended, they were outnumbered in the average congregation more than two to one by adherents and others. Unfortunately little evidence survives of the role of the unconverted majority in the life of the chapel.

The age profile of the membership cannot be reconstructed, but the average age of new converts can be calculated from obituaries in the *Primitive Methodist Magazine*. The average age at conversion of the forty-one men was 30·3, that of the thirty-five women was 32·5. The median age of the men was 26, that of the women was 28. With about half the conversions taking place between 1818

---

[1] The parish registers are kept in the church.

and 1833, and the rest between 1834 and 1867, the trend was towards younger converts in the later period: five of the last six male

	Age at Conversion			
	Men		Women	
Age	1818–33	1834–67	1818–33	1834–67
10–19	3	8	2	3
20–29	8	6	4	10
30–	10	6	12	4

converts were in their teens.[1] Women tended in the later period to convert in their twenties; previously, the thirties and forties had been the most common ages. These small numbers will not support a weighty conclusion, but they do confirm indications from other sources that Primitive Methodism in its early years primarily appealed to adults; the data for the later period are consistent with the speculation that it appealed increasingly to the sons of members and to young married women—perhaps the wives of 'hereditary' members.

The general impression left of the 'ethnography' of Primitive Methodism is that the great majority of the members—and attenders—were labourers, while the higher social ranks were better represented among the leaders and officers. Farmers and craftsmen did not often become members, but when they did they may have been more committed to the sect than labourers were, and were more likely to hold offices, Yet whatever their role, the working-class ethos prevailed throughout the period; only in Primitive Methodism could the list of preachers on a circuit plan be entitled 'Labourers'—as it was on a Gainsborough plan as late as 1874—and the list of chapels, 'Harvest Fields'.[2]

SOME CONSEQUENCES OF SECTARIANISM

On the whole Primitive Methodism may be regarded as having been a modernizing force in rural society, but a far more elaborate investigation would be required to assess anything like its full impact, and the few indirect social consequences that have

---

[1] This tendency finds further support in a report from the Horncastle circuit in 1856 that twenty children under the age of 14 were meeting in class (*P.M.M.* 1856, p. 287).
[2] Gainsborough C.R.

come to light are by no means consistently 'modern' in their implication.

Through the circuit system, Primitive Methodism brought villagers in contact with town preachers, town 'friends', and more generally with town culture—though local market towns were themselves oriented towards the countryside. Town Methodists were at the same time being brought in contact with village Methodism, but in these exchanges it would appear that the villages received more than they gave, as town Methodists were more active both in preaching and in organization. Local preachers tended to form a slightly higher proportion of the membership in the towns than in the villages.[1] And local preachers from the towns seem to have preached more often than their village counterparts—in the Louth circuit in 1839, the town preachers averaged nine services each per quarter, the village preachers only six—and to have preached more often in village chapels than village preachers did in town chapels. Town members also dominated the membership of circuit committees. In the Louth circuit in 1839, for example, the committee comprised ten members from the towns of Alford and Louth and only two from villages (two others were not identified), at a time when there were only two societies in the towns and thirty-four in the villages. Finally, the chairmen at missionary meetings and other special services in the villages were often town leaders if not ministers. Against this, however, is the consideration, as valid for Primitive Methodism in south Lindsey as for Methodism generally, that revivalism, class meetings, and uninhibited personal religion survived longer in the country than in the towns—and that the 'visible' trade deficit between town and country was more than offset by the country's 'invisible' export of emotional religiosity.

Within the villages Primitive Methodism opened the religious opportunity structure not only to the poor but also to women, who indeed were well represented both among the office-holders and among the religious élite more generally. Between 1820 and 1932, ninety-four obituaries of local members appeared in the *Primitive Methodist Magazine*, and 40, or 43 per cent of the total,

---

[1] This was the case in the Market Rasen circuit in 1854, 1863, and 1872, and the Gainsborough circuit in 1874: the only ones for which sufficient data are available.

were those of women, and their careers in Primitive Methodism paralleled those of the men in showing the same broad patterns of piety and service.[1] Nevertheless there was a significant contrast between the offices they held and those held by men. Nearly all the local preachers and society stewards were men, while women tended to be Sunday school teachers and missionary collectors, and they were more often praised in the obituaries for holding services or entertaining preachers in their homes. Thus women played a larger role in Primitive Methodism than in the parish church, but it was still recognizably a 'women's' role, extended from the home to a new setting.

The general secular consequences of 'lay agency' are less clear. A high proportion of Primitive Methodists held office in society or circuit: at the middle of the century local preachers alone amounted to 8.1 per cent of the total membership of the connection,[2] and in south Lindsey the figure was usually well over 10 per cent. In the Alford circuit in 1860 the addition of society stewards brings the proportion to nearly 15 per cent. And even these figures understate the true number of office-holders, for the circuit

Circuit	Date	Local preachers as a percentage of circuit membership*
Lincoln	1831	14·8
Louth	1839	12·9
Louth	1854	9·9
Market Rasen	1854	10·5
Alford	1860	12·7
Market Rasen	1870	10·1
Gainsborough	1874	11·3

* Includes local preachers, preachers on trial, exhorters, and prayer leaders, but not society stewards.

plans from which they are derived never listed the names of class leaders, Sunday school teachers, missionary collectors, and other officials. There is no reason to suppose that this numerous band did not make the most of their opportunities to learn to speak in public and to assume responsibility in an organization. But until the advent of the unions at the very end of the period there were few secular organizations in which these skills could be put to use.

[1] See below p. 252.
[2] Primitive Methodist Conference, *General Minutes*, 1850, p. 13.

At any rate there were no discernible links between Primitive Methodism and politics in south Lindsey. Although most members would not have been qualified to vote, individuals must have had their views, but the connectional 'no politics' rule was strictly observed: even during parliamentary election campaigns, the minute books of the quarterly meetings record no discussions of or allusions to political questions.[1]

The sources are equally silent during the labourers' revolt of 1830, but there are a few pieces of evidence relating to the trade union movement. At the official level Primitive Methodism upheld the rules forbidding the use of chapels for what it regarded as political purposes. The Market Rasen circuit quarterly meeting allowed itself no word of sympathy with union aims when it expressed its disapproval that one of the chapels (in north Lindsey) had been used for a union meeting: 'It is not the proper place . . . and therefore cannot be allowed.' And at a union meeting in Ludford, a village with both Wesleyan and Primitive Methodist chapels, the chairman declared with regret that they would have preferred to meet in a chapel or schoolroom, but the only place offered them was the public house.[2] Individual Primitive Methodists, however, played a major role in the leadership of the unions.[3] It must have been natural for a labourer like George Lyon, chief supporter of the society at Saxby, to emerge as one of the local union organizers.[4] The extent of Primitive Methodist involvement is suggested by a report in 1873 that the Horncastle circuit had 'suffered seriously from removals, caused mainly by the agitation of the labour question—in some cases attempts having been made to starve out families'.[5] The two movements were in any case appealing to largely the same people. A low turnout at a union tea and anniversary at Donington and Benniworth was attributed to

[1] I am indebted to Mr. R. W. Ambler for his findings that the situation was similar in the Kesteven and Holland divisions of the county.

[2] Quarter Day Minute Book, 9 Mar. 1874, Market Rasen C.R.; *Mkt Rasen W.M.*, 15 Feb. 1873. The Primitive Methodist authorities in Alford denied the union the use of a room for a meeting on the subject of emigration (*Labourer*, 24 Dec. 1875). Accounts of some dozens of union meetings, both in the local and in the union press, indicate that they were never held on Primitive Methodist premises.

[3] This is the conclusion for Lincolnshire as a whole reached by Mr. Nigel Scotland in his researches on Methodism and the labourers' unions in the Eastern Counties, 1872–96; I am indebted to his paper on the subject presented at the University of Essex, 7 March 1975.

[4] *Mkt Rasen W.M.*, 29 June 1872.

[5] *P.M.M.* 1873, pp. 183–4.

competition from a Primitive Methodist tea held on the same day.[1] And a labouring family from Sloothby received assistance from both movements when it decided to emigrate: the union helped financially, while the Primitive Methodists presented Bibles to the six children (out of ten) who were scholars in the Sunday school; the entire party of thirteen took fifteen Bibles with them to the New World.[2] Official Primitive Methodism remained silent, neutral, and unco-operative, but unofficially, a high proportion of individual members and office-holders became union activists.

If on public issues and political movements Primitive Methodism was officially neutral, in matters of private conduct it upheld a rigorous moral code which it did not hesitate to enforce. The seriousness and self-discipline it fostered sprang in part from its own internal discipline. Members were subject to a quarterly scrutiny by the preachers, and the preachers to a collective self-scrutiny that was particularly strict. The most frequent offence was to miss an appointment, and while few services were in fact missed, for obvious reasons it was regarded very seriously, and in the Horncastle circuit in 1837 it drew the rather stiff fine of a shilling. Other occasions for admonishment and discipline arose continually. One local preacher was reproved for having been drunk and for neglecting his class; another was required in 1847 to 'sign a pledge to eject his lodgers except they get married in five weeks'. The Alford quarterly meeting strongly disapproved of 'Brother Calthrop's conduct in working on the Railways on the Sabbath Day'; in 1853 a local preacher was suspended for attending the theatre. The surveillance extended to their actual preaching: one was advised in 1845 'to study brevity in his pulpit exercises. . . . When [he] and Brother Dawson are out *together*, and *both* speak at the *same* place, [resolved] that they do not exceed *10* minutes *each*.' More serious was dissension and wrangling between local preachers; it was resolved in the Horncastle circuit in 1840 that 'the first person convicted of speaking evil and keeping up the old grievances shall be put out of society'.[3]

Discipline over ordinary members was less apparent but not lacking. In 1857, for example, it was resolved 'that James and

[1] *Labour League Examiner*, 24 Oct. 1874.

[2] *Labourer*, 16 Jan. 1875.

[3] Quarterly Meeting Minutes, 18 Dec. 1837, 22 June 1840, 26 June 1843, 22 Dec. 1845, 29 Apr. 1853, Horncastle C.R. Quarterly Meeting Minute Book, 17 Dec. 1847, Alford C.R.

Harriott Brown be informed that they cannot be considered members of our society unless they give satisfaction that she is his lawful wife'.[1]

Yet far more important than external discipline were the internal self-discipline, self-respect, and seriousness fostered by Primitive Methodism. These qualities made a sharp break with the old rough labourers' life and its degrading drunkenness and violence. In the first generation of the sect, members were praised for their 'upright walk' or their 'pious walk in the world';[2] later, secular virtues were encouraged. One local preacher 'travelled some 500 miles on the Lord's Day per year, and preached about eighty sermons per year, to make the labouring class of Lincolnshire wise, truthful, industrious, sober, and godly'.[3] In one village the Primitive Methodists succeeded in persuading the labourers not to 'befool' themselves by the rustic antics in which they had been encouraged by the gentlemen of the parish: juvenile, degrading games like sack races, rolling wheelbarrows blindfold, and climbing poles. It was characteristic too that they were the first of the larger branches of Methodism to be consistent teetotallers.[4]

With their seriousness, self-discipline, and other virtues, Primitive Methodists were equipped to rise in society, but how many actually did so, and how far they rose, are open questions. An impression is left that there were more farmers in the membership after 1850 than before, but if that is so, it would be hard to decide what the link was between their religion and their economic status. Two examples of upward and one of downward mobility illustrate some of the complexities of the subject. Robert Tasker was the son of a cottager or small farmer of twelve acres; his parents were both Primitive Methodists and for more than forty years had held services in their house, which was also a preachers' home. At the age of 21, after a conversion in a field at midnight, he too became a member; two years later he became a local preacher, declining an invitation to become a minister because he considered his talents inadequate. He spent thirteen years in farmers' service in Corringham before setting up as a farmer himself. Returned in

---

[1] Quarterly Meeting Minute Book, 26 Jan. 1857, Horncastle C.R. A similar instance in the Alford quarterly meeting minutes, 13 June 1856.

[2] Among many examples, *P.M.M.* 1834, p. 122, and 1849, p. 60.

[3] ibid., 1873, pp. 183–4.

[4] *Mkt Rasen W.M.*, 18 May 1872; H. B. Kendall, *Origin and History*, i. 452–3.

the 1851 Census as a cottager, he was renting 147 acres in 1861 and was 'blest with prosperity': 'In many things Mr. Tasker furnished an excellent example to men commencing business with limited means, industrious, economical, honest and upright, ever respectful to equals and superiors in position and attentively kind to the poor.'[1] A member of the same Corringham society was Matthew Keyworth. Born in Corringham in 1805, son of a 'praying father', he spent twelve years in service, then became manager of the dairy farm at Somerby Hall and later under-gardener. His origins were humbler than Tasker's, and his rise more modest, yet his work ethic was similar. 'He had always felt it his duty to be industrious, careful and honest . . . His advice to all was the motto of his own life: "Never let the expenditure be more than the income."' He was, moreover,

a very kind but strict man; he did not spare the rod and spoil the child; he always taught his children to be honest and speak the truth; he never allowed us to play on the Sabbath-Day, but would say, when we were against the door, 'Come in, boy, and get that Bible.'[2]

Tasker and Keyworth were archetypal—but perhaps not typical. A final example shows that Primitive Methodism could also bring about downward mobility. John Maltby of Louth Park was converted in 1819 at the age of 29; he served locally as class leader, local preacher, and Sunday school teacher, and nationally as the General Missionary Treasurer of the Connection. Inheriting 'considerable wealth' from an uncle, he farmed over 400 acres, yet when he died, 'his property . . . was six times less than it once was', apparently depleted in part by his beneficence to his church.[3] Thus Primitive Methodism could have quite divergent consequences for its members: upward mobility for Tasker and Keyworth, downward mobility for Maltby, trade union militance for George Lyon. The question remains open.

STAGES IN SECT DEVELOPMENT

In a notable earlier work, H. B. Kendall interpreted the history of Primitive Methodism in the nineteenth century as a movement from local diversity to national unity, ascending through succes-

---

[1] P.M.M. 1870, pp. 43–4.
[2] Lidgett and Keyworth, *Life*, p. 3.
[3] P.M.M. 1864, p. 299.

sive levels of church government and organization. The process began with the circuits, continued at mid-century with the districts, and culminated at the end of the century in the Primitive Methodist Church.[1] Kendall's analysis remains fundamental; here an attempt will be made to complement it with an analysis of the sect's inner religious dynamic and its changing social and psychological character.

The heroic early years saw the advance into Lincolnshire of a highly 'aggressive' conversionist sect, evangelizing with great verve and optimism. Its preachers broadcast their message by means of 'missioning' and 'remissioning': preaching without invitation in a parish, in the open air, until conversions took place, a society was formed, and a room was found for services. The resistance and even persecution that the preachers met only stimulated them to further effort, for they considered themselves to be instruments of the Lord and were confident that He was actively advancing His kingdom.[2]

The evangelistic message was 'plain, impressive, and powerful': salvation and sanctification, available to all who would repent and believe. It invited, and received, an explosive emotional response, with all the phenomena of 'enthusiasm'. So demanding a message was directed almost exclusively at adults, as only they could grasp its meaning and consequences; it was their souls that must be saved while time was left.

The ideal laymen in the first generation were the 'saints', distinguishing themselves by their piety and by the sheer fact and intensity of their commitment, their unwavering loyalty despite opposition or persecution. On their deathbed they were confident of heaven and triumphant over pain and despair. Though husbands and wives often were members together and opened their houses for services, the pattern of piety was mainly individual and not yet familial.

The turbulent character of the sect in these years is reflected in the figures for membership and for preaching places. Membership fluctuated violently at every level, connection, circuit, and society. In the Lincoln circuit, for example, after rapid initial growth it fell

---

[1] H. B. Kendall, *Origin and History*, i. 159–61; ii. 357–8 and *passim*.

[2] At Tealby, Benjamin Hemstock 'found the Lord still carrying on his work; sin continued to be destroyed, and the kingdom of Christ enlarged' (*P.M.M.* 1821, pp. 85–7).

from 664 in 1823 to 338 in 1824 and 221 in 1829; the superintendent minister at Louth had to be persuaded not to abandon the circuit as hopeless.[1] Societies too were unstable: the pattern was not one of continuous outward expansion, but rather one in which an initial 'wildcat' expansion was followed by irregular contractions until a settled group of viable societies was found. In the Lincoln and Horncastle area there were services in forty-three different parishes between 1821 and 1851; the maximum, thirty-one, was reached at the very beginning, in 1821. In its first phase the sect was aggressive, ambitious, and speculative; offering itself to villagers 'on approval,' it had many failures. Later, concentrating on well-established societies, it took fewer risks, venturing less and failing less.

The history of particular societies shows many discontinuities at the local level, as societies were founded, flourished briefly, then subsided and even disappeared. This was due partly to the inevitable ebb and flow of excitement, the impossibility of maintaining a high pitch of enthusiasm. Societies also foundered on dissension among their members, which was probably unavoidable in a voluntary and emotional form of association. And a 'family cause' was vulnerable if a single family or individual left the village. In two villages it was claimed that societies were kept alive by a single individual in each who in lean times was the only person present at Sunday services in the chapel.[2]

In its early years, then, the movement swung from extreme to extreme, violently and unpredictably. Circuit membership soared, collapsed, then rose again. Societies oscillated between enthusiasm and neglect. Individuals were converted and backslid. The world was divided not between members and non-members but between 'saints' and 'sinners'. Whether over-optimistic or dejected, expanding or contracting, the sect was dynamic and unstable.

The transition between the first period and the age of revivalism that followed is personified, both for south Lindsey and for the Connection as a whole, by John Stamp, a native of Louth and minister there from 1836 to 1839. He was the last headlong expansionist, a reckless chapel-builder—sixteen chapels were built in the circuit under his direction, many lacking adequate

---

[1] Membership figures from the annual *General Minutes* of the Primitive Methodistn Conference.

[2] Springthorpe and Mumby (*P.M.M.* 1846, pp. 309–10, and 1859, pp. 585–7).

financial support and proper legal title. At the same time, he introduced into Primitive Methodism some of the new American revivalist techniques, the protracted meeting and the penitents' form, which were to set the pattern for the next twenty years, and he was one of the sect's first doctrinaire teetotallers.[1]

Missioning and remissioning continued into the second period, but less frequently and less vigorously; they were overshadowed by the rise of revivalism. If the precondition of the first period had been an open mission field, that of the second was an existing congregation—a lukewarm, declining one.[2] And if it was God who initiated conversions in the first period, now it was self-consciously the preachers. They were confident that revival could break out simply by virtue of their own will-power and prayer-power. In a local preachers' meeting in the Horncastle circuit, it was 'moved and unanimously carried, that we should have 50 souls this quarter'.[3] The protracted meeting, the principal instrument of the new revivalism, aimed not only at winning new converts—which it accomplished with unprecedented effectiveness by means of the penitents' form—but also at rekindling the flame of piety in the old members. The old expansive optimism was not dead—'May showers of blessings come down upon us in every place, and make us a thousand times more than we are'[4]— but the sect was beginning to turn inward.

As outward expansion declined, the household became the new mission field. Parents assembled their families for daily prayers and pressed their children to be converted: the family became a religious unit. The other focus was the chapel. Earlier, services were more often held in barns or cottages, but by 1851 a majority of the congregations worshipped in chapels, and in the following decades nearly every society built its own. The chapels were both cause and consequence of the sect's new position and outlook: they were the products of established congregations, and they involved debts and financial administration that only heightened the need for caution and routine. There was finally a third newly important institution in this period, the Sunday school, which completed the link between family and chapel. Earlier, when

---

[1] H. B. Kendall, *Origin and History*, i. 452–3.
[2] See Kent, 'American Revivalism and England', p. 22.
[3] *P.M.M.* 1856, p. 237.
[4] ibid. 1852, p. 48.

adults had been the evangelistic objective, Sunday schools were rare, but they multiplied in the 1850s—just as children were being separated from adults in the parish churches and in the wider society.

The model layman in the first period was pre-eminently a man of piety; in the second period he was still pious but now notable additionally for his services to the cause, for his contributions as local preacher, class leader, or chief supporter. This shift in ideals can be traced in the changing pattern of qualities praised in obituaries in the *Magazine*.

Piety and Service in Obituaries in the Primitive Methodist Magazine *1820–1932*

	Men			Women		
	Piety alone	Piety and service	Service alone	Piety alone	Piety and service	Service alone
1820–40	7	3	1	5	1	1
1841–60	7	7	1	9	7	3
1861–76	1	11	4	2	3	1
1877–1932	0	1	11	1	1	6

The long-term transition from piety to service, from the saint to the organizer, is clearly indicated. Since the obituaries examined were limited to those of south Lindsey members, the numbers are not large, but the direction of change is consistent from period to period over the century.

The new ideal of service reflected the fact that Primitive Methodism, while still a movement, was now an established organization as well, with chapels, Sunday schools, and missionary societies; besides the local preachers and class leaders there was a host of major and minor functionaries who kept the wheels turning, and whose service was beginning to be recognized and rewarded. Perhaps the most important element in the situation was that the Primitive Methodists now were owners of property— of debt-ridden chapels, which had to be managed carefully and above all financed. As a result there were changes both in the status ranking of offices and in the social pattern of office-holding. The office of society steward was a purely administrative one, but its responsibility for finances gave it a new importance, and it tended increasingly to be held by farmers, from Primitive Methodism's small social élite. Farmers at the same time were less likely to become local preachers. In both Wesleyan and Primitive

Methodism, an earlier 'pluralism'—the holding of more than one important office by the same person—declined; the purely organizational role was increasingly respected and increasingly differentiated from the preaching role, which was more closely related to the ideal of piety; and the social rank of the organizers appears to have risen, while that of the local preachers remained the same or declined.

After the tumult of the first two decades, Primitive Methodism settled into a routine. Booms and slumps were succeeded by the more gentle fluctuations of revivalism; the most marginal and the non-viable societies were gradually given up and dropped from the plan.[1] The liturgical calendar was completed, with its weekly, seasonal, and annual events. The family, previously a source of opposition and instability, was captured for the cause. The alternating recklessness and dejection of the first period were replaced by a more equable mood and temper. But by the same token, the expectations that had propelled the sect forward were reduced, and, with the abandonment of entire sanctification, the dimensions of personal piety were scaled down. Saints became less saintly, sinners less sinful.

The advent after 1860 of the stage of denominationalism is marked most clearly by the declining interest in revivalism. Missioning all but ceased as the outward missionary thrust weakened, was encapsulated, and turned inward. Children, in family and Sunday school, were now the chief missionary field. And revivalism, the historic successor to missioning, also began to decline. Camp meetings survived, but contributed more to nostalgia than to revivalism. Protracted meetings continued through the 1870s and into the 1880s but in a steadily diminishing number of societies.[2] The instruments and occasions of revivalism continued, but revivals ceased. Protracted meetings and class meetings had been attempts to renew and maintain the faith by means of communal feeling and sociability, with faith the end and community the means. In the third period and after, the relation

---

[1] Among the lost causes was Withern, in the Alford circuit. The quarterly meeting dropped it from the plan because there was 'no prospect of any society being established there'; it was recalled that 'many of the local preachers who have been planned there have had no congregation to preach to, and no person to give them a bite to eat' (Quarter Day Minute Book, 11 June 1856, Alford C.R.).

[2] This can be traced in the Market Rasen circuit plans in the collection of Mr. William Leary.

was reversed. Faith provided the means and occasions, while the community and its sociability now were the ends, evacuated of their previous religious content. The communion of saints passed into the 'fellowship' of members.

At the same time, Primitive Methodists were altering their stance towards the outside world. The waning of outward missionary effort, combined with the turning towards children, the concern with chapels and debts, and the members' own collective self-celebration—all implied a new relationship between Primitive Methodism and the wider society. This new relationship found ritual expression in the Sunday school, chapel, and missionary anniversaries—the special services, which contrasted with and partly undermined the means of grace. Primitive Methodists now sought to entertain their fellow villagers rather than to convert them, and asked for their financial contributions rather than their spiritual commitment. Demanding less of themselves, they also demanded less of others, and the sect accommodated itself to the ways of the world.

Not surprisingly, the ideal of saintliness was progressviely abandoned after 1860. For the first time, obituaries praise departed members less for their piety than for their services to the organization. And among office-holders there was less esteem for the local preacher and class leader and more for the society steward—the preachers and pastors were being upstaged by the administrators. Another index of the decline of piety was the decline in the genre of the edifying deathbed. In the obituaries of the 1860s the deathbed began to be treated in a vague and perfunctory manner, in the 1870s half the obituaries omitted it, and by 1890 it had virtually disappeared. No longer was there a place for the member whose career had been brief but pious; service and longevity were now the virtues. The supernatural itself—visions, prophecies, acts of Providence—became rare and distant, as if receding before the prosaic rationality of organization.[1] Piety was challenged from still another quarter by the rising appeal of the secular virtues of thrift, industry, self-discipline, self-improvement, and respectability. To the cult of 'fellowship' was added that of 'character'. The new mood was reflected in the motto from a circuit plan of 1870:

---

[1] The 'Providence Department' in the connectional *Magazine* was discontinued in 1862; the decline of persecution should also be mentioned as a factor.

If you know anything that will make a brother's heart glad, run quickly and tell it, but if it is something that will grieve him and cause him to sigh, bottle it up and keep it. Remember time flies, flowers fade, and the body dies, but character is immortal.[1]

In these circumstances, the 'pious walk in the world' of the early period survived chiefly in its reified and ritualized remnants—sabbatarianism and teetotalism. Thus the 'Ranters' became the 'Prims', and over a wide field there occurred consistent displacements of accent from the religious goals to either the secular means or the secular by-products: from movement to organization; from admonishment to entertainment; from piety to service; from local preacher and class leader to society steward; from evangelism and revivalism to fellowship; from a serious approach to life as a whole to sabbatarianism and teetotalism; from soul-making to character-building. Everywhere the latent secular content of Primitive Methodism was emerging as a primary conscious goal.

Changes were also taking place in Primitive Methodism's relations with other religious groups. It began to see itself less as a sect and more as a denomination, as one among a number of groups equally legitimate, none of them making exclusive claims for itself. Primitive Methodists had always been able to co-operate with Wesleyans; in the second and particularly the third periods, they multiplied their contacts with Baptists and Congregationalists. They began to identify themselves with Dissent, political as well as religious, in opposition to Tories and Anglo-Catholics. Another aspect of the shift from sect to denomination was the elevated status now enjoyed by the ministers, who were increasingly differentiated from the local preachers and from the ordinary lay members. Their pay rose, they were more regularly styled 'Reverend' and referred to as 'ministers' instead of 'itinerant preachers', and after 1870 they received formal academic training. Previously they had often followed their congregations, but now they led them, and strove to give them a stronger sense of identity as Dissenters. The ministers' concerns were apparent in a notice on

---

[1] Market Rasen circuit plan, 16 Jan.–10 Apr. 1870. A motto from a plan of the previous period attacked the characteristically different problem of lukewarmness: 'Slow singing, long praying in public, and late attendance on the means of grace, are indubitable signs of a low state of piety' (Market Rasen circuit plan, 22 Jan.–17 Apr. 1854). Both plans are from the Leary collection.

a Gainsborough circuit plan in 1874: 'The Officials and Members of Society are strongly recommended as Dissenters, in Marriages to respect their own Chapels and Ministers'.[1]

By 1875 Primitive Methodists in south Lindsey had shed much of their dynamic, fervent, revivalist past; they had become more stable and respectable, and perhaps more political. In the future lay Pleasant Sunday Afternoons and the great experiment of political dissent.

CONCLUSION

Until more is learned about the social bases of Primitive Methodism—about its adherents and casual attenders as well as its members—the links between its internal dynamics and the wider social setting will remain uncertain. What follows therefore is suggestive rather than conclusive.

There is to begin with a general over-all correspondence between the stages of sect development and the stages of agrarian social development. This is clearest in the second quarter of the century, when disruptive social change created a 'demand' that sectarian religion could supply. In these decades the traditional village social pattern was broken irreparably, and the labouring poor now had to find a way of honouring values and expectations of a traditional society that could not be restored, and a way of living in the new uncongenial society without fully embracing it. In these circumstances sectarian religion had a powerful appeal and made its most rapid advances. It provided personal values that (indirectly) equipped its members for the new society: it also created a community that answered the need for social solidarity. Both the content of Primitive Methodism—damnation and salvation, sinners and saints—and its style—spontaneous, passionate, direct—suited the mood of the poor in their time of need. When class pressure from above was greatest, the response from below, both rural and urban, was most passionate, the aggression and fervour of Methodism in the villages paralleling the insurgency of Chartism in the towns.

After 1850 the interplay between sect and society continued, but in a more indirect and elusive manner. The easing of social tension created a favourable external setting for what Primitive Methodism was already being led to do by its own internal

[1] Gainsborough C.R.

development: to relax, consolidate, and turn inward. Its challenges came increasingly from different quarters—Catholics in the Church of England, Tories in Parliament, the drink trade—and could be met in ways not requiring an intense and localized all-encompassing social movement.

What then did Primitive Methodism do for its followers? Again the answer is clearest for the early years. Primitive Methodism created a religious counter-culture, with its own values, activities, and community, that offered a response and alternative not only to the new social order, but also to the older village culture and to the Established Church. In response to the capitalist social order it 'adaptively' provided an ethic of individual self-discipline and responsibility; but it also rejected the deferential dependence which the dominant classes sought to instil in the poor. It could not do so directly, for an open attack on farmers and landlords was out of the question; but if there was no social space for a secular working-class movement there was enough for a religious movement making a symbolic, indirect critique of capitalist social relations. And a surrogate target was conveniently at hand in the Established Church, closely allied with the dominant powers in the new order and the spiritual guardian of its social stability. Its very etiquette of subordination, inhibition, and decorum—which symbolized these qualities in the wider society—was also an inviting target. Everything the Primitive Methodists did implied a rejection of the parish church, even if some of them attended the parish church on Sunday before going to the 'means of grace'. At the same time they stood apart from what they saw as the immoral traditional culture of the poor. They rejected drunkenness, then drink itself, and the traditional 'take life as it comes' attitude. For Primitive Methodism meant planning—epitomized in the quart-erly circuit plan of services and preachers—and it meant voluntary commitment, contrasting with the ascribed statuses of the older society. There was also the sense of direction and purpose implicit in having a spiritual career, to which there was no counterpart either in the parish church or in traditional culture. And above all the classic Methodist ideal of holiness—which the 'Ranters' pursued more fervently and ambitiously than anyone else—contradicted the inferior and unregarded status to which labourers were condemned everywhere outside their chapels.

Primitive Methodism thus provided for a small minority of the village poor a comprehensive counter-culture, in reaction simultaneously to the new class society, to the old village ways, and to the Anglican social and religious pattern. It appeared at a critical moment, as the traditional culture was passing but before the subsequent working-class culture had developed to replace it. In this perspective Primitive Methodism may be seen as a religious response to social change which in its turn foreshadowed later developments in the secular culture. Thus in the private realm the 'soul' emerged before the private self (and 'character'), and the religious family, gathered at the 'family altar', anticipated the secular psychological family. In the public realm the 'fellowship' of class meeting and chapel came before the solidarity of trade union and of working class, and this earnest minority affirmed their spiritual worth before laying claim to their social inheritance. If this was modernization, it involved not an abandonment of religion but a deeper and more intense religious commitment than the rural poor had ever known. As for the developments in Primitive Methodism after 1850, their implications are less clear and less important, since the sect was making its peace with the secular world. Perhaps the safest estimate is that Primitive Methodism now was past its period of greatest creativity, and was only one of several religious groups moving in the same direction; that instead of creating new modes of social life, in a period of crisis, it was, in a period of consolidation, affirming its own variant of existing ones.

VI

POPULAR RELIGION

They had a nearer apprehension of the spiritual world than
we have. Their ideas, if not so practical as ours, were far more
poetical.
>   Henry Winn, notebooks. (Winn 3/6, sect. 3, p. 11.)

The decisive consideration was and remains: who is deemed
to exert the stronger influence on the individual in his everyday life, the theoretically supreme god or the lower spirits and
demons? If the spirits, then the religion of everyday life is
decisively determined by them, regardless of the official god-
concept of the ostensibly rationalized religion.
>   Max Weber, *The Sociology of Religion*, trans. E. Fischoff,
>   1964, p. 20.

NEVER had the churches shown more energy and expansive-
ness than in the nineteenth century, and never perhaps had
they attracted more of the village population, yet they were by no
means the sole expression of rural religious life. Villagers might
attend both church and chapel, but their religious realm extended
beyond the churches, indeed beyond Christianity, to encompass an
abundance of pagan magic and superstition.

But before exploring these unofficial beliefs and practices it may
be useful to consider the reasons for regarding them as religious
in the first place. They would not, after all, be included in the
religious realm by the true believer, of the type for whom religion
means Christianity, Christianity Protestantism, and Protestantism
the Church of England as by law established. At the other extreme
they would certainly be included—but along with much else far
more distant from institutional religion—by certain sociologists for
whom religion is virtually coextensive with human culture. Definitions of religion notoriously vary as much as religion itself, but
between the extremes is a broad central view that popular magic
and superstition are indeed religious phenomena in good standing.

The justification for this begins with the observation that

definitions of religion define religion: they do not define the church. Religion is universal in human society; no society is known to be without it. Churches by contrast are a relatively late phenomenon in the history of religion and are far from universal. Religion, the broader category, is prior to the church both analytically and chronologically. Churches appear at a later stage, that of the 'institutionalization of religion'.[1] The institutional church therefore makes a misleading model for analysing religion, and it is necessary to adopt a more diffuse and flexible conception of religion that includes the church as one setting for religion among many.

It may be questioned whether even a broad definition of religion should go so far as to include magic, which has often been distinguished from and contrasted with religion. Recent writings, however, tend to blur the distinction and to argue for an inclusive rather than an exclusive definition of religion. Durkheim's view that religion differs from magic in alone having a 'moral community' has been rejected: Goody points out that 'magic too has its church'. Religion and magic may be 'polar ideal-types', but in practice they are inextricably intertwined. For Lévi-Strauss, 'there is no religion without magic any more than there is magic without at least a trace of religion', and indeed it has become standard to speak of 'magico-religious institutions'.[2]

Religion in this broader sense is to be understood less as a substance or entity than as a quality, and the emphasis shifts from 'religion' to 'religious', from organized cults to 'religious phenomena', 'religious facts', 'a religious quality, present to greater or lesser degree in many situations'.[3] As Durkheim observed, there are religious phenomena—'lower' rather than 'higher', private rather than public, fragmentary rather than integrated—which do not belong to any institutional religion and are particularly abundant in folklore; no definition or discussion of religion would be complete that did not take account of them.[4] However

[1] T. F. O'Dea, *The Sociology of Religion*, 1966, pp. 47–8.
[2] J. Goody, 'Religion and Ritual: the Definitional Problem', *British Journal of Sociology*, xii (1961), pp. 143, 158; W. J. Goode, *Religion Among the Primitives*, 1964, pp. 52–5; C. Lévi-Strauss, *The Savage Mind*, 1966, p. 221.
[3] Emile Durkheim, 'De la définition des phénomènes religieux', *Année Sociologique*, ii (1898), p. 22; J. Milton Yinger, 'A Structural Examination of Religion', *Journal for the Scientific Study of Religion*, viii (1969), p. 91.
[4] *The Elementary Forms of the Religious Life*, 1913, p. 36.

quaint or picturesque they may appear on the surface—religion after all is rich in particularities—they share with organized religion the essential common feature: they too are responses to 'the sacred', to 'supernatural powers', and to 'the continuing, recurrent, "permanent" problems of human existence'.[1]

It is a further characteristic of religious responses, both institutional and 'popular', that they are subject to individual adaptation and variation. Consciously or unconsciously everyone fashions his own religion, even if he does no more than understand the prevailing institutional religion in his own way. Even if he seeks to be nothing more nor less than a Christian, an Anglican, or a Methodist, a personal element intrudes, adapting, distorting, individualizing what comes down from above.[2] The result is a personal *Weltanschauung*, a private theatre of sacred phenomena. And the range of variation is still greater in the case of non-institutional religion.

Yet religion also has a collective and social character. Man makes his own religion, but he does not do so just as he pleases. To the large extent that religion is inherited, he may be limited to the choices available to a particular class and society at a particular time. This is true not only of the churches, which are manifestly social organizations, but also of many non-institutionalized religious phenomena. Magical techniques, for example, are transmitted socially from generation to generation, and depend for their supposed effectiveness on socially shared beliefs and expectations. A social dimension will generally be found in even the most idiosyncratic and private religious experience. Society creates, transmits, and transforms religion, both in its public and its private expressions.

In the present discussion 'popular religion' is defined as the non-institutional religious beliefs and practices, including unorthodox conceptions of Christian doctrine and ritual, prevalent in the lower ranks of rural society.[3] It was not a unitary phenomenon: it can best be understood as an amalgam, a loose combination of unofficial Christianity and a rather larger measure of pagan

[1] Yinger, 'A Structural Examination', p. 91.

[2] Durkheim, 'De la définition', pp. 27–8.

[3] This is not to suggest that the poor never believed or practised institutional religion in a 'correct' manner; it merely highlights the large mass of unauthorized versions. Nor does it suggest that the upper classes were free from superstition: theirs however took a different form, social and political myths about the poor.

'survivals'; and since both these elements diverged significantly from orthodoxy, its relation with official Christianity was complex.[1] This rarely involved direct conflict, for popular religion had no creed, liturgy, or corporate identity; indeed to call it a religion is misleading: it was not a religion among other religions but rather a congeries of religious phenomena. Yet even if it was not hostile to Christianity, the Church could not avoid being hostile to what it regarded as 'superstition', a mass of dimly perceived beliefs that were deviant at best and heathen at worst.[2]

What makes a social perspective necessary is that the disjuncture between Christianity and popular religion was at the same time a social and cultural one between the élite and the poor. Christianity, a 'higher' religion, was closely linked with the higher ranks in society, while its place in the life of the poor was tenuous and problematical: the social distribution of superstition was exactly the opposite. To be sure, on the surface, popular religion appears virtually classless, a medley of superstitions without social content or a social function. But its markedly uneven distribution is of cardinal importance. While the educated classes rejected it, it was rife among the poor; as one contemporary observer noted, 'Those who are not in daily intercourse with the peasantry can hardly be made to believe or comprehend the hold that charms, witchcraft, wise-men, and other like relics of heathendom have upon the people.'[3]

Popular religion, then, was part of popular culture, and in so far as clergymen and other members of the élite were aware of it at all they could not help viewing it from across the great cultural divide that separated them from the poor. This helps to explain some of the inadequacies of the written sources on popular religion and folklore, most of which were the work of élite observers.[4] Collectors of folklore were more interested in the picturesque than in the typical, and preferred to speculate about

---

[1] For the term 'amalgam' see Smith, 'Popular Religion', p. 185, and R. Mandrou, *La France aux XVIIe et XVIIIe siècles*, 1967, p. 277.

[2] Séjourné observes that 'la superstition s'oppose à la religion sur son propre terrain' ('Superstition', in *Dictionnaire de Théologie Catholique*, 1947, xiv, pt. 2, p. 2770); it may also be worth recalling that to the rationalist, Christianity too is a superstition.

[3] Edward Peacock (in north Lindsey), in *Notes and Queries*, 2nd ser. i (1856), p. 415; quoted by K. Thomas, *Religion and the Decline of Magic*, 1971, p. 666.

[4] See the Appendix.

the distant origins of the beliefs and practices they recorded rather than to inquire into their immediate social setting, about which some of them knew but little. There is some assurance that the beliefs and practices themselves were not idiosyncratic and unique to south Lindsey, for popular culture was remarkably homogeneous in rural England, and the local examples could easily be paralleled in other districts. But much about the local social context of popular religion remains obscure. Besides labourers, it seems to have comprised cottagers, craftsmen, small farmers, and old-style farmers, but the proportions are uncertain. Its social functions are even less clear. Thus the limitations of the sources impose limits on the discussion. What follows is a preliminary study: a survey the two sources of popular religion, the Christian and the pagan; an estimate of its place in village society; and finally a sketch of its implications for collective mentalities.

SUPERSTITION: CHRISTIAN

As Christianity passed from the pulpits to the pews and from the churches to the cottages, it underwent many alterations and distortions to suit popular needs and tastes. The question arises whether the results of this process remained within the Christian framework or fell outside it: were they 'cultic' superstition or 'non-cultic'?[1] Cultic practices are defined as those that are directed towards orthodox ends—the worship of the Christian God—but which are either superfluous, like animal sacrifice, or distorted, like the adoration of the hair and nails of Jesus. Non-cultic superstition is directed towards non-Christian ends and employs both Christian and non-Christian means. The category of cultic superstition, which combines orthodoxy and heteropraxy, offers an indirect measure of the extent to which Christianity has established itself in the popular imagination. It is noteworthy therefore that cultic superstition has come to light in south Lindsey in only a trifling number of instances: and in those few it involved the 'piety' of animals rather than men. At midnight on the eve of St. Mark's day (24 April) and on Christmas Eve, cattle and horses were believed to kneel in their stalls, as a sign of reverence.[2] These were two distinct beliefs, but both appear to

---

[1] Séjourné, 'Superstition', p. 2770.
[2] Penny, *Folklore*, p. 75; E. Peacock, *Glossary*, p. 57.

have been firmly and widely held. With regard to the Christmas
Eve kneeling, Edward Peacock wrote in 1877 that 'many persons
have assured me that they have watched and seen the oxen in the
"crew-yard" do this', and he recorded a related custom, formerly
'general' and 'still by no means extinct', of 'giving all animals
better food'.[1] On these two nights the farm animals were more
reverent than the human population of the villages—who disliked
kneeling when they were in church—though the religious significance is more apparent on Christmas Eve, with its echoes of the
Nativity scene, than on St. Mark's Eve, which otherwise was
totally pagan. Apart from these two ambiguous exceptions,
however, the category of cultic superstition proves to be virtually
an 'empty box'. The absence of superfluous or exaggerated
beliefs and devotions is a first indication of the subordinate place
of Christianity in popular religion.

That is not to say that there was no Christian element in popular
religion, only that it was 'non-cultic', redirected towards non-
Christian ends. Indeed there was hardly a Christian rite or observance that was not bent to superstitious purposes, and a sampling
of popular beliefs indicates how extensive this was. Sunday, for
example, which the pious kept holy as the Sabbath, was popularly
regarded as being lucky rather than holy. The sign of the cross,
required of the clergy in the rubric for baptism, also figured in
popular superstition. A person was supposed to cross himself
after seeing a magpie, in order to avert bad luck, and after washing
hands in water in which another person had washed before, in
order to avoid quarrelling with him in the coming year. A servant
girl eager to learn whom she would marry could exploit the
powers of the Bible: she would fasten a house key in the middle of
Bible and rest one side of the key on a finger 'while certain words
are said and all the male Christian names that she can remember
are repeated in succession'. When the right name was said, the
Bible would turn around. The powers of the churchyard were
exploited in an old remedy for ague which included nine worms
taken from a churchyard at midnight.[2] And the Crucifixion itself
was exploited, through sympathetic magic, in a marshland remedy
for the 'shakes'. A lock of hair was cut and wrapped around a

---

[1] Peacock, *Glossary*, p. 57.

[2] ibid., pp. 23, 75; R. M. Heanley, 'The Vikings: Traces of their Folklore in
Marshland', *Saga-Book of the Viking Club*, iii, pt. 1 (1903), pp. 52, 54.

branch of the 'shivver tree' (the black poplar) and the following was recited:

> When Christ our Lord was on the Cross,
> Then thou didst sadly shivver and toss;
> My aches and pains thou now must take,
> Instead of me, I bid thee shake.[1]

Miscellaneous examples of this kind could easily be multiplied, but the place of Christianity in popular religion can be seen more clearly by tracing systematically the popular reinterpretations of the Church's holidays, its rites, and its clergy.

Holidays

For most of the nineteenth century, the holidays of England were still the holidays of the Church of England: Christian in name and origin.[2] But both their content and their functions often proved to be more pagan than Christian.

To the Church, 1 January was the Feast of the Circumcision.[3] But to Lindsey villagers it was New Year's: the day for gift-giving and the day on which it was prescribed that no one should take anything out of a house before something was brought into it, preferably by a 'fair-haired man'.[4] Here was a pattern to recur often: a Christian holiday giving lodging to customs which had nothing to do with Christianity.

Candlemas, 2 February, was for the Church 'The Presentation of Christ in the Temple, Commonly Called the Purification of Saint Mary the Virgin'. Its significance was more meteorological than theological in village society, for it was the time for weather predictions: 'If the sun does shine, Saddle your horses and go buy hay.' (That is, winter will continue.) A fuller and more poetic version:

---

[1] Heanley, 'The Vikings . . .', p. 52.

[2] The 'state services' were exceptions, but they had fallen into disuse, and only the service for the accession of the sovereign was included in the Prayer Book after 1858. Bank Holidays date from 1871. See J. H. Blunt, *The Annotated Book of Common Prayer*, 1893, pp. 578–9.

[3] An educated aristocrat like the 6th Lord Monson, though not at all High Church, was aware of the day's religious significance; see above p. 39.

[4] Winn 3/1, pp. 1–2; Jabez Good, *A Glossary or Collection of Words, Phrases, Place Names, Superstitions, etc., Current in East Lincolnshire*, 1900, p. 108; Heanley, 'The Vikings', p. 41.

If Candlemas Day be gloomy and black,
It will carry ow'd Winter away on it's back;
But if Candlemas Day be bright and gay,
Saddle your horses and go buy hay.[1]

St. Valentine's Day, associated from its origins with the Roman
Lupercalia, had long lost its Christian character, though it remains
a holiday on the Anglican calendar to the present. In Victorian
Lindsey, sweethearts and others (but not schoolchildren) exchanged Valentine cards, 'some of them very coarse and vulgar.'[2]

Shrove Tuesday was another holiday whose religious meaning
had long been obscured. Locally, it was one of the days on which
farm and domestic servants were hired, and hence was known as
'fasten Tuesday' from the 'fasten penny' which the employer gave
to his new servant to confirm the contract.[3] More commonly it
was 'pancake Tuesday' or 'pancake day', from the traditional dish
of the day.[4] After the 'pancake bell' had rung, apprentices ceased
work, and children were dismissed from school. After the feast
there might be cock-fighting or football.[5]

The Feast of the Annunciation of the Blessed Virgin Mary—25
March—was Lady Day in common speech. It seems to have had
little religious significance, except among High Churchmen, but
it was important in farming circles as the terminal day for farm
leases.

Good Friday, by contrast, retained more of its traditional
religious content and indeed was generally observed as a day of
rest, the only such holiday besides Christmas. The ban on work
was reinforced by the sanctions of superstition; a blacksmith once
refused to shoe a horse on Good Friday because he feared that
"'owd Skraat 'ud hev' him sartain sewer, if 'e put hand to hammer
or nails the whole blessed daa"'.[6] But superstition also regarded

---

[1] Winn 3/1, p. 3; Penny, *More Folklore*, p. 18.

[2] Heanley, 'The Vikings', p. 41. Their character can be gauged from the reaction
of a girl who had been converted by the Methodists: she was 'so mad . . . that she
came and burnt all the Valentines' (Winn 5/5, p. 63).

[3] Good, *Glossary*, p. 41; Brogden, *Provincial Words and Expressions*, p. 66; Coulson
Peasant Preacher, p. 14.

[4] E. Peacock, *Glossary*, p. 187; Winn 1/1, pp. 95–6; Penny, *More Folklore*, pp. 4–5.

[5] John Brown, *The Lay of the Clock, and Other Poems*, 1861, pp. 7–8; Winn 3/1,
p. 32; M. Peacock, 'Folklore and Legends', p. 29. See also Francis P. Magoun, Jr.,
'Shrove Tuesday Football', *Harvard Studies and Notes in Philology and Literature*, xiii
(1931).

[6] Heanley, 'The Vikings', p. 42.

Good Friday as a good day for planting—presumably for cultivators of allotments and smallholdings rather than for larger
farmers.[1] This was a second important pattern: the 'merits' of the
Christian holiday were tapped and diverted to secular ends. This
was not secularization, voiding the holiday of its religious
content—it would have been if planting had proceeded on Good
Friday as on any other day in that season of the year; but the fact
that it was regarded as a particularly favourable day for planting
meant that it was still endowed with a power that set it apart from
ordinary days, that it was still religious. Other superstitions in a
similar manner exploited the Christian Good Friday for non-
Christian ends. A hot-cross bun baked on Good Friday would be
preserved for years to protect the house from fire; and anyone
born on the night of Good Friday would grow up immune from
fright. Finally, it may be recalled that the Methodists, in selecting
it as a day for Sunday school anniversaries, also helped to undermine its primary Christian meaning.[2]

Like other holidays, Easter Sunday was the occasion for customs whose connection with Christianity was purely fortuitous.
As late as 1900 a few Marshmen still practised the 'wading of the
sun', for example, a technique of divining the weather: a bucket
of water was placed outdoors at sunrise to catch the first rays of
the sun, and if the image on the surface of the water trembled, a
wet season was forecast, while a steady image indicated a fine
summer.[3] More serious was the way in which superstition diverted
attention from the central Christian meaning of the day. It was
widely believed that it was unlucky not to wear new clothes on
Easter Sunday: anyone imprudent enough to neglect this made
himself vulnerable to aerial bombardment from crows. According
to Henry Winn, children said that 'if they have not something
new to wear the birds will dung upon them'. This superstition
fostered the dignity of worship by encouraging the wearing of
new clothes at church, but in practice concern was shifted from

[1] M. Peacock, 'Folklore and Legends', p. 31. Good Friday may have been the
labourers' day for planting for the additional reason that it was the only free time
at their disposal for this task.

[2] M. Peacock, 'Folklore and Legends', p. 30; *Notes and Queries*, 8th Ser. x (1896),
p. 92. Good Friday was also the day for mass meetings and rallies by the Lincolnshire
Labour League, beginning in 1873.

[3] Heanley, 'The Vikings', p. 42. In western Lindsey Miss Peacock 'heard the
dancing of the sun . . . spoken of . . . but never with any real conviction' ('Folklore
and Legends', p. 31).

the dignity of worship to the indignity of crow-dung, and the greatest Christian festival was known popularly as 'Crow-day'.[1]

Of all the Christian holidays, the most enriched by superstition was the Eve of St. Mark's, 24 April. Its only Christian aspect was the widespread belief that cattle and horses knelt in their stalls at midnight. But it was alive with paganism. It was then that anyone seeking the powers of a 'wise man' or wizard could acquire them, by gathering the 'Devil's harvest'.[2] The aspirant for 'wisdom' would equip himself with three pewter plates, one inside the other, and at midnight would hold them under a bracken fern to catch its seed, which fell 'with sudden force and violence'. Then the Devil rode up on a pig, and one had to be brave not to drop the plate and flee, but anyone who stayed and talked with him would learn all he needed to know to become a wise man.[3] It was also on St. Mark's Eve that witches who were thought to have sold themselves to the Devil could annually renew their powers; this they did by going to the parish church, walking round it backwards three times, looking in a keyhole, and saying 'certain words'.[4] These were specialized pursuits; probably more common was the practice of 'watching the church porch'. It rested on the belief, 'still received with undoubting faith' in the 1870s, that anyone who watched the door of the parish church at midnight would see the spirits of the inhabitants come out of church: the spirits of those who were to marry in the coming year would walk in pairs, but those whose spirits did not appear were destined to die within the year. And once a person started watching the church on St. Mark's Eve, he had to continue doing it on that night, year after year, until he foresaw his own death.[5] It also gave girls another opportunity to learn the names of their future husbands. A girl who picked twelve sage leaves one by one as the clock struck midnight would see her future husband; or she could fast on the Eve and see him in a dream, or sit up with food on the table and the doors open and meet him at midnight walking in for supper. Finally, anyone born on St. Mark's Day would be able to

[1] Winn 3/1, p. 33; M. Peacock, 'Folklore and Legends', p. 31.
[2] M. Peacock, 'Folklore and Legends', p. 33. For wise men see below, pp. 287–91.
[3] Penny, *Folklore*, pp. 32–3.
[4] Ethel H. Rudkin, *Lincolnshire Folklore*, 1936, p. 81.
[5] E. Peacock, *Glossary*, p. 211; Brown, *Lay of the Clock*, pp. 8–10; Penny, *Folklore*, p. 75; Mrs Gutch and Mabel Peacock, *Lincolnshire* (Publications of the Folklore Society No. 63), 1098, p. 136.

see good and evil spirits—and the stars at noon.[1] On this one night the multifarious strands of paganism were drawn together: the Devil, the witch, and the wise man, the 'humanity' of animals, and foreknowledge of love and death. The name of the holiday was Christian but nearly everything else about it was pagan.

Superstition formed round the other holidays as well. On Ascension Day, known as 'Holy Thursday', it was believed that washing clothes would bring a death in the family. Holy Cross Day, 14 September, was like several other holidays in having a popular name different from its official one: 'Hally Loo Day'. Anyone picking nuts then was 'certain to come to grief of some kind'.[2] Michaelmas, 29 September, was the Feast of St. Michael and All Angels; the custom of eating goose for dinner gave the day its popular name of 'goose-feast', and it was remembered by Marshmen as the date after which they would refuse to touch a 'brambleberry' (blackberry). They cited Revelations 12:9 and claimed that the Devil, thrown down to earth, spoiled all the blackberries by means 'too filthy to be mentioned'.[3] St. Martin's Day, or Martinmas, on 11 November, was not a major holiday, and no special observance, whether Christian or pagan, has been discovered for it, but by a typical transformation it became 'Martlemas' in Lindsey dialect to suit the local tongue and ear.

There was a special concentration of unofficial customs in the Christmas season. St. Thomas's Day, 21 December, was noted for the custom of 'mumping' or 'thomassing' in which women went round the farmhouses to beg gifts. It was noted in 1836 that 'the ancient custom of begging on St. Thomas's Day is kept up most extensively by the women of this county'. At Corringham, on the Eve of St. Thomas, horses were believed to lie down reverently at midnight.[4] The last week of Advent was marked not only by preparation for Christmas, but also by the visits of the Morris dancers, with their non-Christian cast that included Tom Fool, the Lady,

---

[1] Gutch and Peacock, p. 137; Penny, *Folklore*, p. 75; *Lincs. N. and Q.*, ii (1890–1), p. 44; E. Peacock, *Glossary*, p. 211.

[2] M. Peacock, 'Folklore and Legends', p. 32; *Notes and Queries*, 4th Ser. ix (1872), p. 225.

[3] Brogden, *Provincial Words and Expressions*, p. 84; Heanley, 'The Vikings', p. 46.

[4] *Linc. Gaz.*, 26 Dec. 1836; M. Peacock, 'Folklore and Legends', p. 49. In the Marsh the privilege of mumping appears to have been limited to widows (Heanley, 'The Vikings', p. 40).

the Fiddler, and the Farmer's Son.[1] At Christmas the 'celebration' seems to have obscured the event ostensibly being celebrated. On Christmas Eve itself religious concerns were muted on what was a pleasant social occasion. Henry Winn recalled that on Christmas Eve, while the oxen knelt in reverence, the young people gathered at the mistletoe and their elders enjoyed a 'quiet game of cards'. Christmas day was a time for the telling of 'nonsense stories'; at Fulletby, 'the young men and boys . . . got up a football match among themselves'.[2]

The state of the Christian holidays in nineteenth-century south Lindsey is instructive for the whole course of religion in England since the Middle Ages. Of the rich traditions associated with the holidays in medieval Catholicism—the miracles of the saints and the legends of the Virgin Mary—almost nothing had survived.[3] But villagers did not ignore the Christian holidays; nor did they simply debase them; still less did they raise up a rival set of pagan festivals to compete with them. Rather, they preserved them, including several which the clergy themselves no longer celebrated—the popular religious tradition was in these instances more tenacious than the clerical. But the process of preservation involved at the least certain displacements of accent from the Christian to the pagan, which even in the principal holidays (Good Friday, Easter Sunday, and Christmas) were considerable. Often the process involved still more, the virtual elimination of Christian content. Yet if some of the holidays were now Christian in name only, they still remained religious. If the Eve of St. Mark's, for example, had nothing to do with St. Mark, it had much to do with the Devil, with 'wisdom', and other pagan religious themes. Even days like Martinmas, with no manifest religious content whether Christian or pagan, were still minimally 'sacred' to the extent that they were remembered, and thus were set apart from ordinary 'profane' days. They were sometimes dechristianized but not yet

---

[1] M. Peacock, 'Folklore and Legends', p. 54; Winn 3/1, p. 31. Marsh villages were visited by sword dancers, representing the alternative tradition in English folk dance (Heanley, 'The Vikings', p. 40). See Joseph Needham, 'The Geographical Distribution of English Ceremonial Dance Traditions', *Journal of the English Folk Dance and Song Society*, iii (1936).

[2] Winn 5/3, p. 41; *Lincs. N. and Q.* ii (1890–1), p. 20. Among other highlights of the Christmas season was the game 'turn-trencher' (Brogden, *Provincial Words and Expressions*, p. 142.)

[3] Except a few 'old oaths of popish times' like 'Marry good faith!' and 'By'r Lady' (Cooper, *Wise Saws*, ii. 126–7).

desacralized. They formed, along with the rites, clergy, churches, and churchyards, a vague reservoir of spiritual potency which was no longer specifically Christian and which could therefore be tapped and directed to non-Christian ends. Paganism was parasitical upon Christianity, but it had grown larger than its host.

Rites and Sacraments

The rites and sacraments of Anglican Christianity were also affected by popular superstition, though not to the extent that might be expected. They were efficacious, quasi-magical performances that ought to have appealed to villagers with a non-mechanistic world view, but in practice they inspired few cultic superstitions, and not many more non-cultic ones. Though the pattern varied from case to case, what stands out most is the fact that sacramental power was not transmuted into popular magic, that it failed to engage the popular imagination.

Paradoxically this failure was most apparent in popular attitudes towards Holy Communion—the most sacramental of the sacraments. Its pre-eminence was granted by all, Churchmen, Methodists, and 'floaters', yet it was singularly barren of popular superstition. The explanation for this would appear to lie in the dual impact of the Reformation and of social change. Since the Reformation the doctrine of Communion in the Church of England (and in Methodism) was a rather 'low' one which downplayed its mystery and supernatural efficacy. As late as 1858 it was celebrated only four times a year in a majority of south Lindsey parishes. There was also a social explanation. If in the early eighteenth century the entire adult population in some parishes were regular communicants, in the middle of the nineteenth the poor rarely received communion.[1] No one knew their attitudes better than Henry Winn, and his view was that to them it was 'so solemn . . . awful and exclusive . . . that they *durst not* presume to take it'.[2] What appears to have made them fearful was not its intrinsic sacramental power but the 'solemn' and 'awful' consequences in store for unworthy and presumptuous recipients. Considering themselves too sinful and unworthy, they mentally reserved it for

[1] Norman Sykes, *Church and State in the Eighteenth Century*, 1934, pp. 251–2. Winn 1/1, pp. 65–6;.
[2] Winn 1/1, pp. 65–6.

the gentry—the 'quality' in local dialect[1]—and other people whose virtue was ensured by their rank in society. That the poor seldom were communicants is to be explained by their self-depreciation, which in turn reflected the dissolution of the village community and the hardening of class lines. Infrequent celebrants who took a low view of its spiritual powers, and social change that confined it to the élite, made Communion psychologically remote from ordinary villagers—too remote to be available even for superstitious uses.

The interplay between clerical and popular religion is also illustrated in their views on the other Anglican sacrament, baptism. It had no fewer than three different names, corresponding with three differing notions of its nature and importance. The correct term 'baptism' was the least heard of the three: only the clergy used it and even they preferred the more popular 'christening'; and there was still a third, rather vulgar word for it, 'naming' —past tense 'nampt'.[2] There were also at least two distinct clerical views on baptism: the High Churchmen believed that it washed away original sin and regenerated the soul of the child, and the moderate and Low Churchmen that it marked his entry into the Church. But neither of these came very close to the popular view that it simply gave him a name, and entitled him to a proper Christian burial. (The souls of the unbaptized were said to wander endlessly in the form of wild geese.)[3] Though the popular view was non-theological it did tend to reinforce the official rule that only the baptized could receive a Christian burial. Two minor superstitions were connected with baptism: if a boy and a girl were presented for baptism at the same time, the boy was to receive the rite first, to prevent the girl from growing a beard; and an infant would die if it did not cry at baptism. Altogether this was a small crop of superstitions, but the basic lay view of baptism was very firmly held.[4]

Confirmation was not a sacrament in the Church of England,

---

[1] E. Peacock, *Glossary*, p. 199.

[2] Brogden, *Provincial Words and Expressions*, p. 133; E. Peacock, *Glossary*, p. 176.

[3] Heanley, 'The Vikings', pp. 40–1. It was widely felt however that charity required a proper burial for the unbaptized as well—not to mention those who had received a Methodist baptism, whom militant High Church parsons sometimes refused to bury.

[4] M. Peacock, 'Folklore and Legends', p. 64; Winn 3/1, p. 15. The contemporary popular view that baptism is 'lucky' may have emerged as a generalization of the more specific effects anticipated in the nineteenth century.

though it was often considered to be a prerequisite for Communion. In practice few recent confirmees made their first Communion and for most it probably marked an end of formal religious practice rather than a beginning. One minor superstition connected with the rite was that a candidate receiving the bishop's left hand would never marry. But the outstanding one was the belief that confirmation was a cure for rheumatism. People of mature and elderly years were known to present and re-present themselves to the bishop at confirmations for his thaumaturgic touch: though few, probably, of the many who held the belief actually acted on it.[1]

Only a single superstition has come to light in connection with the marriage ceremony: the belief that whichever partner knelt first at the altar rail would be the first to die.[2] But there may have been many more than the sources recorded, for they would have been part of the folklore of sexuality which probably was extensive but on which the sources are all but silent.

Like other rites, the 'Thanksgiving of Women after Childbirth' was better—indeed in this case universally—known by its common name: 'churching'. Its popularity, which was great, was due not to the pious desire to render thanks to God, but almost entirely to two superstitions: that it removed the impurity which was thought to taint women after childbirth—'clean' in local dialect referred to 'a woman after being churched'—and that a mother who left her house to go visiting before being churched would give birth to another child within the year—'"an bairns [children] comes quick enif wi'cot encoregin' on 'em"'.[3] Of all the rites, this was the best integrated with its accompanying superstition, but as in the case of confirmation, the motives for

[1] M. Peacock, 'Folklore and Legends', p. 72. This belief was also the object of an outstanding example of popular scepticism. An old gamekeeper told Penny (see Appendix) that he had not been confirmed and did not intend to be: he had heard that bishops could '"cure our rheumatics . . . same as [Woodhall] Spa water"', but he '"niver see'd anybody as was cured by a Bishop"'. When told that the bishop would lay his hands on his head and pray for him, he replied, '"Now look you here . . . see my 'and, and see my ow'd 'at on the table. I puts my 'and on my 'at, now what good 'as my 'and done to my 'at? . . . The Bishop's 'ands can't do more good to my 'ed than my 'and did to my 'at."' (More Folklore, pp. 38–9.)

[2] Winn 5/5, p. 58. It was also reported that some grooms, misunderstanding the phrase in the marriage vows 'with all my worldly goods I thee endow', said instead, 'with all my worldly goods, I, thee, and thou'. (Brown, Literae Laureatae, p. 71 n.

[3] E. Peacock. Glossary p. 60; M. Peacock, 'Folklore and Legends', pp. 64–5. See also F. Thompson, Lark Rise, p. 108.

participating in the rite owed nothing to Christianity and everything to superstition. Christianity provided the ritual, but
paganism gave it its meaning.

The reasons for the sparsity of superstitions about the Anglican
rites are unfortunately obscure. Churching was exceptional in
being both popular and strongly paganized, but the other rites
seem to have evoked no *frisson* whether Christian or pagan.
Marriage may be an exception: the sources are inadequate. But
baptism was desacralized; what popularity confirmation had
(among young people) was not due to religious motives whether
Christian or pagan; and Holy Communion, the centrepiece of the
Anglican sacramental system, repelled most villagers, psychologically and socially if not doctrinally. The psychological
remoteness of the sacraments is consistent with other evidence of
the strength of popular Protestantism, which was hostile not only
to Rome and the Pope but also to the rites and sacraments and
other 'Catholic' features of the Church of England.[1] It would
appear that the purging of the sacraments begun by the Protestant
Reformers was completed by the common people, and so thorough
was it that it denied the Anglican rites not only their Christian
efficacy but also much of their susceptibility to pagan and superstitious uses. If this folk Protestantism retained little of the
Reformation's positive doctrinal content, it was authentically
Protestant in negation.[2]

The Clergy

A third divergence between clerical and popular Christianity
may be seen in their conceptions of the role of the Anglican
clergyman. In his own mind he had two chief roles: clerical (or
ecclesiastical) and secular, in which he performed respectively as
pastor and preacher, and as gentleman and magistrate. Now
villagers not only acknowledged these two roles but fused them.
In Lindsey as elsewhere, a villager when speaking about a parson
habitually used the phrase 'his reverence' and addressed him as

---

[1] e.g. Henry Winn's attack on Anglo-Catholicism: 'Idolatry in England lifts her
head, And *priests* now make us *gods* of bits of *bread*' (Winn 4/5, p. 139). See also
G. F. A. Best, 'Popular Protestantism in Victorian Britain', in R. Robson (ed.),
Ideas and Institutions of Victorian Britain, 1967.

[2] Protestant also was the popular regard for the Bible as the source and sign of
true religion: to be reckoned a 'Bible parson' or 'gospel minister' was to receive the
highest praise.

'your reverence'.[1] These expressions were presumably formed on analogy with 'his lordship' and 'your lordship' and thus combined religious and secular formulas of deferential address. But popular religion occasionally added a third, pagan role: the clergyman as exorcist, caster of spells, and wielder of power over the pagan world of spirits. It was believed that the most effective way of dealing with haunted houses or with satanic possession was to summon a 'church clergyman with a Bible' or better, several clergymen.[2] And when a certain wheelwright approached R. M. Heanley in one of his Marshland parishes he had a similar role in mind. He asked Heanley to '"say a few wuds"' over a sow which he thought had been '"overluked"' by a witch. When Heanley refused, he asked for a piece of wicken (the ash tree) from his garden; when refused that too, he took it later when Heanley was not looking, put it over the sty—and the pig recovered.[3] The magical aura of the Anglican parson hardly compared with that of the Irish Roman Catholic priest, who did nothing to discourage the superstitious reverence in which he was held by his flock; and since for most parsons the fact that they were gentlemen was at least as significant as their priestly function, they were unlikely to invest themselves with magical powers. But there was always the possibility that they might unwillingly or unwittingly be invested with them by uninstructed villagers.

There was one further discrepancy between official and popular views of the Anglican clergy. In classic Anglicanism, as stated by George Herbert, for example, the parson was the *persona* of his parish, its representative man, representing his people before God and God before his people. Evidence suggests however, and not only for south Lindsey, that at the popular level this representative role was not acknowledged, nor was a sharp distinction drawn between the clergy and ministers of other denominations. People regularly spoke not only of 'church parsons'—implying that non-church parsons existed—but also explicitly of 'Methodist parsons' as well as 'black coats'—i.e. 'anyone who preaches'.[4] This is not to

[1] Brogden, *Provincial Words and Expressions*, p. 166; Cooper, *Wise Saws*, i. 186.

[2] M. Peacock, 'Folklore and Legends', p. 159; Rudkin, *Lincolnshire Folklore*, p. 33.

[3] Heanley, 'The Vikings', p. 49.

[4] Winn 5/3, p. 103; *Notes and Queries*, 4th Ser. vi (1870), p. 566; Booth to Kennedy, 8 Apr. 1832, 3 ANC 7/23/25/12; E. Peacock, *Glossary*, p. 25; Brogden, *Provincial Words and Expressions*, p. 42.

suggest that clergy and ministers were regarded as interchange-able[1] but only that the ideal of the parson, of which the Church of England was so proud, was not accepted by the people for whose benefit it was intended—who may well have found it implausible after centuries of pluralism and absenteeism.

The Devil

If belief in the Devil had been abandoned by the educated classes, he was still a living presence in the villages. It would be an exaggeration to draw an absolute contrast between an élite oriented towards God and lower classes oriented towards the Devil, but the divergence was apparent, and reflected real differences in class cultures.

The Devil was rarely spoken of by his proper name, which was itself part of his malignant reality. Instead, there were nicknames—Samwell, the Owd Lad, Old Nick, Old Harry, Old Sam, the Old 'Un—which suggest that the popular attitude towards him was not unequivocally one of revulsion. Indeed, he was spoken of 'in a mixture of familiarity, affection, and awe . . . [He is] very bad and not a bit respectable, but still they had better keep right with him.'[2] This ambivalence may have been due to the fact that he represented not only external evil but also ordinary human weakness.

In several of the stories told about him, he served to embody the vices and desires of the individuals who confronted him; he was a distorting mirror in which they saw their own faults exaggerated. Thus a drunkard in the habit of coming home and beating his wife was confronted one night after a drinking session by 'a tall man dressed in black looking very sternly at him'; recognizing his visitor as the Devil, he begged him for mercy and promised not to drink or beat his wife again. A tailor who worked on Sundays ('"I would as soon measure anyone on a Sunday as a wattle [week] day"') began to measure a 'gentleman' who inadvertently exposed a cloven hoof: the tailor was converted to the Baptists

---

[1] The distinction was certainly recognized by the larger farmers and gentry; at agricultural dinners the usual toast to 'the Bishop and clergy of the diocese' was sometimes extended to include 'the ministers of all denominations'.

[2] Penny, *Folklore*, p. 50; see also Rudkin, *Lincolnshire Folklore*, pp. 71–2. According to Edward Peacock, *Glossary*, p. 86, 'old-fashioned' people in the late eighteenth century used the word 'devil' when reading the Bible or speaking about religion, but in oaths and on lighter occasions 'were careful to say Divil'.

and never violated the Sabbath again.[1] If, as Feuerbach said, men projected their virtues on God, he might have added that they projected their vices on the Devil.

Another source of ambivalent feelings was one of the Devil's more pagan roles—the dispenser of 'wisdom'. Those seeking occult or magical power might have to make a pact with him; on the Eve of St. Mark, for example, they bargained with him after reaping the 'Devil's harvest'. He in turn tempted people with money or other rewards to come under his power and become his servant. An old man returning penniless after a night of drinking stopped on the road to pick up some half-crowns, whereupon a man in a blue smock-frock stepped up to ask him to become his servant: he could have all the half-crowns he wanted, though he would have to be branded. But the man said he was the servant of God Almighty, at which the Devil fled.[2] This role was an extension of the first, but simultaneously much more attractive and much more dangerous.

When the Devil swooped in to carry some poor sinner off to hell, his role was unambiguously evil. Yet the anecdotes—seemingly authentic—which illustrate this role are overlaid by a second theme, surprising but distracting. In most of the stories told of him, the Devil had the appearance of a gentleman dressed in black: the same as a clergyman. On two occasions actual clergymen were mistaken for the Devil come to perform his awful mission. In what appears to be an autobiographical sketch, Penny describes how this happened when he went to visit a certain old man for the first time. Knocking at the cottage door, he received no answer; then, as he walked away, the door opened slightly and

the very frightened face of an old man appeared, but instantly disappeared with a cry of terror before the clergyman could say more than 'I', and the poor old man sank back into a chair ... with a groan ... Thinking he was going to faint ... the clergyman asked ... 'Shall I fetch your daughter?' 'Oh! no, no ... take me sooner than her if you must take somebody.'

When finally the clergyman identified himself, the old man said, that he had had a dream in which the Devil, dressed in

---

[1] Penny, *More Folklore*, pp. 7–8, 44–5.
[2] Penny, *Folklore*, p. 50. In another story a Wesleyan minister dispersed a pack of devils by similar means (pp. 73–4).

black like a clergyman, had appeared, saying, "'I am come to take you.''

'I thought you was the ow'd lad come to take me, for I had such an awful dream last night, and I was afraid to come to the door . . . and I only opened it when you knocked again to prevent the ow'd lad breaking it down; and when I saw you all in black and you began "I", just as he did, I was sure my dream had come true.' 'I am so glad you did not drag me after you for ever so far, and when the earth suddenly opened throw me into a burning fiery furnace as I dreamt the ow'd lad did.'[1]

Penny also records a second incident of this kind. A bishop entered a barn in which two men were threshing grain; looking up, they assumed from his dress ('shovel hat, apron, and gaiters') that he was the Devil; they fell to their knees and cried, '"Oh! Mr. Devil! Mr. Devil! have mercy on us and don't take us away so soon."' The bishop then identified himself, but the men, still on their knees, cried out, '"How was we to know you was our Bishop if you dressed up like the Devil."'[2] Whether these mis-identifications were anything but fortuitous is a mystery whose resolution awaits further research. But there is no mistaking the terror which the Devil was capable of inspiring.

In this as in other respects the Devil was a phenomenon of village culture rather than of élite clerical culture, and a major discontinuity is apparent here between the two. Though Devil beliefs had evolved in the early Church and had been introduced into popular life by the Church, most parsons now were silent about the Devil, if indeed they still thought he existed, while villagers appear to have had few doubts on this score. Yet their view of the Devil was not a mere 'survival' of some earlier clerical one. There is nothing in the local evidence about the Devil's sexual dealings with women—one of the teachings of theologians in the classic age of witchcraft—and his connection with witchcraft was no more than marginal. And if in clerical Christianity the Devil tended to be regarded as a solution to an abstract problem of theodicy, in popular religion he was a person, not a principle; he was a familiar, with nicknames, whom one met face to face. But while he belonged to the popular religious world he was invulnerable to its magic and manipulation; men were his

---

[1] Penny, *More Folklore*, pp. 63–4.   [2] ibid., pp. 64–5.

playthings, not he theirs. This combination—terrifying external menace and the intimacy of a psychological 'double'—gave popular religion not merely a dramatic but also a moral and psychological dimension.

*   *   *

Popular Christianity in south Lindsey was no mere derivative or debased version of the clerical faith. Its libretto was not written by bishops or by Fellows of Oriel or by Regius Professors of Divinity. What villagers understood as Christianity was never preached from a pulpit or taught in Sunday school, and what they took from the clergy they took on their own terms.

By the same token the clergy were unable or unwilling to adapt Christianity to suit popular taste. Although the Church of England was a 'national' church it had become too closely associated with the élite and with élite culture to be attractive to most villagers. The clergy, who now ranked as gentlemen, were in village society but not of it. And the Church was almost entirely lacking in religious institutions of the middle range— monks, nuns, saints, shrines, processions, pilgrimages, rosaries, candles—which might have reduced the gap between a transcendent deity and ordinary villagers. The Anglican texture was too thin to have much popular appeal; the Church offered no 'moral equivalent' to the magic and superstition that proliferated in the villages.

Since the clergy were incapable of shaping a more popular version of the faith, villagers were left to do so themselves. A ceremony like churching flourished only for reasons which the parsons would have disapproved of, had they known them. The Devil was a powerful figure in the popular religious world long after he had faded from the clerical. The observance of Easter was reinforced by superstition, but at the expense of depreciating its Christian meaning. There were also holidays like the Eve of St. Mark's which had to give lodging to pagan myths and practices of an entirely alien kind. Virtually every feature of Anglican Christianity suffered the indignity of being treated as a mere packet of magical power which was at the disposal of anyone who cared to exploit it, for ends that had nothing to do with Christianity. It was in this deformed state that Christianity survived in the popular religious scene.

SUPERSTITION: PAGAN

To use the term 'paganism' for the non-Christian elements in popular religion is convenient but misleading, since like popular religion as a whole, it was not a distinct and conscious movement or organization but a loose agglomeration of religious phenomena. It was not a counter-religion to Christianity; rather, the two coexisted and complemented each other. Nevertheless, before inquiring into their psychological and social functions it is pertinent to ask Weber's question: which was the effective, decisive force, the higher god or the lower? Villagers freely combined Christian and pagan elements in varying proportions, but in most cases it was the pagan element that predominated.

In an episode recorded by Heanley Christian and pagan mingled in something like even proportions. Visiting a little boy suffering from ague, he offered to give him some quinine, but the boy's parents refused; they asked Heanley to look at three horseshoes they had nailed to the footboard of the bed, and explained that

when the Old 'un comes to shaake 'im yon ull fix 'im as fast as t' chu'ch steeaple. He weant niver nivver pass yon . . . it's a chawm. Oi teks the mell i' my left hand, and Oi taps they shoes an' Oi saays— 'Feyther, Son and Holy Ghost, Naale the divil to this poast. Throice I smoites with Holy Crok, With this mell Oi throice dew knock, One for God, An' one for Wod, An' one for Lok.'[1]

While Christianity clearly contributed much, the magical techniques and the syncretism itself were personal and pagan.

Another incident from the Marsh reflects a pagan dominance over Christianity. When Heanley noticed a 'kern baby'—a doll made of barley straw—perched on a sheaf facing a wheat field, an 'old dame' explained it to him thus:

Yis, she be thear to fey away t' thoon'er an' lightning' an' sich-loike. Prayers is good enuff ez fur as they goas, but t' Awmighty mun be strange an' throng wi' soa much corn to look efter, an' in these here bad toimes we moan't fergit owd Providence. Happen, it's best to keep in wi' both parties.[2]

[1] Heanley, 'The Vikings', p. 53.

[2] ibid., pp. 45–6. 'Strange' forms the superlative in Lindsey dialect. (Oxley, *Lindsey Dialect*, p. 62.)

'Providence' was a Christian word, but its content was the pagan idea of fate, and the woman acted as though fate was more effective than God. On still another occasion, when the cattle plague reached Lincolnshire in 1866, Christianity and paganism were mutually exclusive alternatives. The clergy explained that it was God's way of punishing the people for their sins, and sought to end it by asking them to repent and pray for God's forgiveness. One clergyman told his congregation that 'it was a visitation of God for the many sins we have committed, and strongly advised us to repent of them, and lead a new life'.[1] But the farm servants in the Marsh, not trusting to prayers, took matters into their own hands and set up crosses of wicken in their farmyards to ward off the plague. 'Not a single cowshed in Marshland but had its wicken cross over the door'. A more drastic measure was tried on one farm in the Wolds: a calf was killed and buried, feet upwards, facing the threshold of the cowshed—but it failed, according to one explanation, because the calf chosen was a sick one, and likely to die anyway, whereas a healthy one would have worked.[2] These farm servants did not repudiate Christianity, but they acted as though there were surer ways than prayer of coping with misfortune.

In its totality the pagan universe was a large, loose, pluralistic affair without any clear unifying principle. It encompassed superhuman beings and forces, witches and wise men, and a mass of low-grade magic and superstition. The whole was less than the sum of its parts, for it was not a cosmos to be contemplated or worshipped but a treasury of separate and specific resources to be used and applied in concrete situations.

Perhaps it was this popular utilitarianism that explains why most of the old pagan pantheon was virtually extinct by the nineteenth century. Wod and Lokk survive only in fugitive references, though the notion of fate is more apparent. Much lower in the hierarchy there may possibly have been more life in the 'boggarts'. When Heanley asked an old man to help him open a barrow outside his garden hedge at Wainfleet, he refused: '"The king of the boggarts is shutten up inside that thear, an' if thou lets un out on

---

[1] Haxby, Diary, 18 Feb. 1866, Thimbleby 4/11, L.A.O. Methodists too held services to ask divine assistance against the cattle plague, and R. D. B. Rawnsley's sermon on the subject at Halton Holegate was published (*The Cattle Plague*, 1866).

[2] Heanley, 'The Vikings', p. 50. This was the explanation offered by the garthman on Heanley's father's farm.

it 'ud tek aal the parsuns i' the Marsh a munth o' Sundays to lay
'un again.'" [1] Evidence is more abundant for the 'old Lady' or
'Old Gal' who presided over the safety of the elder tree. Marshmen
were reluctant to chop elder wood without first asking '"the Old
Lady's leave"' or '"the Old Gal's leave"'. When a baby became ill
in its cradle, blame fell on the man who had made a rocker of elder
wood for the cradle without asking her permission. And a servant
of Heanley's attributed his illness to his having chopped elder
wood without reciting the proper request for permission: 'Owd
Gal, give me of thy wood, an' oi will give some of moine, when I
graws iner a tree.' [2] Here was expressed in a highly specific manner
the pagan theme, so alien to the biblical tradition, of man's
dependence upon nature.

At a lower level there was still more activity among the spirits
and ghosts. Not always consistently distinguished, spirits usually
belonged to the living, ghosts to the dead. Stories involving
spirits are not numerous, apart from their chief role, which was to
emerge from the church porch on the Eve of St. Mark's. But
belief in ghosts appears to have been widespread, at least down to
the middle of the century. A sampling can be taken for just one
village, Fulletby, through the diaries and reminiscences of Henry
Winn. In 1844 he wrote in his diary, 'I have seldom talked with a
peasant that did not fancy he had either seen or heard something
of the kind [ghosts] at some period of his life.' The next day he
heard 'some strange tales of certain old houses being haunted from
a person that firmly believes in such reports'. The explanation,
which 'I have heard scores of times before', was 'that some person
had been murdered in the house and could not rest until the
remains of their body was removed to a place of greater sanctity—
or some former occupant of the house had some money hid there
and could not rest until it was discovered, and become the property of the rightful heir'. He also recounts several ghost stories of
a familiar type. A place near Fulletby was haunted by the ghost (in
the form of a white rabbit) of a girl who died in 1766 after a fall
from a horse. The rectory at Fulletby was haunted, so it was said,
because a skull from an earlier parsonage in the village was built
into the chimney; it ceased to be haunted when the chimney was

---

[1] Heanley, 'The Vikings', p. 39. A boggart was a spectre or ghost, often haunting
a well or some other particular place. See Tennyson, 'Northern Farmer: Old Style'.
[2] Heanley, 'The Vikings', pp. 55–7.

taken down. In another story from Fulletby a young man was so frightened by a ghost that he refused to leave the house; the ghost spoke with him and identified itself as his father, and said that it would have a message for him the next night at midnight in the churchyard; the boy tried to hang himself, but was saved just in time, and the ghost no longer bothered him. All this, from one village with a population of less than 300 in 1851, suggests a superabundance of ghost beliefs in the area as a whole. The clue to the meaning of ghosts was given by Winn himself when he referred to 'a place of greater sanctity' and 'rightful heir'. Ghosts were embodiments (or disembodiments) of conscience; they represented either the guilt of an individual (as in the case of the boy and the ghost of his father) or the social memory of past wrong and injustice (as suggested by Winn himself).[1] They were not primarily an individual creation, for private visions of conventional images like ghosts depend on the socially created expectations that they will occur; they depend, moreover, on the existence of a *moral* community with a collective memory and concern for ancient wrongs and injustices.[2] Popular paganism was no mere collection of mindless magic or of vain fantasies: it had a conscience, which it commonly projected and personified in the Devil or in ghosts. It did not teach a distinct moral code of its own, but rather gave dramatic expression to the common conscience, both individual and collective.

Witchcraft

To leave the world of spirits is not unfortunately to reach more solid empirical ground, for the pre-eminent human figures in popular religion were also the most problematical: the witches. Though the educated élite ceased to find witchcraft credible after 1700, it was still flourishing in the nineteenth century among Lindsey villagers.

It flourished partly because it provided an explanation for misfortune: for anything from the fatal to the trivial. Later in the century it was recalled that 'fwoakes' bairns was hover-looked and

[1] Winn, Diary, 23 and 24 Sept. 1844; Winn 3/6, sect. 3, pp. 6–9. Similarly Penny, *Folklore*, pp. 30–1.

[2] This was apparent in the belief that the sons were punished for the sins of the fathers, and more specifically that misfortune would befall the descendants of those who enclosed common land around 1800. (M. Peacock, 'Folklore and Legends', p. 199.)

the poor things withered away',[1] and a woman at Tetford was
supposed to have bewitched people 'for the pleasure of seeing
them suffer' and to have caused the deaths of her own son,
daughter, and sister. In the 1840s a blacksmith at Stixwold was
tormented by a black cat which scared his horse as he passed
through Horsington. It also harassed his pigs and other animals,
until a certain old woman in the adjoining parish of Bucknall died.
A woman who was 'always seeing a magpie' feared she was being
bewitched by her mother-in-law. A boy at Sotby, having grown
uncontrollably fat, until he was almost too fat to walk, suspected
witchcraft.[2] The most common of these misfortunes occurred in
the farm dairy: whenever the butter failed to come in the churn,
witchcraft was suspected.

> How the housewives dreaded the witches pow'r,
> And fearfully work'd each spell.
> The husband with curses both loud and long,
> With fury his breast would burn,
> When told by his good old trembling dame,
> That the witch was in the churn.[3]

The misfortunes of animals as well as those of men were ascribed
to witchcraft; in an agricultural economy witches could harm men
by harming their animals. Cows and pigs were 'overlooked', and
witches were often blamed when horses refused to move or to go
past a certain house.[4] Witches themselves often took the form of
hares and other animals. A witch at Sloothby ran about as a hare
which no one could catch or shoot—unless they had used a silver
bullet. And a certain squire, addicted to hare-coursing, paying
anyone a shilling who could guide him to a hare, came to suspect
that a boy who had collected many shillings from him was
actually leading him to his mother, a witch.[5]

The misfortunes attributed to witchcraft can be believed, but
what of the witches? Were there actually women who considered
themselves to be witches? Witchcraft can be unconscious as well
as conscious, and Miss Peacock claimed without citing examples
that popular belief recognized both varieties.[6] The woman at

[1] H. D. Rawnsley, *Memories of the Tennysons*, p. 35.
[2] Penny, *Folklore*, pp. 13, 24–5, 36–7.
[3] Brown, *Lay of the Clock*, p. 9.
[4] *Lincs. N. and Q.* i (1889), p. 170; H. D. Rawnsley, *Memories of the Tennysons*, p. 35.
[5] Rudkin, *Lincolnshire Folklore*, pp. 79–81, 84–5; Penny, *Folklore*, pp. 72–3.
[6] M. Peacock, 'Folklore and Legends', p. 127.

Tetford was said to have done harm deliberately, and the same is implied in the story of the mother-in-law responsible for the magpie. In other cases it is not at all clear whether the witchcraft was intentional or not. Perhaps the question is not important: whether or not witchcraft was a conscious idea and intention in the mind of the witch, it was undoubtedly present in the mind of the victim, who blamed it for his misfortune and could take countermeasures against it. Whatever its relationship to witches, witchcraft provided the victims and accusers with a practical explanation of life's misfortunes.

And more than an explanation: in at least two cases the witchcraft accusation seems to have sprung from a pre-existing personal conflict between the victim and the witch.[1] This may well have been true in other cases, particularly when the complaint of the 'victim' was relatively trivial, but unfortunately the sources rarely discuss the relations between victim and witch before the accusation. Two exceptions are the stories cited above involving women and their mothers-in-law, a situation with limitless possibilities for conflict, not the least of which was the desire of the younger couple to take over the house of the mother-in-law. In accusing her of witchcraft, the daughter-in-law simultaneously projected and displaced her own resentment.[2] The suspicion of witchcraft at the butter churn may have reflected not only the perverse slowness of the butter to form, but also the inevitable conflict between mistress and servant. Instead of venting their frustration and aggression on each other, they could displace it on to a third party, the witch. In other cases, witch and victim appear to have been strangers to each other, sometimes living in different parishes, but the possibility that a familial or other kind of tension was present is not precluded. The limitations of the sources make further inquiry difficult.

By the end of the nineteenth century witchcraft was said to be declining;[3] it was in any event changing its character, completing a long-term process of depersonalization. As late as the 1830s, to be bewitched was to be 'overlooked' by the 'evil eye' of a known

---

[1] See K. Thomas, *Religion and the Decline of Magic*, 1971, pp. 552–61.

[2] cf. J. Demos, 'Underlying Themes in the Witchcraft of Seventeenth-Century New England', *American Historical Review*, lxxv (1970), p. 1325.

[3] Winn 3/6, sect. 3, p. 12. One of H. D. Rawnsley's informants told him around 1890, 'Well you know witches is clean gone by' (*Memories of the Tennysons*, p. 46).

witch.[1] It was a personal relation between witch and victim. Later in the century, references to the 'evil eye' decrease; and the relation between witch and victim, while still personal, was less intense, now that the eye of the witch was no longer fixed on her victim. People still feared being overlooked, but no longer were aware of the eye. Subsequent stages of the process are illustrated by the history of the butter churn and its witchcraft. Late in the century, witchcraft was blamed when the butter failed to form, but the accusers had not only forgotten the evil eye, but also dispensed with the need for a particular witch: they instead blamed the abstraction 'witchcraft'. It was witchcraft without witches. A further stage was reached when dairymaids, still placing their remedial sprigs of wicken over the churn, no longer knew why they did so: they no longer knew about witches or witchcraft.[2] It was a ritual without a myth, degenerating into mere luck.

Among the many remedies for witchcraft the most significant was the one that was *not* available: the assistance of a clergyman. Otherwise the most common was a piece of wicken put near the butter churn to keep the witches out. (Like other remedies for witchcraft, it was credited with a wider effectiveness against all kinds of misfortune: it was put in a thatched roof to prevent fire or kept in one's pocket for good luck.) Another specific against witches in the churn was to throw a pinch of salt in the churn and another into the fire.[3] A mother and daughter whose butter had been turned by a witch into 'fuzz balls' responded by wearing pieces of wicken in a bag round their necks. The harassed blacksmith put wicken in his keyhole, on his chimney, and on the roof. A more idiosyncratic antidote was attempted by the woman troubled by the magpie: she stuck pins in a cork and put it in a bottle containing some liquid, hoping it would force the witch to call off the magpie—or else kill her with dropsy.[4] If a suspected witch could be made to bleed, her nefarious activities would be checked, at least against the person who inflicted the wound. When a witch asked a woman to take a thorn out of her finger, the woman had the presence of mind to prick her with the needle,

[1] ibid., p. 46. In Henry Winn's youth a witch at West Ashby was said to have a 'witch-pap' as well.

[2] M. Peacock, 'Folklore and Legends', p. 136.

[3] Brown, *Lay of the Clock*, p. 9; M. Peacock, 'Folklore and Legends', pp. 136, 210; E. Peacock, *Glossary*, pp. 43. 66-7, 275.

[4] Penny, *Folklore*, pp. 13-14, 24-6.

drawing blood, and thereby rendering her powerless to harm her in the future. For this purpose the victims of a witch often contrived to place pins in her chair.[1] This could have its dangers: the wheelwright who asked Heanley to '"say a few wuds"' over a sow he thought was overlooked was afraid to try this tactic because the witch would take him up to the Spilsby magistrates, who would '"be that iggnerant"' as to make him pay a fine. When the witch took the form of a hare, a pin or needle was useless, as she was impossible to catch except by a 'spayed bitch'. When the squire who loved hare-coursing set one after the hare, it failed to draw blood but bit the hare in the back—and the witch suffered backaches ever after. He could also have tried a crooked sixpence, or a more certain and poetic weapon, a silver bullet.[2] There were, then, animal, vegetable, and mineral weapons against witchcraft; the most potent, however, was the human weapon: the wise man.

The Wise Man

'I' my young daays theer wur a deal of hover-looking . . . by the hevil eye, and fwoakes had to go to the wise man.
J. C., an elderly inhabitant of Somersby, c. 1890. (H. D. Rawnsley, *Memories of the Tennysons*, p. 46.)

If the witch was the most evil human figure in paganism, the man was the most beneficent; and if witches were elusive and problematical, the wise men were public figures known over wide areas, their work attested to in a variety of sources. They had long careers and practised their skills as self-conscious professionals. Besides thwarting witchcraft, they told fortunes and identified thieves and recovered stolen property. Their techniques, which they acquired variously by inheritance, by study, or by pacts with the Devil, included astrology, magic, and 'the gift of sight', but most of them seem to have relied in some degree on their own shrewdness and knowledge of human nature.

Two successive wise men of unusual gifts made Louth as important in the pagan world as it was in Methodism. After 'Johnny o' the grass' came the celebrated Stainton, who had a high

---

[1] Rudkin, *Lincolnshire Folklore*, p. 80; Penny, *Folklore*, pp. 25–6; H. D. Rawnsley, *Memories of the Tennysons*, p. 47.
[2] Heanley, 'The Vikings', p. 49; Penny, *Folklore*, pp. 72–3; Rudkin, *Lincolnshire Folklore*, pp. 84–5.

reputation throughout south-east Lindsey, villagers often travel-
ling many miles to seek his services.[1] One of his clients was the fat
boy who came ten miles from Sotby to consult him; diagnosing a
case of witchcraft, Stainton promised to cure the boy by setting
the witch on fire. When he returned home, he found her running
in flames from her cottage, and he recovered from his obesity soon
afterwards. The magpie-tormented woman sent her husband to
Stainton, who for £2 gave him a bottle of pills. In another case a
rather simple-minded man who suspected that his wife was a
prostitute went to Stainton and paid him a guinea to be told the
truth. Stainton told him that '"no good looking woman like your
wife is safe, or ugly ones either, from being accused of being a
——, but your wife is not a —— . . . if she should go wrong I will
punish her."'[2]

Another practitioner, with a more local clientele, was 'Fiddler'
Fynes of Kirkstead. He was remembered for the case of a farm
servant who asked him to recover his stolen watch; Fynes
not only succeeded in this, identifying the thief as one of his
client's fellow servants, but also detected the attempt of a third
servant to poison him with arsenic: and all this he performed for
the standard fee of five shillings. On another occasion, three
Stixwold men found their scythe blades missing; they went to
Fynes, and for half a crown each he told them where to find
them.[3]

It is not recorded whether all wise men told fortunes, or only
the astrologers. While the latter handled all kinds of cases—witchcraft and theft, as well as divination—their special technique set
them apart from their colleagues, though they were all equally
'wise men' in the popular mind. Foremost among them was John
Worsdale of Lincoln, author of several books on astrology, who
was much sought after by villagers as well as fellow-townsmen.
What he promised, in casting a horoscope, was

to calculate the Nativity of any Person, when the true time and place of
birth is communicated to him [Worsdale] . . . to point out, and ascertain
the time and quality of every important event during the life of any
individual, both past, present, and to come.[4]

[1] Penny, *Folklore*, pp. 64–5; H. D. Rawnsley, *Memories of the Tennysons*, p. 36.
'Johnny o' the grass' had gained his powers by gathering the 'Devil's harvest'.
[2] Penny, *Folklore*, pp. 13–15, 37; *More Folklore*, p. 52.
[3] Penny, *Folklore*, pp. 46, 53–4, 71.
[4] Worsdale, *Astronomy and Elementary Philosophy*, 1819, p. 55.

His books contain scores of examples of his forecasts, most of them pessimistic and all of them, apparently, proved true by events. He also issued an invitation to people suffering from illness to send him a note of the time and place of their birth, promising in return an astrological diagnosis of their illness and a remedy. He dealt with ordinary cases of theft as well: consulted by the wife of a farmer from Stixwold (twelve miles from Lincoln) about a theft of money from the farmhouse, he succeeded in identifying the thief as one of the farm servants.[1] A contemporary of his was 'Cussitt,' the 'wise man of Welton', whose reputation and clientele were extensive. Several people from Fulletby, well over ten miles away, 'sought his professional aid'. Cases of theft were a large part of his practice. Consulted by a man about three stolen sheep, he showed him the thief's face in a mirror. While receiving (and refusing) many requests from clients to 'cast their nativities', he could use conventional, non-astrological methods as well, and in fact preferred to work by his intuitive understanding of human nature, consulting his astrological reference books only on special occasions.[2]

Ranking below the wise men with their all-round competence were men with lesser talents, limited to particular types of cases. A certain blacksmith of South Ormsby, for example, had a particular mastery of 'all the witches and wizards'. When a man complained to him that his cows were bewitched, he had him sit close to the fire and began reading from a mysterious big book which resembled the Bible but was not; at length a stranger came and joined them, also sitting near the fire, but as the heat gradually became too intense for him, he found himself powerless to move, and as his trousers began to smoke, he cried for mercy; the blacksmith warned him not to trouble the cows again, on pain of being burnt to a cinder: he fled, and the cows lived in peace thereafter.[3] Another such specialist was a woman (apparently the sole woman with a socially valuable pagan talent) at Fenton in Kettlethorpe parish, who was adept at making reluctant foals begin suckling. When a worried farmer sought her help, she would ask him when the foal was born and whether it was during the day or night; she

[1] Penny, *Folklore*, p. 8. Worsdale's other works were *Genethliacal Astrology*, 2nd edn., 1798, and *Celestial Philosophy*, 1828.

[2] Cooper, *Wise Saws*, i. 61–3 Winn 3/6, sect. 3, p. 12; H. D. Rawnsley, *Memories of the Tennysons*, p. 46.

[3] Penny, *Folklore*, pp. 34–5.

then told him to return home, and he would usually find the foal sucking healthily. In 1889, after her death, a farm foreman went to consult her son, but he '"was not scholar enuf"' to be able to help.[1]

Much about wise men unfortunately remains obscure: the precise nature of their methods (when not astrological) and the numbers and kinds of clients. A few scraps of evidence suggest that they nourished certain grievances against society. Fiddler Fynes, while 'a regular and devout attendant' at Kirkstead parish church and a respectable manager of a school, considered himself a gentleman, and 'used to say all Kirkstead ought to belong to him'. Cusworth, who 'followed husbandry' as his main occupation, milking his own cows, often turned rich men away, declining to 'cast their nativities' in spite of their lucrative offers.[2] Worsdale was inclined to radical political views; in a work completed in June, 1819, not long before Peterloo, he wrote:

I frequently view with astonishment, the elevated and dignified positions of the Celestial Bodies at be [*sic*] time when North America obtained her independence; the superior stations of those Astral Significators ... most clearly forbode, that the time will arrive, when THAT EMPIRE shall give Laws to all Nations, and establish FREE-DOM and LIBERTY in every part of the habitable Globe.[3]

He was bitter against 'SOME CLERGYMEN, of the Established Church' who collected their tithes on Sunday before celebrating Holy Communion, and recalled that it was 'a Bishop, who, for thirty pieces of silver, betrayed the Redeemer of the World'. 'Celestial Philosophy', he promised, would break 'all the forged *shackles of Priestcraft*' and liberate 'all those who are slaves to refined Popery'.[4] These are the only wise men for whom there is any evidence; in so far as they regarded the clergy as rivals they may have been moved into hostility to the social and political as well as the ecclesiastical Establishment, but what relation there was if any between their activities as wise men and their other views is unclear.

The parallels between their role and that of the clergy invite

---

[1] *Lincs. N. and Q.* i (1889), p. 131.
[2] Penny, Folklore, p. 46; Cooper, *Wise Saws*, i. 62.
[3] Worsdale, *Astronomy*, pp. 46–7.
[4] ibid., p. 39; *Celestial Philosophy*, pp. xvii–xviii.

comparison. They charged fees for their services, creating a professional–client relationship rather than that of a shepherd and his
flock—or of a prophet and his followers. Like the clergy, they
were subject to 'indelible orders', for, 'once a wizard, always a
wizard', as Stainton said, adding, 'the Devil has hold of you'.[1] In
some ways they were a shadow clergy; and they sometimes used a
big book which resembled the Bible—but wasn't. And like the
clergy they sometimes dealt with personal psychological problems. A wise man had clients, while the parson had parishioners;
he saw them singly, while the parson usually met his parishioners
communally, in public worship. But he drew his clientele from a
wide area, while the parson was confined to a single parish. His
authority derived from his personal gifts, while the parson owed
his to his office. He received fees for his services from clients who
came to him on an individual basis, while the parson received
income from tithes whose payment was legally enforceable.
Contrasted as he was with the parson, however, he did not directly
compete with him; he offered no alternative to the rites of the
church and to public worship, but at the same time he was not
challenged by the parson in his own specialities.

The other significant relationship was that between wise men
and witches. If the effects ascribed to witchcraft were real, the
witches themselves were problematic; while with the wise men
the pattern was reversed: they were real, but the effects attributed
to them—their antidotes to witchcraft—were problematic. The
two linkages of cause and effect were themselves linked: the
strength of the popular will to believe in wise men depended on
the strength of the fear of witches. Consequently, as witchcraft
underwent depersonalization in the course of the century, the
need for a personal antidote to it declined, and much less is heard
of wise men at the end of the century than at the beginning.

Oracles, Magic, and Luck

Oracles and divination, standard features of primitive religion,
respond to the human desire to know the future, to face it with
confidence, to minimize the anxiety and uncertainty about the
outcome of particular projects or of one's life as a whole. This is
no less a religious need than the need for explanation and consolation at the recognized 'breaking points' of suffering and death, but

[1] Penny, *Folklore*, p. 65.

since Christianity had little to offer besides prayer, it was answered by pagan means: by astrology, and by a variety of omens, oracles, and portents.

A special set of oracles was at the disposal of girls anxious to discover who their future husbands would be—and to attract them.[2] A girl at Mumby removed the entrails from a live pigeon and put them over her door in order to attract a lover—and succeeded. A servant girl at Horncastle tried a variety of charms: she put a toad in a bottle, covering the top with paper, then stuck pins through the paper and buried the bottle for nine days and nights; that failing, she fastened a spider in a paper and put it under her pillow for nine nights; and finally she tried scratching her left wrist and writing in blood on a paper which she buried in the garden as the church clock struck twelve—but the wrong spirit appeared and scared her. There were also the techniques employing the house key and the Bible and the sage leaves at midnight on St. Mark's Eve. Remarkably, only one example has survived of a man attempting to discover the identity of his future wife.[3]

Among the many other omens some of the most familiar were connected with the days of the week. The most general in application was 'Monday for health, Tuesday for wealth, Wednesday the best day of all, Thursday for losses, Friday for crosses, Saturday no luck at all'. As for birthdays, 'Monday's child is fair of face, Tuesday's child is full of grace, Wednesday's child is a child of woe, Thursday's child has far to go, Friday's child is loving and giving, Saturday's child must work for its living. A child that is born on the Sabbath is lucky and happy, and good and gay.' Finally,

> A man had better ne'er be born
> Than have his nails on Sunday shorn
> Cut them on Monday, cut them for health
> Cut them on Tuesday, cut them for wealth
> Cut them on Wednesday, cut them for news

---

[1] Séjourné ('Superstition', p. 2807) is one of the few Christian writers to point out the insufficiency of Christianity in this regard, and to suggest that is anything but a virtue.

[2] Including one of which Miss Peacock notes delicately that it 'does not bear printing, and is evidently of great antiquity' ('Folklore and Legends', p. 175).

[3] *Lincs. N. and Q.* ii (1890–1), p. 41; Penny, *Folklore*, p. 66; M. Peacock, 'Folklore and Legends', p. 166.

Cut them on Thursday, for a pair of new shoes,
Cut them on Friday, cut them for sorrow,
Cut them on Saturday, see your sweetheart tomorrow
Cut them on Sunday, cut them for evil,
For all the week long will be with you the Devil.[1]

Like many other aspects of popular paganism these omens set up structures of meaning in daily life; at the same time they had religious implications. For they amounted to exceptions to the sovereignty of God, and to attribute favourable and unfavourable influences to anything created was to limit and dishonour the Creator.

Another pagan oracle was dreams. They are commonly regarded in traditional societies as privileged sources of illumination and prophecy, and the fragmentary surviving evidence suggests that this was true also of village society in nineteenth-century Lindsey. All dreams were meaningful; most could be interpreted according to the principle that they 'go by contraries': death meant a wedding, and so on. In addition there was a special category of 'serious visions during which much time is spent with one person'. After such a 'vision in a dream' the dreamer would often say the next morning, 'I have been a deal with —— in the night'.[2] It was as though the dreamer was actually present with the person in the dream. An example of this kind of dream was the one the old man had of the Devil, with frightening consequences the next morning. Dreams thus made possible a nightly encounter with the supernatural for which there was no counterpart in Christianity. It also was characteristic of popular religion to find significance in an involuntary activity; Christianity on the other hand only acknowledged voluntary acts, whether in worship or conduct.

Equally characteristic of popular religion were its resources of magic, of which only one small part, folk medicine, will be sampled here. Though physicians became more numerous in the countryside in the course of the century, their fees were high—except for members of friendly societies—and most villagers had

[1] Good, *Glossary*, p. 107; Rudkin, *Lincolnshire Folklore*, pp. 18–19; Winn 3/1, pp. 7–9.

[2] M. Peacock, 'Folklore and Legends', p. 194. The 'contraries' theory was by no means confined to the poor of south Lindsey; see, e.g., John Keats to Fanny Brawne, 15 (?) July 1819; Hyder Edward Rollins (ed.), *Letters of John Keats*, 1958, ii. 129.

no alternative to the time-honoured therapies of sympathetic magic. A child with a sore throat—a 'frog'—was to suck a live frog, holding it by the leg, until it died. Henry Winn also mentions a village remedy for whooping cough: to have an 'entire horse' breathe down the child's throat. When a wound was caused by something made of iron, it was treated by removing the dirt and rust from the iron.[1] Whatever the virtues of particular remedies, they rested upon the principle that was fundamental to the popular pagan outlook: that there were continuities of influence and action both within nature and between men and nature.

The last and lowest form of superstition—but also paradoxically the most modern and secular—was luck. Lacking any connection with mythology, deities, or higher rationality, it was the religious view of the world at its lowest energy level: but it was none the less religious, since even in the most trivial bit of luck was a spark of efficacy that derogated from the majesty of God. So pervasive was it that only a minimal sampling is possible. To be born with a caul was good luck, in Lindsey as the world over.[2] Stones possessed special powers—some of them were even garnished by legend.[3] A stone with a hole in it was considered lucky: when Heanley found one, an old neighbour advised him to 'hing 'im up over thy bed an' thou'll nivver hev no rewmatiz'. Among other substances bringing good luck was iron, notably in horseshoes and nails: schoolboys sealed bargains with each other by lifting a foot and touching a nail in their boots. The favourable influence of peacock feathers also was recognized: most labourers at the statute hiring fairs wore one with a rosette and ribbons in their hats. Shopkeepers were in the custom of spitting on the first money taken in the day's business.[4] In general terms the 'world of experience' of south Lindsey villagers, as for Hoggart's urban working class, was 'mapped at every point . . . in two colours, into those things which "mean good luck" and those which

---

[1] Winn 3/1; Heanley, 'The Vikings', p. 55.

[2] M. Peacock, 'Folklore and Legends', p. 63; Winn 3/1, p. 15; Thomas Rogers Forbes, *The Midwife and the Witch*, 1966, p. 95.

[3] Rudkin, *Lincolnshire Folklore*, pp. 56–70. Mircea Eliade notes that 'it is not a question of actually worshipping the stones; the stones are venerated precisely because they are not simply stones but hierophanies, something outside their normal status as things.' (*Patterns in Comparative Religion*, 1958, p. 13.)

[4] Heanley, 'The Vikings', pp. 51, 54–5; M. Peacock, 'Folklore and Legends', p. 189; *Notes and Queries*, 8th Ser. v (1894), pp. 75–6; Winn 3/1.

"mean bad luck"'. What remained of paganism in its last evolutionary stage, after being demythologized and depersonalized,
was luck: superstition in its most modern, adaptable and acceptable form.[1]

DEATH

References to the subject of death have already been numerous,
for of all the themes of superstition, it was one of the most richly
elaborated. And since the transformation in attitudes to death is
one of the greatest discontinuities between the nineteenth century
and the twentieth, it deserves special study.

Portents of death were very numerous, and taken very seriously.
After Henry Winn was awakened one night by a dog howling
under his window, 'some women . . . began to console me . . . that
it was a sure and certain sign of a speedy death in the family; and
as usual adduced a number of instances in support of their
opinion'.[2] 'A green Christmas makes a fat churchyard' was a
commonplace. Other portents included a solitary white pigeon,
bees swarming on a dead tree, Christmas holly withering, diamond-
shaped folds in a tablecloth, a 'shroud' or 'coffin' or 'corpse' seen
in the flame of a candle.[3] Watching the church porch on St. Mark's
Eve has already been described. These portents were objectively
implausible but taught a valid subjective truth; they acted as a
memento mori in an age and society in which death often came
suddenly, unpredictably, and early in life. (They had a precise
Christian parallel in the numerous sermons, particularly in the
first half of the century, devoted to the theme of sudden death and
the necessity of repentance and conversion.)

Popular religion offered detailed guidance during the final
hours of life. It was an 'almost universal belief in Marshland that
deaths mostly occur during the falling of the tide'.[4] And through-

---

[1] Hoggart, *Uses of Literacy*, p. 29. For a similar view of the modernity of luck, see
E. R. Dodds, *The Greeks and the Irrational*, 1964, p. 242. The Opies offer an example
of a still longer evolution: the nursery rhyme 'Cushy cow, bonny, let down thy
milk', which had begun as a 'charm used by milkmaids to induce refractory or
bewitched cows to give milk' and 'degenerated into a nursery rhyme by the
beginning of the nineteenth century'. (Iona and Peter Opie (eds.), *Oxford Dictionary
of Nursery Rhymes*, 1951, p. 137.)

[2] Winn 1/1, p. 46 (7 Sept. 1845).

[3] Winn 3/1, pp. 4, 13–14; Gutch and Peacock, *Lincolnshire*, p. 237; Penny, *Folklore*, pp. 56–7; M. Peacock, 'Folklore and Legends', pp. 89, 186.

[4] Heanley, 'The Vikings', p. 57. Dickens mentions a similar belief in *David
Copperfield*, ch. 30, in his account of the death of Barkis.

out Lindsey, as in England generally, it was accepted that a person could not die so long as he was lying on a bed or mattress which contained pigeon feathers; to put a dying person in such a bed was wrong, since it denied him an early release from his suffering—and by the same token, dying persons might be moved out of their beds to hasten the end: Henry Winn recalled that he had 'heard this asserted scores of times'.[1] The breath of the dying person could be tested with a mirror, but once he died, it was imperative to turn it so that its face was concealed; otherwise, anyone looking into it would see the dead man's face and their own death as well. After death, a window was to be opened to let the spirit of the deceased escape; a grandfather clock was to be stopped and veiled. Precautions thus were necessary to prevent further deaths.[2]

The night of a death in a household was one of the appropriate times for the remarkable custom, common not only in Lindsey but also over much of England, of 'telling the bees'. It was important to go out to the hive and inform the bees of a death, particularly the death of the head of the household; if this was neglected, either the bees would die or a further death would occur in the household.[3] In 1859, in the night following the death of a rich farmer near Alford, some of his domestic servants went out to tell the bees of their master's death; they reported that the bees answered by giving a ' "solemn hum" '. Two years later, after the death of another Marshland farmer, the bees were not told, and they subsequently died.[4] Another occasion for telling the bees was during the funeral feast after the burial. The hives having been put in mourning, the new head of the household would take a dish from the feast to the hives and tell the bees, ' "I have brought you a bit and a sup of all that's on the table, and I hope you will be pleased." '[5] This custom reflected the fact that agriculture was a

---

[1] Winn 3/1, p. 14.

[2] Heanley, 'The Vikings', p. 58; M. Peacock, 'Folklore and Legends', pp. 74–5.

[3] Gutch and Peacock, *Lincolnshire*, pp. 29–30; Good, *Glossary*, p. 108; E. Peacock, *Glossary*, p. 20. One woman was supposed to have lost twenty hives because she 'mocked advice to knock each hive with the front door key and tell them her husband had died' (Penny, *Folklore*, p. 57).

[4] The newspaper noted, however, that many hundreds of hives died during that severe winter; the moral was 'the necessity of greater exertions in the spreading of sound education and common sense amongst the rising generation in the Marsh' (*Louth Adv.*, 23 Feb. 1861).

[5] Heanley, 'The Vikings', p. 60.

co-operative enterprise involving animals as well as people. When the human side was disrupted, it was vital for the succeeding generation to renew the partnership with its animal members. This was accomplished by an offering, an act of communion. To omit the custom was to deny symbolically the vital interdependence of men and animals.[1]

The next stage was the preparation for the funeral. It was important not to wait too long before the burial: 'Two or more people are soon buried if a corpse lies unburied on a Sunday.' And if a corpse turned limp before the funeral or had a 'soft fleshy feeling' there would be another death in the family before long.[2] All cuttings of hair and nails from the corpse were either to be preserved and buried with the body, or else burnt, in order to prevent improper magical use being made of them. When the coffin arrived it was supposed to be brought into the house foot-first.[3] When the corpse was placed inside, its feet were to be tied, in order to prevent its untimely return. After an aunt of Heanley's at Croft had neglected this precaution early in the 1870s, his cousin reported in some distress that 'mother's in a rare doment: she clear fergot to tie grandfeyyther's feet, and he's cummed agin, and set himself in his owd corner, and we daredn't shift him wersens, not if it were ever so.'[4] In general these customs reflect fear of the dead: fear of their return to the society of the living, fear of their deadly contagion.

On the day of the funeral, the coffin was usually carried 'under-hand': being carried shoulder high was only for those of high status. According to an old but declining tradition, those carrying the coffin should be of the same sex and marital status as the deceased: the coffin of a married man should be carried by married men, and so on. A mother who died in childbirth might be accorded a 'white funeral' in which the bearers wore some white with their mourning black.[5] For young unmarried women, there were sometimes funeral wreaths, made of metal, white paper or

---

[1] The social distribution of beekeepers is unfortunately obscure, but in Dorset, at least, labourers were known to keep hives (Hardy, 'Dorsetshire Labourer', p. 178), as did Flora Thompson's mother in Oxfordshire (*Lark Rise*, pp. 77–8).

[2] Penny, *More Folklore*, p. 47; E. Peacock, *Glossary*, p. 69; Winn 3/1, p. 14.

[3] M. Peacock, 'Folklore and Legends', pp. 75–6.

[4] Heanley, 'The Vikings', p. 58. He was said to have appeared in the form of a large toad.

[5] M. Peacock, 'Folklore and Legends', p. 76.

flowers.[1] In Trentside villages, when the funeral procession began its way from the house to the church, no one was to head it until the parson met it inside the churchyard. The custom of singing the dead to the grave seems to have declined and disappeared in the course of the century.[2]

The funeral service—the 'Burial of the Dead'—was of course an integral part of the whole proceedings; to be buried without it, 'like a dog', was abhorrent. But its promise of a 'spiritual body' at the 'general Resurrection in the last day' was too remote and insubstantial to accord with popular taste.

Burial for the poor was usually in a grave with either an insubstantial wooden marker or none at all. As elsewhere in England the churchyard north of the church was reserved for the bodies of suicides and the unbaptized. But Lincolnshire people were apparently unique in considering it sacrilegious to bury two corpses in the same grave, even when they were of husband and wife.[3]

After the funeral came the funeral feast, a central institution in the subculture of death. It was even suggested that 'when th' parson hed read oot as far as 'dust to dust', an' thaay'd nothing at all on the'r minds but wurnering if th' caakes wo'd ha' hed time to get fer th' tea by thaay was hoame agean.'[4] Mourners were served special biscuits, 'long, narrow, finger-shaped', which it was a 'great offence' to refuse. Conversation touched on 'the virtues it is polite to attribute to the deceased, and earlier bereavements'.[5] After the death of the head of the household, this feast was known as the 'heir-ale', the heir taking his place at the head of the table; this was also an occasion for telling the bees. The feast in general may be supposed to have helped the survivors to adjust to the loss and to reaffirm the solidarity of the community and its will to live.

It is unfortunate that evidence for popular conceptions of the afterlife has rarely been preserved. At least one villager was capable of telling his parson, ' "What you say be all very true for them that's strange an' good or strange an' bad-like, but i' my

[1] Gutch and Peacock, *Lincolnshire*, p. 236. One survives in Springthorpe parish church.
[2] Rudkin, *Lincolnshire Folklore*, p. 15; M. Peacock, 'Folklore and Legends', p. 79.
[3] *Notes and Queries*, 8th Ser. ii (1892), p. 386.
[4] Mabel Peacock, *Taales fra Linkisheere*, 1889, pp. 41–2.
[5] Heanley, 'The Vikings', p. 60; M. Peacock, 'Folklore and Legends', p. 81.

opinion best part goes nowhere." "[1] More common, however, was
the concrete, materialist understanding of the afterlife which was
given picturesque expression by one of Heanley's parishioners at
Wainfleet. When her husband died she had put 't' groat in his
mouth to pay his footing' but had forgotten to include his
favourite mug and jug in the coffin, so she now had broken them
and placed the pieces on his grave.

An' whativver he'd do wi'out 'em I can't think. So I goes and does t'
next best: I *deads* 'em both over his grave, an', says I to mysen, 'my old
man, he set a vast o' store, he did, by yon mug and jug, he'd knaw 'em
out o' a thousand, and when their ghastesses gets over yon side, he'll
holler out, "Yon's mine, han' 'em over to me"; and I'd jest like to see
them as would stop him a' having of 'em an' all, for 'e were an' handy
wi' 'is fistesses, so be 'e were crossed above a bit, 'e were.'[2]

Superstition laid down a complete etiquette of death from its first
portents to the funeral feast. But more than an etiquette was
involved, for manners reflect morals and morals reflect fundamental attitudes. Three such attitudes, partly overlapping, can be
discerned. The first was the desire to honour the dead. This was
clearest in the long procession to the churchyard, the funeral
service, and the wearing of mourning. But since the dead inspired
fear—that further deaths might occur—as well as respect, a second
motive, related to the first, was the desire to avoid the contagion
of the dead. Hence the concern about mirrors, about opening the
window, tying the feet, telling the bees, and burying the corpse
before Sunday. Care had to be taken lest the one death cause
further deaths. This led naturally to the third motive, the desire to
ensure the continuance of the society of the survivors. This was
accomplished not only by taking care to avoid further deaths, but
also by the funeral feast, in which the community affirmed its will
to carry on.[3] This was a motive also for telling the bees, which
secured the continuing indispensable co-operation between men
and their animals.

[1] E. Peacock, *Glossary*, pp. 22–3. For contemporary English conceptions of the
afterlife, many of them unorthodox, see Geoffrey Gorer, *Exploring English Character*,
1955.
[2] Heanley, 'The Vikings', p. 61. Another of Heanley's vignettes (pp. 59–60)
reveals an equally vivid and equally materialist conception of the afterlife.
[3] This is memorably described by Raymond Williams in a scene in his novel
Border Country, 1960, p. 323.

SOCIAL DISTRIBUTION

The 'ethnography' of superstition, because it was ignored by the
folklore collectors, is difficult to map out with precision. What is
certain is that superstition was widespread, especially among the
labouring class. A local clergyman observed that 'with the poor',
belief in ghosts, witches, warning dreams, miracles and the like
was 'all but universal'.[1] But it was not confined to labourers. It
reached upward to the craftsmen and tradesmen and even into the
ranks of the farmers. Customs like the telling of the bees presupposed a standard of living which was perhaps as likely to be
found among small farmers as among labourers. Among the
clients of Worsdale, the wise man, was a farmer's wife, and it was
farmers who went to the woman at Fenton for help with their
foals. Farmers' wives, supervising the work of their dairymaids at
the butter churn, must either have put up the wicken themselves
or approved their servants' doing so. Superstition was probably
stronger among 'old-style' farmers—readers of *Old Moore's
Practical Almanack*, with its astrological predictions—than among
'new-style', and stronger among women—less well educated, less
under the influence of the rationalism of the cash nexus, culturally
more conservative—than their husbands.[2] The evidence for
artisans and craftsmen is slightly firmer. It was a tailor who asked
Heanley's co-operation against a witch, a blacksmith who feared
'owd Skraat' on Good Friday, another blacksmith who was
'overlooked' by a witch in the next village, and a tailor who was
confronted by the Devil while working on the Sabbath. Still more
significantly, those who reported these examples betray no surprise that anyone of the rank of a craftsman should give credence
to superstition.

Nevertheless, the labourers were the chief bearers of superstition. In the folklore collections examined for this chapter, any
belief or custom not otherwise attributed may safely be ascribed to

[1] Mossman, 'The Church in Lincolnshire', p. 269.

[2] The illiterate daughters of an old-style Marsh farmer around 1850 'told tales of
witches and ghosts' (C. E. Heanley, *Toll of the Marshes*, p. 50), and it was Tennyson's
'Northern Farmer: Old Style' who recalled his encounter with a 'boggle' (boggart).
A contemporary study concludes that women are more superstitious and religious
than men, while men are more likely to believe in luck (Nicholas Abercrombie *et al.*,
'Superstition and Religion: the God of the Gaps', in D. Martin and M. Hill (eds.),
A Sociological Yearbook of Religion in Britain 3, 1970.

them. Within this class the most superstitious group appears to have been the farm and domestic servants. The latter were keen practitioners of charms and other techniques for attracting husbands as well as of anti-witchcraft measures at the butter churn. And the farm servants, who raised the wicken crosses to ward off the cattle plague, were a byword for ignorance and credulity. But superstition was not limited to a particular age group or occupational status: it was taken for granted, an unremarkable part of the village atmosphere.

CONCLUSION

Superstition was real, as real as Christianity—perhaps more so. It was no 'mere survival'—any more than Christianity itself was. What then was the balance between Christianity and paganism in popular religion?

The weakness of Christianity at the popular level has become apparent. Many features of Anglican Christianity—the remoteness of its high God, the social elevation of its clergy, its deficiency in institutions of the 'middle range'—made it unsuited for the populace, who distorted and 'edited' it before they could accept it. Its holidays, rites and sacraments, churches, and clergy all were subjected to popular interpretations in which vital Church doctrines were ignored or repudiated. Popular Christianity therefore differed drastically from clerical Christianity.

This was due not only to 'paganism' but also to a folk Protestantism that had pursued the logic initiated by official Protestantism to 'illogical extremes', redirecting it against Christianity itself. It was probably some such combined effect of official and popular Protestantism that accounts for one of the most striking features of popular religion: the virtual absence from it of the figure of Jesus Christ. Not even His miracles engaged the popular imagination. (The Third Person of the Trinity was still less evident—except of course in Methodism.) In the clerical faith, by contrast, Christ was central. Rival schools of theology and churchmanship formed behind the great complementary but rival doctrines of the Atonement and the Incarnation; Christian apologetics relied heavily on the argument from the miracles of Jesus Christ; and the obsession with Christ in certain Evangelical circles verged on a 'unitarianism of the Second Person'. The reasons for the eclipse of Christ in popular religion are uncertain, but the influence of

Protestantism may be suspected. Elite Protestantism replaced the crucifix with the cross; and one may speculate that popular Protestantism completed the process, abandoning Christ as it had neutralized the sacraments.[1] Whatever the origins—which like the consequences have hardly been explored—popular Christianity was a Christianity without Christ.[2]

There was a similar contrast between clerical and popular views with respect to the role of magical forces in Christianity and in nature. According to Weber, Protestantism brought about the 'disenchantment of the world', draining nature of magic, myth, and pagan forces, leaving it a neutral autonomous realm amenable to dispassionate scientific study and rational manipulation. But while Protestantism may have contributed to this change in the outlook of the clerical and educated élite—though the influence of science itself probably was greater—its effect upon the outlook of the majority was quite different. In south Lindsey, popular Protestantism worked paradoxically to bring about the demystification of Christianity—particularly of the sacraments—while leaving nature still saturated with magical forces. It may be that villagers were too close to nature, too dependent upon it and vulnerable to it for Protestantism to alter their attitudes towards it. In any event they were psychologically still part of a pagan, animate natural world. For them nature was alive, and the Christian sacraments were dead; magic operated in nature but not in church. The clergy, however, like other educated Christians of the time, still attributed some vestigial efficacious power—magic —to the sacraments, though denying it altogether to external nature; for them, nature was dead, the sacraments still alive.

The origins of these contrasting outlooks lay in the growing divergence between élite and popular culture since the seventeenth century. At the very beginning of its history Christianity had not denied the existence or the power of the pagan demons but on the contrary had promised deliverance from them. Later it made its compromise peace with the pagan gods and festivals. But in the seventeenth and eighteenth centuries the world view of the

[1] For certain intellectuals atheism has been the final stage of Protestantism.

[2] This is not to suggest that the human character of Christ has invariably been prominent in official Christianity. In the second and third centuries, according to E. R. Dodds, 'the human qualities and human sufferings of Jesus play singularly little part in the propaganda of this period; they were felt as an embarrassment in the face of pagan criticism.' (*Pagan and Christian in an Age of Anxiety*, 1965, p. 119.)

educated classes, as it became mechanistic, Newtonian, and desacralized, increasingly departed from that of the populace, and by the nineteenth century little common ground was left between them. Though the clergy remained faithful to biblical cosmology they too belonged to the enlightened post-Newtonian élite, and they found themselves unable to enter into the mental world of the villagers, still dominated by pagan forces. Thus it was the villagers, not the clergy, who were closer to the mythologized outlook that had prevailed in the early Christian centuries—and to whom the Bible still spoke with force and immediacy, as the Methodists had discovered. The clergy, if obscurantist by German standards, were secular and rational by those of their flocks, and to make matters worse, they were largely unaware of the real character of popular religion. Paganism dominated the outlook of the poor but they were to hear no promise of deliverance from its toils from a clergy to whom it was either unknown or unintelligible. Perhaps the message would have been rejected, but it never was offered.

If the parsons said little about the spirits and demons, they did not neglect urging upon their flocks the duty of good works—and the correlative doctrine that misfortune was due to sin. Together these notions gave a strong moralistic tone to official Christianity.[1] Popular religion rejected the link between sin and misfortune but accepted the call to good works, though not without drawing conclusions from it which were not intended by the clergy. It was popularly understood to mean that a Christian was defined by his moral qualities—that he was fair, honest, unselfish—all of which were possible without attending church. Yet by this time class divisions had led villagers to consider themselves morally unworthy of being communicants, contrary to the wishes of the clergy. Thus at the popular level the Church's moral teachings, like its Christology, its holidays, and its sacraments, were either distorted or abandoned. Nevertheless Christianity provided both a framework and raw material for popular pagan religious expression.

The pagan contribution to the amalgam of popular religion was larger than the Christian, but it was also more diffuse, and its character can best be elucidated in comparison with Christianity.

---

[1] This development in earlier Anglican theology is examined by C. F. Allison, *The Rise of Moralism*, 1966.

At first sight a contrast suggests itself between Christian communalism and pagan individualism. It is true that paganism never assembled congregations, but this does not mean that it was any the less *social* than Christianity, for it too rested on expectations and conventions that were socially created and shared.

One function which paganism and Christianity both served was to provide explanation and meaning for death, illness, evil, and misfortunes of all kinds. Christianity referred them all to the will of God and His displeasure with the sins of men, but it also proclaimed a gospel by which to transcend them. Paganism lacked a soteriology, but then too it lacked a doctrine of sin. And instead of a high god it deployed many explanatory devices of a lower order, pitching its explanations at a humbler and perhaps more convincing level. Among its patterns of explanation was witchcraft, which alone could account for the death of people or the illness of farm animals or the failure of the butter to form in the churn. Some explanations were frankly *ad hoc*—a hundred little misfortunes too trivial for God could be traced along the networks of superstition to a hundred quirks of bad luck. But still they were explanations, better than meaninglessness, and perhaps more comprehensible than the will of God.

If both Christianity and paganism undertook to explain misfortune, paganism alone ventured to predict the future, thereby answering a human craving ignored by Christianity. The Church assured people of God's love and protection; it could encourage them to pray for the fulfilment of their wishes, if God was willing. But among its rites and sacraments were no techniques of divination, no oracles.[1] Prophecy was dangerous ground, but wise men rushed in where Anglicans feared to tread, and paganism provided the means of foreseeing everything from the weather to the identity of a future spouse to the manner of one's own death. What mattered was not so much the accuracy of a prediction but the building of confidence, and here the concreteness and precision of paganism were more effective than the vague assurances offered by the clergy.

Where the Church was unrivalled was in its public rites and

---

[1] Evangelicals, however, indulged in prophecies of national and world history, extrapolating from the Book of Revelations; e.g. B. D. Bogie, *The Crisis*, 1836, and *The Crisis is Come*, 1843. Bogie was rector of Lusby, 1828–82.

ceremonies, above all those that marked the principal stages of the life cycle—baptism, confirmation, marriage, churching, and burial. Pagan superstition embellished these rites (not necessarily their specific Christian meaning) without challenging them. But in coping with things less momentous than birth, marriage and death—with the ordinary exigencies of life—paganism was supreme, providing magic and meaning which Christianity neither challenged nor embellished. There were techniques to be employed in cases of illness, theft, and other misfortunes. There were also petty rituals to express and enhance the meaning of a great variety of situations and events—spitting on the first coin taken in the day's business, touching iron to confirm an agreement, the etiquette of death and mourning. Although these sometimes resembled private neurotic rituals, they were usually enacted in a social setting and their meaning was social, not individual. They filled the vacuum left when the Reformation repudiated the saints and magic of the medieval Church.

There was a somewhat similar division of labour between paganism and Christianity in the realm of morality. The Church possessed an explicit moral code and sought to instil in the people general principles of conduct, a consistent moral outlook. Paganism contained no coherent moral principles in its miscellany of superstition. But if superficially it was amoral, it was not without moral implications. First, through ghosts and the Devil, it helped dramatize and personify the moral convictions of the community and thus served to give expression to the traditional moral sense. Second, it set up certain *ad hoc* codes of behaviour of its own, like wearing new clothes on Easter or asking permission before chopping elder wood. Its networks of good and bad luck gave informal guidance to choices in everyday life.

The place of worship in paganism was similarly tenuous at first sight but not negligible. There was no collective worship, no Morning and Evening Prayers in paganism. But in acknowledging the power of the 'Old Gal' or of wicken or of iron, a villager was performing a kind of mental genuflection towards them. Similarly, days of the week, stones with holes in them, pigeon feathers, and so on possessed their lesser but real powers: to recognize and respect them amounted to an act of worship.

It is hard to avoid the conclusion that paganism was dominant and Christianity recessive in popular religion. Paganism was rarely christianized, but Christianity was often paganized. Those parts of Anglican Christianity which were not exploited by paganism were, like the sacraments, emasculated by popular Protestantism. And outside the Christian framework was the enormous proliferation of purely pagan beliefs and customs. To be sure, the village poor considered themselves to be Christians, but the answer to Weber's question is that 'the stronger influence on the individual in his everyday life' was pagan not Christian. If this conclusion is confirmed in other areas, then the 'ptolemaic' theory of popular religion—with Christianity at its centre and paganism at the fringes—will need to undergo a 'copernican revolution'.

On the surface, popular religion was a mass of particulars without logic or a unifying myth. Yet it is possible to infer from the particulars certain general modes of perception and response— the outlines of a collective mentality. In the present state of knowledge this construct can be no more than highly tentative, not only because there were so many different kinds of superstition to take account of, but because there were different ways of being super-stitious—a subject that has hardly been explored.[1] Superstition was real, and pervasive, but it was not uniformly real for everyone. Though everyone knew the lore and many accepted it implicitly, the intensity and quality of acceptance varied from item to item and from individual to individual, and exotic items like pacts with the Devil were probably treated as 'talking points' more often than they were 'believed', let alone acted upon. Still, there is some assurance that the general outlook was constant, even if it was subject to a certain amount of individual variation.

What villagers found in popular religion was a pluralistic, polymorphous universe in which power was fluidly distributed among a multitude of beings—from God, whose authority in principle was limitless, to the 'Old Gal', whose responsibility was limited to elder trees, to peacocks' feathers, which were merely 'lucky'. The clergy had influence over it, but so did 'Johnny o' the grass' and his colleagues, as well as any dairymaid putting a piece of wicken over the churn.

This universe was the result of syncretism—the universal

---

[1] One of the complexities is pointed out by Gustav Jahoda: that people will simultaneously be sceptical about some superstitious custom and ashamed of their belief in it, yet still practise it. (*The Psychology of Superstition*, 1969, p. 62.)

religion of the peasant—which combined elements from the 'higher' religion and the 'lower' religion without regard for logical compatibility. It involved no inconsistency for a villager to attend the parish church on Sunday morning and the Methodist chapel in the evening—and with equal conviction to put up a horseshoe over the door or ask the permission of the 'Old Gal' before chopping elder wood. Nor was there any inconsistency when a woman washing a tablecloth after a Methodist tea meeting was frightened at seeing a diamond shape in the folds—a superstitious portent of death. In some respects Christianity and paganism were mutually exclusive, but usually the logic governing them in the popular mind was 'both-and' not 'either-or'. On Good Friday there were both the Crucifixion and potato-planting, on Easter Sunday both the Resurrection and the crows.

More fundamentally villagers envisioned a Nature that was still alive, that had not been neutralized or desacralized by the Reformation or by science. It was still saturated with the traditional meanings and powers, and though villagers did not find it friendly, it was not autonomous or inaccessible. For between the natural world and the human there were continuities, correspondences, designated channels for action.

The cosmos of the educated and pious classes, with its Newtonian laws and its evidences of Design, was more conducive to admiration, contemplation, and scientific investigation, but the animate and animistic nature of the villagers was more responsive to human initiative, a greater encouragement to action.[1] If nature affected men's affairs—usually for the worse—men could still affect, and participate in, Nature. Although villagers had little control over the circumstances of their lives, they could respond to hardship in ways other than prayer and passivity, by taking advantage of favourable luck and by performing magical techniques. Objectively these were ineffectual gestures, but subjectively they bolstered morale, for disappointment was better than

---

[1] Thus for the élite it was the vertical continuities between God, the Creator, and Nature that mattered, while for villagers it was the horizontal ones between Nature and man. The role of Primitive Methodism is noteworthy in this regard. While its doctrine of providence brought it close to the popular view of Nature as a realm of signs and wonders, it also attempted to inculcate the educated outlook: one of the regular departments in the *Magazine* was 'Works of Creation', devoted to natural history and natural theology. It continued to appear after 1862 when the 'Providence Department' was discontinued.

powerlessness. They presupposed an individualistic 'activism' that ran in a separate, lower track from the various forms of collective activism—traditional agrarian protest, Methodism and the friendly societies, and the trade unions.

In the short term, therefore, paganism abounded in expedients which implied not only activism but also optimism: Christianity by contrast was pessimistic, as it could only advise prayer and resignation. In the long term, however, the positions were reversed: paganism was pessimistic, while Christianity foresaw the life everlasting and imperishable bliss. These twin polarities were the basic emotional alternatives within popular religion.

Still, it might be questioned whether there could be any parallel to the role of feeling in Christianity—described eloquently by Feuerbach—in popular religion. That it had a role is certain: even magic at its most instrumental also served expressive needs. But was popular religion merely an outlet for feeling or did it have its own emotional style? Was one even possible among so many unconnected phenomena, with no overarching myth to give them coherence? Answers to these questions are made no easier by the lack of personal testimony from those who believed pagan beliefs and practised pagan practices. Yet there was at least one constant in popular religion: its pessimism, which predominated over the restricted optimism of luck and magic. It was from this pessimism that popular religion acquired its characteristic 'structure of feeling'.

At the very least the general experience with the invisible world was one of 'great annoyance and inconvenience'.[1] Still gloomier was the larger sense of life that emerged: that it was surrounded by danger and misfortune which were impossible to avoid. At the butter churn there was the likelihood that witches would impede the forming of the butter, but it was equally a misfortune if it came too quickly: 'quick to butter, quick to bairns'. (A large family was by no means invariably regarded as a good thing.) After death, if the hair of the deceased was given away, it might pass into the hands of a witch, who could work spells with it—but to keep it was equally unlucky.[2] The pessimistic logic implied by popular belief was that whatever anyone did, they were likely to

---

[1] Winn 3/6, sect. 3, p. 11.
[2] M. Peacock, 'Folklore and Legends', pp. 197–8, 317.

suffer, that life was at best a narrow path with evil threatening on every side. Superstition thus gave indirect but faithful expression to the insecurity of the rural poor, their powerlessness in the face of adversity. Like Christianity, it assumed that life was a 'vale of tears', but was even more precise in its pessimism.

But while Christianity responded to suffering with a promise of salvation, of transcendence, the pagan response remained at the level of the stimulus; it offered not a soteriology but a technology, a way of coping with misfortunes rather than a deliverance from them. Its imagination was incurably earthbound. What is more, it insistently directed men's thoughts to death—its ubiquity, inevitability, and imminence—but offered no triumph over it. The afterlife it envisioned was a continuation of life on earth—with the same mugs and jugs—rather than something qualitatively different. It abounded in omens of death but gave little promise of the life after death: at most it delayed death with rising tides and pigeon feathers.

Another aspect of popular pessimism was the tendency to regard the very words of their language as 'living powers' for good or evil—mostly for evil. 'The very naming of trouble,' Miss Peacock noted, 'seems to attract it.' Villagers were careful not to mention the proper name of the Devil and not to boast of escape from misfortune. Yet trouble perversely was also attracted by the naming of its very opposite: expressions of happiness, success, and well-being were believed to invite misfortune. 'To admire or praise any person or thing in a marked manner, even without the slightest envy, will bring ill-luck on what is extolled.' In the same spirit villagers 'cautiously said "Middling" in answer to . . . "How do you do?"'[1] Whatever they said, whatever they did, they were likely to suffer.

Finally, pessimism extended even to the remedies against misfortune: the very 'wisdom' of the wise men was double-edged. Astrology, for example, gave foreknowledge of the future, but if Worsdale's prophecies were typical, they were usually pessimistic, even morbid.[2] Anyone who began watching the church porch on St. Mark's Eve was compelled to continue until he foresaw his own death. Wise men likewise were under a compulsion: 'Once a wizard, always a wizard,' said Stainton, 'the Devil has hold of

---

[1] ibid., p. 210.
[2] As was the sole recorded prophecy of Cussitt (Cooper, *Wise Saws*, i. 64–71).

you.' And Cussitt was supposed to have said on his deathbed, 'I've lived a wise man but I shall die a fool.'[1] It was as though all 'wisdom' came from the Devil and though desirable in itself was fatally cursed by its origins; it involved an irrevocable commitment and an inevitable misery in the end.

Thus a general outlook was implicit in the minutiae of popular magic and superstition. It comprised an animate, polymorphous universe which, while responsive to local manipulation, was predominantly hostile. Not merely actions but words and pagan 'wisdom' itself were all felt to be double-edged; no matter what villagers did or said they were vulnerable to misfortune. They were surrounded by dangers which they could cope with but not transcend. Their pessimism was the subjective truth that lay beneath the fanciful surface expressions of popular religion: a piecemeal optimism of expedients and a deep-seated pessimism of conditions.

* * *

It remains to trace a few last connections between popular religion and its social setting. Since most of the superstitions current in the nineteenth century were of ancient origin and were widely distributed geographically, there can be no question of establishing special links with south Lindsey. But they were not entirely independent of society either; besides reflecting the deprivations of the rural poor they presupposed certain structural features in the agrarian economy and society.

Though popular religion lacked a church and had no congregations, it rested upon a moral consensus and a moral community. It was the values of such a community that found expression in ghosts beliefs, for example. Not only was this a moral community, but also an economic one that embraced all who depended upon each other and upon the fortunes of agriculture. Thus it included animals as well as men; superstition reflected in a superficially quaint or bizarre manner their profound mutual dependence. It was from these economic and social realities that the desire arose to draw animals into the moral and even into the religious community—hence the custom of telling the bees and the belief that farm animals knelt in reverence on Christmas Eve. But both the

---

[1] Penny, *Folklore*, p. 65; H. D. Rawnsley, *Memories of the Tennysons*, p. 48.

village community and superstition itself were changing, and to uncover further links between superstition and society it is necessary to turn to the parallel evolutionary paths they followed in the course of the century.

If there was a central theme in the history of superstition in the nineteenth century it was depersonalization, best seen in the evolution of witchcraft. The passage from the intensely personal 'evil eye' to witchcraft without witches to a final stage in which the traditional magical remedies were used not to counter witches or witchcraft—both now forgotten—but to bring good luck, or to avoid the bad luck that would come if they were omitted: this was the central sequence of change. By a parallel process, wise men—the personified antidote to personified evil—lost their popularity in the second half of the century. Belief declined also in other personal beings like ghosts.[1] Unfortunately the evidence for other aspects of popular religion is too uneven to yield any firm conclusions. But it seems clear that the process of depersonalization, which had begun long before with the decline of the mythical figures, was now largely completed. Superstition subsided to the level of luck, its impersonal lowest common denominator.

This was probably the most important set of changes in popular religion since the Reformation, and it is tempting to look for an explanation in social change, which in a comparable manner was more rapid and more severe in its effects on the village poor in this period than in any previous one. A tentative explanation begins with the observation that the personal figures in popular religion retained their plausibility as long as ordinary personal relations in village society were in the traditional mode, direct, face-to-face, and 'manystranded'. But with the advent of a fully developed class society, the traditional relations between individuals were overshadowed by 'singlestranded' relations between classes. It seems more than a coincidence that when persons as persons were no longer so salient in village social life, they gradually lost their salience in popular religion. Their position was also undermined when new-style farmers rejected popular superstition and considerably enlarged the non-superstitious minority (of which the gentry had been the original and for a long period the only members); beliefs about witches and wise men were probably the least likely to withstand the active disapproval of the dominant

[1] Winn 3/6, sect. 3, p. 12.

classes. And when the farmers became a class, with their own class values, they rejected traditional moral values, shattering the traditional moral consensus: superstitions like ghost beliefs that had expressed that consensus inevitably declined.[1]

Popular religion was therefore not an autonomous realm: neither was it a simple reflex of social conditions. Its origins remain obscure, but its later history invites a social interpretation. For beneath its colourful surface phenomena were certain social assumptions which were those of the superstitious classes in agrarian society, and when the 'social being' of the village poor altered, superstition would eventually alter as well. When it dwindled into the residual category of luck, it was because the more complex forms and expressions of the recent past no longer corresponded with felt social realities. The timeless appearance of magic and superstition was deceptive; popular religion—like institutional religion—could not avoid being affected by the rise of class society.

---

[1] N. Abercrombie et al., 'Superstition and Religion', p. 114, speculate that 'superstitions are a vestigial expression of community'—while 'the church is an institution in a society of institutions'. This is entirely consistent with the conclusions of the present work.

VII

CONCLUSION

THE religious life of south Lindsey cannot be 'reduced' to its social foundations, but it is unintelligible without them. The transformation of traditional agrarian society into a society of classes transformed religion as well.

But before turning to the social classes themselves and their religious outlooks, it is instructive to consider some of the related social changes that accompanied the rise of classes. One of the most notable was the emergence of the family as an enclosed, self-sufficient setting for social life. When the farmers, like the gentry earlier, formed themselves into a conscious class, they withdrew from community and crowd into the private life of the family. Relations between husbands and wives and between parents and children became closer, more 'psychological'; and families which had become social and psychological units easily became religious units. Family prayers thus were the religious aura of a new type of family sentiment. Among the farmers, where the new pattern was most apparent, husband and wife tended to form a religious unit: if one was a Methodist, both were; among the labourers, where the traditional pattern of less intense family relations still held, husband and wife were more likely to go their separate religious ways.

A less direct consequence of the rise of class society was the opening of the way for greater religious activity by women. In so far as church attendance had been regarded as a public duty in the traditional society, it appears to have been principally a duty of the husband, as 'representative' of his family and household. When the rise of classes made communal obligations obsolete, religious practice became a matter of individual decision, and women now were free to play a more active role. This was most apparent in Methodism—particularly in Primitive Methodism, where there were a few female local preachers and class leaders—but even in the parish churches more girls were confirmed than boys, and the west gallery orchestras were replaced by predominantly female choirs.

Equally significant was the new prominence of children, who emerged from the traditional 'crowd' to form a distinct group in class society. Quick to respond, the churches identified children as a new field for evangelistic conquests—though their efforts were not always crowned with success. When the clergy attempted to reintroduce catechizing into the Sunday service, they met with resistance, not grasping that precisely because children were now a distinct social group adults did not want to see them in the regular service. But all the churches sought to win, or capture, the younger generation. The Church of England, which had fallen behind the Methodists, conceded them the adults but hoped to recover by gaining the children, and seems to have been first in the field with Sunday schools. The Methodists, who in their earlier phases had concentrated on adults, shifted to children, partly to meet Anglican competition, partly because children were the last remaining and accessible target group in an era of declining adult revivalism. In any event Sunday schools multiplied in all denominations, particularly after 1850. In Primitive Methodism the average age of conversion dropped sharply, and juvenile conversion formed the chief exception to the general shift in denominational ideals from piety to service. Nevertheless, the churches' efforts to christianize the children fell well short of total success. This was so probably because most children were from the labouring class, where traditional social patterns retarded the emergence of children as a distinct social group, and where children's Sunday as well as day schooling was interfered with by exploiting farmers. Farm servants remained unresponsive to the initiatives of the clergy, and jeered at the moral pretensions of the chapels. Most of the young people who were confirmed in the Church of England either did not go on to make their first communion or else communicated once and then stopped. What the clergy envisioned as the beginning of mature religious practice was for the young people rather the beginning of the freedom not to attend church. Even so, never before had piety been expected, sought, or found among children on so large a scale, and the Sunday and day schools sponsored by the churches gave institutional form to a distinct youth subculture. Thus the general reordering of family and youth in class society had important implications for religious life.

But the cardinal feature of the new society was after all the classes, and as they emerged, with their separate class cultures, they developed distinctive religious styles. Among the gentry, a virtually *ex officio* commitment to the Church of England was qualified—and compromised—by other class values and interests.[1] They were indeed regular attendants at public worship —at the morning service of respectability—but they regarded it, justifiably, not only as a religious exercise but also as the pre-eminent ritual of social stability. Furthermore, having long since withdrawn from village social life, they also withdrew their practice of religion as much as possible from the public to the private sphere. They preferred marriage by licence to marriage by banns,[2] and their baptisms were private, family affairs; in church they secluded themselves from the rest of the congregation in family pews. Even their tombs, which lay within the walls of the church, were separate from the other graves, in the churchyard; they awaited the general Resurrection in splendid isolation. As landlords, they followed their landlords' instinct to be masters in their own parishes, and did their best to keep the church itself under control, thwarting if necessary the rising pretensions of the clergy. Their favourite recreations, field sports, were at the heart of an élite male counter-culture, more pagan than Christian, which indeed at times subjected Christianity to outright desecration. The ideal of the gentleman, which embodied the highest aspirations of gentry culture, diverged from the Christian moral ideal; even in death it compromised the gentry's Christian identity. The inscriptions on their tombs and funerary monuments almost never included biblical texts (unlike those of Methodists and of farmers), and equally characteristically were 'retrospective' in content, commemorating the virtues and actions of the deceased during their life on earth, rather than 'prospective', looking forward to the afterlife.[3] It would seem that the prospect of heaven,

[1] It may be worth mentioning that conversion to Roman Catholicism, which was becoming a recognized option for those of unusual religious fervour in the upper classes, held little appeal for the south Lindsey gentry. Before 1875 the only converts were C. J. H. Massingberd-Mundy of South Ormsby (1864) and one of the daughters of Charles Tennyson d'Eyncourt (1846). (W. Gordon Gorman, *Converts to Rome*, 1910, pp. 85, 187.)

[2] Sir Charles Anderson was a self-conscious exception.

[3] For the contrast between prospective and retrospective orientations see Erwin Panofsky, *Tomb Sculpture*, 1964, p. 16. It was also characteristic of the gentry that they remained faithful to the pagan Greek style in the design and lettering of funeral monuments, while the clergy were being converted to a Gothic style. A good

after a life of privilege and ease, was not a compelling one.[1] In any event the gentry, more than any other class, give the impression of fitting religious observance and religious sentiment into the places appointed for them in a larger conventional pattern of life.

The religiosity of the farmers was by contrast less well defined; it was a mixed, transitional affair, reflecting the old-style farmer as well as the new, rather than a wholly consistent and mature style. Nevertheless, the 'new' elements predominated. The substantial wealth of the larger farmers underlaid their characteristic roles in Methodism: society stewards, leading supporters, employers of Methodist labourers, dealers with Methodist merchants and tradesmen, generous contributors to chapel, circuit, and connectional funds. As the dominant class in most villages they set a high value on their respectability, and accordingly favoured the morning church service, the service of respectable 'necessity'. Their emergence as a class was further apparent in their preference for private baptism and marriage by licence—signs of their withdrawal from the village community. By the same token they held the new 'class' conceptions of family life and of the role of children. The farming family became a religious unit; Methodist farmers presided over 'holy households' and led children and servants into membership. If a very small Anglican sample is representative, the farmer and his wife tended to follow identical patterns at Communion, whether they both received the sacrament or both were absent. New-style farmers may also have been more likely to make an exclusive commitmnt to one denomination or another, and less likely to float from church to chapel and back. At the same time, however, more traditional values also influenced the farmers' religious life, above all their allegiance to Methodism. Many farmers did not want to cut themselves off from fellow

---

example of a retrospective inscription appears in a tablet dating from 1821 in Knaith Church; it commemorates the former squire of the parish, Henry Dalton, 'owner of the manor of Knaith and of considerable estates . . . For nearly half a century he resided in this parish and as a landlord and a master largely contributed to the comforts and welfare of his tenants and dependants whose happiness formed his principal gratification.' After praising his 'kindness and benevolence' and the 'endowments of a highly cultivated mind' it concluded that 'he elevated and adorned the character of an English country gentleman by a range of talents and extent of erudition which would distinguish him as a statesman or a man of letters'.

[1] Living in a benign environment, they found the notion of a benevolent God plausible and congenial, and that of Satan uncongenial and unnecessary. Something like the reverse was true among the poor.

villagers, and in the chapels they regularly mixed with their social inferiors. They listened to sermons from labourers and shop-keepers and in class meetings they exposed to them their intimate religious experiences. In the traditional village, this kind of fellow-ship and psychological intimacy between persons of different ranks was unremarkable, but it was completely at odds with the class segregation favoured in the new society. The recent and incom-plete nature of the transition from the old-style farmer to the new thus left its mark on the farmers' religious life.[1]

The place of craftsmen and shopkeepers in south Lindsey society is obscure, but they were very prominent in its religious life, above all in Methodism, to which they contributed more than their proportionate share of members, hearers, and officials. In Wesleyan Methodism they were particularly active as local preachers and were also over-represented among the stewards and class leaders. In certain parishes over half the families of craftsmen and shopkeepers rented seats in Wesleyan chapels. In Primitive Methodism they supplied nearly a third of the local preachers. Most were classified with the poor, yet unlike the labourers they had at least a measure of independence. What impelled them into Methodism is unclear: perhaps a combination of resentment at a Church of England which had no use for their abilities and ener-gies and the grievances of little men at the dominant classes.

Since the labourers were the last to establish themselves as a class, their religious outlook was the most traditional of all the groups in society; but by the same token it was also the most exposed to the capitalist assault on tradition.

It was non-institutional superstition, with its mitigating expedi-ents in a world of misfortune, that best represented the general conditions of the labourers' existence: their poverty, their con-tinual vulnerability to misfortune, their closeness to nature, their concern with the immediate and the practical, and their pessimism. But their social values—particularly their traditional regard for

---

[1] The farmers were in an intermediate position, between gentry and labourers, in death as in life. The poor were buried in the churchyard, but they could not afford gravestones; their graves were therefore public but anonymous. The graves of the farmers were also public, but were 'individualized' by permanent gravestones. The tombs of the gentry were individual in this sense, but as they were usually inside the church they were separate from the graves of the other classes, and when they were in special chapels they were private as well. Thus the qualities of the graves echoed those of the social values of each class.

the communal and public realm in village life—were more apparent in their dealings with the churches. It was probably the labourer's values, and not merely their poverty, that made them the least likely to make an exclusive commitment to one church or another. No doubt they had an incentive both to stay on good terms with a beneficent parson and to avoid the expense of formal Methodist membership; they appear to have been less likely than other classes to rent seats in Wesleyan chapels, and in at least one village they were more likely to 'shop around' for baptisms, or to be guided by convenience. But the notion that church and chapel were equally legitimate, equally integral to the community, was one that would have come most easily to labourers, for whom the community was prior to the individual, to the family, and to any other minority; they would have been the least eager to set themselves apart from their fellows by making a total commitment to a partial association. A related belief in the supremacy of the public realm over the private led them to prefer marriage by banns (though again finance was a consideration): it announced a private event to congregation and community, who, on the third time of asking, replied with their approval, 'God speed them well.' For similar reasons baptism too was more likely to be public than private in labouring families.

In more general terms the labourers inherited from traditional society a diminished Christianity, which precisely in its attenuations and alterations reflected the vitality of the culture of the labouring poor and their considerable independence from élite culture. Just as the gentry's class values compromised their Christianity, so the poor compromised it by their traditional paganism and by altering it to suit their own needs. In this spirit they looked to the clergy less for piety than for charity, and for a readiness to be at their service, even (as some parsons complained) at their beck and call, though this last appears not to have survived long in the era of new-style clergy. It is apparent that the labourers' traditional religious style was conditioned to a large extent by their poverty, but it was not solely an economic matter. In the case of baptism, where expense was not a consideration, they preferred public celebrations for purely social reasons.

The second social determinant of the labourers' religious outlook was the farmers' attack on traditional values and their emergence as a class. A significant measure of this process was the contrast in their dealings with their servants between the 1820s and the 1850s. In the earlier period they had insisted that their farm servants should attend church; later, they disliked having them in the house, and though they included female domestic servants in family prayers they were 'too high' to sit with them in church, and seem not to have cared whether they attended church at all. The elevation of the farmers meant a further decline in the status of the labourers, the 'joskins' and 'clodhoppers' whose reluctance to receive Communion was only one aspect of their sense of unworthiness, which itself reflected the contempt in which they were held by the dominant classes. And while the farmers were defining themselves as a class, harshly repudiating traditional ties with their labourers, traditional popular recreations were at the same time coming under fire from the moralizers. Thus a comprehensive attack was made on the labourers' way of life, and their needs were urgent and equally comprehensive; in the circumstances of the times they could only be met by Methodism. Significantly, the period of maximum pressure from above, the second quarter of the century, was also the period of maximum revivalistic excitement in Methodism; when the pressure eased, after 1850, Methodism relaxed as well. But labourers were attracted by Methodism throughout the period. Its appeal was all-embracing: communal fellowship, protest (indirect) at the new social regime, free emotional expression, self-respect based on piety and moral rigour, entertainment, the means of learning one's way in the new society.

In a district in which Old Dissent had been weak, the rise of Methodism was the most important event in the religious life of the poor since the Reformation, creating an alternative to the Established Church that was fundamentally different in spirit and structure, and far more attractive to labourers. Yet however great the contrast, most labourers approached Methodism in the same selective way as they did the Church; though they felt more at home in the chapels than in the churches, they only accepted from Methodism what suited them, and not everything that ministers or preachers offered. They regarded the chapel as a source of entertainment just as they regarded the parson as a source of half-crowns and confirmation as a remedy for rheumatism. They evidently knelt in chapel though they refused to do this in church. But in both places they drew the line at the more serious demands made upon them by the religious professionals. For the majority of labourers, Anglican confirmation was acceptable, partly because a 'treat' came with it, but not 'the sacrament', except for old people. In Methodism they enjoyed sermons and special services but declined to 'find liberty' and to become 'converted members', much less 'saints'. Thus they characteristically remained 'floaters', seeking 'variety and novelty' rather than 'pardon' or 'purity', and their religious style continued to be syncretistic. To the existing pagan and Anglican mixture they now added a large measure of Methodist ingredients, but the blend remained their own.

The three class cultures, along with the emerging subgroups based on age and family, rendered the new social order considerably more differentiated than the traditional village had been. Its over-all effect on religion—on practice, more than belief—was consequently to fracture it, to make it more adaptable to the parts of society, less expressive of the whole. Thus religion too became more differentiated, and even in the middle of the nineteenth century the process involved individuals as well as classes and other groups. In this regard it was the 'floaters' who played the most prophetic role: guided by personal preference rather than by fear or by external obligation, they were able to take religion or leave it, and to take *from* it only what suited them. Though they were 'traditional' in their unwillingness to make exclusive commitments, they were modern in their individualism. And for a similar reason it was superstition, the most archaic form of religion, which turned out to be the most modern: not in its content, but because it was the most malleable, the most amenable to personal preference. It prefigured the 'invisible religion' becoming apparent towards the end of the century—the miscellaneous religious notions that individuals assemble privately for themselves from the common cultural stock[1]—by giving freest play to the individualizing tendencies inherent in the new society.

To the churches, however, the increasing social differentiation of religious practice was by no means a uniformly encouraging prospect. The rise of class religious styles in particular symbolized the problem that all the churches had identified as the major one: how they were to maintain or create religious communities when

---

[1] See Durkheim, *Elementary Forms*, p. 46 (who cites earlier works by Spencer and Sabatier), and T. Luckmann, *The Invisible Religion*, 1967.

the wider secular community was disintegrating. What made their position still more difficult was that they were threatened not only by class division but also by the more subtle corrosion of economic individualism. In practice each church resisted only one of the threats and entered into partial complicity with the other.

For the clergy, individualism was the greater threat, and they disliked it in all its forms, religious as well as economic. They condemned Methodism for individualistic excesses like extemporaneous prayers and the cult of feeling, and they feared ambition and self-assertion as a threat to their ideal of a stable hierarchy. Class divisions and inequality, however, they regarded as a positive good and a social necessity. But social conflict, arising from a discontented proletariat, was a great evil, and they exhorted landlords to do their paternalist duty and labourers to endure their poverty without complaining. Two additional concerns were the rise of Methodism and the personal responsibility they felt, as the representatives of a state church, for the preservation of social order. Their tasks therefore were: to rebuild their congregations, to discourage individualism, to minimize class conflict, to safeguard class divisions and inequality, and to secure general social tranquillity.

What gave coherence to this programme was the role that the clergy assigned to the Church itself as a prime agent of social integration. Within the churches, congregations were to be made more communal and unified, partly by eliminating signs of class separateness, such as private baptism and box pews, partly by encouraging all parishioners to become communicants and by reintroducing public catechizing; congregations could then give a more effective assent to the signs of hierarchy and submission that the clerical reforms had not touched. The seating plan, with or without box pews, continued to symbolize and justify the wider social hierarchy, and Anglican decorum and self-restraint symbolized the corresponding secular virtues. Thus a united, polite, but manifestly unequal congregation would ritually enact in church the stabilizing qualities wished for in the wider society. Whatever the success of this strategy, it represented an ambitious, almost paradoxical attempt to create religious unity in defiance of social divisions—in order to preserve them.

The Methodists, on the other hand, responded to the twin threats of class society in exactly the opposite manner to that of the clergy. Far from being disturbed by its assertive individualism, they fostered within the denomination a religious individualism that eventually intersected with the economic variety. It was class divisions that they feared, and their whole 'project' was an effort to exclude, deny, or circumvent them.[1] Like the clergy, the Methodists sought to build religious communities, but theirs were to be based entirely on voluntary religious commitment, independent of the secular class hierarchy. The Methodist 'society' was drawn from village society but stood apart from it in a specifically Methodist circuit structure; the Methodist 'class' eclipsed social class. At every level in Methodism one's religious identity as 'brother' or 'friend' cut across the hardening class lines in the wider society. In a more traditional manner the special services mixed people of different ages, sexes, and occupations without regard to class. Even in the period of greatest social tension Methodism succeeded in overcoming class divisions.

But if the Methodists denied class they found the individualism of the new society—both its economic form and its underlying psychological rationale—positively attractive. (They had also accepted and built upon the other social correlatives of class: the new prominence of family, women, and children.) From the beginning Methodism had laid great emphasis on individualism in the realms of religious experience and moral conduct, and in time it became apparent that the underlying psychological rationale of religious individualism was much the same as that of economic individualism; on this common ground Methodist preachers in the 1860s formally endorsed the doctrines of character and self-help.

This ethic of self-realization probably owed more to the Methodist than to the capitalist background. In the realm of conduct Methodism enforced a rigorous moral code that not merely condemned the traditional evils of violence and drunkenness—and Methodistic vices like dancing and Sabbath-breaking—but also more positively demanded responsibility and self-respect. Wesleyans and Primitives alike urged labourers to give up the childish games by which they made fools of themselves in the eyes

---

[1] This is clearly more true of the Wesleyans, whose religious congregations were a reasonable cross-section of secular society, than of the Primitive Methodists, who were drawn largely from a single class. The discussion that follows therefore relates chiefly to Wesleyan Methodism.

of farmers. In the realm of religious experience individualism was even more highly developed. Methodists underwent the intensely individual experience of conversion, made a personal commitment to become members, and in class meetings gave a novel and constant attention to their own private experience. Feeling was regarded as the very test and essence of religion, much to the disgust of the clergy. A Methodist thus acquired a multiple sense of selfhood, as a responsible moral agent, and as the bearer of a unique personal experience and spiritual autobiography. And he felt a moral duty to himself, in secular as well as religious matters, which before 1860 was becoming increasingly explicit. The acceptance of the formal doctrines of character and self-help in the following decade was the natural conclusion.

What then were the dangers of individualism to Methodist religious communities? It fostered an excessive self-consciousness and concern for privacy that was incompatible with the self-exposure required by the class meeting. And in its later forms it was objectively secularizing; it ranked character equal with soul, and self-development even superior to what had been known as 'growth in grace'. Class divisions by contrast had threatened religious unity more directly, by making it impossible for people to meet on terms of religious equality when their relationship outside the place of worship was one of authority and subordination, and by generating divergent class religious styles that could not be accommodated within a common pattern of worship.

Thus the reactions of the clergy and the Methodists to the twin forces of social disunity were remarkably parallel, each resisting one while embracing a partly tamed version of the other. The clergy disliked individualism but accepted class divisions—stabilized so as to avoid class conflict; the Methodists rejected class divisions but accepted individualism—moralized so as to avoid competitiveness. For a considerable period the churches maintained their cross-class appeal, but in retrospect it seems unlikely that they could have prevailed over the centrifugal effects of the new society, with its class divisions, its calculating and private individualism, its lack of a moral consensus. And when the labourers' class culture matured after 1850, it tended if anything to widen their distance from organized religion. Their growing taste for privacy accorded poorly with the demands of Methodism, and their expanding political consciousness led to a disaffection from the clergy, whom they regarded as agents of the dominant classes. The full establishment of capitalism, not only as an economic but also as a social and cultural system, blighted any prospects the churches may have had of constituting themselves as genuine communities. Even if they had been more uncompromising it seems doubtful whether they could have held together the classes that capitalism had put asunder.

There remains one final question. Rural society and religious life were transformed: were they also secularized? The answer is by no means obvious, and not only because of deficiencies in the sources. The very notion of secularization is problematical, as it draws upon three separate sources of confusion: inconsistencies in the definition of religion itself, *a priori* theories of the drift of modern culture, and the practical difficulties inherent in the measurement and analysis of cultural change.[1] Some proponents of extremely broad definitions of religion would even deny that secularization is possible, arguing that religion permeates human existence and that it consequently never declines but only changes its forms. But it seems more reasonable to assume that the religious sphere does not include everything, that it has boundaries, which can contract and expand. On this view secularization becomes a possibility (as does 'resacralization') but not an inevitability. The local evidence relates both to formal religious institutions and to the dimensions of individual belief and consciousness.

In the realm of formal religion a broad shift from religious to secular values was apparent in Methodism. In Primitive Methodism, for example, evangelism yielded to entertainment, the community of 'saints' to 'fellowship', and soul-making to character-building. There was nothing comparable in the Church of England, where the clergy's social gospel of paternalism and obedience was no novelty. The harvest thanksgiving represented a shift within the religious sphere from Christian to pagan rather than an instance of secularization. The decline of religious concerns appears to have gone further in Methodism—from a higher starting-point—than anywhere else in the religious scene, and is the best documented.

As for formal practice, the Religious Census showed that the

[1] For some of these questions see D. Martin, *The Religious and the Secular*, 1969, and L. Shiner, 'The Concept of Secularization in Empirical Research', *Journal for the Scientific Study of Religion*, vi (1967).

over-all levels of church attendance in south Lindsey were high, but other indicators suggest a less optimistic picture. The figures for communicants in the parish churches—the clergy's own standard of 'membership'—were generally low; communicants and attendants alike were relatively most numerous in small close parishes where the decisive influence was landlord pressure rather than devotion. In Methodism the level of membership was high, but the majority of attendants in the chapels were not members but adherents, who while renting seats and attending regularly declined the responsibilities of membership. Indeed a majority of the village population as a whole refused to make a serious commitment to either church or chapel. The clergy were pleased if the communicants in a parish amounted to 10 per cent of the population: the same figure was the Methodists' target for membership. Even if both denominations had achieved their quotas in a given village, the great majority of the population would have remained outside, and as long as Methodists were in the habit of receiving Communion in the parish church, the total élite group would have been even smaller. Probably the majority of attendants were the floaters seeking 'variety and novelty' rather than the salvation of their souls. Compared with the earlier period, the years after 1825 probably saw a rise in the level of church attendance, reflecting both the 'aggression' of the Methodists and the Anglican counter-attack. More generally it corresponded with a favourable but transitory set of social conditions— the tensions of an emerging class society, new-style farmers unsure of their respectability, the delay in the transformation of the labouring poor into a working class, and the hiatus between traditional and modern popular leisure.

Whatever the level of attendance at Sunday services, the churches' demands on the laity in this period increased. Methodism not only required attendance at class meetings as well as at Sunday services, but also offered an assortment of prayer meetings, protracted meetings, and lovefeasts, not to mention the special services. The clergy also raised the standard expected of the laity by insisting upon regular communion as the proof of churchmanship. And in church and chapel alike congregations were subjected to unprecedented financial demands. Over-all demands, spiritual as well as financial, rose early in the century in Methodism, after 1850 in the Church of England, and perhaps declined after 1870, particularly in Methodism. But for most of the century the trend was clearly the opposite of secularizing.

There was probably a similar pattern in the churches' varying influence on social life, with an increase until about 1870, then a gradual decline. It was Methodism that made the greatest impact, creating for its members an all-encompassing way of life that broke decisively with traditional village mores. This was most apparent in the early years, before the special Methodist code of behaviour began to relax. But the decline in intensity within the circle of membership was more than offset in the wider village scene when Methodism after 1850 actually extended its influence over leisure, providing special services and other entertainments. Economic life too was drawn into the religious sphere via the Methodist trading and employment networks. Methodist influence on politics is obscure, but may have increased as Methodists gained the franchise and as Methodism drew further away from Tory Anglicanism. The general impression is that Methodist influence on social life was broader in the third quarter of the century but deeper before: that it expanded at the sacrifice of its religious content.

The influence of the Established Church was probably smaller in the nineteenth century than it had been earlier, not only because of the rise of the Methodists, but also because the clergy, though resident, had become too remote from their parishioners. They slowed the decline by more vigorous pastoralia, but in the long run they abandoned the broad aim of promoting the temporal as well as the spiritual welfare of their parishioners. Only through the schools did they expand the Church's influence.

What indeed was significant was that the influence of Methodism and Church alike came to be differentiated by age group, and actually increased over children while it was diminishing over adults. Sunday schools were established by all denominations, day schools chiefly by the Established Church, and Methodism encouraged early conversions and juvenile piety.

The churches were able to exert a wide influence on village life in this period chiefly because they faced little competition outside the beerhouse and friendly society. They expanded into an institutional vacuum between the decline and repression of the traditional popular recreations and the later pattern of secondary associations and leisure activities.

Religious belief and knowledge of Christian doctrine were unprecedentedly widespread, owing to the Methodists and the Sunday schools, but at the same time there was considerable ignorance of Christian fundamentals, which regularly dismayed new clergymen upon entering their parishes. And popular participation in the rites and sacraments of the Established Church was motivated by unofficial and quite unorthodox beliefs. In the long run religious instruction in Sunday and day schools improved the basic level of knowledge, but the higher religious aspirations declined with the waning of Methodist fervour. Compared with the twentieth century, the nineteenth presented a far greater range: the devout were more devout, the ignorant more ignorant. It should be noted, however, that along with varying proportions of faith and unbelief, knowledge and ignorance, there was much outright hostility to formal religion, to particular churches, and to religious professionals, particularly the clergy. At one social extreme there was gentry anti-clericalism (and blood sport sacrilege); at the other, farm servants insulted chapel-goers and scorned the moral pretensions and magical efficacy of organized religion. The general reputation of the clergy for piety was not high, and not only among Methodists. But it is uncertain whether these attitudes were more common in 1875 than they had been in 1825, except in the case of the Primitive Methodists, who after being persecuted in their early years later became an accepted part of the village scene.

The realm of individual consciousness, the most fundamental to religion, is also the most elusive, and since evidence of change over time is particularly scarce, only a few suggestions can be offered here.

Again the evidence is clearest in Methodism. The decline in 'enthusiasm' and zeal in all branches of Methodism in the course of the century is unmistakable. In itself this was not secularization, perhaps, but it suggests that the emotional bases of religion were contracting.

A tendency towards secularization is also suggested by the evidence that religion was increasingly regarded as an individual, even a private matter, of no concern to other people. In general terms this would have involved a long-term shift from public duty to personal inclination as the determinant of religious practice, with the consequence that withdrawing from religious activity—

if not from belief—would require not a defiance of public opinion but a purely individual decision. That a change of this kind took place is suggested by the decline and disappearance of opposition to Methodism; and it is consistent with what is known of social change in the villages; but the best source of evidence on this point, lists of communicants in the parish churches, remain to be studied. In any event religious practice itself was being privatized. Like the gentry before them, farmers asked for private baptism and marriage by licence, and at the end of the period a taste for privacy became apparent even among the labourers, who had been the most communal in outlook of the three classes. This was symbolized in their social life by the abandonment of nicknames and the adoption of 'Mr.' and 'Mrs.', and in religion by their growing dislike of congregational baptisms. In Methodism the emphasis on individualism would later undermine the class meeting; by the end of the century Methodists would recoil from drinking from the communal loving cup in lovefeasts. Though organized religion had been for many the basis of social identity, it slowly retreated from the public to the private sphere. As with the decline of enthusiasm in Methodism, this in retrospect appears to have been more than a change in the mode of being religious: it made it easier to be only minimally religious, or not religious at all.

In the field of popular magic and superstition it is tempting to assume that the religious consciousness exists in a 'steady state', that as one superstition fades another moves in to take its place, the underlying outlook remaining constant. But as Keith Thomas has noted for the seventeenth century, popular superstition is 'conservative' in a rather different sense: as old stock declines, it is ordinarily *not* replaced by new growth.[1] And in the nineteenth century the forms and objects of belief changed in a consistent manner that suggests change in the underlying outlook as well. When the human figures in paganism declined and disappeared—witches, wise men, ghosts, and spirits—no new ones arose to take their place; the degeneration of magic into luck was irreversible. Thus there were unilinear, long-term changes in the forms of belief; they indicate a contraction in the scope and range of super-natural agency. For it seems doubtful whether luck could have expanded to cover the kinds of misfortunes that witches and

[1] K. Thomas, *Religion and the Decline of Magic*, p. 656.

witchcraft had been invoked to explain; still less was it capable of performing an expressive function as witchcraft had done, providing an outlet for guilt and hostility. And compared with the magic that had come before, it was less specific and much less powerful. It had always been part of popular superstition: it now dominated it.

The result of these changes was a popular superstitious mentality that had become quite different at the end of the century from what it had been at the beginning. A narrower range of phenomena were now explained by means of magical and supernatural forces; and they were explained less dramatically and anthropomorphically. By the same token the human power to affect and control the external world was diminished. And as magic and 'wisdom' declined, so too did the ambivalence and pessimism which had previously been associated with them. Indeed it would appear that superstition engaged and expressed a diminishing range and depth of emotion of any kind. The tone became cooler, less intense, more neutral and impersonal. Thus with the waning of the personal and dramatic elements in popular religion, there was a decline in three of its major functions—the explanatory, the efficacious, and the expressive—and as a result the popular outlook was less influenced by this kind of religion than it had been in the past. It may not have become more scientific, but it was more secular.

What is remarkable is that parallel and complementary changes can be identified in institutional religion as well; local religious life, when re-examined from the vantage point of secularization, discloses common tendencies in its two sectors. In the first half of the century, there was a significant amount of overlap between institutional religion, dominated by Methodism, and popular religion. In both, external powers were envisioned as intervening in human life; both were outlets for a considerable range and intensity of emotion; wise men and clergy played analogous roles, and the two worlds were linked by Satan. But in the second half of the century Christianity and popular religion both receded, in opposite directions, from their common ground. The decline in the belief in special acts of providence had its parallels in the realm of superstition; what can be thought of as the lower reaches of Christianity and the upper levels of paganism both were affected, leaving Christianity more transcendent, superstition more submerged in particulars. A broader zone of both natural and human activity was now out of range of supernatural intervention, whether Christian or pagan. And partly for the same reason the joint emotional level declined. Methodists ceased to experience 'powerful visitations of the Holy Spirit', the religion of the heart grew cooler, and the emotional scope of paganism was reduced. Institutional and popular religion together were comprehensively weakened: in their power of explanation and meaning, in their power of supernatural agency, and in their power of feeling. The joint religious domain not only abandoned territory but held what remained less securely.

*　　　*　　　*

Secularization, easier to document than to interpret, remains the riddle of modern religious history. In a long perspective it is clear that Christianity had never fully established itself in European society, either as a belief system or as a pattern of worship and observance, that it shared the field with superstition. Yet whatever the balance between them, they can be seen in south Lindsey both to have prospered together, in the same kind of agrarian social setting, and to have declined together, during a period of disruptive social change. The broad correspondence between social and religious change is apparent; what remains elusive is the precise ways in which the new social and cultural influences actually operated to bring about the contraction in the religious realm. Perhaps the most suggestive clue was offered by Henry Winn, who observed that the ideas of his adult contemporaries, in the second half of the century, were more 'practical', while those of the villagers of his youth, who consequently had 'a nearer apprehension of the spiritual world', had been 'far more poetical'.[1] For this decline in 'poetry'—which involved both the popular religious imagination and the imaginative faculty of common language on which it was based—was not limited to south Lindsey or to popular culture. It calls to mind Macaulay's related observation that a different yet related kind of poetry—the medium of formal literary expression—grew out of the same linguistic origins, and that it too had declined in modern times, having been superseded in effect by prose, with its greater affinity for the scientific and the

[1] Winn 3/6, sect. 3, p. 11.

practical.[1] What is more, Macaulay's explanation of this change—the advance of 'civilisation'—also has its bearing on the problem of popular religion. For the countryside, no less than the towns, felt the impact of the 'new civilisation'—its acquisitive drives and class divisions as well as its mundane rationalism. In these circumstances the 'nearer apprehension of the spiritual world' that Henry Winn discerned in the villagers of the 1820s could not long survive: the 'poetry' in their religious outlook, Christian and superstitious alike, could only fade, once deprived of its sustaining conditions in the intimacy and communality of traditional village life.

[1] T. B. Macaulay, essay on Milton, in *Edinburgh Review*, xlii (1825), pp. 306–10.

APPENDIX

SOURCES FOR SOUTH LINDSEY FOLKLORE

The advance of scholarship into the history of popular culture has revealed the richness of a subject formerly regarded as trivial or undocumented. Yet it is unfortunate that an important (and easily accessible) source has not yet been more fully exploited. Local collections of folklore, though sometimes dismissed as mere arbitrary compilations of the quaint and picturesque, offer, at their best, an unrivalled record of popular belief and custom.

They are not of course free from shortcomings. Most collectors, in south Lindsey as elsewhere, were more interested in the origins than in the functions of the customs they studied, and they rarely plotted their distribution or placed them in their social context. They also neglected subjects as important as the folklore of agricultural work, which must have been extensive; less surprisingly, the folklore of sexuality, probably as extensive and certainly as important, was also neglected, though traces survive in a few children's songs and in folksongs.[1]

Yet the arguments for the authenticity of the folklore collections are persuasive. At the national level it is most significant that the folklore collectors uncovered the same beliefs and customs in county after county. (In France, by contrast, regional folklores and subcultures were much more salient.) This mutually confirming and reinforcing testimony is no less abundant for the folklore of Lincolnshire. 'The only striking characteristic of Lincolnshire folk-lore is its lack of originality. Nearly every superstition and custom of the county appears to be a local variant of something already familiarly known in other parts of the British Islands, or beyond their limits.'[2] And the sources for south Lindsey inspire confidence on these same grounds, for they represent every important region and yield multiple recordings of particular beliefs and customs in different regions. Local folklore and superstition were not a miscellany of individual curios or parochial idiosyncrasies but widely distributed social facts. These considerations not only argue the reliability of the sources used in this study but also

[1] The works of George Ewart Evans are a treasury of agricultural folklore from Suffolk; for sexual folklore see G. Legman, 'Misconceptions in Erotic Folklore', *Journal of American Folklore*, lxxv (1962).

[2] Gutch and Peacock, *Lincolnshire*, p. v.

suggest that its conclusions may have some value beyond the boundaries of south Lindsey.

The biographies of the five chief local collectors give further reason to trust the authenticity of their findings. Four were natives of the area, and one, Henry Winn, though not superstitious himself, belonged socially to the 'superstitious classes'. Altogether they lived in a total of three centuries in the county and studied its folklore from the vantage-point of long familiarity; their accounts are no mere travellers' tales. Most parsons and squires were completely cut off from folk culture, but the Lindsey collections bear the mark of intimate local knowledge.[1]

BIOGRAPHICAL NOTES ON THE PRINCIPAL COLLECTORS

Heanley, Robert Marshall (1848–1915). A native of south Lindsey, he was the eldest son of Marshall Heanley of Croft, one of the largest and most influential farmers in the Marsh. Taking his B.A. at Queen's College, Oxford, in 1871, he entered the Church and became assistant curate at Burgh-le-Marsh in 1875 and rector of Wainfleet All Saints and perpetual curate of Wainfleet St. Thomas in 1880. He left Wainfleet at the end of 1889. His article on 'The Vikings: Traces of their Folklore in Marshland' draws on boyhood memories of Croft as well as his clerical experience.

Peacock, Edward Shaw (1831–1915). Squire and lord of the manor of Bottesford in north Lindsey (near Scunthorpe), he was an antiquary, a collector of folklore, and a student of local dialect, beginning his studies about 1850. His *Glossary of Words used in the Wapentakes of Manley and Corringham, Lincolnshire*, published by the English Dialect Society, is a superior example of its type; it not only explains its entries but also illustrates them with examples of their use in local speech, and contains notes on folklore as well.

Peacock, Mabel. Daughter of Edward Peacock, she continued his studies into the twentieth century and wrote several works in dialect in addition to the most comprehensive study of Lincolnshire folklore. She lived at Bottesford and at Kirton Lindsey until her death in 1920.

---

[1] The remoteness of the dominant classes from popular culture is illustrated repeatedly in the history of the 'discovery' of English folksong at the end of the nineteenth century. C. L. Marson, who introduced Cecil Sharp to folksong, was an unusually energetic and devoted parish clergyman, but in his first eight years in his Somerset parish he heard only one folksong, and that entirely by accident. 'Folksong,' he wrote, 'unknown in the drawing-room, hunted out of the school, chased by the chapel deacons, derided by the middle classes ... takes refuge in the fastnesses of tap-rooms, poor cottages, and outlying hamlets ... It comes out very shyly, late at night, and is heard when the gentry have gone to bed ... You can live for years within a few yards of it and never suspect its existence.' (C. Sharp and C. L. Marson, *Folk Songs from Somerset*, 1904, i, p. xiii.) Similarly, Augustus Jessopp, a generally well-informed country parson in Norfolk, claimed that 'we have no local songs or ballads' (*Trials of a Country Parson*, 1890, pp. 47–8)—not long before Vaughan Williams published *Folk Songs from the Eastern Counties* (1908).

Penny, James Alpass (c. 1856–1944). The son of a Somerset parson, he took his B.A. at St. Catharine's College, Cambridge, in 1878 and was vicar of Stixwold 1888–95 and vicar of Wispington 1895–1914. Suffering from blindness, he lived his later years at Woodhall Spa. His two collections of folklore include much besides folklore: popular memories of persons and events of the neighbourhood and incidents from Penny's own experience as a parish clergyman.

Winn, Henry (1816–1914). The son of a shoemaker, he at first followed his father's trade but later made his living primarily as a grocer, draper, and 'general dealer'. A lifelong resident of Fulletby, in the South Wolds, he taught in the church Sunday school and was parish clerk for seventy-six years. As poet, diarist, and chronicler of the local scene, he had a limitless curiosity about his fellow villagers and the changing society in which they lived. His papers span the better part of a century and contain a wealth of contemporary observation and later reflection on village life.

BIBLIOGRAPHY

I   MANUSCRIPT SOURCES

A. *Public and Institutional Collections*

1. Lincolnshire Archives Office
    a. Diocesan records
        'Conference of Rural Deans 1873–77' Minute Book
        Confirmation Papers
        Correspondence of Bishop John Kaye
        Schools Questionnaire 1855
        Specula
        Visitation Returns, 1858, 1873, 1879, 1886
        Wills proved in the Court of the Dean and Chapter, Lincoln
            Consistory Court, Prebendal Court of Corringham, and
            Stow Archdeaconry Court
    b. Parish records
        South Carlton
        Faldingworth
        Fillingham
    c. Wesleyan and Primitive Methodist circuit records
        Alford   Lincoln
        Bardney   Louth
        Gainsborough   Market Rasen
        Horncastle   Spilsby
    d. Other deposits
        Ancaster   Larken
        Anderson   Layng (Misc. Dep. 165)
        Brownlow   Massingberd
        Cragg   Massingberd Mundy
        Land tax   Monson
        Rashdall diary (Misc. Don. 125, copy of original in Bodleian
            Library)
        School Records   Toynbee, Larken and Evnas
        Scorer   Tweed and Peacock
        Stubbs   West
        Tennyson d'Eyncourt Winn
        Thimbleby
2. Public Record Office
    Agricultural Returns of 1867 (M.A.F. 68/135)

Census enumerators' books, 1841, 1851, 1861 (H.O. 107 and R.G. 9)
Friendly society rules (F.S. 1 and 3)
Religious Census, 1851 (H.O. 129/428–32 and 434)
Tithe Files (I.R. 18)

3. Methodist Archives and Research Centre
   Wesleyan ministers' correspondence
   Circuit plans
   Lincoln and Hull District meeting minute books

4. Bodleian Library
   Correspondence of Samuel Wilberforce
   (with Sir Charles Anderson)

5. Vaughan Williams Memorial Library, English Folk Dance and Song Society
   Percy Grainger papers (copies of originals in Percy Grainger Library, University of Melbourne)

6. Church Commissioners
   Queen Anne's Bounty papers

7. Magdalen College, Oxford
   Estate correspondence

8. Lincoln Cathedral Library
   Wraggoe Rural Deanery Minute Book

B. *Church of England Parish Records in the Custody of the Incumbents*

Aisthorpe	Ormsby, South
Burton	Panton
Donington	Rand
Driby	Springthorpe
Horsington	Torrington, East

C. *Private Collections*

Mrs. G. G. V. Duncombe, Helmsley, Yorks.
   Helmsley MSS. Diaries of Sir Charles Anderson
Mr. Terence Leach, Dunholme, Lincoln
   MS. sermons of Arthur Wright
   Dunholme and neighbourhood parish magazines
Mr. William Leary, Riseholme, Lincoln
   Methodist circuit plans

II OFFICIAL PUBLICATIONS

Annual Reports of the Registrar-General

Parliamentary Papers
   1831 Census Returns 1833, xxxvi
   Report on Allotments of Land 1843, vii

Report on the Employment of Women and Children in
Agriculture 1843, xii

Report on Popular Education 1861, xxi, pt. 5

Seventh Report of the Medical Officer of the Privy Council
1865, xxvi

Sixth Report of the Commission on Children's Employment
1867, xvi

Report on Employment of Children, Young Persons and
Women in Agriculture 1867-8, xvii

1871 Census Returns 1873, lxx, lxxi

Return of Owners of Land 1874, lxxii

III   NEWSPAPERS AND PERIODICALS

A. *Local Newspapers*

> *Boston, Stamford, and Lincolnshire Herald* (Boston)
> *East Lincolnshire Times* (Louth)
> *Horncastle, Spilsby and Alford News* (Horncastle)
> *Lincoln Gazette*
> *Lincoln Journal*
> *Lincoln, Rutland, and Stamford Mercury* (Stamford)
> *Lincolnshire Chronicle* (Lincoln)
> *Lincolnshire Times* (Lincoln)
> *Louth and North Lincolnshire Advertiser*
> *Market Rasen Weekly Mail*
> *Retford, Worksop, Isle of Axholme and Gainsburgh News* (East
> Retford)

B. *Newspaper Clippings*

> Newspaper Cuttings, Vol. B, Local History Collection, Lincoln
> Public Library

C. *Denominational Newspapers and Periodicals*

> *Church Union Gazette*   *Primitive Methodist Magazine*
> *The Methodist*   *The Watchman*
> *Methodist Recorder*   *Wesleyan Methodist Magazine*

IV   OTHER PRINTED SOURCES

The place of publication is London unless stated otherwise.

A. *Church of England.* Chiefly by and about the clergy of south Lindsey

BAYLEY, H. V., *Charge Delivered to the Clergy of the Archdeaconry of Stow*,
Gainsborough, 1826.

BLENKINSOPP, E. L., 'Catholic and Protestant', in Orby Shipley (ed.), *Studies in Modern Problems by Various Writers*, 1874.

BOGIE, B. D., *The Crisis*, 1836.

——, *The Crisis is Come*, Edinburgh, 1843.

BONNEY, H. K., 'Sacred Music and Psalmody Considered', in *Practical Sermons by Dignitaries and Other Clergymen of the United Church of England and Ireland*, 1846.

——, *Bonney's Church Notes*, ed. N. S. Harding, Lincoln, 1937.

CARR, J., *The Duties of the Parochial Clergy*, Lincoln, 1842.

Clergy List, 1841.

CONYBEARE, W. J., 'Church Parties', *Edinburgh Review*, xcviii (1853).

DALE, H. P., *Life and Letters of Thomas Pelham Dale*, 2 vols., 1894.

FLOWERS, F., *A Plan for Increasing the Usefulness of Parish Clerks in Small Country Villages*, 1829.

Free and Open Churches, 1876.

GREGORY, ROBERT, *A Plea in Behalf of Small Parishes*, 1849

HAWKE, LORD, *Recollections and Reminiscences*, 1924.

HEANLEY, R. M., *A Memoir of Edward Steere*, 1890.

HURCOMB, F. B., *Sermons*, 1877.

JACKSON, JOHN, *Charge Delivered to the Clergy of the Diocese of Lincoln, at his Primary Visitation, in October, 1855*, 1855.

——, *Charge Delivered to the Clergy and Churchwardens of the Diocese of Lincoln*, 1858.

——, *Charge Delivered to the Clergy and Churchwardens of the Diocese of Lincoln at his Triennial Visitation in October 1861*, 1861.

——, *Charge Delivered to the Clergy and Churchwardens of the Diocese of Lincoln at His Triennial Visitation in October 1864*, 1864.

——, *Rest Before Labour*, 1859.

KAYE, J. *Works*, 8 vols., 1888.

KAYE, W. F. J., *Sermon Addressed to the Churchwardens of the Parishes within the Archdeaconry of Lincoln*, Lincoln, 1859.

KING, EDWARD, *Charge Delivered to the Clergy and Churchwardens of the Diocese of Lincoln, at the Primary Visitation, October, 1886*, Lincoln, 1886.

List of Churches and Chapels, Built, Rebuilt, Restored, or Enlarged in the Diocese of Lincoln since 1840, Lincoln, 1875.

MARTIN, SAMUEL, *Family Sermons*, 1838.

MASON, WILLIAM, *Sermons Preached in the Parish Church, Bilsby*, 1858.

MASSINGBERD, F. C., *Lectures on the Prayer Book*, 1864.

——, *A Real Diocesan Synod as the Remedy for Present Difficulties*, 1868.

MOSSMAN, T. W., 'The Church in Lincolnshire', *Union Review*, iii (1865).

NEAVE, D., 'Letters of Edward Steere', *Lincolnshire History and Archaeology*, no. 2 (1961).

NEVINS, W., *The Clergy's Privilege and Duty of Daily Intercession*, 1847.

——, *The Scriptural Doctrine of the Holy Communion*, 1855.

OVERTON, J. H., and WORDSWORTH, E., *Christopher Wordsworth*, 1888.

PENROSE, J., *Fifty-four Sermons*, 1851.

RAWNSLEY, R. D. B., *Christian Exhortation*, 3rd ser. 1871.

——, 'The Feast Refused', in E. Fowle (ed.), *Plain Preaching*, 1873.

——, *Sermons Preached in Country Churches*, 2nd ser. 1867.

SMITH, JOHN BAINBRIDGE, *The Consistency and Faithfulness of Ministerial Character*, 1840.

STEERE, E., *Notes of Sermons*, ed. R. M. Heanley, 3 vols., 1884–90.

STONEHOUSE, W. B., *A Stow Visitation*, ed., N. S. Harding, Lincoln, 1940.

TROLLOPE, E., 'The Churches of Horncastle and Other Parishes, Visited by the Society, on the 14th and 15th of June, 1876' (Lincoln Diocesan Architectural Society), Associated Architectural Societies, *Reports and Papers*, xiii (1876).

WILKINSON, C. A., *The Last Act in the Drama of Sixhills*, Lincoln, n.d.

WORDSWORTH, C., *Miscellanies: Literary and Religious*, 3 vols., 1879.

——, *A Pastoral to the Wesleyan Methodists in the Diocese of Lincoln*, 1873.

WRAY, J., *A Voice from the Church*, 1835.

B. *Methodist*. Works by and about Wesleyan and Primitive Methodist ministers and laymen in south Lindsey.

BAILEY, JOSEPH, *Life's Crowning Ornament, or Excellence of Character and How to Acquire It*, 1871.

BEECH, J. H., *Outer Life of a Methodist Preacher*, 1884.

BROADBENT, J. W., *The People's Life of Charles Garrett*, Leeds, n.d.

BUSH, J., *Elizabeth Riggall: A Memorial*, Derby, 1893.

COULSON, J. E., *The Peasant Preacher: Memorials of Mr. Charles Richardson* 2nd edn. 1866.

FEATHERSTONE, P., *Reminiscences of a Long Life*, 1905.

GREGORY, B., *Life of Frederick James Jobson, D. D.*, 1884.

HALL, JOSEPH, *Hall's Circuits and Ministers 1765–1912*, 1914.

HILL, WILLIAM, *Alphabetical and Chronological Arrangement of Wesleyan Ministers*, 1905.

HOYLE, A., *Joseph Bush: A Memorial*, 1907.

HUDSON, W., *An Answer to Bishop Wordsworth's Pastoral to the Wesleyan Methodists in the Diocese of Lincoln*, 2nd edn. 1873.

HUGHES, T., *The Conditions of Membership in the Christian Church*, 2nd edn. 1873.

HURT, W., 'Eminent Piety', *Sermons by Wesleyan-Methodist Ministers*, 1851.

JOBSON, F. J., *A Mother's Portrait*, 1855.

KENDALL, C., *The Christian Minister in Earnest*, 1854.

KENDALL, J., *Eccentricity*, 1859.

——, *Ministerial Popularity*, 1847.

——, *Remarks on Pastoral Visiting among the Wesleyans*, 1852.

LIDGETT, W., and KEYWORTH, W., *Life of the Late Matthew Keyworth*, Misterton, 1890. (Copy in Gainsborough Public Library.)

LINDLEY, W., *A Reply to the Bishop of Lincoln's Pastoral to the Wesleyan Methodists in the Diocese of Lincoln*, 4th edn. 1873.

LUNN, H. S., *Chapters from My Life*, 1918.

Primitive Methodist Conference, *General Minutes*.

SHAW, G., *Life of Rev. Parkinson Milson*, 1893.

SMITH, MARY, *Raithby Hall*, 1859.

SMITH, THORNLEY, *A Christian Mother: Memoirs of Mrs. Thornley Smith*, 1885.

TINDALL, S., *The Means of Obtaining Materials for the Pulpit*, 1849.

UNSWORTH, W., *Self-Culture and Self-Reliance: or, the Poor Man's Help to Elevation on Earth and in Heaven*, Alford, 1861.

'Wesleyan Ministers in the Gainsborough Circuit' (T. S. Gregory and others), *Two Letters to the Bishop of Lincoln*, Gainsborough, 1873.

WHITEHEAD, J., *The Evangelist and Pastor: Autobiography and Reminiscences*, 1879.

WILLIS, J., *The Class and the Congregation*, 1869.

C. *Other*. Relating to the folklore, etc., of south Lindsey.

ANDERSON, CHARLES H. J., *Lincoln Pocket Guide*, 1880.

BROGDEN, J. E., *Provincial Words and Expressions Current in Lincolnshire*, 1866.

BROWN, JOHN, *The Lay of the Clock, and Other Poems*, Horncastle, 1861.

——, *Literae Laureatae*, Horncastle, 1890.

——, *Neddy and Sally, or the Statutes Day, a Lincolnshire Tale*, Lincoln, 1841.

CLARKE, J. A., *On the Farming of Lincolnshire*, 1852.

COLMAN, H., *European Agriculture and Rural Economy*, vol. i, Boston, 1846.

COOPER, T., *Life of Thomas Cooper*, 4th edn. 1873.

——, *Wise Saws and Modern Instances*, 2 vols., 1845.

Directory of the Ancient Order of Foresters' Friendly Society and Almanack 1868–69, Wolverhampton, 1868.

ELLISON, R., *Kirkstead! or the Pleasures of Shooting*, 1837.

A Farming Tour, or Handbook of the Farming of Lincolnshire, Lincoln and Market Rasen, 1854.

GOOD, J., *A Glossary or Collection of Words, Phrases, Place Names, Superstitions, etc., Current in East Lincolnshire*, 1900.

GRESSWELL, F., *Bright Boots*, 1936.

GUTCH, Mrs., and PEACOCK, M., *Lincolnshire* (Publications of the

Folk-Lore Society, no. 63; Printed Extracts VII, County Folk-Lore), 1908.

HEANLEY, C. E., *Toll of the Marshes*, 1929.

HEANLEY, R. M., 'The Vikings: Traces of their Folklore in Marshland', *Saga-Book of the Viking Club*, iii, pt. 1 (1903).

Lincolnshire Notes and Queries, i-ii (1889–91).

PEACOCK, E., *A Glossary of Words Used in the Wapentakes of Manley and Corringham, Lincolnshire* (English Dialect Society, Ser. C, Original Glossaries VI), 1877.

PEACOCK, M., 'Folklore and Legends of Lincolnshire', typescript in Folklore Society Library, University College London.

——, *Tales fra Linkisheere*, Brigg, 1889.

PENNY, J. A., *Folklore Round Horncastle*, Horncastle, 1915.

——, *More Folklore Round Horncastle*, Horncastle, 1922.

Poll Book (Lindsey division, 1835), Stamford, 1835.

Poll Book for the Parts of Lindsey in the County of Lincoln, August, 1841, Lincoln, 1841.

Poll Book of the North Lincolnshire Election Taken in July, 1852, ed. T. Fricker, Boston, n.d.

RAWNSLEY, H. D., *Memories of the Tennysons*, 2nd edn. Glasgow, 1912.

STREATFEILD, G. S., *Lincolnshire and the Danes*, 1884.

TENNYSON, A., *Poems*, ed. C. Ricks, 1969.

——, *Poems and Plays*, 1965.

WALKER, GILBERT, *Tales of a Lincolnshire Antiquary*, ed. W. A. Cragg, Sleaford, 1949.

WALTER, J. C., *Records, Historical and Antiquarian, of Parishes round Horncastle*, Horncastle, 1904.

WHITE, WILLIAM, *History, Gazetteer, and Directory of Lincolnshire*, Sheffield, 1842, 1856, 1872.

WORSDALE, J., *Astronomy and Elementary Philosophy*, 1819.

——, *Celestial Philosophy*, 1828.

V   SECONDARY SOURCES

ABERCROMBIE, N., and others, 'Superstition and Religion: the God of the Gaps', in D. Martin and M. Hill (eds.), *Sociological Yearbook of Religion 3*, 1970.

ARIÈS, P., *Centuries of Childhood*, trans, R. Baldick, New York, 1965.

ASHBY, M. K., *Joseph Ashby of Tysoe*, Cambridge, 1961.

BAKER, FRANK, *Methodism and the Love-Feast*, 1957.

BECKWITH, I., 'The River Trade of Gainsborough, 1500–1850', *Lincolnshire History and Archaeology*, no. 2 (1967).

BEST, G. F. A., 'Popular Protestantism in Victorian Britain', in R. Robson, (ed.) *Ideas and Institutions of Victorian Britain*, 1967.

——, 'The Road to Hiram's Hospital', *Victorian Studies*, v (1961).

——, *Temporal Pillars*, Cambridge, 1964.

BOURNE, GEORGE, *Change in the Village*, 1955.

BOWMER, J. C., 'Church and Ministry in Wesleyan Methodism, from the Death of Wesley to the Death of Bunting', unpublished Ph.D. thesis, Leeds University, 1967.

CHADWICK, W. O., *Edward King*, Lincoln, 1968.

——, *The Victorian Church*, Part I, 1966.

CHAMBERS, J. D., and MINGAY, G. E., *The Agricultural Revolution 1750–1880*, 1966.

CURRIE, R., *Methodism Divided*, 1968.

DITCHFIELD, P. H., *The Parish Clerk*, 1907.

DUNBABIN, J. P. D., 'The Incidence and Organization of Agricultural Trade Unionism in the 1870s', *Agri. Hist. Rev.* xvi (1968).

——, 'The "Revolt of the Field": the Agricultural Labourers' Movement in the 1870s', *Past and Present*, no. 26 (1963).

DURKHEIM, E., *The Elementary Forms of the Religious Life*, trans. J. W. Swain, 1915.

EDWARDS, K. C., 'A Lincoln Industrial Centenary', *East Midland Geographer*, i (1954).

GILBERT, ALAN, 'The Growth and Decline of Non-conformity in England and Wales, with Special Reference to the Period before 1850', unpublished D.Phil. thesis, Oxford University, 1973.

GRAINGER, P., 'The Impress of Personality in Traditional Singing', *Journal of the Folk-Song Society*, no. 12 (1908).

HABAKKUK, H. J., 'La Disparition du paysan anglais', *Annales: E.S.C.* xx (1965).

HARDY, T., *Thomas Hardy's Personal Writings*, ed. H. Orel, 1967.

HARRISON, B., *Drink and the Victorians*, 1971.

HOBSBAWM, E. J., and Rudé, G., *Captain Swing*, 1969.

HOLDERNESS, B. A., 'Rural Society in South-east Lindsey, 1660–1840', unpublished Ph.D. thesis, Nottingham University, 1968.

——, '"Open" and "Close" Parishes in England in the Eighteenth and Nineteenth Centuries', *Agri. Hist. Rev.* xx (1972).

HURT, J. S., 'Landowners, Farmers, and Clergy and the Financing of Rural Education before 1870', *Journal of Educational Administration and History*, i (1968).

KENDALL, H. B., *Origin and History of the Primitive Methodist Church*, 2 vols., n.d.

KENT, J., 'American Revivalism and England in the Nineteenth Century', in *Papers Presented to the Past and Present Conference on Popular Religion, 7 July 1966*.

——, Review of E. P. Thompson, *The Making of the English Working Class*, in *Proceedings of the Wesley Historical Society*, xxiv (1964).

KERR, B., 'The Dorset Agricultural Labourer 1750–1850', *Proceedings of the Dorset Natural History and Archaeological Society*, lxxxiv (1963).

LEACH, T. R., 'The Methodist Squire of Raithby', *Epworth Witness and Journal of the Lincolnshire Methodist History Society*, i (1970).

LINTON, D. L., 'The Landforms of Lincolnshire', *Geography*, xxxix (1954).

LÖWITH, K., 'Can There Be a Christian Gentleman?' *Theology Today*, v (1948).

MCCLATCHEY, D., *Oxfordshire Clergy 1777–1869*, Oxford, 1960.

MALCOMSON, R. W., *Popular Recreations in English Society, 1700–1850*, Cambridge, 1973.

MARTIN, D., *The Religious and the Secular*, 1969.

——, *Sociology of English Religion*, 1967.

——, 'Interpreting the Figures', in M. Perry, (ed.), *Crisis for Confirmation*, 1967.

MILLS, D. R., 'English Villages in the Eighteenth and Nineteenth Centuries: A Sociological Approach', *Amateur Historian*, vi (1965).

MINGAY, G. E., *English Landed Society in the Eighteenth Century*, 1963.

MOIR, E., *The Justice of the Peace*, Harmondsworth, 1969.

MORRIS, G. M., 'Primitive Methodism in Nottinghamshire, 1815–1932' unpublished Ph.D. thesis, Nottingham University, 1967.

OLNEY, R. J., *Lincolnshire Politics 1832–1885*, Oxford, 1973.

OXLEY, J. E., *The Lindsey Dialect*, Leeds, 1940.

PERKIN, H., *Origins of Modern English Society*, 1969.

PEVSNER, N., and HARRIS, J., *Buildings of England: Lincolnshire*, Harmondsworth, 1964.

PICKERING, W. S. F., 'The 1851 Religious Census—a Useless Experiment?', *British Journal of Sociology*, xviii (1967).

——, 'Religion—a Leisure-time Pursuit?' in D. Martin (ed.), *Sociological Yearbook of Religion in Britain*, 1968.

PINCHBECK, I., *Women Workers and the Industrial Revolution*, 1930.

RACK, H. D., 'The Decline of the Class Meeting and the Problem of Church-Membership in Nineteenth-Century Wesleyanism', *Proceedings of the Wesley Historical Society*, xxxix (1973).

RUDKIN, E. H., *Lincolnshire Folklore*, Gainsborough, 1936.

RUSSELL, REX C., *A History of Schools and Education in Lindsey, Lincolnshire, 1800–1902*, Pts. 1–4, Lincoln, 1965–7.

——, *The 'Revolt of the Field' in Lincolnshire*, Lincoln, n.d. [1956].

——, Review of E. J. Hobsbawm and G. Rudé, *Captain Swing*, *Agri. Hist. Rev.* xviii (1970).

SÉJOURNÉ, P., 'Superstition', in A. Vacant (ed.), *Dictionnaire de théologie catholique*, vol. xiv, pt. 2, Paris, 1941.

SHINER, L., 'The Concept of Secularization in Sociological Research', *Journal for the Scientific Study of Religion*, vi (1967).

SHRIMPTON, C., 'Landed Society and the Farming Community of Essex in the Late Eighteenth and Early Nineteenth Centuries', unpublished Ph.D. thesis, Cambridge University, 1965.

SMITH, A. W., 'Popular Religion', *Past and Present*, no. 40 (1968).

STEPHENSON, A. M. G., *The First Lambeth Conference 1867*, 1967.

STONE, L., 'Literacy and Education in England, 1640–1900', *Past and Present*, no. 42 (1969).

STURGESS, R. W., 'The Agricultural Revolution on the English Clays', *Agri. Hist. Rev*, xiv (1966).

THIRSK, J., *English Peasant Farming: The Agrarian History of Lincolnshire from Tudor to Recent Times*, 1957.

THOMAS, K., *Religion and the Decline of Magic*, 1971.

THOMPSON, DAVID, 'The Churches and Society in Leicestershire, 1851–1881', unpublished Ph.D. thesis, Cambridge University, 1969.

——, 'The 1851 Religious Census: Problems and Possibilities', *Victorian Studies*, xi (1967).

THOMPSON, E. P., '"Rough Music": Le Charivari anglais', *Annales: E.S.C.*, xxvii (1972).

THOMPSON, FLORA, *Lark Rise to Candleford*, 1945.

THOMPSON, F. M. L., *English Landed Society in the Nineteenth Century*, 1963.

WEBB, R. K., 'The Victorian Reading Public', in B. Ford (ed.). *Pelican Guide to English Literature: From Dickens to Hardy*, Harmondsworth, 1958.

——, 'Working Class Readers in Early Victorian England', *English Historical Review*, lxv (1950).

WILSON, BRYAN, *Religion in Secular Society*, 1966.

——, (ed.), *Patterns of Sectarianism*, 1967.

WOLF, E. R., *Peasants*, Englewood Cliffs (N.J.), 1966.

YINGER, J. M., 'A Structural Examination of Religion', *Journal for the Scientific Study of Religion*, viii (1969).

INDEX

(Places are in south Lindsey unless otherwise indicated.)

labourers—*cont.*
modes of address, 93, 99, 101
self-discipline and self-respect, 80–1,
101–2
religious behaviour of, 128, 136,
141–2, 145–6, 153, 157, 165,
317–20
and Methodism, 195–6, 202, 242
and superstition, 300
see also children; farm servants; confined labourers; unions
Lady Day, 266
Lafargue, Revd, R. A., 118
land ownership, 9–10
landlords, *see* gentry
Langton-by-Horncastle, 107
Larken, Revd. E. R., of Burton, 174 n.
Legbourne, 199
Lincoln, 4, 5, 131
Lincoln circuit:
Wesleyan, 184, 185, 193, 196
Primitive Methodist, 238, 244, 249
Lincoln diocese, 104
Lincolnshire:
situation, 2
Parts of, 2
folklore, 333
Lindsey, south:
defined, 2;
as setting for religion, viii
Lord's Supper, *see* Communion
Louth, 2, 4, 201, 287
Grammar School, 54
Louth circuit:
Wesleyan, 184, 185, 186, 196;
Primitive Methodist, 243, 244
Loutit, Revd. James, Wesleyan minister, 186
lovefeasts, 204 n., 227
luck, 294, 312
Ludford, 81, 245
Lunn, Henry, 188, 205–6
Lusby, 35, 168
Lyon, George, of Saxby, 245

Mablethorpe, 2, 17
magic, and religion, 260
magistrates, clerical, 32
Maltby, John, of Louth Park, 232, 248
Manby, 163
Manduell, Revd. Matthewman, 118
Mareham-le-Fen, 166, 169

Mareham-on-the-Hill, 108
Market Rasen, 2, 4
Market Rasen circuit:
Wesleyan, 184, 196;
Primitive Methodist, 244
marriage, 315, 316, 318
Anglican, 135–7
superstitions about, 273
Marsh, 6, 16, 20, 53, 77, 119, 126, 153, 237
see also Middle Marsh; Outer Marsh
Martin, Revd. Samuel, 138
Massingberd, Revd. F. C., of South Ormsby, 123, 124–5, 142, 144, 146, 165, 168, 170
Massingberd-Mundy, C. J. H., of South Ormsby, 33, 315 n.
Methodism, 142, 319
local advantages, 9, 21–2
dominant position in south Lindsey, 168, 183
'aggression', ix, 249
'Methodist' synonymous with 'religious', 103, 183
circuits, 5–6
ministers, 275
discipline, compared with Anglican, 162
members and adherents, 197, 241
and the village community, 99, 322
attitudes towards money, 206–8, 229, 230, 251
see also Wesleyan Methodism; Primitive Methodism; chapels and chapel-building; ministers; sermons; conversion; revivalism; church attendance; baptism; Communion; Sunday schools; entertainment, noise
Middle Marsh, 6, 8, 10, 15, 16, 19, 31, 47, 51, 77
see also Marsh
migration, 18, 21, 59
ministers (Methodist):
Wesleyan, 185–7
Primitive Methodist, 222, 223, 255
preachers' homes, 200–1, 234
see also clergy
Minting, 130, 169
Molson Revd. William, of Hogsthorpe, 171
Monson family, of Burton, 34, 199
William, sixth baron, 39–40
Mossman, Revd. T. W., 110 n., 168